New Religious Movements

Nashville
Public Library
Foundation

*This book added
to the library's collection
through the generosity of
the Joyce Family Foundation*

New Religious Movements

A Documentary Reader

<small>EDITED BY</small>

Dereck Daschke and W. Michael Ashcraft

New York University Press

<small>NEW YORK AND LONDON</small>

NEW YORK UNIVERSITY PRESS
New York and London
www.nyupress.org

Library of Congress Cataloging-in-Publication Data
New religious movements : a documentary reader / edited by Dereck
Daschke and W. Michael Ashcraft.
p. cm.
Includes bibliographical references and index.
ISBN 0-8147-0702-5 (cloth : alk. paper)
ISBN 0-8147-0703-3 (pbk. : alk. paper)
1. Sects—United States—History—Sources. 2. Cults—United States—
History—Sources. 3. United States—Religion—History—Sources.
I. Daschke, Dereck. II. Ashcraft, W. Michael, 1955–
BL2525.N4865   2005
209—dc22   2005002330

New York University Press books are printed on acid-free paper,
and their binding materials are chosen for strength and durability.

Manufactured in the United States of America

c 10 9 8 7 6 5 4 3 2 1
p 10 9 8 7 6 5 4 3 2 1

Contents

Acknowledgments

The idea for a reader containing primary documents from New Religious Movements (NRMs) was first suggested several years ago by Jennifer Hammer, editor at New York University Press, to several NRM scholars. Eventually Phillip Charles Lucas and W. Michael Ashcraft agreed to edit such a reader. When Lucas had to leave the project, Ashcraft invited Dereck Daschke to join him as co-editor. We are grateful to Hammer, Lucas, and others who participated in discussions in the early stages of this book's development. Their foresight and vision set in motion a process that has culminated in what we hope will be a useful, reliable, and handy one-volume source of information about various NRMs as found in documents from the movements themselves.

The cooperation of those associated with NRMs was critical. Without their advice and guidance, this book would not exist. We would like to thank Sally A. Ulrich of the Church of Christ, Scientist; Beth Collings and Anna Jamerson; Will Thackera of the Theosophical Society, Pasadena; Guy McCloskey of Soka Gakkai–USA; Oberon Zell-Ravenheart; Karen Karsten of Llewellyn Worldwide Publishers; Marta Morena Vega of The Frank H. Williams Caribbean Cultural Center; Lonnie Davis and Claire Borowik of The Family International; Michael L. Mickler of the Unification Theological Seminary; the staff of the Watch Tower Bible and Tract Society of Pennsylvania; and Ryan Cook of the University of Chicago Chen Tao Research Cadre.

The advice of other NRM scholars has made our job as co-editors far easier than it could have been. We asked many scholars with expertise on specific NRMs to suggest where we might include those groups in the reader, and also to suggest which documents we might use. We could not always follow the advice that was offered so freely and graciously, but we deeply appreciate those who gave us the benefit of their many years of scholarship: James Chancellor, the Southern Baptist Theological Seminary; Mary Ann Clark, University of Houston at Clear Lake; Brenda Denzler,

Chapel Hill, North Carolina; John Simmons, Western Illinois University; and Catherine Wessinger, Loyola University New Orleans. Other scholars who provided assistance include Allan Anderson, University of Birmingham; Eileen Barker, London School of Economics; Brenda E. Brasher, University of Aberdeen; Michael F. Brown, Williams College; Bret Carroll, California State University, Stanislaus; George Chryssides, University of Wolverhampton; Chas S. Clifton, University of Southern Colorado; Cynthia Eller, Montclair State University; Gareth Fisher, University of Virginia; Eugene Gallagher, Connecticut College; Terryl L. Givens, University of Richmond; Irving Hexham, University of Calgary; Jeffrey Kaplan, University of Wisconsin, Oshkosh; Scott Lowe, University of North Dakota; J. Gordon Melton, Institute for the Study of American Religion; Rebecca Moore, San Diego State University; James Penton; Ian Reader, Lancaster University; Richard Salter, Hobart and William Smith Colleges; and Brad Whitsel, Pennsylvania State University, Fayette. Many thanks to all of these scholars. They made the reader far better than it would have been without their suggestions. We are especially grateful to Douglas E. Cowan of the University of Missouri, Kansas City, for writing the appendix to the reader. We also thank Jacob Nelson and Kawtar El Alaoui, students at Truman State University, for their assistance in editing and proofreading, and all the workers in the Social Science Division office at Truman State who contributed their assistance.

And finally, two personal notes: Daschke would like to thank Jennifer Creer for all she has done, regarding this book and otherwise, and for putting up with the mountains of perplexing books around the house. Ashcraft would like to thank his wife, Carrol Davenport, and his children, Brittany and Kathleen, for their love and support.

Introduction

Origins of the Study of New Religious Movements

In the introduction to *The New Religions* (1970), now a classic in the study of New Religious Movements, Jacob Needleman recalled a conversation with the famous Jewish scholar Abraham Heschel. At the time, Heschel was translating an old Jewish text, and in a dramatic moment in their conversation, he "pounded his finger on a stack of manuscript in front of him and quoted something he had just translated: 'God is not nice, He is not an uncle. God is an earthquake.'"[1] Needleman found this to be an apt description of the experiences of many people who joined New Religious Movements in California in the 1960s. "Earthquake" continues to be a useful metaphor for understanding those attracted to various groups labeled "cults," "sects," "emergent religions," "alternative religions," or the term used in this volume, "New Religious Movements" (hereafter NRMs). People who join such groups have experienced an earthquake. Something has been shaken: their understanding of family or other forms of human community, their sense of evil and suffering, their larger picture of the cosmos and their place in it, or a combination of these and many other aspects of human awareness. Whatever the motivating factors for seeking and joining NRMs—and these factors are as varied as the individuals who seek and join—people in NRMs leave behind older and less useful ways of conceiving of themselves and their world because they have felt the earth move and sense that they must move with it or fall off the edge.

The term "New Religious Movement" is now used by most scholars who study such groups because "cult" has become a pejorative in the media and among anticultists (those who align themselves against religious groups they label as dangerous or even evil).[2] The descriptors used for these movements have come primarily from the sociology of religion, although other disciplines—notably theology, history, religious studies, cultural anthropology, and social psychology—have also contributed to

NRM study. Building on the early work of two noted German scholars, the sociologist Max Weber (1864–1920) and the theologian Ernst Troeltsch (1865–1923), early twentieth-century sociologists of religion uneasily placed groups later called NRMs somewhere along a spectrum of categories that included "church," a religious organization that accommodates itself to the host culture; "sect," a smaller religious organization that usually splits off from a church and rebels against the norms of mainstream culture and society; and "cult," a more countercultural group than a sect that has a fluid organizational structure and usually centers around a charismatic leader.[3]

Today, the terms "sect" and "cult" are often used interchangeably with "New Religious Movement," but in fact the latter term was initially coined to describe innovative religious groups that appeared in the West, particularly in the United States, in the 1960s and 1970s. After U.S. restrictions on immigration from South and East Asia were lifted in 1965, teachers of religious traditions from those parts of the world came to the United States, as well as other Western nations, and cultivated movements largely composed of Western converts. The earliest Western members of the Unification Church, the International Society for Krishna Consciousness (ISKCON), and other Asian imports tended to be white, middle-class adolescents and young adults. These spiritual seekers turned to Asian religious teachers and traditions because they were dissatisfied with the answers provided by mainstream Western religious traditions, primarily Judaism and Christianity, to life's deepest questions. Other religious groups that were not Asian in origin, but whose views of the world unquestionably ran counter to prevailing religious and cultural norms, also arose during this period. Scientology, for example, relied upon psychotherapeutic concepts and language. The Church Universal and Triumphant, on the other hand, echoed Western occult and esoteric traditions with centuries-long pedigrees.

The issue of perception is crucial in any discussion of NRMs. With the emergence of so many new groups in the 1960s and 1970s, clergy, journalists, government officials, academics, and concerned parents of youth who joined NRMs began to conceive of the religious scene as a stage upon which a veritable phalanx of alternative religious organizations were sweeping America's youth off of their feet. For the younger generation and its observers an earthquake had occurred, and they were not certain when it would stop or what the cultural and religious landscape would look like once the earth again stood still.[4]

Older groups that had been challenging the Christian mainstream in the United States since the nineteenth century, such as Christian Science, Seventh-day Adventism, and the Jehovah's Witnesses, were often considered alongside NRMs that emerged in the 1960s. Older Afro-Caribbean groups that centered on African-derived ritual and belief (such as Santería or Vodou) or used concepts of blackness and Afrocentrism in their founding myths (such as the Nation of Islam) were also added to this mix. Thus, "NRM" came to denote any and all alternative or emergent religious groups.

The inclusion of so many diverse groups under the term "New Religious Movements" raises several questions. First, were all of these groups new? Many NRMs claimed that they were restoring ancient truths in the present. Theosophy, Wicca, and the Church of Jesus Christ of Latter-day Saints, for example, base their identity on this idea, and part of their appeal lies in their supposed antiquity. As noted above, groups such as Christian Science had been in existence since the 1800s, and even some of the newer movements had already been in the United States for several decades by the mid-twentieth century. Groups that began in the 1960s can now look back on a history of forty years or so. How long must a religious group exist before it is no longer considered new? No clear consensus exists among scholars on this matter.

Second, were these groups religious? Many NRMs rejected any association with religion, a term they identified with older traditions that had ceased, in their opinion, to provide meaningful direction to modern people. Scientology, for example, initially presented itself as a therapeutic group whose prescriptions for life's problems were completely devoid of religious content, although the group later identified itself in more religious terms. Other groups, whose origins clearly hearkened back to particular religious traditions, nevertheless claimed not to be "religions." A notable example was Transcendental Meditation (TM), brought to the United States by the Hindu guru Maharishi Mahesh Yogi (b. 1917). Advocates of TM said that their meditative practice need not be accompanied by any particular religious belief. Although this assertion derives from the modern Hindu insight that mystical experience can be divorced from religious community and ritual and still be quite legitimate, TM practitioners made these claims at a time in the mid-twentieth century when NRM discourse often contained a strong component of religious denial or a downplaying of religious elements.[5]

Third, were these groups movements? As NRM scholar George D. Chryssides pointed out, a movement is a fluid social grouping within larger society, while an organization has clearly delineated boundaries and structures, including membership rules and leadership hierarchy. Most NRMs have some degree of organization.[6] The New Age movement, for example, began as a nebulous conglomeration of teachers, texts, and practices bearing scant resemblance to one another. However, New Age groups eventually coalesced into organizations, complete with in-group rules for behavior; doctrinal boundaries; conflicts over correct interpretation of a leader's legacy; budgetary worries; and systematic purchase and use of property, facilities, and equipment.

NRMs, then, are new (or old) religious groups that may or may not claim to be religious, and that are organizations more often than they are movements. Although an imperfect label, "NRM" continues to be the most helpful one available, and it has achieved a level of acceptance in general discourse about religion that other labels have not. Conceived by mid-twentieth-century observers of American and, more broadly, Western religious events, the category of NRM is useful because it includes both the innovative newer religious groups and the older alternative groups, which, taken together, form a spectrum challenging both mainstream religious traditions and secular society.

Significant Factors in the Study of New Religious Movements

The study of NRMs has been shaped by many factors. One such factor has been the opposition these movements have generated. Those who join NRMs, of course, do so because they find a purpose, a sense of belonging, perhaps even a little adventure. For the most committed believers, the NRM is their new life, their new family, and they intend never to regret their decision to join. But most NRMs have had relatively few long-term members. Many seekers shuffle among various groups, and most ultimately reject NRM affiliation altogether. Nonetheless, some observers of these trends during the 1960s and especially the 1970s and later saw NRM growth as a dangerous threat to social and moral order. Parents of young adults who joined NRMs began to form networks of "anticultists" (or "countercultists" if they were evangelical Protestant Christians concerned about NRM-based alternatives to the their particular version of Christian salvation). These networks coalesced into national organizations such as the now-defunct Cult Awareness Network (CAN) and the still-active American Family Foundation (AFF). In order to combat the influence of NRMs, anticultists argued that the leaders of such groups relied upon devious methods, variously called "brainwashing," "mind-control," or "thought reform," to impair the initiative and decision-making capacity of members. Therefore, the key to extracting people from NRMs was an equally deliberate course of action to reverse the effects of brainwashing. This action, called "deprogramming," involved kidnapping, isolation, verbal barrages, and sometimes even more dire methods to persuade NRM members that their mental and emotional dispositions had been tainted.[7]

Gender has been another significant factor in NRM study. Historically, women have accounted for the majority of participants in American religious groups, if not always the majority of leaders.[8] NRMs have been no exception to this rule. Most seekers and joiners have been women, although plenty of men have engaged in this activity as well. Using gender as a category of analysis, NRM scholars have clarified a number of important aspects of NRM organization, belief, and ritual practice that otherwise would remain hidden from view. Some NRMs incorporate gendered images into their most basic beliefs and have been on the cutting edge of women's leadership. Others have reasserted patriarchal attitudes, relegating women to subservient roles. NRMs are not consistent in their perceptions or treatment of women, but in this they are no different from mainstream religions. Any understanding of NRMs, however, must take gender and sexuality into account.[9]

A third important aspect of NRM study is violence. In 1978, an exceptionally disturbing religious earthquake shook Americans and the world. Nine hundred and fourteen people were killed or committed suicide in Jonestown, Guyana, under the leadership of Jim Jones (1931–1978). Jones's Peoples Temple was already a newsworthy group, having evolved from a Pentecostal congregation with a liberal social agenda into an NRM with decidedly isolationist and apocalyptic leanings. Jones and the core leaders around him perceived certain actions taken by ex-members and concerned relatives to be hostile, especially when a delegation led by Congressman Leo Ryan visited the Jonestown site, where the group had relocated from California in 1977. As Ryan was leaving with some members, he and four others in his party were attacked and killed. Exiting this life became the only perceived option for many Peoples Temple members, but it was a violent exit that stunned Americans and moved many to ask why such a thing had happened. Jonestown and later violent incidents, such as the 1993 federal siege and storming of a religious community called the Branch Davidians outside Waco, Texas, and the dramatic 1997 group suicide by members of Heaven's Gate, who expected deliverance by UFOs, have spiked interest in NRMs and especially in violence and NRMs. Scholarly interest in this area of NRM study has been further heightened by the current grappling with religiously absolute terrorist organizations from the Islamic world. This area of study continues to attract many NRM scholars, while the controversy surrounding brainwashing has receded in significance, if not in dramatic appeal. Questions about the causes of NRM violence, whether that violence is directed inwardly toward members or outwardly against the world at large, require considerable study and reflection.[10]

A fourth important element in NRM study has been a greater focus on groups outside the United States. Experiences with NRMs in Europe, both American imports and home-grown varieties, have differed significantly from those in the United States. France, for example, has passed stringent laws against NRMs, usually called "sects" in the French context. The fall of Communism in the former Soviet Union has led to the introduction of numerous religions, which have not always been welcomed by secularized Russians or by a resurgent Russian Orthodox Church.[11] In Japan, NRMs have existed since the late nineteenth century, when various organizations reworked traditional Shinto and Buddhist elements into new organizational and ritual forms. Since the 1970s, a newer wave of Japanese NRMs —called "New New Religions" to distinguish them from older new religions—have appeared.[12] In sub-Saharan Africa, thousands of NRMs have arisen since the nineteenth century, combining the beliefs and practices introduced by Christian missionaries with older indigenous religions or, more recently, innovatively reconstituting Pentecostal and Charismatic methods and emphases imported from the West. These diverse organizations are collectively called African Initiated (or Independent) Churches, or AICs.[13] In these and many other places around the world, the amazing variety of religious expressions across national, ethnic, regional, and continental boundaries provocatively challenges older assumptions derived mainly from sociological and theological study of NRMs in the United States. This facet of NRM study promises to expand significantly into the twenty-first century, giving to the discipline the global perspectives and scope that NRMs themselves already exhibit.[14]

The study of NRMs carries its own unique challenges. The specific cases that fall under the heading of NRM do not rest easily there. Most

members of NRMs, for example, either do not accept
reluctantly, making the scholar's task difficult. In add
prolific. Thousands, if not hundreds of thousands, of su
often embedded in social and cultural settings that make
recognize, much less study, unless they choose to reveal
beyond a target audience of potential recruits. In additio
existed long enough that some members have themselves be
and can effectively study their own group while exchangin
scholars from other NRMs or those not aligned with any g
tionally, many NRM scholars are reassessing their own status
observers. Recent trends in ethnography and anthropology ha
questions about the objectivity of the scholar and have revealed the multiple ways that scholars of NRMs incorporate their own personal, religious,
cultural, and social assumptions into their study. The day of the aloof, dispassionate observer of a religious group is over—if, in fact, it ever existed
—and NRM scholars acknowledge more readily than ever before the
importance of factoring their predilections and orientations into their
analysis and interpretation of NRMs.[15]

The Purpose of This Volume

The aftershocks of the religious earthquake of the 1960s and 1970s that
shook younger Americans from their roots and introduced them to alternative visions of the world offered by NRMs are still felt in our society
today. Interest in NRMs has never been greater. Publishers produce numerous volumes every year on NRMs. Professional societies for the study
of religion hold NRM conferences or include NRM-related presentations
in their annual meetings. The Federal Bureau of Investigation (FBI) and
other government agencies are increasingly concerned about NRMs, particularly volatile ones that could become violent. Hollywood celebrities
attract considerable attention by their adherence to various NRMs. Anticult groups continue to warn the public about the dangers of NRMs, but
the movements that successfully survive their first decade or more have
learned to respond effectively to anticult attacks with media tools, and
sometimes with litigation. In short, our culture is very aware of NRMs'
existence.

NRMs continue to fascinate students, and many colleges and universities offer courses on the subject. This volume is designed to facilitate

discussion of NRMs in college-level courses, although we have approached it with the general reader in mind as well. Contained in these pages are the words and ideas of representatives from fourteen different NRMs, as well as an appendix by Douglas E. Cowan that surveys the anticult/countercult scene. We hope that by giving voice to NRM founders, leaders, members, and ex-members we can contribute to the ongoing task—so vital in a free and open democratic society—of understanding groups and individuals who have been grossly misunderstood and tragically stereotyped. Those who speak out of various NRM contexts are neither angels nor demons. They are human beings who make complex decisions to join NRMs and embrace their teachings. They need to be heard. Equally important, the reader of this volume needs to know what NRMs themselves can tell us. Genuine understanding that leads to tolerance can only begin when people are heard on their own terms. Yet this book also has a specific design. The voices from NRMs are filtered through a particular structure, and it is to that structure that we now turn.

There Are Typologies and Then There Are Typologies

A "typology" is a deliberately organized categorization of religious phenomena, groups, beliefs, individuals, or other aspects of religious life so that those aspects can be compared and contrasted and some meaningful conclusions can be drawn about religious life in general. The church/sect/ cult categories alluded to above have formed the historical basis, in the sociology of religion, for numerous typologies that attempt to catalogue religious organizations along a spectrum so that they can be studied. NRMs have been ordered according to numerous typologies in the last forty years. Drawing on the older church/sect categories of Weber and Troeltsch, Bryan Wilson, a pioneer in the study of NRMs, offered a compelling typology of sects according to the means of salvation they offer. *Conversionist* sects, for example, see the world as evil and believe that salvation is only possible when the individual convert experiences a profound alteration of self-identity, while *reformist* sects believe that the world's evils can be overcome through social reform.[16] Another early scholar of NRMs, Roy Wallis, classified groups according to their relationship with the larger society. *Affirming* groups accept the values of society, while other groups reject those values and yet others accommodate to them.[17] These classifications are sociological in nature—that is, they are based upon a religious group's relationship to society and measure that group's degree and direction of dissent from mainstream values.

NRM scholars who are not trained in sociology, or who are not interested in privileging sociological themes and methods in their work, have found ways of typing NRMs that incorporate other themes without neglecting social location altogether. (Although sociological typologies do not ignore other factors, they do foreground social dynamics as the basis for categorizing religious groups.) One of the most formative, and most famous, of the typologies that departs from an exclusively sociological approach was devised by J. Gordon Melton for his landmark reference work, *The Encyclopedia of American Religions,* first published in 1978 and appearing in six subsequent editions. Melton divided all religious groups in the United States, including NRMs, into "families" that were defined by "a common heritage, thought world (theology in its broadest sense), and lifestyle." Melton believed that this way of typing religious groups would enable the observer to comprehend more fully than had been permitted by older church/sect typologies the wide range of American religious groups.[18]

Melton's family typology reflected the insights brought to NRM study by scholars in religious studies, history, and other disciplines. Today, many major surveys of NRMs offer, in some form or another, a family typology.[19] The advantage of expanding a typology's basis beyond a given religious group's relationship to society is obvious: if religious groups are compared according to several characteristics, the student of NRMs can achieve a more holistic understanding of the diverse ways that these groups exist in relationship to one another, as well as to larger society.

However, the very method of typing points to Western values. As Jeff Kenney notes in a discussion of the problems associated with categorizing Islamic groups, "types reflect the cultural reality that they are supposed to explain." Kenney found that church, sect, and cult are concepts based upon a religious group's orientation to the Western, predominantly secular, social world in which they exist. In Islamic societies, on the other hand, a particular subgroup's relationship to social institutions is premised on far different categories.[20]

No typology can escape the predominant social and cultural values sustaining the discipline or disciplines that give birth to typologies. With this in mind, we seek to be as comprehensive as possible in the typology we offer in the present volume. Although our typology draws primarily from the sociological models that highlighted NRMs' organizational structures and relationships to larger society, we were also influenced by the efforts of Melton and others who looked to the histories, beliefs, rituals, and daily practices of NRMs. Ultimately, we hope that our typology will help to raise the broadest possible questions about NRMs in the broadest possible contexts.

Any NRM creates what William E. Paden calls a "religious world." This is "not just a matter of conceptual representation, but also a specific form of habitation and practice—the structure of meaningful relationships in which a person exists and participates." Religious worlds "are cultural systems that organize language and behavior around engagement with postulated superhuman agencies."[21] As such, religious worlds are all-encompassing, taking into account the full range of human activity at all levels of interaction. NRMs

> show how the language of spirituality constantly recreates itself to address the needs of emerging cultural identities. The enormous variety of these innovative systems shows the naturalness of religious world building, each group reconstituting a cosmology, manufacturing a revised version of history, offering a new set of ontological markers and new interactive objects of authority and communication. They do this as naturally and inevitably as any species will form a habitat.[22]

NRMs are earthquakes—and they react to earthquakes. That is, they shape the world in which their members exist by shaking the foundations of older worlds, but they also react to the constant shaking of worlds that is the ongoing work of religious life in general. We believe that the student of NRMs can observe this continuous process of earthquakes by looking at NRM activity under five general types or categories, which also comprise the basic outline of this volume. Each type brings into focus a particular way that a given NRM reconstitutes its world by rearranging social relationships, by reconfiguring basic myths and perspectives, and by recasting ethical prescriptions. In very broad terms, it may be argued, groups have historically offered certain religious benefits along five distinct pathways, arranged here from "inner" to "outer": a new *understanding* of the true nature of the cosmos; a new, transformed, healthier, and/or more spiritually advanced *self*; a new, better-connected, more loving and caring *family*; a newly ethical *society*, more concerned with public morality or equitable justice; and finally a new *world*, one where the corruption of cosmic evil, the effects of human fallibility or short-sightedness, or the burdens of material existence have been erased forever or simply left behind. These five categories reflect themes of newness typically found in NRMs (and traditional religions, for that matter). A particular NRM will emphasize one or more of these themes in its communication with members and the larger world, including and especially in any texts it holds sacred. For our purposes here, we might call these themes "nexuses of novelty" that offer something appealing and compelling around which an identity can be constructed in contradistinction to other socially available options, both for the group as a whole and for individual members. Let us look at some of the defining qualities of groups centered around each of these types of novelty.

- *New Understanding*: A group that emphasizes a new understanding of the cosmos primarily seeks to address the illusions and errors that plague people's experience of life—mainly the limitations of human sensory perceptions and our constant confrontations with difference, disharmony, and separation. Beyond the everyday world we experience—what we know as "this world"—is an infinite, interconnected spiritual realm, say these groups. Furthermore, this realm is accessible to all people, if only they can find their way through to it. Seeing the spiritual realm either as infused with the material world or as superceding it gives the member of an NRM of this type a completely transformed understanding of the nature of the cosmos, how it works, and the human individual's role in it. Not surprisingly, many groups of this type are influenced by or transplants of Eastern religions, especially Hinduism and Buddhism, although influences from all major religious traditions are evident.
- *New Self*: A group that promotes a path to a new self as a primary feature views the human being (or, sometimes more precisely, "being human") as the cornerstone of cosmic existence. Seeing a potential for unlimited spiritual growth as inherent to all humans, New Self groups claim to offer the secret to unlocking this potential and to transforming the individual's apparently weak, imperfect, and insignificant traits into the perfect, powerful, and vital forces into which they are destined to evolve. This spiritual progress is often seen in a therapeutic light, as an education about and a liberation from destructive bonds that keep us trapped in a corrupt, material world, or in an unhappy past, or in patterns of unhealthy behavior. New Self groups often speak of the godliness of all individuals

and the possibility of becoming a god or godlike oneself. New Self groups, like New Understanding groups, quite often show a distinct Eastern influence, especially the spiritual goals of the Hindu discipline of yoga, but one also may find certain Western Gnostic notions, such as the "spark of the divine"—not to mention a good deal of modern, humanistic psychology.

- *New Family*: As NRMs that constitute themselves as "new families" for their members, New Family groups may reproduce the nuclear family structure and will sometimes use the language and rhetoric that define traditional families to make explicit the relationships among members of the group. Leaders are to be seen as adults—parents, "mothers" and "fathers"—while others are "children" who seek the guidance and protection of their wise and powerful "elders." To a large degree, it is the New Family groups that inspire the ire and fear of parents, religious leaders, and politicians. Seeing the ways in which these NRMs construct alternative families may help us make sense of the long-standing public battles involving certain NRMs. For someone to join a new family, in these cases, is to reject the old one, to claim that those who have raised this person have failed to prepare him or her for the world. This rejection applies to society's surrogate families, religion and the state, where leaders are often more or less explicitly regarded as parental figures. Hence, when individuals pursue an alternative spiritual path that reinforces their individuality, as in the New Understanding and New Self groups, the communal structures—especially the looser ones in America—are not as openly threatened. Yet when a group seeks to replace those same structures *at their very core* by redefining the family, those who represent or support the maintenance of social norms feel threatened.

- *New Society*: In contradistinction to the New Family groups, which tend to be insular, other NRMs do not so much reject society outright as seek to reform it. These groups promote a new, comprehensive moral code or social justice imperative, thus working to transform the existing institutions and mores into ones that achieve a unified higher purpose while improving the daily lives of the needy or deserving within the social sphere. New Society NRMs view their own group structure not just as an exemplar for society as a whole—even globally—but often, in fact, as the catalyst that will ultimately create a permanent perfect society. Very frequently, these NRMs will self-identify with the biblical Zion, Israel, or Promised Land, imparting a sacred sanction to their efforts. Therefore, their own social relations and personal ethics are held to a divine standard; moral failings could jeopardize nothing less than the promise of a hard-won paradise on earth. With this goal at the forefront, recruitment and evangelism may focus on larger themes of oppression, injustice, moral decay, and marginalization, making these groups at times overtly political and activist. Furthermore, these groups quite often are Afrocentric, defining their social struggles in terms of black racism and the imperative to restore the African descendents of slaves to a sovereign nation of their own.

- *New World*: A group anticipating the total transformation of the planet and its inhabitants is typically labeled *apocalyptic,* and indeed the very source of that term, the biblical Book of Revelation, or the Apocalypse of St. John, famously envisions "a new heaven and a new earth" (Rev. 21:1). Thus, apocalyptic groups in the Christian mold, who await a final battle between Good and Evil (Armageddon), anticipate a total transformation of the world, both socially and physically, at the End of Time. Yet many NRMs not overtly linked to Christian ideology similarly see the only hope for the future in the promise of a new earth, either through the complete revitalization of the planet as a living being itself (Gaia), or through casting off this planet for some more perfect place in the cosmos, generally as a result of the intervention of a superior alien civilization. These two diametrically opposed goals, in essence, split the Christian promise in two, promising a perfect earth without a heaven and vice versa.

These nexuses of novelty clearly are interrelated. Hence, a "new family" will require a "new self" and will engender a "new understanding"; envisioning a "new society" follows from the desire for a "new world" (or vice versa). As each nexus of novelty in this schema is progressively more comprehensive, there is often an implicit or explicit transformation of the categories that precede it. On the other hand, this continuum could also be seen not as linear, but as *circular* (a step beyond re-envisioning the earth is to understand the cosmos in a new way) and *reversible* (a new understanding of the cosmos could demand a rejection of the world as it is, including society, family, and one's old self). Ultimately, the best way to conceptualize the relationship among these five types is as a *matrix*: to achieve the fullest comprehension and analysis, any given NRM can be viewed primarily through the lens of one of these categories, but then the diligent investigator must trace the multifarious connections between one nexus of novelty and any others that might be pertinent.

The groups and texts anthologized in this collection, then, are organized according to their core nexus of novelty, that is, the innovation on the available existential answers that most primarily or fundamentally sets the group apart and makes it a fresh, distinct option appropriate for certain individuals' religious sensibilities. In this way, we can achieve a depth, breadth, and cohesiveness in our understanding of a particular NRM's stances. Moreover, this way of organizing groups should facilitate comparison and contrast among those of the same and different types, enhancing an overall picture of the diversity of NRMs while bringing into focus what they have in common, why they share these traits, and what that might mean to any student of religion. To present a clear and accurate picture of the groups categorized by a specific nexus of novelty, we have attempted to include two or three representatives of each type.[23]

How to Use This Volume

This volume is not intended to be the ultimate or only source of information about NRMs. Rather, it should be used as a complement to the many useful texts, essays, reference works, and monographs about NRMs. Although our typology is unique, it is not the first or only one to categorize NRMs according to certain basic themes and presuppositions, and individuals seeking a deeper understanding of these groups will benefit from comparing our approach with other typologies. In this section we consider how the reader might use this volume most effectively in conjunction with other sources of information about NRMs.

NRMs themselves produce a seemingly endless stream of material: books, pamphlets, newsletters, magazines, videotapes and DVDs, audiotapes and CDs, and Websites. This volume offers only a small sampling of the multitude of NRM resources available to the curious student. We have selected materials from certain NRMs to represent not only those particular groups, but also the nexus of novelty that we think a given NRM reflects. One way to use this volume when exploring the vast sea of NRM materials is to keep our typology in mind as you explore. For example, when examining the Website of ISKCON, an NRM not found in this volume, ask which nexus of novelty best describes the emphases you find there. Are the devotees of Krishna in ISKCON most concerned about con-structing a New Family, propagating a New Understanding of life, or forming a New Self? How might these various emphases intertwine in a group like ISKCON?

A similar strategy may be helpful when you read anticult or countercult literature. Like NRMs, anticult and countercult movements have produced a massive amount of information accessible in numerous forms, from printed matter to internet sources. Anticult and countercult writers and apologists have very specific perspectives on NRMs that determine how they see and interpret them. Their viewpoints can be usefully compared with the typology in this volume. For example, Walter R. Martin, who was "regarded by many as the most influential countercult apologist of the post–World War II period,"[24] had a decidedly theological perspective. That is, he focused upon the beliefs of NRMs, to the exclusion of other features, in making judgments about the value of the groups and those who joined them. Martin saw NRMs as "false prophets," a phrase he borrowed from Matthew 7:15. In this way, Martin categorized all NRMs as deceptive orga-nizations that clearly departed from Christian truth.[25] To use our typolog-ical terms, Martin was most interested in New Understanding (which he would undoubtedly have preferred to label "false understanding")—that is, with the metaphysical worldview of NRM members. Other typological categories from this volume would have been less important to Martin. For example, he probably would not have been especially interested in the New Society that a given NRM might foster, except as that vision of soci-ety was part of the theological error of an NRM's worldview. Other advo-cates of the anticult and countercult movements focus on other nexuses of novelty. Margaret Thaler Singer formulated a psychologically based theory to explain how people who joined NRMs were supposedly deprived of free agency, or the ability to make decisions for themselves. In the appendix to this volume, Cowan highlights Singer's three-part explanation: cultic lead-ers are charismatic and dictatorial, their organizations are tightly con-trolled by leaders, and members who join are forced into regimented behavior and thinking.[26] To use the typological terms in this volume, for Singer the most important nexus of novelty was perhaps New Self, or even New Family. Singer was most concerned about the alteration of an in-dependent, free-thinking individual into a self that was robotic and men-tally and emotionally stifled. Arguably, she was also dismayed by the new familial relationships that replaced the old ones when someone joined a NRM. In Singer's view, all members of NRMs severed prior relationships to friends and family and adopted a new family, albeit one that, in Singer's view, was unhealthy and potentially destructive.

If you are interested in learning about NRMs, you most likely will read not only the literature produced by NRMs and their opponents in the anticult and countercult movements, but also scholarly interpretations and analyses published by researchers whose goal is neither to defend the specific truth claims of any particular group nor to condemn NRMs from an anticult or countercult viewpoint. Such scholarly research, in sociology of religion and other fields, is usually published by academic presses affiliated with universities, or by reputable general presses with academic subdivisions devoted to producing works of a scholarly nature. Many NRM scholars have published their books or collections of essays in these venues.

Without question, one of the most useful general introductions to the study of NRMs is John Saliba's *Understanding New Religious Movements,* now available in a second edition. Saliba's book "is based on the assumption that examining the new religions from different academic perspectives is a necessary preliminary step for understanding their presence in our age and for drafting an effective response to their influence."[27] Each of Saliba's chapters considers NRMs from a different vantage point: history, psychology, sociology, the law, Christian theology, and counseling. The present volume could profitably be read alongside Saliba's book by comparing his chapter on the sociological interpretation of NRMs with the New Family nexus of novelty, for example, or by comparing his chapter on the psychological interpretation of NRMs with the New Self nexus of novelty. Or, the reader might work through both texts simultaneously, seeing how the history of NRMs as described by Saliba has affected various groups in all of the nexuses of novelty, or by comparing various issues related to law and NRMs in Saliba's book with legal issues as they arise in the present volume.

Many, perhaps most, scholarly books about NRMs rely upon the sociology of religion. One of the best of the recent offerings in this category is Lorne L. Dawson's *Comprehending Cults: The Sociology of New Religious Movements.* Each chapter of Dawson's book raises a significant question asked by many observers of NRMs, scholarly and nonscholarly alike. The creative reader could consider the questions posed by Dawson and search for the various ways that NRMs have answered them in all five nexuses of novelty in our volume. For example, the organizing question for Dawson's third chapter is "Who Joins New Religious Movements and Why?"

This question is paramount in several examples from the present volume: Theosophy in New Understandings, Wicca in New Selves, and The Family International in New Families. Dawson's fifth chapter is concerned with the question "Why Do Some New Religious Movements Become Violent?" This question is germane in other examples from our volume: UFO experiencers in New Understandings, Peoples Temple in New Societies, and the Adventist Branch Davidians as well as Heaven's Gate in New Worlds.

Although sociology of religion is crucial to NRM study, other academic disciplines also play important roles. A collection of essays edited by Timothy Miller entitled *America's Alternative Religions,* for example, considers history and doctrine more than the sociological aspects of NRMs. Contributors to Miller's volume cover over one hundred NRMs in forty-three chapters. A given NRM was included if it was religious, of "considerable public interest," and represented "some notable departure from the religious mainstream."[28] Although we did not consciously go by these criteria when selecting NRMs, we certainly could have. Almost all of the NRMs in our volume (the exception being those in our section on the year 2000) are discussed in Miller's volume.[29] A reader of both books could compare the ways that NRMs in Miller's category of "Established Christian Alternatives," for example, appear in various places in our volume. These "Established Christian Alternatives" include the Jehovah's Witnesses (in New Worlds) and Christian Science (in New Understandings). Both Jehovah's Witnesses and Christian Scientists "are rooted in Christianity but have added new or unusually nuanced doctrines, scriptures, or practices to the Christian tradition."[30] That places them within the same category in Miller's volume. Yet in our volume we see them as examples of two different nexuses of novelty. Both means of understanding these two groups —in terms of their family resemblances as alternatives within Christianity and in terms of their differing nexuses of novelty—are important. Miller's way of conceptualizing NRMs and the one we rely upon in this volume do not cancel one another out. NRMs are too varied, too fluid, and too unpredictable to be studied through only one disciplinary or conceptual lens.

In summary, *New Religious Movements: A Documentary Reader* is designed to complement other scholarly works available to the NRM student today. This volume contains not only primary documents in which leaders and members of NRMs speak in their own voices, but also a typology that is flexible enough to allow readers to contrast and compare it with other typologies.

NOTES

1. Jacob Needleman, *The New Religions* (Garden City, N.Y.: Doubleday, 1970), 6.

2. Catherine Wessinger, *How the Millennium Comes Violently: From Jonestown to Heaven's Gate* (New York: Seven Bridges Press, 2000), 4. See the Appendix to this reader, "Constructing the New Religious Threat: Anticult and Countercult Movements" by Douglas E. Cowan, for an extended discussion of these issues.

3. Enlightening discussions of these terms can be found in Lorne L. Dawson, "Creating 'Cult' Typologies: Some Strategic Considerations," *Journal of Contemporary Religion* 12.3 (1997): 363–81; James T. Richardson, "Definitions of Cult: From Sociological-Technical to Popular-Negative," *Review of Religious Research* 34.4 (June 1993): 348–56; and David V. Barrett, *A Survey of Sects, Cults, and Alternative Religions* (London: Cassell, 2001).

4. The literature on the seemingly sudden appearance of many NRMs or alternative religions in the United States in the 1960s is voluminous. Useful discussions of this period in American religious history can be found in books written for teaching purposes, including Lorne L. Dawson, *Comprehending Cults: The Sociology of New Religious Movements* (Don Mills, Ontario: Oxford University Press Canada, 1998); and John A. Saliba, *Understanding New Religious Movements*, 2d ed. (Walnut Creek, Calif.: AltaMira Press, 2003).

5. See Gene R. Thursby, "Hindu Movements since Mid-Century: Yogis in the States," in *America's Alternative Religions*, ed. Timothy Miller (Albany: State University of New York Press, 1995): 193–95.

6. George D. Chryssides, *Exploring New Religions* (London: Cassell, 1999), 16–17.

7. For a useful introductory explanation of the brainwashing controversy, see Dawson, *Comprehending Cults*, chap. 4. A helpful review of the scholarship can be found in Larry D. Shinn, "Who Gets to Define Religion? The Conversion/Brainwashing Controversy," *Religious Studies Review* 19.3 (July 1993): 195–207. To date the most significant scholarly volume on this topic is Benjamin Zablocki and Thomas Robbins, eds., *Misunderstanding Cults: Searching for Objectivity in a Controversial Field* (Toronto: Toronto University Press, 2001). The definitive study of countercultists is Douglas E. Cowan, *Bearing False Witness? An Introduction to the Christian Countercult* (Westport, Conn.: Praeger, 2003). Some of the most notable anticult and countercult experts include Ron Enroth, Margaret Singer, and Steven Hassan. Margaret Singer and Janja Lalich's *Cults in Our Midst: The Hidden Menace in Our Everyday Lives* (San Francisco: Jossey-Bass, 1995) is an excellent example of anticult literature.

8. See Ann Braude, "Women's History *Is* American Religious History," in *Retelling U.S. Religious History*, ed. Thomas A. Tweed (Berkeley: University of California Press, 1997).

9. See Susan Jean Palmer, *Moon Sisters, Krishna Mothers, Rajneesh Lovers: Women's Roles in New Religions* (Syracuse, N.Y.: Syracuse University Press, 1994); Catherine Wessinger, ed., *Women's Leadership in Marginal Religions: New Roles Outside the Mainstream* (Urbana: University of Illinois Press, 1993); and Thomas Robbins and David G. Bromley, "What Have We Learned about New Religions? New Religious Movements as Experiments," *Religious Studies Review* 19 (July 1993): 209–16.

10. Again, Dawson's discussion in *Comprehending Cults* constitutes one of the best introductions to the issues involved. To date one of the best scholarly treatments of this ongoing area of study is Wessinger's *How the Millennium Comes Violently*. Another excellent scholarly source is David G. Bromley and J. Gordon Melton, eds., *Cults, Religion, and Violence* (Cambridge: Cambridge University Press, 2002).

11. See "*Nova Religio* Symposium," *Nova Religio* 4.2 (April 2001): 172–350; and Robert Towler, ed., *New Religions and the New Europe* (Aarhus, Denmark: Aarhus University Press, 1995).

12. See H. Byron Earhart, "New Religions," in *Kodansha Encyclopedia of Japan* (Tokyo: Kodansha Ltd., 1985), 5:366–67; and Shimazono Susumu, "New New Religions and This World: Religious Movements in Japan after the 1970s and Their Beliefs about Salvation," *Social Compass* 42.2 (1995): 194.

13. See Allan Anderson, *African Reformation: African Initiated Christianity in the 20th Century* (Trenton, N.J.: Africa World Press, 2001).

14. The most exciting new study of NRMs across multiple boundaries is Phillip C. Lucas and Thomas Robbins, eds., *New Religious Movements in the 21st Century: Political and Social Challenges in Global Perspective* (New York: Routledge, 2004).

15. See David G. Bromley and Lewis F. Carter, eds., *Toward Reflexive Ethnography: Participating, Observing, Narrating* (Amsterdam, N.Y.: JAI, 2001).

16. Chryssides, *Exploring New Religions,* 6. Bryan Wilson explained his typology in his *Sects and Society: A Sociological Study of the Elim Tabernacle, Christian Science and Christadelphians* (Berkeley: University of California Press, 1961).

17. Lorne L. Dawson, "Creating 'Cult' Typologies," 367.

18. J. Gordon Melton, "Selections from the Introduction to the First Edition," in *The Encyclopedia of American Religions,* 5th ed., ed. J. Gordon Melton (Detroit: Gale Research, 1996), xviii.

19. See, for example, Miller, ed., *America's Alternative Religions*; Chryssides, *Exploring New Religions*; and Saliba, *Understanding New Religious Movements.*

20. Jeff Kenney, "The Politics of Sects and Typologies," *Nova Religio* 6.1 (October 2002): 138.

21. William E. Paden, "World," in *Guide to the Study of Religion,* ed. Willi Braun and Russell T. McCutcheon (London: Cassell, 2000): 334–35.

22. Ibid., 343.

23. Certain groups presented obstacles to inclusion in this reader. For example, groups such as Falun Gong and Transcendental Meditation instruct followers in a specific meditative or yogic practice intended to allow the "True Self" to emerge, and could have been included in that section of the book. However, these groups insist that they are not, in fact, religions at all; rather, they merely offer a pragmatic technique for self-transformation. Other groups originate from the teachings of a single revered individual, which are closely guarded against misuse and misrepresentation by outsiders. The protection of sacred writ and a founder's legacy is paramount, for instance, for the Church of Scientology. Other groups are simply closed off to outsiders. Finally, the use of many instructive documents from NRMs in non–English speaking countries has been limited by a variety of cultural and geographic factors.

24. Cowan, p. 320 below.

25. Walter Martin, *The Kingdom of the Cults,* rev. and expanded ed. (Minneapolis: Bethany House, 1985), 15.

26. See Cowan, p. 318 below.

27. Saliba, *Understanding New Religious Movements,* vii.

28. Miller, editor's introduction to *America's Alternative Religions,* 7.

29. One other exception is the Japanese NRM Soka Gakkai, but its emphasis on the emergence of a metaphysical "true self" through a meditative practice corresponds to the concerns and techniques of many of the Hindu-based movements examined in chapters 17 and 18 of Miller's book.

30. Miller, editor's introduction to *America's Alternative Religions,* 11.

FOR FURTHER READING

Bednarowski, Mary Farrell, *New Religions and the Theological Imagination in America* (Bloomington: Indiana University Press, 1989). This unique study compares six NRMs—Mormonism, the New Age, Theosophy, Christian Science, Scientology, and the Unification Church—according to four theological concerns: the nature of God, the nature of humanity, the afterlife, and ethics.

Chryssides, George D., *Exploring New Religions* (London: Cassell, 1999). A thorough survey of major NRMs and their context by a noted British scholar.

Dawson, Lorne L., *Comprehending Cults: The Sociology of New Religious Movements* (Don Mills, Ontario: Oxford University Press Canada, 1998). An excellent introduction to the sociological issues that define the contemporary study of NRMs.

Dawson, Lorne L., ed., *Cults in Context: Readings in the Study of New Religious Movements* (New Brunswick, N.J.: Transaction, 1998). Brings together contributions from NRM scholars on many theoretical issues: recruitment, the brainwashing controversy, violence, gender, and the cultural importance of NRMs.

Miller, Timothy, ed., *America's Alternative Religions* (Albany: State University of New York Press, 1995). Forty-three chapters provide sketches of NRMs ranging from Native American to Asian, Christian to New Age, Middle Eastern to African diaspora traditions.

Religious Movements Homepage Project, University of Virginia, http://religious movements.lib.virginia.edu. This scholarly resource provides information on virtually every NRM in the world.

Saliba, John A., *Understanding New Religious Movements*, 2d ed. (Walnut Creek, Calif.: AltaMira Press, 2003). The best introduction to NRMs available, comprehensive yet written for the general reader. Published in the United Kingdom under the title *Perspectives on New Religious Movements* (London: Cassell, 1995).

Stein, Stephen J., *Communities of Dissent: A History of Alternative Religions in America* (New York: Oxford University Press, 2003). A brief but informative survey of the significant NRMs in American history and culture.

Wessinger, Catherine, *How the Millennium Comes Violently: From Jonestown to Heaven's Gate* (New York: Seven Bridges Press, 2000). The now-classic survey of NRMs that have made headlines because of violence: Jonestown, the Branch Davidians, Aum Shinrikyo, the Montana Freemen, Solar Temple, Heaven's Gate, and Chen Tao.

Part I

New Understandings

Chapter 1

Christian Science

The Church of Christ, Scientist, also known as Christian Science, was founded in 1879 by Mary Baker Eddy (1821–1910). Christian Science cannot be understood apart from Eddy's life story, and her life story cannot be understood without some attention to the religious context of her day. Many Americans in the mid-nineteenth century were attracted to a range of alternative spiritualities that existed outside the boundaries of Protestant and Catholic churches and usually are called metaphysical or harmonial religions. Although these metaphysical faiths differ from one another in many ways, they generally insist that God is absolute Mind and that humans are manifestations of that Mind. The origins of such views owe much to the speculations of the Swedish mystic Emanuel Swedenborg (1688–1772), who wrote that the divine and nature are one and that the spiritual world provides the forms and patterns for all manifestations in the physical world. Metaphysical religions were also influenced by Franz Anton Mesmer (1734–1815), an Austrian physician and showman who insisted that a subtle fluid called animal magnetism flowed through all things and that one could effect healing—or most anything else—by tapping into and controlling the flow of this fluid. During the Enlightenment, many French thinkers accepted Mesmer's explanation as a rational way to harness what previously had been seen as occultic or superstitious forces. By the mid-nineteenth century, Mesmerism had become a fad in the United States. It provided both religious and nonreligious people with a way to understand the universe. For the non- or antireligious person, Mesmerism was a scientific means of explaining both the visible and the invisible in nature. For the religious person, Mesmer's ideas were relatively easy to graft onto a theological understanding of the cosmos: God exists, God created animal magnetism, and God works through it to affect all things according to God's will.

One American of this era who participated in the spread of metaphysical ideas, and who played a dramatic role in Eddy's life, was Phineas

Parkhurst Quimby (1802–1866), a Maine clockmaker who became interested in Mesmerism and began to heal people using Mesmeric methods. Quimby eventually realized that his healings were successful because his clients believed that animal magnetism worked. He therefore decided that the key to healing was not to be found in some universal fluid, but rather in the mental attitude of those who were healed. In the antebellum Yankee spirit of his time and place, Quimby was a pragmatic rationalist. He was not a religious man, nor was he given to philosophical speculation, and he did not write about mind and healing in a systematic fashion. Nevertheless, his influence on Eddy was enormous, in part because she discovered him at an auspicious time in her own life.

Eddy was a weak and nervous child and spent much of her childhood suffering from various physical and psychological ailments. In rural New Hampshire, where she was born and raised, the problem of illness was addressed by a combination of folk medicine and strong Calvinist theology inherited from the Puritan period in New England. If one was sick, then God willed it; little could be done to alter the course of illness, except by using some folk remedies or by resorting to one of a number of medical therapies that later would be labeled "alternative" to the allopathic, or mainstream, medical practice that eventually triumphed in the battle of medical therapies that lasted throughout much of the nineteenth century.

During her periods of convalescence, Eddy became an avid reader, especially of the Bible. When she was twenty-one she married George Glover, who died that same year. Eleven years later, in 1853, she married Daniel Patterson, a traveling dentist who was away from home much of the time. Eddy was often alone and ill during his prolonged absences. In 1873 they divorced. Throughout this long and difficult period of childhood and adulthood, Eddy experimented with various alternative medical therapies, but nothing seemed to help. In 1862, while looking for yet another way to address her persistent health difficulties, she discovered Quimby. His prescription of a positive mental attitude worked wonders for Eddy, who spent long hours in conversation with him. Although Quimby was not sympathetic to the strong religious strain in her life and thought, Eddy nonetheless found Quimby's approach to be revolutionary. The general trend in her thinking toward mental cure for disease was cemented when, in 1866, she fell on the ice and suffered terribly as a result (see "The Great Discovery" below). While in pain, she read from the

New Testament about Jesus' miracles, and when she realized that Jesus' healing was effected through positive mental attitudes, her own condition improved dramatically.

For the next nine years Eddy wrote and taught classes on her evolving explanations for illness and healing. The end result was *Science and Health with Key to the Scriptures,* first published in 1875. Originally this project began as an extended commentary on the Bible, hence the "Key to the Scriptures" in the title, but the book eventually became more than this as she compiled many writings reflecting her years of thought about illness and healing. She was not willing to surrender her Protestant heritage or biblical worldview, but she recast both in metaphysical terms that gave rise to a unique NRM still alive today, Christian Science.

The "Christian" aspect was, for Eddy, always important. She did not interpret her approach as being a departure from Christian theology, but as an elaboration on it that corrected previous errors. She called her movement "Science" because she was convinced that her approach could be scientifically verified. In an era before science and religion radically parted company, many found her science, which we might today call "scientism," to be entirely compatible with both rationality and religion. Eddy insisted that all of her claims could be confirmed by rational observation and experimentation, and the many success stories included in her book (see "A Case of Mental Surgery" and "A Remarkable Case" below, for example) attested to the practicality of Christian Science in healing ills and injuries.

In 1877 she married Asa Eddy. When he died five years later of heart disease, she was convinced that one of her students had sent negative thoughts toward him and was responsible for his death. These and several other difficult and controversial relationships plagued Eddy as her movement became increasingly successful.

As Christian Science reached its mature form, the main points in Eddy's teaching took shape as follows. She taught that God is absolute Mind, and that the only reality is God. God made the world, but the materiality that our five senses indicate as being real is, in fact, an illusion, filled with pain and death. Although God is absolute Mind, God also has personal characteristics, especially Love, and through Love humans can know God. This happens when humans are healed; they cannot know God and God's Love otherwise. Illness participates in the illusory world of the material. When one realizes that illness or any other suffering is merely illusory, then one sees God clearly and enjoys God's Love purely. When one is healed from sin or suffering, the real reason for such healing is not to rectify some wrong or relieve pain, but to reveal the glory of God.

Humans, Eddy taught, have two purposes: to realize that God is Mind, and to effect healing in our lives and in the lives of others. Our material existence is ultimately not real, despite what our five senses tell us about our flesh and blood and bones. In practical terms, when a person experiences pain from an illness or injury, a Christian Science expert called a "practitioner" helps that person readjust his or her thinking in order to overcome the pain and achieve a deeper realization of one's true nature in God. For many people, simply reading from *Science and Health with Key to the Scriptures* during times of illness effects this transformation.

Science and Health with Key to the Scriptures is not written like a systematic theology, in which one idea follows another in linear fashion. Rather, Eddy returns repeatedly to the same basic themes, using different language and perspectives. For the Christian Scientist, an individual reading from this text is being exposed to correct thinking as embedded in its words. A skeptic might dismiss this assumption that the act of reading from a text could have salutary effects on one's health as merely magical thinking. But for Christian Scientists, Eddy's book contains the distilled wisdom of the ages regarding God and human existence. Therefore, repeated exposure to these concepts through prolonged reading has the positive effect of transforming erroneous thoughts into correct ones.

Eddy hoped that by reading her words we would finally realize that we are free from sin and sickness, which she defined as illusory and transitory states of mind. When a person accepts this truth, said Eddy, then sin and sickness dissipate like mist in the morning sunlight. Death, too, is an illusion for Eddy. While trapped into wrong thinking about the reality of matter, many people fear death as a transition to some unknown or threatening state of existence. But Christian Scientists understand that just as matter is not real, neither is death as it is conventionally conceived. Eddy used biblical concepts such as resurrection, heaven, and hell, but reinterpreted them. In Christian Science, Resurrection is Jesus' means of bringing to people the realization that all is absolute Mind and freeing them from the grip of death. Hell is perpetual bondage to illusory thinking, while heaven is total acceptance of absolute Mind, so that physical death, as such, is merely a short interlude between one radiant life and another. Life with God in heaven, then, is a full realization, not a shift from the material dimension to the nonmaterial.

In 1879 Eddy founded the Church of Christ, Scientist, in Lynn, Massachusetts, to give institutional expression to her growing movement of Christian Scientists. At first she encouraged the formation of local congregations, but when many of these proved too rebellious, she reorganized the church in 1892 with full control centered in the Mother Church in Boston, of which the local congregations became branches. Lay leaders, rather than pastors, led congregations at the local level. They did not preach sermons, but read prescribed passages from the Bible and *Science and Health with Key to the Scriptures* each Sunday during worship. Eddy provided all rules for the church in the *Manual of the Mother Church*. This tightly controlled NRM thus journeyed successfully into the twentieth century, with women in the overwhelming majority.

Eddy's successes were marred, however, by controversy and the misunderstanding of the general public. In 1908 she began what became *The Christian Science Monitor,* a newspaper that she hoped would clarify Christian Science teaching for others. Eventually the newspaper evolved into one of the most journalistically responsible news organs in the United States, far exceeding its original mandate as a mouthpiece for Christian Science. The movement has also suffered negative publicity, especially when Christian Science children fall ill or receive injuries and their parents refuse medical treatment that might save their children's lives. A number of court cases have resulted from this unfortunate state of affairs, with no clear pattern, judicially speaking, having yet emerged.

Clearly, Christian Science emphasizes the necessity for a New Understanding. Erroneous thinking must be erased so that the individual has the correct understanding about God, the world, and humanity. Christian Science assumes that a New Self—one that correctly dismisses sin and suffering as illusory—will result from this New Understanding. Christian Science says relatively little, especially compared to other NRMs, about a New Family, a New Society, or a New World. Presumably all of these would result from all people coming to the New Understanding that Christian Science teaches, but the importance of understanding remains central to Christian Science activity.

The following excerpts highlight the New Understanding of Christian Science teaching. The first is taken from a collection of Eddy's writings that postdate *Science and Health with Key to the Scriptures.* Included in this collection is "The Great Discovery," Eddy's version of her crucial fall on the ice in 1866 and the realizations that followed it. The second excerpt begins with a series of questions and answers taken from a catechism that

Eddy used to teach Christian Science, and which she also included in *Science and Health with Key to the Scriptures*. In her answers, Eddy summarizes many basic concepts in Christian Science thought. The second excerpt closes with two of the many testimonies written by nineteenth-century Americans who put Eddy's practices to use. In the first instance, a man applied Christian Science principles to the treatment of his broken arm, while in the second a mother applied them to her son's medical condition. In both cases, satisfactory results were achieved.

From *Retrospection and Introspection*

Mary Baker Eddy

The Great Discovery

It was in Massachusetts, in February, 1866, and after the death of the magnetic doctor, Mr. P. P. Quimby, whom spiritualists would associate therewith, but who was in no wise connected with this event, that I discovered the Science of divine metaphysical healing which I afterwards named Christian Science. The discovery came to pass in this way. During twenty years prior to my discovery I had been trying to trace all physical effects to a mental cause; and in the latter part of 1866 I gained the scientific certainty that all causation was Mind, and every effect a mental phenomenon.

My immediate recovery from the effects of an injury caused by an accident, an injury that neither medicine nor surgery could reach, was the falling apple that led me to the discovery how to be well myself, and how to make others so.

Even to the homeopathic physician who attended me, and rejoiced in my recovery, I could not then explain the *modus* of my relief. I could only assure him that the divine Spirit had wrought the miracle—a miracle which later I found to be in perfect scientific accord with divine law.

I then withdrew from society about three years,—to ponder my mission, to search the Scriptures, to find the Science of Mind that should take the things of God and show them to the creature, and reveal the great curative Principle,—Deity.

The Bible was my textbook. It answered my questions as to how I was healed; but the Scriptures had to me a new meaning, a new tongue. Their spiritual signification appeared; and I apprehended for the first time, in their spiritual meaning, Jesus' teaching and demonstration, and the Principle and rule of spiritual Science and metaphysical healing,—in a word, Christian Science.

I named it *Christian*, because it is compassionate, helpful, and spiritual. God I called *immortal Mind*. That which sins, suffers, and dies, I named *mortal mind*. The physical senses, or sensuous nature, I called *error* and *shadow*. Soul I denominated *substance*, because Soul alone is truly substantial. God I characterized as individual entity, but His corporeality I denied. The real I claimed as eternal; and its antipodes, or the temporal, I described as unreal. Spirit I called the *reality*; and matter, the *unreality*.

I knew the human conception of God to be that He was a physically personal being, like unto man; and that the five physical senses are so many witnesses to the physical personality of mind and the real existence of matter; but I learned that these material senses testify falsely, that matter neither sees, hears, nor feels Spirit, and is therefore inadequate to form any proper conception of the infinite Mind. "If I bear witness of myself, my witness is not true." (John v. 31.)

I beheld with ineffable awe our great Master's purpose in not questioning those he healed as to their disease or its symptoms, and his marvelous skill in demanding neither obedience to hygienic laws, nor prescribing drugs to support the divine power which heals. Adoringly I discerned the Principle of his holy heroism and Christian example on the cross, when he refused to drink the "vinegar and gall," a preparation of poppy, or aconite, to allay the tortures of crucifixion.

Our great Way-shower, steadfast to the end in his obedience to God's laws, demonstrated for all time and peoples the supremacy of good over evil, and the superiority of Spirit over matter.

The miracles recorded in the Bible, which had before seemed to me supernatural, grew divinely natural and apprehensible; though uninspired interpreters ignorantly pronounce Christ's healing miraculous, instead of seeing therein the operation of the divine law.

Jesus of Nazareth was a natural and divine Scientist. He was so before the material world saw him. He who antedated Abraham, and gave the world a new date in the Christian era, was a Christian Scientist, who needed no discovery of the Science of being in order to rebuke the evidence. To one "born of the flesh," however, divine Science must be a discovery. Woman must give it birth. It must be begotten of spirituality, since none but the pure in heart can see God,—the Principle of all things pure; and none but the "poor in spirit" could first state this Principle, could know yet more of the nothingness of matter and the allness of Spirit, could utilize Truth, and absolutely reduce the demonstration of being, in Science, to the apprehension of the age.

I wrote also, at this period, comments on the Scriptures, setting forth their spiritual interpretation, the Science of the Bible, and so laid the foundation of my work called Science and Health, published in 1875.

If these notes and comments, which have never been read by any one but myself, were published, it would show that after my discovery of the absolute Science of Mind-healing, like all great truths, this spiritual Science developed itself to me until Science and Health was written. These early comments are valuable to me as waymarks of progress, which I would not have effaced.

Up to that time I had not fully voiced my discovery. Naturally, my first jottings were but efforts to express in feeble diction Truth's ultimate. In Longfellow's language,—

> But the feeble hands and helpless,
> Groping blindly in the darkness,
> Touch God's right hand in that darkness,
> And are lifted up and strengthened.

As sweet music ripples in one's first thoughts of it like the brooklet in its meandering midst pebbles and rocks, before the mind can duly express it to the ear,—so the harmony of divine Science first broke upon my sense, before gathering experience and confidence to articulate it. Its natural manifestation is beautiful and euphonious, but its written expression increases in power and perfection under the guidance of the great Master.

The divine hand led me into a new world of light and Life, a fresh universe–old to God, but new to His "little one." It became evident that the divine Mind alone must answer, and be found as the Life, or Principle, of all being; and that one must acquaint himself with God, if he would be at peace. He must be ours practically, guiding our every thought and action; else we cannot understand the omnipresence of good sufficiently to demonstrate, even in part, the Science of the perfect Mind and divine healing.

I had learned that thought must be spiritualized, in order to apprehend Spirit. It must become honest, unselfish, and pure, in order to have the least understanding of God in divine Science. The first must become last. Our reliance upon material things must be transferred to a perception of and dependence on spiritual things. For Spirit to be supreme in demonstration, it must be supreme in our affections, and we must be clad with divine power. Purity, self-renunciation, faith, and understanding must reduce all things real to their own mental denomination, Mind, which divides, subdivides, increases, diminishes, constitutes, and sustains, according to the law of God.

I had learned that Mind reconstructed the body, and that nothing else could. How it was done, the spiritual Science of Mind must reveal. It was a mystery to me then, but I have since understood it. All Science is a revelation. Its Principle is divine, not human, reaching higher than the stars of heaven.

Am I a believer in spiritualism? I believe in no *ism*. This is my endeavor, to be a Christian, to assimilate the character and practice of the anointed; and no motive can cause a surrender of this effort. As I understand it, spiritualism is the antipode of Christian Science. I esteem all honest people, and love them, and hold to loving our enemies and doing good to them that "despitefully use you and persecute you."

From *Science and Health with Key to the Scriptures*

Mary Baker Eddy

Chapter XIV. Recapitulation

Questions and Answers

Question. – What is God?
Answer. – God is incorporeal, divine, supreme, infinite Mind, Spirit, Soul, Principle, Life, Truth, Love.

Question. – Are these terms synonymous?
Answer. – They are. They refer to one absolute God. They are also intended to express the nature, essence, and wholeness of Deity. The attributes of God are justice, mercy, wisdom, goodness, and so on.

Question. – Is there more than one God or Principle?

Answer. – There is not. Principle and its idea is one, and this one is God, omnipotent, omniscient, and omnipresent Being, and His reflection is man and the universe. *Omni* is adopted from the Latin adjective signifying *all.* Hence God combines all-power or potency, all-science or true knowledge, all-presence. The varied manifestations of Christian Science indicate Mind, never matter, and have one Principle.

Question. – What are spirits and souls?

Answer. – To human belief, they are personalities constituted of mind and matter, life and death, truth and error, good and evil; but these contrasting pairs of terms represent contraries, as Christian Science reveals, which neither dwell together nor assimilate. Truth is immortal; error is mortal. Truth is limitless; error is limited. Truth is intelligent; error is non-intelligent. Moreover, Truth is real, and error is unreal. This last statement contains the point you will most reluctantly admit, although first and last it is the most important to understand.

The term *souls* or *spirits* is as improper as the term *gods.* Soul or Spirit signifies Deity and nothing else. There is no finite soul nor spirit. Soul or Spirit means only one Mind, and cannot be rendered in the plural. Heathen mythology and Jewish theology have perpetuated the fallacy that intelligence, soul, and life can be in matter; and idolatry and ritualism are the outcome of all man-made beliefs. The Science of Christianity comes with fan in hand to separate the chaff from the wheat. Science will declare God aright, and Christianity will demonstrate this declaration and its divine Principle, making mankind better physically, morally, and spiritually.

Question. – What are the demands of the Science of Soul?

Answer. – The first demand of this Science is, "Thou shalt have no other gods before me." This *me* is Spirit. Therefore the command means this: Thou shalt have no intelligence, no life, no substance, no truth, no love, but that which is spiritual. The second is like unto it, "Thou shalt love thy neighbor as thyself." It should be thoroughly understood that all men have one Mind, one God and Father, one Life, Truth, and Love. Mankind will become perfect in proportion as this fact becomes apparent, war will cease and the true brotherhood of man will be established. Having no other gods, turning to no other but the one perfect Mind to guide him, man is the likeness of God, pure and eternal, having that Mind which was also in Christ.

Science reveals Spirit, Soul, as not in the body, and God as not in man but as reflected by man. The greater cannot be in the lesser. The belief that the greater can be in the lesser is an error that works ill. This is a leading point in the Science of Soul, that Principle is not in its idea. Spirit, Soul, is not confined in man, and is never in matter. We reason imperfectly from effect to cause, when we conclude that matter is the effect of Spirit; but *a priori* reasoning shows material existence to be enigmatical. Spirit gives the true mental idea. We cannot interpret Spirit, Mind, through matter. Matter neither sees, hears, nor feels.

Reasoning from cause to effect in the Science of Mind, we begin with Mind, which must be understood through the idea which expresses it and cannot be learned from its opposite, matter. Thus we arrive at Truth, or intelligence, which evolves its own unerring idea and never can be coordinate with human illusions. If Soul sinned, it would be mortal, for sin is mortality's self, because it kills itself. If Truth is immortal, error must be mortal, because error is unlike Truth. Because Soul is immortal, Soul cannot sin, for sin is not the eternal verity of being.

Question. – What is the scientific statement of being?
Answer. – There is no life, truth, intelligence, nor substance in matter. All is infinite Mind and its infinite manifestation, for God is All-in-all. Spirit is immortal Truth; matter is mortal error. Spirit is the real and eternal; matter is the unreal and temporal. Spirit is God, and man is His image and likeness. Therefore man is not material; he is spiritual.

Question. – What is substance?
Answer. – Substance is that which is eternal and incapable of discord and decay. Truth, Life, and Love are substance, as the Scriptures use this word in Hebrews: "The substance of things hoped for, the evidence of things not seen." Spirit, the synonym of Mind, Soul, or God, is the only real substance. The spiritual universe, including individual man, is a compound idea, reflecting the divine substance of Spirit.

Question. – What is Life?
Answer. – Life is divine Principle, Mind, Soul, Spirit. Life is without beginning and without end. Eternity, not time, expresses the thought of Life, and time is no part of eternity. One ceases in proportion as the other is recognized. Time is finite, eternity is forever infinite. Life is neither in nor of matter. What is termed matter is unknown to Spirit, which includes in

itself all substance and is Life eternal. Matter is a human concept. Life is divine Mind. Life is not limited. Death and finiteness are unknown to Life. If Life ever had a beginning, it would also have an ending.

Question. – What is intelligence?
Answer. – Intelligence is omniscience, omnipresence, and omnipotence. It is the primal and eternal quality of infinite Mind, of the triune Principle, —Life, Truth, and Love,—named God.

Question. – What is Mind?
Answer. – Mind is God. The exterminator of error is the great truth that God, good, is the *only* Mind, and that the supposititious opposite of infinite Mind—called *devil* or evil—is not Mind, is not Truth, but error, without intelligence or reality. There can be but one Mind, because there is but one God; and if mortals claimed no other Mind and accepted no other, sin would be unknown. We can have but one Mind, if that one is infinite. We bury the sense of infinitude, when we admit that, although God is infinite, evil has a place in this infinity, for evil can have no place, where all space is filled with God.

We lose the high signification of omnipotence, when after admitting that God, or good, is omnipresent and has all-power, we still believe there is another power, named *evil.* This belief that there is more than one mind is as pernicious to divine theology as are ancient mythology and pagan idolatry. With one Father, even God, the whole family of man be brethren; and with one Mind and that God, or good, the brotherhood of man would consist of Love and Truth, and have unity of Principle and spiritual power which constitute divine Science. The supposed existence of more than one mind was the basic error of idolatry. This error assumed the loss of spiritual power, the loss of the spiritual presence of Life as infinite Truth without an unlikeness, and the loss of Love as ever present and universal.

Divine Science explains the abstract statement that there is one Mind by the following self-evident proposition: If God, or good, is real, then evil, the unlikeness of God, is unreal. And evil can only seem to be real by giving reality to the unreal. The children of God have but one Mind. How can good lapse into evil, when God, the Mind of man, never sins? The standard of perfection was originally God and man. Has God taken down His own standard, and has man fallen?

God is the creator of man, and, the divine Principle of man remaining perfect, the divine idea or reflection, man, remains perfect. Man is the expression of God's being. If there ever was a moment when man did not express the divine perfection, then there was a moment when man did not express God, and consequently a time when Deity was unexpressed—that is, without entity. If man has lost perfection, then he has lost his perfect Principle, the divine Mind. If man ever existed without this perfect Principle or Mind, then man's existence was a myth.

The relations of God and man, divine Principle and idea, are indestructible in Science; and Science knows no lapse from nor return to harmony, but holds the divine order or spiritual law, in which God and all that He creates are perfect and eternal, to have remained unchanged in its eternal history.

The unlikeness of Truth,—named *error,*—the opposite of Science, and the evidence before the five corporeal senses, afford no indication of the grand facts of being; even as these so-called senses receive no intimation of the earth's motions or of the science of astronomy, but yield assent to astronomical propositions on the authority of natural science.

The facts of divine Science should be admitted,—although the evidence as to these facts is not supported by evil, by matter, or by material sense,—because the evidence that God and man coexist is fully sustained by spiritual sense. Man is, and forever has been, God's reflection. God is infinite, therefore ever present, and there is no other power nor presence. Hence the spirituality of the universe is the only fact of creation. "Let God be true, but every [material] man a liar." . . .

Question. – What is man?
Answer. – Man is not matter; he is not made up of brain, blood, bones, and other material elements. The Scriptures inform us that man is made in the image and likeness of God. Matter is not that likeness. The likeness of Spirit cannot be so unlike Spirit. Man is spiritual and perfect; and because he is spiritual and perfect, he must be so understood in Christian Science. Man is idea, the image, of Love; he is not physique. He is the compound idea of God, including all right ideas; the generic term for all that reflects God's image and likeness; the conscious identity of being as found in Science, in which man is the reflection of God's image and likeness; the conscious identity of being as found in Science, in which man is the reflection of God, or Mind, and therefore is eternal; that which has no separate mind from God; that which has not a single quality underived from Deity; that which possesses no life, intelligence, nor creative power of his own, but reflects spiritually all that belongs to his Maker.

And God said: "Let us make man in our image, after our likeness; and let them have dominion over the fish of the sea, and over the fowl of the air, and over the cattle, and over all the earth, and over every creeping thing that creepeth upon the earth."

Man is incapable of sin, sickness, and death. The real man cannot depart from holiness, nor can God, by whom man is evolved, engender the capacity or freedom to sin. A mortal sinner is not God's man. Mortals are the counterfeits of immortals. They are the children of the wicked one, or the one evil, which declares that man begins in dust or as a material embryo. In divine Science, God and the real man are inseparable as divine Principle and idea.

Error, urged to its final limits, is self-destroyed. Error will cease to claim that soul is in body, that life and intelligence are in matter, and that this matter is man. God is the Principle of man, and man is the idea of God. Hence man is not mortal nor material. Mortals will disappear, and immortals, or the children of God, will appear as the only and eternal verities of man. Mortals are not fallen children of God. They never had a perfect state of being, which may subsequently be regained. They were, from the beginning of mortal history, "conceived in sin and brought forth in iniquity." Mortality is finally swallowed up in immortality. Sin, sickness, and death must disappear to give place to the facts which belong to immortal man.

Learn this, O mortal, and earnestly seek the spiritual status of man, which is outside of all material selfhood. Remember that the Scriptures say of mortal man: "As for man, his days are as grass: as a flower of the field, so he flourisheth. For the wind passeth over it, and it is gone; and the place thereof shall know it no more."

When speaking of God's children, not the children of men, Jesus said, "The kingdom of God is within you;" That is, Truth and Love reign in the real man, showing that man in God's image is unfallen and eternal. Jesus beheld in Science the perfect man, who appeared to him where sinning mortal man appears to mortals. In this perfect man the Saviour saw God's own likeness, and this correct view of man healed the sick. Thus Jesus taught that the kingdom of God is intact, universal, and that man is pure and holy. Man is not a material habitation for Soul; he is himself spiritual. Soul, being Spirit, is seen in nothing imperfect nor material.

Whatever is material is mortal. To the five corporeal senses, man appears to be matter and mind united; but Christian Science reveals man as the idea of God, and declares the corporeal senses to be mortal and erring illusions. Divine Science shows it to be impossible that a material body, though interwoven with matter's highest stratum, misnamed mind, should be man,—the genuine and perfect man, the immortal idea of being, indestructible and eternal. Were it otherwise, man would be annihilated.

Question. – Is materiality the concomitant of spirituality, and is material sense a necessary preliminary to the understanding and expression of Spirit?

Answer. – If error is necessary to define or to reveal Truth, the answer is yes; but not otherwise. *Material sense* is an absurd phrase, for matter has no sensation. Science declares that Mind, not matter, sees, hears, feels, speaks. Whatever contradicts this statement is the false sense, which ever betrays mortals into sickness, sin, and death. If the unimportant and evil appear, only soon to disappear because of their uselessness or their iniquity, then these ephemeral views of error ought to be obliterated by Truth. Why malign Christian Science for instructing mortals how to make sin, disease, and death appear more and more unreal?

Emerge gently from matter into Spirit. Think not to thwart the spiritual ultimate of all things, but come naturally into Spirit through better health and morals and as the result of spiritual growth. Not death, but the understanding of Life, makes man immortal. The belief that life can be in matter or soul in body, and that man springs from dust or from an egg, is the result of the mortal error which Christ, or Truth, destroys by fulfilling the spiritual law of being, in which man is perfect, even as the "Father which is in heaven is perfect." If thought yields its dominion to other powers, it cannot outline on the body its own beautiful images, but it effaces them and delineates foreign agents, called disease and sin.

The heathen gods of mythology controlled war and agriculture as much as nerves control sensation or muscles measure strength. To say that strength is in matter, is like saying that the power is in the lever. The notion of any life or intelligence in matter is without foundation in fact, and you can have no faith in falsehood when you have learned falsehood's true nature.

Suppose one accident happens to the eye, another to the ear, and so on, until every corporeal sense is quenched. What is man's remedy? To die, that he may regain these senses? Even then he must gain spiritual understanding and spiritual sense in order to possess immortal consciousness. Earth's preparatory school must be improved to the utmost. In reality man never dies. The belief that he dies will not establish his scientific harmony. Death is not the result of Truth but of error, and one error will not correct another.

Jesus proved by the prints of the nails, that his body was the same immediately after death as before. If death restores sight, sound, and strength to man, then death is not an enemy but a better friend than Life. Alas for the blindness of belief, which makes harmony conditional upon death and matter, and yet supposes Mind unable to produce harmony! So long as this error of belief remains, mortals will continue mortal in belief and subject to chance and change.

Sight, hearing, all the spiritual senses of man, are eternal. They cannot be lost. Their reality and immortality are in Spirit and understanding, not in matter,—hence their permanence. If this were not so, man would be speedily annihilated. If the five corporeal senses were the medium through which to understand God, then palsy, blindness, and deafness would place man in a terrible situation, where he would be like those "having no hope, and without God in the world;" but as a matter of fact, these calamities often drive mortals to seek and to find a higher sense of happiness and existence.

Life is deathless. Life is the origin and ultimate of man, never attainable through death, but gained by walking in the pathway of Truth both before and after that which is called death. There is more Christianity in seeing and hearing spiritually than materially. There is more Science in the perpetual exercise of the Mind-faculties than in their loss. Lost they cannot be, while Mind remains. The apprehension of this gave sight to the blind and hearing to the deaf centuries ago, and it will repeat the wonder.

Question. – Will you explain sickness and show how it is to be healed?
Answer. – The method of Christian Science Mind-healing is touched upon in a previous chapter entitled Christian Science Practice. A full answer to the above question involves teaching, which enables the healer to demonstrate and prove for himself the Principle and rule of Christian Science or metaphysical healing.

Mind must be found superior to all the beliefs of the five corporeal senses, and able to destroy all ills. Sickness is a belief, which must be annihilated by the divine Mind. Disease is an experience of so-called mortal mind. It is fear made manifest on the body. Christian Science takes away this physical sense of discord, just as it removes any other sense of moral or mental inharmony. That man is material, and that matter suffers,—

these propositions can only seem real and natural in illusion. Any sense of soul in matter is not the reality of being.

If Jesus awakened Lazarus from the dream, illusion, of death, this proved that the Christ could improve on a false sense. Who dares to doubt this consummate test of the power and willingness of divine Mind to hold man forever intact in his perfect state, and to govern man's entire action? Jesus said: "Destroy this temple [body], and in three days I [Mind] will raise it up;" and he did this for tired humanity's reassurance.

Is it not a species of infidelity to believe that so great a work as the Messiah's was done for himself or for God, who needed no help from Jesus' example to preserve the eternal harmony? But mortals did need this help, and Jesus pointed the way for them. Divine Love always has met and always will meet every human need. It is not well to imagine that Jesus demonstrated the divine power to heal only for a select number or for a limited period of time, since to all mankind and in every hour, divine Love supplies all good.

The miracle of grace is no miracle to Love. Jesus demonstrated the inability of corporeality, as well as the infinite ability of Spirit, thus helping erring human sense to flee from its own convictions and seek safety in divine Science. Reason, rightly directed, serves to correct the errors of corporeal sense; but sin, sickness, and death will seem real (even as the experiences of the sleeping dream seem real) until the Science of man's eternal harmony breaks their illusion with unbroken reality of scientific being.

Which of these two theories concerning man are you ready to accept? One is the mortal testimony, changing, dying, unreal. The other is the eternal and real evidence, bearing Truth's signet, its lap piled high with immortal fruits.

Our Master cast out devils (evils) and healed the sick. It should be said of his followers also, that they cast fear and all evil out of themselves and others and heal the sick. God will heal the sick through man, whenever man is governed by God. Truth casts out error now as surely as it did nineteen centuries ago. All of Truth is not understood; hence its healing power is not fully demonstrated.

If sickness is true or the idea of Truth, you cannot destroy sickness, and it would be absurd to try. Then classify sickness and error as our Master did, when he spoke of the sick, "whom Satan hath bound," and find a sovereign antidote for error in the life-giving power of Truth acting on human belief, a power which opens the prison doors to such as are bound, and sets the captive free physically and morally.

When the illusion of sickness or sin tempts you, cling steadfastly to God and His idea. Allow nothing but His likeness to abide in your thought. Let neither fear nor doubt overshadow your clear sense and calm trust, that the recognition of life harmonious—as Life eternally is—can destroy any painful sense of, or belief in, that which Life is not. Let Christian Science, instead of corporeal sense, support your understanding of being, and this understanding will supplant error with Truth, replace mortality with immortality, and silence discord with harmony.

Chapter XVIII. Fruitage

A Case of Mental Surgery

I have felt for some time I should give my experience in mental surgery. In May, 1902, going home for lunch, on a bicycle, and while riding down a hill at a rapid gait, I was thrown from the wheel, and falling on my left side with my arm under my head, the bone was broken about half-way between the shoulder and elbow. While the pain was intense, I lay still in the dust, declaring the truth and denying that there could be a break or accident in the realm of divine Love, until a gentleman came to assist me, saying, he thought I had been stunned. I was only two and half blocks from home, so I mounted my wheel again and managed to reach it. On arriving there I lay down and asked my little boy to bring me our textbook. He immediately brought Science and Health, which I read for about ten minutes, when all pain left.

I said nothing to my family of the accident, but attended to some duties and was about half an hour late in returning to the office, this being my only loss of time from work. My friends claimed that the arm had not been broken, as it would have been impossible for me to continue my work without having it set, and carrying it in a sling until the bone knit together. Their insistence almost persuaded me that I might have been mistaken, until one of my friends invited me to visit a physician's office where they were experimenting with an X-ray machine. The physician was asked to examine my left arm to see if it differed from the ordinary. On looking through it, he said, "Yes, it has been broken, but whoever set it made a perfect job of it, and you will never have any further trouble from that break." My friend then asked the doctor to show how he could tell where the break had been. The doctor pointed out the place as being slightly thicker at that part, like a piece of steel that had been welded. This was the first of several cases of mental surgery that have come under my notice, and it made a deep impression on me.

For the benefit of others who may have something similar to meet, I will say that I have overcome almost constant attacks of sick headaches, extending to my earliest recollection.

—L. C. S., Salt Lake City, Utah.

A Remarkable Case

Nine years ago my only child was hovering between life and death. Some of the best physicians in Boston had pronounced his case incurable, saying that if he lived he would always be an invalid and a cripple. One of the diseases was gastric catarrh.[1] He was allowed to eat but very few things, and even after taking every precaution, he suffered to the extent that he would lie in spasms for half a day. He also had rickets;[2] physicians saying that there was not a natural bone in his body.

It was while he was in what seemed to be his greatest agony, and when I was in the darkest despair, that I first heard of Christian Science. The bearer of the joyful tidings could only tell me to come and hear of the wonderful things that Christian Science was doing. I accepted the invitation, for I was willing to try anything to save my child, and the following Friday evening I attended my first meeting, which was in The Mother Church of Christ, Scientist. Long before the service began every seat was filled, which was amazing to me, being an ordinary weekly meeting, and that night I realized from the testimonies given that Christian Science was the religion for which I had been searching for years. The next day I went to find a practitioner, but was unable to get the one who had been recommended, he being too busy. On my way home I thought of some of the testimonies which I had heard the night before,—of people being healed by simply reading Science and Health. I resolved at once to borrow a copy, and not dreaming of the sacrifice that my friend would make by conferring such a favor, I went and asked her for a loan of Science and Health. I never saw any one part so reluctantly with a book as my friend did with her copy of the textbook.

I read it silently and audibly, day and night, in my home, and although I could not seem to understand it, yet the healing commenced to take place at once. The little mouth which had been twisted by spasms grew natural and the child was soon able to be up, playing and romping about the house any child should. About this time we decided to move to the far West.

I was young in Science at the time, and my husband greatly feared that the journey would cause a relapse for the child, but instead, he continued to improve. I constantly read the Bible, Science and Health, and Miscellaneous Writings, the two weeks we traveled, and we were the only ones in our car who, throughout the journey, did not get train sick. The child's limbs grew perfectly straight, he ate anything he wanted, and for years he has been a natural, healthy child in every way. He has passed through some of the worst forms of contagion untouched and unharmed.

I had been reading Science and Health several months, before I gave any thought to myself and my numerous complaints. I had never been very strong, and some of my ailments were supposed to be hereditary and chronic, hence I dragged through many tedious years with a belief in medical laws and hereditary laws resting upon me. Just before I commenced reading Science and Health I spent a half day in having my eyes examined by one of the leading oculists[3] in Boston. His verdict was that my eyes were in a dreadful condition, and that I would always need to wear glasses. In the meantime I commenced to read Science and Health, and when I thought of my eyes, I had no need for glasses. The years that I have been in Science I have used my eyes incessantly, night as well as day, doing all kinds of trying work and without requiring the aid of glasses. I was healed of all my complaints whilst seeking the truth for my child, and many of them have never returned. Those that appeared simply came to the surface to be destroyed. Teeth have been restored and facial blemishes removed, unconsciously, simply by reading Science and Health. All of this is, however, nothing to compare with the spiritual uplifting which I have received, and I have everything to be thankful for.

—M. T. W., Los Angeles, Cal.

NOTES

Excerpt from Mary Baker Eddy, *Retrospection and Introspection* (Boston: The First Church Of Christ, Scientist, 1891, 1892); reprinted in *Prose Works Other Than "Science and Health with Key to the Scriptures"* (Boston: The First Church Of Christ, Scientist, 1925). Reprinted by permission of the publisher.

Excerpt from Mary Baker Eddy, *Science and Health with Key to the Scriptures* (Boston: Trustees under the Will of Mary Baker G. Eddy, originally published 1875), pp. 465–71, 475–77, 484–87, 493–95, 605–7, 612–14. Reprinted by permission of the publisher.

1. Inflammation of mucous membranes.
2. A childhood disease that causes bones to soften and deform.
3. A medical doctor who specialized in treatment of the eyes.

FOR FURTHER READING

Church of Christ, Scientist, http://www.tfccs.com. The official Website of the Church of Christ, Scientist (Christian Science).

Fraser, Caroline, *God's Perfect Child: Living and Dying in the Christian Science Church* (New York: Henry Holt, 1999). A readable and moving account by someone who grew up in Christian Science then left it.

Gill, Gillian, *Mary Baker Eddy* (Reading, Mass.: Perseus, 1998). The standard scholarly biography of Eddy.

Gottschalk, Stephen, *The Emergence of Christian Science in American Religious Life* (Berkeley: University of California Press, 1973). A treatment of the Christian Science movement by a Christian Science scholar.

Chapter 2

Theosophy

The term "theosophy" (from the Greek words for "divine" and "wisdom") refers to a particular type of knowledge found among certain thinkers in monotheistic mystical traditions, as well as in Western esoteric traditions such as Hermeticism and in occult practices such as alchemy and astrology. A theosopher was someone who had attained experiential knowledge of the divine, or God, and could thus understand the arcane mysteries of the universe hidden from the awareness of most human beings. However, in this volume, Theosophy refers to a latter-day tradition, as embodied in various organizational forms that usually go by the name Theosophical Society. These Theosophists borrowed the term "theosophy" to apply to their own unique blend of esoteric, Asian, and monotheistic mystical, as well as modern scientific, traditions.

The Theosophical Society was founded in 1875 by Helena Petrovna Blavatsky (1831–1891) and Henry Steel Olcott (1832–1907) in New York City. The first participants in Theosophical Society meetings were urban middle-class professionals and intellectuals interested in comparative religions, Spiritualism, the occult, and the relationship between science and religion. For three years Blavatsky, Olcott, and the fledging Society held regular meetings in which they discussed religious, scientific, and esoteric topics. In 1878, Blavatsky and Olcott journeyed to India, where they hoped to expand the work of the Society among a population whom they deemed naturally suited to embrace the Theosophical message.

The basic teachings of Theosophy have remained relatively unchanged throughout the years. Much of Theosophy resembles ideas found in Hinduism and Buddhism. Theosophists say that each individual is an eternal soul that reincarnates through endless lifetimes, in various forms that become more advanced as the eons pass. The present human forms that souls take will ultimately give way to more spiritual entities who nonetheless share an essential oneness with matter. Souls are subject to karma, the law of cause and effect, which unerringly determines the status of a soul in this life and the next. Theosophy teaches that there is no God, in the monotheistic sense of that term, but rather an overriding divine will or plan that guides all things. In every era, certain advanced individuals, or Masters, serve as guides and shepherds for the masses of reincarnating souls. Blavatsky claimed that she was guided by Masters in her lifetime, especially through letters that they supposedly wrote and magically passed along to her and to other Theosophists. These letters constituted the earliest layer of Theosophical texts.

Blavatsky, Olcott, and others started the Theosophical Society in India and Ceylon (later Sri Lanka). Olcott was instrumental in the revival of Buddhism on Ceylon, and he and Blavatsky took the Three Refuges, a ritual recitation that signified their acceptance of Buddhism. Meanwhile, Blavatsky expounded her ideas in numerous articles for her magazine, *The Theosophist,* as well as a later Theosophical magazine called *Lucifer.* These magazines were crucial in disseminating Theosophy to a wide reading audience in India, the United States, Europe, and Australasia—as, too, were Blavatsky's books, especially *Isis Unveiled* (1877) and her magnum opus, *The Secret Doctrine* (1888).

In the United States, interest in Theosophy waned until one of the first members of the Society, the Irish-born attorney William Q. Judge (1851–1896), revived Theosophical activity in the 1880s. From that time until his death, the Theosophical Society grew significantly, with lodges in many American cities hosting large public meetings and initiating hundreds of members. Under Judge's leadership, a monthly periodical called *The Path* paralleled Blavatsky's magazines in reaching out to spiritual seekers.

In 1884–85, Blavatsky was involved in a scandal in India in which she was accused of producing letters attributed to the Masters. She relocated to Europe and spent the final years of her life in London, where she established a powerful inner circle of leaders—most notable among them the journalist and social activist Annie Besant (1847–1933). After Blavatsky's death in 1891, Besant and Judge became involved in a heated dispute about the veracity of certain letters that Judge claimed to have received in a paranormal way from the Masters. This dispute, known as the "Judge case" within the movement, resulted in 1895 in Judge declaring all Theosophical lodges in the United States independent of the Theosophical Society elsewhere. When Judge died the following year, he was succeeded by social reformer Katherine Tingley (1847–1929), who led the American Theosophists in Judge's tradition from New York City, and later from Point Loma, near San Diego, California. Several Theosophical organizations split off from the Judge/Tingley tradition, such as the United Lodge of Theosophists, founded by Robert Crosbie (1849–1919). Meanwhile, the Theosophists who remained loyal to Besant were led by her and Charles W. Leadbeater (1837–1934).

Besant lived for many years in India, where Blavatsky and Olcott had established a headquarters at Adyar, near Chennai (Madras) in South India. There, they conducted occult experiments, clairvoyantly delving into the past lives of individuals and writing about their findings. Eventually their books became the most significant literature in the Besant, or Adyar, tradition of Theosophy. In 1906, Leadbeater was himself involved in scandal in Australia for teaching boys under his tutelage to masturbate, which outraged fellow Theosophists and tainted the Society's public image. Besant defended him, and ultimately Leadbeater retained his connections with Theosophy, but the scandal followed Besant throughout her career.

In 1909, Besant and Leadbeater declared a young Hindu man, Jiddu Krishnamurti (1895–1986), to be the next bodhisattva, or "World-Teacher," for this age and started a Theosophically related organization called the Order of the Star of the East to promote him. In the 1920s Krishnamurti disassociated himself from the Theosophical claims made for him and eventually followed his own unique trajectory as a teacher of Hindu themes.

In the United States, most Theosophical activity during the early decades of the twentieth century focused on the community at Point Loma. Theosophists there raised and educated hundreds of children, who were seen as the vanguard for a new cycle in human evolution. After Tingley died, she was succeeded by Gottfried de Purucker (1879–1942), who supervised the group's relocation to the Los Angeles area during World War II. Today the Judge/Tingley tradition is maintained by the California-based Theosophical Society, Pasadena, while the Adyar tradition is maintained in the United States by the Theosophical Society in America, headquartered in Wheaton, Illinois.

Theosophy's heyday lasted from approximately 1880 to 1930. Many middle- and upper-class Americans, Europeans, Indians, and Australasians were attracted to the group's optimistic cosmology, which taught that the world inevitably gets better as the cycles of evolution, containing millions of souls, follow their course. People attracted to Theosophy, especially in North America and Europe, typically had rejected the Christianity (and in some cases Judaism) of their families (see Alice Bolting, "Why I Became a Theosophist," below). Theosophy gave these converts a sense of the mystery of the world, but Theosophists were also convinced that their understanding of the cosmos was scientifically verifiable. Where the science of their day disputed that understanding, Theosophists believed that in the future science would see the error of its ways and affirm their teachings.

Theosophy offered to converts a New Understanding that in many cases radically altered the life stories of those who embraced its ideals. In both the Judge/Tingley and the Adyar traditions of Theosophy, published conversion accounts repeat the same story line: the convert discovers Theosophy, feels that they have come home to the truth, and consequently makes choices about careers, friends, and locations in which to live based on their new life in Theosophy. Theosophy also projected a New Society, especially when supporting specific social–reform causes—such as anti-vivisection, opposition to capital punishment, and rescue of orphans in cities—and certainly a New World in the distant future. But the immediate result for anyone who decided to call him or herself a Theosophist was a New Understanding of the cosmos and one's place in it. Religious groups that were influenced by, or were even descended from, the Theosophical Society—including the I Am Religious Activity, the Church Universal and Triumphant, and the New Age movement in general—all retain this emphasis on an altered understanding of the world as the most significant change that can come from a study of their ideas.

The first excerpt below, taken from a Point Loma Theosophical magazine, is the text of a speech given by a woman who was repulsed by the answers to her youthful questions about good and evil given by her Sunday-school teacher and pastor. Her story dates from the turn of the last century and gives us a glimpse of the radical New Understanding that was so exciting for many Theosophical converts in that era. Her convictions, founded upon her rejection of one religious system and embrace of another, sound surprisingly contemporary. Many converts to today's NRMs provide similar testimonials when speaking of their decision to join a NRM. The other excerpts in this section are taken from Judge's popular book *The Ocean of Theosophy* (1893). Judge was remarkably adept at expressing complex Theosophical ideas in the vernacular of the day. Many Theosophists who might not have the patience or intellectual ability to read Blavatsky's books—filled as they are by countless references to myths and legends from the world's religions as well as to scholarly works in many disciplines—could easily comprehend the core teachings of Theosophy by reading Judge's rendition of them. The first excerpt from Judge's book provides a brief introduction to Theosophy, the second describes the Masters, the third and fourth address the nature of the soul, the fifth and sixth consider reincarnation, and the last excerpt deals with the great cycles of time in which souls reincarnate.

From "Why I Became a Theosophist"

Alice Bolting

From infancy I was brought up in the Episcopal faith.

It was some time after my confirmation that I was attending a usual Sunday-school session, when the teacher of the class told in a quivering and pathetic voice that the young man who, as librarian, had passed us our books every Sunday for more than two years, was that day locked in jail.

Consternation and pity struck the class, as the boy in question was one of the most popular in the Sunday-school, and came from a highly respected family.

My wonderment was aroused and, after learning the nature of the offense, I asked, "What will become of that boy for stealing from his employer?" With a grave countenance the teacher replied, "He has broken one of the commandments and therefore cannot enter the kingdom of Heaven!"

This answer startled me as the pictured horrors of the "other place" flashed before my mind, and I felt a deep concern for the young librarian. I had brothers and a thought akin to anxiety occurred to me—suppose one of my brothers should sometime make a similar mistake and he should be consigned to a terrible punishment. The mere suggestion was sufficient to arouse the keenest sense of injustice, and I arose before the teacher and class and said: "If a brother of mine ever makes such a mistake and he should be condemned to hell, I'll go with him!"

It is needless to say the teacher was shocked, and was probably justified in every attempt to remonstrate with such a woeful determination.

"What and where are Heaven and hell?" I asked. She tried to answer my question, and finally called the superintendent of the school to her aid, and when they both failed to satisfy me with their answers, based as they were on their creeds and tenets, they called for the minister.

This clergyman was then and is now in charge of one of the largest, wealthiest and most aristocratic churches in the country, and was noted for a brilliant intellect.

I was little more than a child, but was evidently not supposed to ask questions, so a quietus was put upon the discussion. When the reverend gentleman, looking over his glasses, said to me, "Why do you want to know anything about Heaven and hell? Have you friends in either place whom you do not care to meet?"

I had been truly serious in my queries and this satirical retort left a sting which was destined to smart for some time. Moreover, before the afternoon was over I had quite decided I did not care to attend a Sunday school.

It happened the following week, on the afternoon preceding Easter Sunday, I chanced to be with a friend and I remarked with a sigh, "I should be so happy if I did not have to attend that 6 o'clock service tomorrow morning." The reply which followed quite startled me, as I would most naturally have expected a censure for such an utterance, especially regarding as it did an Easter Sunday service.

"Why do you go if you feel like that?" was the answer. In utter amazement, I asked, "What church do you attend?" and in her answer, "I am a Theosophist," I heard the word Theosophy for the first time.

The answer to my next question, "What is your belief?" lifted a veil which covered a path most desirable to a neophyte seeking truth.

"Theosophists," she said, "believe as you do that Jesus Christ was a Great Soul and that the Kingdom of Heaven is within and is to be attained by one's own spiritual efforts." And I knew that that answer suggested great breadth of thought and resolved instantly to investigate for myself those principles which I soon learned threw great light upon the questions and problems which had been so puzzling and unanswered by the ministers. And I found that, according to the Wisdom Religion, Theosophy, man was placed on his own responsibility and that no petty law could deny him the Kingdom of Heaven, nor could any man-made law condemn him to everlasting punishment, but that each man had within himself the spark of divinity which should illuminate his consciousness. And if man strove through his own divinity to live according to the spiritual laws understood and taught by all the great Saviors of Humanity, he would be his own judge—continually guarding against such thoughts and acts as might injure himself or his fellow men.

I learned of the public meetings of a Theosophical society, and after enlisting the interest of some friends of my family we together attended some lectures, and there I found my questions were not only answered, but all I desired to ask cordially solicited.

The opposition I met from friends and acquaintances, at this juncture, who learned of my new researches, or as they put it, "reckless rambling from the church and your maker," and the prayers which were offered for my salvation by the Sunday-school teacher and minister, if detailed, would prove the verity of the statement that opposition to Theosophy is nothing short of dogmatic prejudice.

A few years later I applied for membership in the Theosophical Society and in due time was the proud possessor of a diploma admitting me a member of that society.

From *The Ocean of Theosophy*

William Q. Judge

Theosophy is that ocean of knowledge which spreads from shore to shore of the evolution of sentient beings; unfathomable in its deepest parts, it gives the greatest minds their fullest scope, yet, shallow enough at its shores, it will not overwhelm the understanding of a child. It is wisdom about God for those who believe that he is all things and in all, and wisdom about nature for the man who accepts the statement found in the Christian Bible that God cannot be measured or discovered, and that darkness is around his pavilion. Although it contains by derivation the name God and thus may seem at first sight to embrace religion alone, it does not neglect science, for it is the science of sciences and therefore has been called the wisdom religion. For no science is complete which leaves out any department of nature, whether visible or invisible, and that religion which, depending solely on an assumed revelation, turns away from things and the laws which govern them is nothing but a delusion, a foe to progress, an obstacle in the way of man's advancement toward happiness. Embracing both the scientific and the religious, Theosophy is a scientific religion and a religious science.

It is not a belief or dogma formulated or invented by man, but is a knowledge of the laws which govern the evolution of the physical, astral, psychical, and intellectual constituents of nature and of man. The religion of the day is but a series of dogmas man-made and with no scientific foundation for promulgated ethics; while our science as yet ignores the unseen, and failing to admit the existence of a complete set of inner faculties of perception in man, it is cut off the immense and real field of experience which lies within the visible and tangible worlds. But Theosophy knows that the whole is constituted of the visible and the invisible, and perceiving outer things and objects to be but transitory it grasps the facts of nature, both without and within. It is therefore complete in itself and sees no unsolvable mystery anywhere; it throws the word coincidence out of its vocabulary and hails the reign of law in everything and every circumstance.

That man possesses an immortal soul is the common belief of humanity; to this Theosophy adds that he is a soul; and further that all nature is sentient, that the vast array of objects and men are not mere collections of atoms fortuitously thrown together and thus without law evolving law, but down to the smallest atom all is soul and spirit ever evolving under the rule of law which is inherent in the whole. And just as the ancients taught, so does Theosophy; that the course of evolution is the drama of the soul and that nature exists for no other purpose than the soul's experience. The Theosophist agrees with Prof. [Thomas] Huxley in the assertion that there must be beings in the universe whose intelligence is as much beyond ours as ours exceeds that of the black beetle, and who take an active part in the government of the natural order of things. Pushing further on by the light of the confidence had in his teachers, the Theosophist adds that such intelligences were once human and came like all of us from other and previous worlds, where as varied experience had been gained as is possible on this one. We are therefore not appearing for the first time when we come upon this planet, but have pursued a long, an immeasurable course of activity and intelligent perception on other systems of globes, some of which were destroyed ages before the solar system condensed. This immense reach of the evolutionary system means, then, that this planet on which we now are is the result of the activity and the evolution of some other one that died long ago, leaving its energy to be used in the bringing into existence of the earth, and that the inhabitants of the latter in their turn came from some older world to proceed here with the destined work in matter. And the brighter planets, such as Venus, are the habitation of still more progressed entities, once as low as ourselves, but now raised up to a pitch of glory incomprehensible for our intellects.

The most intelligent being in the universe, man, has never, then, been without a friend, but has a line of elder brothers who continually watch over the progress of the less progressed, preserve the knowledge gained through aeons of trial and experience, and continually seek for opportunities of drawing the developing intelligence of the race on this or other globes to consider the great truths concerning the destiny of the soul. These elder brothers also keep the knowledge they have gained of the laws of nature in all departments, and are ready when cyclic law permits to use it for the benefit of mankind. They have always existed as a body, all knowing each other, no matter in what of the world they may be, and all working for the race in many different ways. In some periods they are well known to the people and move among ordinary men whenever the social organization, the virtue, and the development of the nations permit it. For if they were to come out openly and be heard of everywhere, they would be worshipped as gods by some and hunted as devils by others. In those periods when they do come out some of their numbers are rulers of men, some teachers, a few great philosophers, while others remain still unknown except to the most advanced of the body. . . .

The Elder Brothers of Humanity are men who were perfected in former periods of evolution. These periods of manifestation are unknown to modern evolutionists so far as their number are concerned, though long ago understood by not only the older Hindus, but also by those great minds and men who instituted and carried on the first pure and undebased form of the Mysteries of Greece. The periods, when out of the Great Unknown there come forth the visible universes, are eternal in their coming and going, alternating with equal periods of silence and rest again in the Unknown. The object of these mighty waves is the production of perfect man, the evolution of soul, and they always witness the increase of the number of Elder Brothers; the life of the least of men pictures them in day and night, waking and sleeping, birth and death, "for these two, light and dark, day and night, are the world's eternal ways."

In every age and complete national history these men of power and compassion are given different designations. They have been called Initiates, Adepts, Magi, Hierophants, Kings of the East, Wise Men, Brothers, and what not. But in the Sanskrit[1] language there is a word which, being applied to them, at once thoroughly identifies them with humanity. It is Mahatma. This is composed of *Maha* great, and *Atma* soul; so it means great soul, and as all men are souls the distinction of the Mahatma lies in greatness. The term Mahatma has come into wide use through the Theosophical Society, as Mme. H. P. Blavatsky constantly referred to them as her Masters who gave her the knowledge she possessed. They were at first known only as the Brothers, but afterwards, when many Hindus flocked to the Theosophical movement, the name Mahatma was brought into use, inasmuch as it has behind it an immense body of Indian tradition and literature. At different times unscrupulous enemies of the Theosophical Society have said that even this name had been invented and that such beings are not known among the Indians or in their literature. But these assertions are made only to discredit if possible a philosophical movement that threatens to completely upset prevailing erroneous theological dogmas. For all through Hindu literature Mahatmas are often spoken of, and in parts of the north of that country the term is common. In the very old poem the *Bhagavad-Gîtâ,* revered by all Hindu sects and admitted by the western critics to be noble as well as beautiful, there is a verse reading, "Such a Mahatma is difficult to find." . . .

The teachings of Theosophy deal for the present chiefly with our earth, although its purview extends to all the worlds, since no part of the manifested universe is outside the single body of laws which operate upon us. Our globe being one of the solar system is certainly connected with Venus, Jupiter, and other planets, but as the great human family has to remain with its material vehicle—the earth—until all the units of the race which are ready are perfected, the evolution of that family is of greater importance to the members of it. . . .

The universe evolves from the unknown, into which no man or mind, however high, can inquire, on seven planes or in seven ways or methods in all worlds, and this sevenfold differentiation causes all the worlds of the universe and the beings thereon to have a septenary constitution. As was taught of old, the little worlds and the great are copies of the whole, and the minutest insect as well as the most highly developed being are *replicas* in little or in great of the vast inclusive original. Hence sprang the saying, "as above so below" which the Hermetic[2] philosophers used.

The divisions of the sevenfold universe may be laid down roughly as: The Absolute, Spirit, Mind, Matter, Will, Akasa or Aether, and Life. In place of "the Absolute" we can use the word Space. For Space is that which ever is, and in which all manifestation must take place. The term Akasa, taken from the Sanskrit, is used in place of Aether, because the English language has not yet evolved a word to properly designate that tenuous state of matter which is now sometimes called Ether by modern scientists. As to the Absolute we can do no more than say IT IS. None of the great teachers of the School[3] ascribe qualities to the Absolute although all the qualities exist in It. Our knowledge begins with differentiation, and all manifested objects, beings, or powers are only differentiations of the Great Unknown. The most than can be said is that the Absolute periodically differentiates itself, and periodically withdraws the differentiated into itself.

The first differentiation—speaking metaphysically as to time—is Spirit, with which appears Matter and Mind. Akasa is produced from Matter and Spirit, Will is the force of Spirit in action and Life is a resultant of the action of Akasa, moved by Spirit, upon Matter.

But the Matter here spoken of is not that which is vulgarly known as such. It is the real Matter which is always invisible, and has sometimes been called Primordial Matter. In the Brahmanical system it is denominated *Mulaprakriti*.[4] The ancient teaching always held, as is now admitted by Science, that we see or perceive only the phenomena but not the essential nature, body or being of matter.

Mind is the intelligent part of the Cosmos, and in the collection of seven differentiations above roughly sketched, Mind is that in which the plan of the Cosmos is fixed or contained. This plan is brought over from a prior period of manifestation which added to its ever-increasing perfectness, and no limit can be set to its evolutionary possibilities in perfectness, because there was never any beginning to the periodical manifestations of the Absolute, there never will be any end, but forever the going forth and withdrawing into the Unknown will go on.

Wherever a world or system of worlds is evolving there the plan has been laid down in universal mind, the original force comes from spirit, the basis is matter—which is in fact invisible—Life sustains all the forms requiring life, and Akasa is the connecting link between matter on one side and spirit-mind on the other.

When a world or a system comes to the end of certain great cycles men record a cataclysm in history or tradition. These traditions abound; among the Jews in their flood; with the Babylonians in theirs; in Egyptian papyri; in the Hindu cosmology; and none of them as merely confirmatory of the little Jewish tradition, but all pointing to early teaching and dim recollection also of the periodical destructions and renovations. The Hebraic story is but a poor fragment torn from the pavement of the Temple of Truth. Just as there are periodical minor cataclysms or partial destructions, so, the doctrine holds, there is the universal evolution and involution. Forever the Great Breath goes forth and returns again. As it proceeds outwards, objects, worlds and men appear; as it recedes all disappear into the original source.

This is the waking and the sleeping of the Great Being; the Day and the Night of Brahma;[5] the prototype of our waking days and sleeping nights as men, of our disappearance from the scene at the end of one little human life, and our return again to take up the unfinished work in another life, in a new day.

The real age of the world has long been involved in doubt for Western investigators, who up to the present have shown a singular unwillingness to take instruction from the records of Oriental people much older than the West. Yet with the Orientals is the truth about the matter. It is admitted that Egyptian civilization flourished many centuries ago, and as there are no living Egyptian schools of ancient learning to offend modern pride, and perhaps because the Jews "came out of Egypt" to fasten the Mosaic misunderstood tradition upon modern progress, the inscriptions cut in rocks and written on papyri obtain a little more credit today than the living thought and record of the Hindus. For the latter are still among us, and it would never do to admit that a poor and conquered race possesses knowledge respecting the age of man and his world which the western flower of culture, war, and annexation knows nothing of. Ever since the ignorant monks and theologians of Asia Minor and Europe succeeded in imposing the Mosaic account of the genesis of earth and man upon the coming western evolution, the most learned even of our scientific men have stood in fear of the years that elapsed since Adam, or have been warped in thought and perception whenever their eyes turned to any chronology different from that of a few tribes of the sons of Jacob. . . .

But the Theosophist knows why the Hebraic tradition came to be thus an apparent drag on the mind of the West; he knows the connection between Jew and Egyptian; what is and is to be the resurrection of the old pyramid builders of the Nile valley, and where the plans of those ancient master masons have been hidden from the profane eyes until the cycle should roll round again for their bringing forth. The Jews preserved merely a part of the learning of Egypt hidden under the letter of the books of Moses, and it is there still to this day in what they call the cabalistic[6] or hidden meaning of the scriptures. But the Egyptian souls who helped in planning the pyramid of Gizeh, who took part in the Egyptian government, theology, science, and civilization, departed from their old race, that race died out and the former Egyptians took up their work in the oncoming races of the West, especially in those which are now repeopling the American continents. When Egypt and India were younger there was a constant intercourse between them. They both, in the opinion of the Theosophist, thought alike, but fate ruled that of the two the Hindus only should preserve the old ideas among a living people. . . .

Respecting the nature of man there are two ideas current in the religious circles of Christendom. One is the teaching and the other the common acceptation of it; the first is not secret, to be sure, in the Church, but it is so seldom dwelt upon in the hearing of the laity as to be almost arcane for the ordinary person. Nearly everyone says he has a soul and a body, and there it ends. What the soul is, and whether it is the real person or whether it has any powers of its own, are not inquired into, the preachers usually confining themselves to its salvation or damnation. And by thus talking of it as something different from oneself, the people have acquired an underlying notion that they are not souls because the soul may be lost by them. From this has come about a tendency to materialism causing men to pay more attention to the body than to the soul, the latter being left to the tender mercies of the priest of the Roman Catholics, and among dissenters the care of it is most frequently put off to the dying day. But when the true teaching is known it will be seen that the care of the soul, which is the Self, is a vital matter requiring attention every day, and not to be deferred without grievous injury resulting to the whole man, both soul and body.

The Christian teaching, supported by St. Paul, since upon him, in fact, dogmatic Christianity rests, is that man is composed of body, soul, and spirit. This is the threefold constitution of man, believed by the theologians but kept in the background because its examination might result in the readoption of views once orthodox but now heretical. For when we thus place soul between spirit and body, we come very close to the necessity for looking into the question of the soul's responsibility—since mere body can have no responsibility. And in order to make the soul responsible for the acts performed, we must assume that it has powers and functions. From this it is easy to take the position that the soul may be rational or irrational, as the Greeks sometimes thought, and then there is but a step to further Theosophical propositions. This threefold scheme of the nature of man contains, in fact, the Theosophical teaching of his sevenfold constitution, because the four other divisions missing from the category can be found in the powers and functions of body and soul. . . . This conviction that man is a septenary and not merely a duad, was held long ago and very plainly taught to every one with accompanying demonstrations, but like other philosophical tenets it disappeared from sight, because gradually withdrawn at the time when in the east of Europe morals were degenerating and before materialism had gained full sway in company with scepticism, its twin. Upon its withdrawal the present dogma of body, soul, spirit, was left to Christendom. . . .

What then is the universe for, and for what final purpose is man the immortal thinker here in evolution? It is all for the experience and emancipation of the soul, for the purpose of raising the entire mass of manifested matter up to the stature, nature, and dignity of conscious god-hood. The great aim is to reach self-consciousness; not through a race or a tribe or some favored nation, but by and through the perfecting, after transformation, of the whole mass of matter as well as what we now call soul. Nothing is or is to be left out. The aim for present man is his initiation into complete knowledge, and for the other kingdoms below him that they may be raised up gradually from stage to stage to be in time initiated also. This is evolution carried to its highest power; it is a magnificent prospect; it makes of man a god, and gives to every part of nature the possibility of being one day the same; there is strength and nobility in it, for by this no man is dwarfed and belittled, for no one is so originally sinful that he cannot rise above all sin. Treated from the materialistic position of Science, evolution takes in but half of life; while the religious conception of it is a mixture of nonsense and fear. Present religions keep the element of fear, and at the same time imagine that an Almighty being can think of no other earth but this and has to govern this one very imperfectly. But the old theosophical view makes the universe a vast, complete, and perfect whole.

Now the moment we postulate a double evolution, physical and spiritual, we have at the same time to admit that it can only be carried on by reincarnation. This is, in fact, demonstrated by science. It is shown that the matter of the earth and of all things physical upon it was at one time either gaseous or molten; that it cooled; that it altered; that from its alterations and evolutions at last were produced all the great variety of things and beings. This, on the physical plane, is transformation or change from one form to another. The total mass of matter is about the same as in the beginning of this globe, with a very minute allowance for some star dust. Hence it must have been changed over and over again, and thus been physically reformed and reimbodied. Of course, to be strictly accurate, we cannot use the word reincarnation, because "incarnate" refers to flesh. Let us say "reimbodied," and then we see that both for matter and for man there has been a constant change of form and this is, broadly speaking, "reincarnation." As to the whole mass of matter, the doctrine is that it will all be raised to man's estate when man has gone further on himself. There is no residuum left after man's final salvation which in a mysterious way is to be disposed of or done away with in some remote dust-heap of nature. The true doctrine allows for nothing like that, and at the same time is not afraid to give the true disposition of what would seem to be a residuum. It is all worked up into other states, for as the philosophy declares there is no inorganic matter whatever but that every atom is alive and has the germ of self-consciousness, it must follow that one day it will all have been changed. Thus what is now called human flesh is so much matter that one day was wholly mineral, later on vegetable, and now refined into human atoms. At a point of time very far from now the present vegetable matter will have been raised to the animal stage and what we now use as our organic or fleshy matter will have changed by transformation through evolution into self-conscious thinkers, and so on up the whole scale until the time shall come when what is now known as mineral matter will have passed on to the human stage and out into that of thinker. Then at the coming on of another great period of evolution the mineral matter of that time will be some which is now passing through its lower transformations on other planets and in other systems of worlds. . . .

This [reincarnation] is the most ancient of doctrines and is believed in now by more human minds than the number of those who do not hold it. The millions in the East almost all accept it; it was taught by the Greeks; a large number of the Chinese now believe it as their forefathers did before them; the Jews thought it was true, and it has not disappeared from their religion; and Jesus, who is called the founder of Christianity, also believed and taught it. In the early Christian church it was known and taught, and the very best of the fathers of the church believed and promulgated it.

Christians should remember that Jesus was a Jew who thought his mission was to Jews, for he says in St. Matthew, "I am not sent but unto the lost sheep of the house of Israel."[7] He must have well known the doctrines held by them. They all believed in reincarnation. For them Moses, Adam, Noah, Seth, and others had returned to earth, and at the time of Jesus it was currently believed that the old prophet Elias was yet to return. So we find, first, that Jesus never denied the doctrine, and on various occasions assented to it, as when he said that John the Baptist was actually the Elias of old whom the people were expecting. All this can be seen by consulting St. Matthew in chapters xvii, xi, and others.

In these it is very clear that Jesus is shown as approving the doctrine of reincarnation. And following Jesus we find St. Paul, in Romans ix, speaking of Esau and Jacob being actually in existence before they were born, and later such great Christian fathers as Origen, Synesius, and others believing and teaching the theory. In Proverbs viii, 22, we have Solomon saying that when the earth was made he was present, and that, long before he could have been born as Solomon, his delights were in the habitable parts of the earth with the sons of men. St. John the Revelator[8] says in Revs. iii, 12, he was told in a vision which refers to the voice of God or the voice of one speaking for God, that whosoever should overcome would not be under the necessity of "going out" any more, that is, would not need to be reincarnated. . . .

Reincarnation being the great law of life and progress, it is interwoven with that of the cycles and karma. These three work together, and in practice it is almost impossible to disentangle reincarnation from cyclic law. Individuals and nations in definite streams return in regularly recurring periods to the earth, and thus bring back to the globe the arts, the civilization, the very persons who once were on it at work. And as the units in nation and race are connected together by invisible strong threads, large bodies of such units moving slowly but surely all together reunite at different times and emerge again and again together into new race and new civilization as the cycles roll their appointed rounds. Therefore the souls who made the most ancient civilizations will come back and bring the old civilization with them in idea and essence, which being added to what others have done for the development of the human race in its character and knowledge will produce a new and higher state of civilization. This newer and better development will not be due to books, to records, to arts or mechanics, because all those are periodically destroyed so far as physical evidence goes, but the soul ever retaining in *Manas* [mind] the knowledge it once gained and always pushing to completer development the higher principles and powers, the essence of progress remains and will as surely come out as the sun shines. And along this road are the points when the small and large cycles of Avatars [descents] bring out for man's benefit the great characters who mold the race from time to time.

The Cycle of Avatars includes several smaller ones. The greater are those marked by the appearance of Rama and Krishna among the Hindus, of Menes among the Egyptians, of Zoroaster among the Persians, and of Buddha to the Hindus and other nations of the East. Buddha is the last of the great Avatars and is in a larger cycle than is Jesus of the Jews, for the teachings of the latter are the same as those of Buddha and tinctured with what Buddha had taught to those who instructed Jesus. Another great Avatar is yet to come, corresponding to Buddha and Krishna combined. Krishna and Rama were of the military, civil, religious, and occult order; Buddha of the ethical, religious, and mystical, in which he was followed by Jesus; Mohammed was a minor intermediate one for a certain part of the race, and was civil, military, and religious. In these cycles we can include mixed characters who have had great influence on nations, such as King Arthur, Pharaoh, Moses, Charlemagne reincarnated as Napoleon Bonaparte, Clovis of France reborn as Emperor Frederic III of Germany, and Washington the first President of the United States of America where the root for the new race is being formed.

NOTES

Excerpt from Alice Bolting, "Why I Became a Theosophist," *New Century*, August 10, 1902, 8.

Excerpts from William Q. Judge, *The Ocean of Theosophy* (Pasadena, Calif.: Theosophical University Press, 1973; originally published 1893), pp. 1–4, 6–8, 15–19, 32–33, 68–70, 71–72, 134–35. Reprinted by permission of the publisher.

1. The ancient and holy language of Hinduism.
2. Early esoteric thinkers, named after Hermes Trismegistus, a legendary Greek figure associated with secret knowledge, first mentioned in a second-century C.E. text.
3. Probably a reference to the "Elder Brothers," or Masters.
4. From the Sanskrit for "root nature," or one's most essential self or being.
5. From Hindu texts called *Puranas*, a reference to the Hindu creator god Brahma, who as the god Vishnu creates and destroys the universe continually. The Day of Brahma is a period of several million years, divided into cycles. This is followed by an equally long period, the Night of Brahma, in which the world remains unmanifest and uncreated.
6. A reference to Kabbalah, or Jewish mysticism.
7. Matthew 15:24.
8. The author of the Book of Revelation in the New Testament.

FOR FURTHER READING

Besant, Annie Wood, *Theosophy* (London: T.C. & E.C. Jack; New York: Dodge, 1912). A popular introduction by a major Theosophical writer and early leader of the movement.

Blavatsky, Helena Petrovna, *The Secret Doctrine: The Synthesis of Science, Religion, and Philosophy*, 2 vols. (Pasadena, Calif.: Theosophical University Press, 1988; originally published 1888). The magnum opus of the founder of the Theosophical Society.

Cranston, Sylvia, *HPB: The Extraordinary Life and Influence of Helena Blavatsky, Founder of the Modern Theosophical Movement* (New York: Putnam's, 1993). The definitive biography of Blavatsky.

Mills, Joy, *100 Years of Theosophy: A History of the Theosophical Society in America* (Wheaton, Ill.: Theosophical Publishing House, 1987). A history of the movement by a noted Theosophical writer.

Prothero, Stephen R., *The White Buddhist: The Asian Odyssey of Henry Steel Olcott* (Bloomington, Ind.: Indiana University Press, 1996). An excellent scholarly biography of the man considered by many to be the cofounder, with Blavatsky, of the Theosophical Society.

The Theosophical Society in America, http://www.theosophical.org. The official Website of one of the major Theosophical organizations in the United States.

The Theosophical Society, Pasadena, http://www.theosociety.org. The official Website of one of the major Theosophical organizations in the United States.

Chapter 3

UFO Religious Groups

Many groups of UFO (an acronym for Unidentified Flying Objects) advocates and aficionados would be uncomfortable with labeling their activities "religious" because they see themselves as scientists conducting research on UFOs (a pursuit generally called ufology), or at least as people who are scientifically informed. For them, UFOs point to a new understanding of the cosmos, but a cosmos that is nonetheless governed by scientific laws. The religious, spiritual, or metaphysical has little or no bearing on that new understanding. But belief in UFOs spans many perspectives. Other UFO believers are religiously motivated, if religion is understood broadly as the human drive for transcendental meaning apart from any specific institutional expression of that meaning. These believers link UFOs and the supposed non-terrestrial beings who operate them to a new awareness of humanity's place in the universe.

This chapter is primarily concerned with this religious subset of the UFO community. Although their beliefs and practices vary widely, we have chosen to label them by the general term *UFO religious groups.* They share some ideas. First, they all say that the future of human civilization is guided by, or heavily influenced by, aliens whose intelligence is far greater than ours. These aliens may be beneficent or malicious, or a combination of both, but their superiority is rarely questioned by members of UFO religious groups. Second, these groups share an appreciation for scientific means of discovering facts about UFOs and their alien occupants, but their stance regarding science remains ambivalent. They reject the materialistic explanations that scientifically inclined ufologists favor, yearning instead for the mysterious and insisting that reality is always far more complex and wonderful than science will ever be able to explain. Third, they encourage everyone who hears the message of UFOs to internalize the deeper philosophical and religious truths that come from that knowledge. Here again, specific beliefs vary widely across the broad spectrum of UFO religious groups, but in general they teach that humans must do something in response to the presence of aliens and UFOs in our world. Usually this involves an inward change of orientation not so different from those taught by many world religions with regard to individual encounters with the divine: a more profound sense of one's place in, and oneness with, the universe; a deeper appreciation of the intrinsic worth of one's fellow humans; and a call to higher service to all entities, human and nonhuman.

Humans have wondered at sights in the night sky for millennia, and UFO advocates search the scriptural traditions of world religions, as well as chronicles dating back over the many centuries of human history, for signs of UFO visitors in the past. But the modern period of UFO interest began in 1947, when a pilot named Kenneth Arnold, flying over Mt. Rainier in western Washington state, reported sighting several disc-like objects flying in formation at great speed. His description of their shape led news media to label them "flying saucers." Soon others, in the United States and elsewhere, reported seeing flying objects that had no humanly associated identity. Sometimes the objects were shaped like discs, other times like cigars.

Flying saucers, or UFOs, captured the popular imagination in the United States. Soon the sightings of UFOs had taken the form of a craze, complete with scoffers and true believers, as well as people of every shade of conviction in between. It was during these early days of UFO speculation that Roswell, New Mexico, first appeared in newspaper headlines, and it would later become the single most important locale in UFO lore. In July 1947 a farmer outside Roswell reported finding strange metallic pieces covering a considerable area. The United States Air Force quickly sealed the area and released a public statement explaining that a weather balloon whose design had been top secret had fallen from the sky, and that its remains were the pieces that the New Mexican farmer had discovered. Although many UFO advocates found this explanation somewhat suspicious, Roswell would not become a controversial topic of widespread public interest until the 1980s, when renewed research into the circumstances of the 1947 incident raised new questions about the military's involvement in what many now thought was a government conspiracy to keep knowledge of UFOs and aliens from the general public.

Meanwhile, certain individuals began to report encounters with aliens. These "contactees" supposedly received visits from aliens and even accompanied them into their spaceships. Arguably at this point the vehicles themselves ceased to be UFOs, since the acronym "UFO" points to something that is unidentified, and contactees claimed that they could identify these objects. However, the explanations of contactees are not universally accepted, even within UFO-related groups, and most likely the term UFO has achieved a permanent place in the vocabulary of religious and scientific interest in extraterrestrial visitors. One of the most important early contactees was George Adamski (1891–1965), a Polish immigrant who led an occult group in California. Following the famous Arnold sightings, Adamski said that he also saw UFOs and that in 1952 he was introduced to an alien named Orthon from the planet Venus. Adamski published his conversations with Orthon in a series of books, in which he described the Venusian in terms reminiscent of those used by the Theosophists to describe the Masters (see Chapter 2 above). The influence of Theosophy on twentieth-century UFO contactees such as Adamski is apparent. Adamski claimed that aliens, like the Masters of Theosophy, had advanced far beyond humans and wanted to help humans evolve to higher levels of consciousness. Also like the Masters, Orthon was not seen as a god, but rather as an entity who had evolved through many stages over numerous lifetimes before achieving his present status.

The UFO religious groups of the 1950s and 1960s reflected this generally Theosophical worldview. The ways they configured contact with extraterrestrials also reveal possible Spiritualist influences. Contactees, like Spiritualist mediums in an earlier era who transmitted information from dead people to the living, often passed along messages from advanced alien beings while in trancelike states, a phenomenon that predated yet dovetailed with the New Age phenomenon of "channeling" that became increasingly popular in the 1970s and 1980s. Although these UFO aliens often instructed humanity in terms that may sound vague and generic to twenty-first-century individuals, in the mid-twentieth century these teachings seemed startlingly new and revolutionary. Adamski and other contactees claimed that aliens wanted humans to pay attention to the one spiritual reality pervading the entire universe, a concept introduced some decades earlier in Theosophical literature. Once enough humans had done this, a new era of human progress would dawn, in concert with alien assistance. Although this promise of a new era also had Theosophical antecedents, UFO religious groups did not explain aliens by resorting to Theosophy, other than to offer the earlier movement as a sympathetic parallel to their own worldview. Rather, they said that aliens' physical existence could be scientifically verified under the right conditions. That scientists refused to grant contactees the credibility they deserved was merely a temporary delay in the unfolding of greater truth.

Aligned with this positive assessment of alien contact was a subsidiary development that, for many UFO-related individuals and groups, took on central importance in their worldview. The "ancient astronaut" hypothesis, first made popular in the publications of German writer Erich von Däniken (b. 1935), became central to the worldview of many UFO religious groups. According to these believers, aliens had visited the earth numerous times over the last several million years, biologically manipulating life on the planet so that the human species would eventually evolve, and also intervening in human history at various points to make sure that the species would progress according to the aliens' plans. This sense of a caring alien culture behind all human life echoes the compassion of Theosophical Masters. But von Däniken and other advocates of this position look to prehistory and ancient history rather than to Theosophical texts for confirmation of their views, insisting that ancient astronauts are ultimately verifiable by scientifically accepted standards.

One of the most controversial UFO religious groups to attract public attention was the Heaven's Gate community, who committed group suicide in 1997. Although they postdate the classic UFO religious groups of the mid-twentieth century, much of their belief structure resembles that of earlier groups. Begun in the 1970s by Marshall Herff Applewhite (1931–1997) and Bonnie Lu Truesdale Nettles (1924–1985), Heaven's Gate taught that compassionate aliens wanted to free humans from their physical bodies so that humanity could join the aliens in doing good in the universe. This ultimate state of existence was called The Evolutionary Level Above Human ("T.E.L.A.H."). Heaven's Gate members believed that Nettles, who had died twelve years earlier, was returning to get them in a spaceship following the Hale-Bopp comet that passed near the earth in 1997. They timed their exit from the physical realm by committing suicide, so that they could be translated spiritually to Nettles's spaceship and achieve T.E.L.A.H. (For more on Heaven's Gate, see Chapter 14 below.)

By the 1980s, a new phase in the history of UFO religious groups had begun. Those who claimed contact with aliens reported that they were taken against their wishes, that the aliens then performed experiments on them that were not always pleasant, and that they could not remember everything that happened during the time they were with the aliens. The widely accepted term for this type of encounter was "abduction," and people involved were called "abductees." More recently, the term "experi-encer" replaced abductee, mostly because the latter term had negative con-notations from its use in the media. Experiencers constituted a different brand of UFO religious group from the more Theosophically influenced contactee groups of the 1950s and 1960s. Experiencers often had no prior religious background or, if they did, their religious beliefs did not seem to affect their descriptions of the experiences in any recognizable way. Some experiencers could not understand why the aliens behaved in certain ways, while others attributed the aliens' behavior to nefarious plans to control, manipulate, or destroy humans. The author Whitley Strieber (b. 1945) became one of the best-known advocates of this new sense of the meaning of UFOs. Popular culture, in the form of science fiction novels, television shows like *The X-Files,* and movies, also reflected this new turn in UFO religious life. Not all experiencers concluded that aliens were evil. Some retained the earlier contactee emphasis on the goodness of aliens and the hope that by doing as aliens wished, humanity would ultimately benefit. Nonetheless, abduction experiences were typically described as stressful, if not painful, whatever the moral intentions of the aliens supposedly responsible for those experiences.

In terms of the categories used in the present volume, all UFO religious groups emphasize New Understanding. That is, they assert that the pres-ence of UFOs in human history calls for a new way of looking at reality. Now that we have this knowledge of UFOs, advocates argue, we cannot settle for older explanations, whether they are religious or scientific. For believers in UFOs, humanity has crossed a threshold. We must look to the future with greater awareness of our place in the universe and our rela-tionship to the other species who inhabit it, such as the alien visitors who have come among us.

The excerpts that follow are from a book by two UFO experiencers, Beth Collings and Anna Jamerson.[1] Collings and Jamerson reported that they experienced repeated abductions beginning in childhood, although they did not meet one another until well into their adult lives. Both women recalled unpleasant emotions from their abductions but could not recall the details of these encounters. However, as time passed they recov-ered some of their memories, and the more they remembered, the more disturbing they found the seemingly inscrutable patterns of alien behav-ior to be. Collings and Jamerson realized that they had been used, as had members of their families from previous generations, in alien exper-iments to breed humans who had been altered to include elements of the alien species. Why the aliens were doing this remained unclear, and Collings and Jamerson retained a somewhat ambivalent attitude toward them. What is clear, however, is that their experiences compelled them to accept a New Understanding of the universe and their place in it, and that for them this New Understanding had come about because of powers far greater than any human could withstand. Although neither woman had been especially religious in the conventional sense of that term, through their experiences with aliens both of them eventually realized that life had spiritual dimensions. The aliens in their story are not purveyors of spiritual wisdom like Orthon and other kindly extraterrestrials in early contact literature. In fact, in Collings's and Jamerson's accounts, the aliens' motivations remain beyond human comprehension. Nevertheless, both Collings and Jamerson changed in ways that other humans could recognize.

The first excerpt, by Collings, is taken from the beginning of their book. Collings indicates her awareness of the cultural context of UFOs and argues that her own experience cannot be explained in terms other than those she has concluded: that she has been abducted by aliens. The second excerpt, by Jamerson, also is taken from the beginning of their book. Jamerson also attests to her awareness of the place of UFOs in social and cultural discourse, but her animosity toward aliens is more evident than in Collings's opening remarks. The third excerpt, by Collings, attests to the difficulties she faced in adjusting her worldview to accommodate to a reality—UFOs, aliens, and her abductions—that she could not deny. The fourth excerpt, also by Collings, relates her experiences attending the Abduction Study Conference held at the Massachusetts Institute of Technology (M.I.T.) in Cambridge in June 1992. She recounts the explanations of other attendees, including other experiencers, and finds herself questioning those explanations. In the fifth excerpt, Jamerson describes a session she had in 1993 with the hypnotist Norris Blanks to attempt to uncover repressed memories of abduction experiences. Blanks tends to interpret these experiences from a generally New Age viewpoint, but Jamerson rejects that interpretation. In the transcript of their session, which is included here, Jamerson claims to relive an abduction in which she was taken to a planet far away from earth. She knows that she has been selected for some purpose, and she is not sure whether the aliens are benevolent. In the sixth excerpt, Collings rejects monotheistic beliefs as unhelpful in understanding her experiences, talks about the futility of resisting the abductions, and concludes that a sense of humor is helpful in enduring them. The seventh excerpt, from the book's conclusion, is by Jamerson. She articulates a New Understanding of the world, and it is not a happy one. For Jamerson, the aliens are intent on a future that is not good for humans, but she realizes that she cannot stop this and as a result learns not to control people and things around her. In the eighth excerpt, also from the book's conclusion, Collings, too, says she is convinced that the aliens are not friendly to humans. But Collings's New Understanding includes the affirmation that humanity is valuable because humans seek knowledge.

From *Connections: Solving Our Alien Abduction Mystery*

Beth Collings and Anna Jamerson

1. Collings

This is the most difficult thing I have ever done, putting down in words what even I myself find fantastic, if not bordering on the bizarre. It is made doubly onerous by the subject's very nature: alien abductions. This is a topic more likely to be bantered about by children trying to frighten themselves with ghost stories and tales of witches and ghouls than by a mature woman who has (until recent times) had a firm grip on reality and all it entails. There was no question of who I was, how I came to be, or that my destiny was in my hands alone. I was to discover these "knowns" were not necessarily static—or real.

What has brought about this reshaping of my reality? Aliens.

Incredible? Unbelievable? Indeed.

Nothing short of solid, irrefutable proof could have convinced me that such things existed in our realm. The subject of UFOs was no more than a euphemism, a way for the human mind to categorize something with which it could not relate or identify. The subject, fascinating as it might be, held little interest for me—before.

I saw the movie *E.T. The Extraterrestrial.* I stood in line in the rain for over an hour to see *Close Encounters of the Third Kind* just to verify that the special effects were as good as the critics claimed. I enjoyed both of these movies, have even watched them again on television. But that's fantasy. That's the movies.

I've always entertained the belief that we cannot be alone in this vast universe. The human race is but a mere speck of sand on an endless beach, so to assume our little planet contains the universe's only sentient species is utterly ridiculous. It is certainly plausible that UFOs exist (and many people may have seen them), so perhaps in the not-so-distant future we may encounter otherworldly species in our continuing exploration of our planetary system—and beyond.

But I stopped short of considering any possibility that alien beings might have come to us first. Ha! What hogwash! No one in his or her right mind would believe that there were real ETs in the back yard scrambling for Reese's Pieces. And, of course, none are.

These aliens scramble for no one. They have their own agenda and will abide by it whether or not we humans cooperate. They do not offer friendship, compassion or loyalty; they are not cute and helpless. They do not follow our expectations of how aliens should look or behave. They are alien in every sense of the word.

It is this frightening reality that has turned my sane world into one of total chaos and uncertainty. What is real? What is fantasy? What is *crazy*? How can one tell the difference when faced with such unearthly creatures? Witnessing a UFO zip over your house or buzz your car becomes a fascinating story to tell friends and family, an experience that when related in the company of total strangers is now considered socially acceptable. These days, describing unidentified lights in the night sky (or even possessing video tapes *proving* what you claim to have seen) generates little more than bored yawns from once captivated listeners who have heard it all before, and probably seen it before, too. A series of television programs have been dedicated to this subject for a number of years; commercials using UFO and alien themes abound; magazines and newspapers report sightings, encounters and even bizarre tales of alien intervention. If one has access to any media these days, the odds of remaining ignorant on the subject (whether one is a believer or not) are extremely slim.

But what happens when one relates a story about encounters with small gray slender beings with oversized heads, huge black eyes and no toes who float their paralyzed human victims through closed bedroom windows in the wee hours of morning? I'll tell you what happens: The teller is unceremoniously categorized as *crazy as a rabid hound*, a person to be *shunned*, a person in dire need of *professional counseling*, even a person who is possibly a victim of childhood abuse.

The abductee (or experiencer) is given few options when faced with these presumptions. My first reaction was to deny anything unusual had ever occurred. (I return to this protective mechanism on a regular basis.) From that point I moved on to exploring other possible explanations for the phenomenon, more earthly interpretations that included lucid dreaming, exhaustion, stress, eye strain, flights of fancy, low self-esteem, paranoia, etc. The list went on and on, but eventually these had to be abandoned in favor of a less popular theory: mental illness. Though not desired, this explanation was preferable to alien intervention. Besides, mental illness was treatable with a good chance of complete recovery. I could expect to return to a normal, alien-free existence, put all this non-sense behind me and go back to the process of living. I could even discuss my illness and treatment in public since mental illness was far more acceptable. This would have been the final chapter had the therapists found any pathology, anything at all that might explain these events in psychological terms. But they found none.

Well, there was always frontal lobe disorder or some other physiological malfunction causing these weird visions. This would be my next avenue of investigation. After numerous—and costly—physical exams by qualified (and baffled) physicians, I was told there was nothing wrong with me, but perhaps I should get more rest. This, I was certain, was their way of saying, "We can't treat psychoses. You need to see a shrink."

With these alternatives gone, I was faced with the one explanation that I just couldn't bring myself to accept: I was being routinely abducted by aliens, had been since early childhood, and there was not one thing I could do about it. I could not dial 911 for help; I could not take a pill and hope it would all go away; I could not ignore the fact that something truly myste-rious was going on. In order to deal with it, I would have to change my whole way of interpreting reality.

Even so, my mind refused to surrender to the idea of an alternate real-ity. In defiance, I declared it was a case of vivid imagination. I would sim-ply deny the existence of little gray aliens who went around abducting humans for experimentation—no matter what strange memories plagued me. I would force myself to forget, command my memories of unex-plained and frightening events to cease and desist, and generally *get a life.*

But human curiosity does not fade away on command, and my nature was of the most inquisitive kind. I come from a family of artists and explorers, a people who have for generations been unable to resist challenging the unknown, learning all that can be learned, striving for greater knowledge, no matter what the sacrifice. I have followed in their footsteps; my grown son has followed in mine; my granddaughter has taken her first steps on that same path. Who was I to think I could circumvent the inevitable? I needed to know what was happening. I needed to believe in one thing or the other. These experiences were either real (strange as they may be) or they were imaginary. They could not be both.

Armed with this new determination, I began documenting everything. Each and every unexplained wound, bruise, burn and scar was photographed and catalogued. I confided in my parents and took notes on their experiences, questioned them relentlessly in an effort to clarify many disturbing childhood memories. I discovered soon after (and to my great dismay) that my granddaughter, Noel,[2] had been enduring her own alien-related episodes since the tender age of three.

The more I learned, the less I felt I could handle. Things were far more complex than I had at first surmised—and far more widespread. How many others out there were going through the same types of experiences?

Thousands, perhaps millions, I learned. I was not alone after all. This understanding, if nothing else, prevented me from collapsing under the strain of continued interference by the aliens. I planned to survive all this. I would survive it by documenting, by striving to assimilate, by confiding openly with friends and family, and by taking advantage of my own innate tenacity.

The aliens may be able to maintain complete control while I'm in their domain, but in mine I will take charge!

2. Jamerson

Tired of the same old thing day after day? In a rut? Looking for some excitement in your life? Being abducted by aliens will surely change your life, but almost any alternative is preferable. I long for the sameness and boredom I used to detest. Excitement, fascination, depression and terror seem to overwhelm me almost daily as I begin to accept a new reality that the majority of the population has little reason to believe exists. I never believed anything like this existed outside the covers of science fiction novels, cult magazines and the fantasy worlds of television and the movies

—until my best friend started telling weird tales of experiences that were very disturbing to her. My sense of what was real and possible changed almost overnight.

Until January of 1992, I never really believed in UFOs. Intellectually, logically, I knew that UFOs were probably real, too many people had reported seeing strange lights in the sky at night—all of them couldn't be misinterpretations of normal phenomena—and they couldn't all be crazy. The odds against our world being the only planet in the galaxy inhabited by sentient beings (with the most advanced civilization) are overwhelming. I've always considered myself to be open-minded, and am willing to suspend disbelief until I have enough information to make an informed choice. Besides, I grew up in the TV generation where news and fiction used to be separate events. I eagerly watched Neil Armstrong's first steps on the moon—I had no illusions that what I saw was real. It opened many avenues for my imagination to follow, when I had time—later. I watched *Star Trek* emerge as a science fiction cult phenomenon, but did not become a "Trekkie"—I had no illusions that what I saw was not real. I was fascinated by the creatures and the story lines; besides, Spock always appealed to me with his cold, calm logic in any situation. But to actually believe that we could work with (or against) sentient beings from other planets and galaxies within my lifetime—no way. A hundred years from now, yes. But not now. Please, not now.

I had intellectually accepted the possibility that UFOs were probably visiting the earth. It was an interesting phenomenon, one I hoped to see some day, but I never took the next logical step—that UFOs could be occupied. What little I knew about humans being in contact with alien entities was based on bits and pieces of movies, books and tabloid headlines. I hate scary movies; I never watch them all the way through. Most alien contact movies fall into that category. No, thanks, not for me. I prefer adventure, nature, comedy and the occasional psychological thriller.

I loved *Alfred Hitchcock Presents* and *The Twilight Zone* when I was growing up. The psychological twists in the plots kept my interest. No, I never saw *Close Encounters of the Third Kind* or even *E.T.* until a few months ago. I watched *E.T.* on TV and thought it was cute, but not realistic. I rented *Close Encounters* because I couldn't remember what happened and people kept asking if I'd seen it. I watched it and realized that the reason I couldn't remember what happened was because I had never seen the whole movie, only previews for it on television. I enjoyed the movie, although there were several places in it that made me very uncomfortable.

(Too close to my own experiences?) The bright lights in the beginning at the railroad tracks made my skin crawl, and the views of the mother ship were disturbing, although beautiful.

My tastes in books run to murder mystery, science fantasy, James Michener, Dick Francis, Anne McCaffrey or technical books related to horse farms. Most of the magazines I'd read were horse related.[3] Not a book or magazine in my extensive library had anything to do with UFOs or abductions. These were two subjects that I had never taken time to study. I considered UFOs as probably real, but anyone who claimed contact with alien beings had to be lying, crazy or just plain weird. Tabloid headlines proved it—flying saucer cults and little green Martians were all the product of demented or avaricious minds. I tended to stay away from people who were too far out of the mainstream of American life.

I still have a hard time believing that I am not in control of my life, that "little gray shits"[4] have had a role in directing my life, and still do to this day. I'm frustrated and angry. How dare they! They never even asked my permission. I know now that I would never give it. They take my body and mind, perform unknown experiments on both, return me to this reality with hardly a memory, but with a body that suffers bruises, cuts, exhaustion, digestive disturbances and occasional false(?) pregnancy.

I accept and reject their existence daily. I can believe in them when I know I have been abducted the night before, but that only lasts for a few weeks. When they become inactive for a month or so, I'm sure I made all this stuff up. I go back to denying that they are really abducting me. It doesn't change my belief that they are abducting others, I'm just not involved. Beth calls it my denial phase. I go through it continuously it seems. Whenever something happens to upset my comfortable, scientifically detached investigation of this phenomenon, I become panicked, or depressed, where I withdraw from everything and everyone around me until I can regain some equilibrium. I'm not sure I ever will really accept my involvement with the aliens; it's just too bizarre, too far from the reality I have known for all of my life. But, if I don't accept their reality in my life, I probably will go crazy.

Whatever happens in the future, I am going to continue to fight against the gray shits. I'll fight for my sanity, for my right to choose to live my life without interference from them, for your right to know what is happening to me and thousands of your friends and neighbors, and for abductees' rights to be taken seriously in their quest for physical, emotional and mental support in dealing with their personal alien invasion.

Now, I am forced to acknowledge the existence of UFOs and their occupants.

3. Collings

Seeing is not necessarily believing. Though we had been advised by Rob and Don[5] not to indulge our curiosities by reading UFO-related material, Anna and I could not resist doing some amateur investigating of our own. Even so, we discovered our built-in belief systems were well established, and found it difficult to accept some of these accounts, no matter how well presented. Perhaps it was because we didn't want to believe. After all, by accepting the possibility of truth, we would need to greatly modify our perceptions of reality.

I, for one, could not imagine myself as a member of this exclusive club for alien abductees. I could accept—even believe—that UFOs exist since too many responsible (and *sane*) people have reported seeing them, but I was still unwilling to embrace the alien abduction theory. It wasn't that I suspected these "victims" of creating a hoax; I truly felt they were poor misguided people who had seen or experienced something unexplained and their minds had filled in the blanks with fantasy and false memories. This self-defense mechanism made more sense to me than that ordinary people were routinely being taken hostage by aliens.

In the "real world" if an offender was tried and proven guilty of kidnapping, he would be subjected to harsh penalty, likely imprisonment for up to thirty years. So, I reasoned, how could this kidnapping by aliens be going on right under the noses of law enforcement? If the claims of abductees were justified, why weren't the authorities notified and action taken to protect the victims of these assaults?

Later, as my understanding of the abduction phenomenon expanded, I realized all my previously accepted strategies for dealing with such violations no longer applied. It had been tried before by other victims, resulting in humiliation, embarrassment and frustration over law enforcement's inability to take these reports seriously. And I could hardly fault them for their reluctance to investigate these claims. From my own scanty memories of events, I could appreciate how difficult it would be to report an abduction—after the fact.

First of all, there was the problem of believability; the mere description of these abductors would be enough to classify the victim as deranged.

Second, explaining how the kidnapping was accomplished (often while in a vehicle, in bed or behind locked doors) stretches the credibility of the witness to extremes. How did the offender force the victim to stop his or her car on a lonely road, get out of the vehicle and go with the abductor, and then be returned safely if the victim was not a willing party to the abduction?

If the abduction took place in the wee hours of the morning while the victim was in bed, how had the abductor(s) gotten inside if not invited? And how would one explain a bedroom abduction succeeding despite the presence of the victim's spouse, sleeping undisturbed in the same bed? How would a victim of one of these abductions explain being floated through locked doors, closed windows or solid walls? If I was having trouble believing what little I recalled of these strange events, what was the likelihood of the police accepting them?

It was time to reevaluate my position. I would need to set guidelines as to what was acceptable for me and what was not. These guidelines were not to be set in stone (even early on I realized that my horizons were continually expanding), but they were necessary if I was to function in this reality. The more I could assimilate, the easier it would be.

But I couldn't seem to assimilate. Nothing in my experience had prepared me for having to blend two such unrelated realms. If I could accept one as the true reality while packaging the other as a curious (yet unproven) phenomenon, I might find it easier to cope. It was extremely important to me that I continue on with my life with as few uncertainties as possible. As I saw it, living day to day was enough of a challenge. So I learned to compartmentalize instead.

This prepackaging worked well, for a while, until things began to pick up. Interference in my recently accepted reality became more frequent, again presenting me with a dilemma for which I was less than prepared.

4. Collings

An Abduction Study Conference? Who were they kidding?

When Dick Hall[6] called to tell us about an abduction conference scheduled for June at M.I.T., I laughed aloud. What was there to confer about? No one knew anything; no one could explain anything; nobody had any realistic suggestions on how to stop these intrusions.

Who would be going to this conference? I asked Anna afterward.

Investigators, researchers, scientists, therapists, medical doctors, and, of course, experiencers (both abductees and contactees), she replied. We had also been invited.

What for?

So we could find out more about what was happening, meet others who were going through the same traumas, and maybe even make contact with therapists who could help us deal with it. This, apparently, seemed like a golden opportunity for Anna!

I didn't feel the same way. Why should we go all the way to Boston to expose ourselves to ridicule, when we could be ridiculed right here at home? Besides, I had no interest in being confused even more by the Doomsday theorizing of self-proclaimed contactees! I had limited knowledge of the claims of contactees, it was true, but from what I did understand, it appeared they believed themselves to have been chosen by these aliens as emissaries. These chosen ones were to spread the word, so to speak, of an imminent world-wide annihilation—an ending that would eventually assure the survival of our human race. How this would be accomplished was vague, but believers proclaimed that the aliens were only trying to help us save ourselves, that they had the most sincere and selfless motives, and that their interference in our society and evolutionary process had been going on since before recorded history. The role of these contactees was to relay this alien message to the rest of the world. "Space Brothers" was a term repeatedly connected with this camp. An interesting hypothesis, but a little too bizarre for my taste!

Anna seemed taken aback by my disinterest in attending the conference, saying that if I wouldn't go, *she couldn't*. "And why can't you?" I asked her.

"Because *you're* the abductee," she said pointedly, as if I had knowingly committed an embarrassing social faux-pas. "The only reason I was invited was so that you would go."

I didn't believe this, still feeling strongly that Anna was just as involved, but I promised to think about it anyway.

In May the invitation from M.I.T. arrived, along with a tentative schedule for the four-day conference. Included in this outline was a planned Abductee Panel, hinting that organizers of the conference would like to have "experiencers" volunteer to sit on this panel. *Ho boy!* I thought. No abductee is going to voluntarily expose him or herself to a few hundred strangers! They'd never get anyone to agree to that, I was sure–except perhaps for the contactees; they had already exposed themselves.

Soon after the arrival of the invitation, one of the conference's organizers called to ask if Anna and I would be willing to join the Abductee Panel. Another opportunity for a guffaw! I was assured that our anonymity would be protected, our true names not used without our permission, and that what we decided to reveal during our few minutes in the limelight was entirely up to us. Guffaw, guffaw!

I tried to explain to the organizer that Anna and I were still very new to this business and I, for one, didn't feel there was anything I could contribute to the panel or the further understanding of the observers. We hadn't even decided if we were going to attend!

Here I must add that only *I* had not decided. Anna was determined and I was almost convinced that it couldn't do any harm to go—but that was as an observer, not a participant! It didn't seem fair to deprive Anna of the experience, since she was obviously very excited over the prospect, and I was pretty sure she wouldn't go without me. So I agreed to go. How bad could it be?

And the Abductee Panel? Well, since we were guaranteed anonymity, and it was highly unlikely anyone other than Dick Hall would know our true identities, perhaps it would be an ideal forum for educating the therapists and encouraging their participation. Therapists knowledgeable about the phenomenon were in short supply, we all agreed. This might be the best way to gain access to them.

The panel participants were asked to submit typewritten material in advance, describing the planned topics of discussion. These would later be included in the published proceedings scheduled for release to the conference attenders later in the year. Although my original submission was sent as requested, the computer file copy I had planned to reprint here was mysteriously deleted from the data base during the "computer tamper days" (as described in a later chapter).

Briefly, I wrote of my family's connection with the phenomenon; about my father's, uncle's, son's and granddaughter's similar experiences. I wrote Noel's description of her poster board drawing[7] and the puzzle of my entire family's apparent involvement. Writing all this down was not as difficult—or traumatic—as I had expected it to be, but then I did not take into account that I would have to relate these things aloud in front of a room full of total strangers—believers and skeptics alike. I would be in for a real surprise, so it was probably best that early on it seemed to be a simple, harmless exercise.

We arrived in Boston a day early. I wanted to drive around and check out the old neighborhood. I had lived in the Boston suburbs from 1972 until 1981 but hadn't been back since. It felt good to see how little had changed, but even so I had trouble getting around with any confidence. After a few hours sight-seeing, we drove farther west of the city and found a quiet, inexpensive motel not too far out for the daily commute to M.I.T.

The next morning we made an appearance at M.I.T., registered and picked up our name tags. (We had agreed to use only first names for identification purposes.) I didn't see anyone I knew, but Anna recognized a few names from her many books on the phenomenon. Feeling stiff and out of place, I found myself searching for a familiar face! I knew Richard Hall was supposed to be there, but I didn't see him initially. I did notice that Anna was tense as well and wondered if my uneasiness had rubbed off on her. I was truly hoping this experience would provide the evidence I so wanted to find: That I was not an abductee; that I was probably crazy; and that Anna was suffering from sympathy pains.

I was continually wafting back and forth on the subject of insanity! Some days I couldn't discount the memories, my family's connection with those memories, and my feelings about Anna having been my friend since childhood; then, usually after a lull in the intrusions, I would again wish for insanity, deny anything unexplained had ever happened either to me or to my family, and embrace the belief that the connection was nothing more than hereditary mental illness. I theorized how easy it would be to commit myself for treatment. All I need do was convince a psychiatrist of my insanity and then I could relax and concentrate on getting better. It would be so nice not to have to worry about this stuff any longer! People would take care of me, keep me out of trouble, give me pills to dull the psychic pain, and erase the little gray shits from my mind! That was the only way to get rid of them once and for all!

But then something would happen: An unexplained cut or puncture, a fragmented memory of having been floated *through* my bedroom window, a shared "dream" with Anna. Whoosh! I was back in that other reality yet again.

Being at the conference was going to make this uncertainty even harder to control.

I noticed how many experiencers were registering during that first morning and felt as if I'd dropped into a scene from *Star Trek*. No . . . that's not quite right. These experiencers were just like us; normal average people who looked as uncomfortable as I did. They seemed just as insecure, just as nervous. This wasn't a scene from some futuristic movie, this *was* the future.

The Abductee Panel convened on the second day, and Anna and I joined them at the long table set up in front of the lecture hall. I was as jittery as I could ever remember being, thinking I had made a fatal mistake by coming to this conference. As each of us were introduced to the audience, I kept my eyes diverted, not wanting to see those wolfish faces glaring down on us. I had learned there were some invited reporters in the audience (though we had been assured no cameras would be permitted), and envisioned tiny spy cameras trained on the panel, clicking away and recording our faces (and identities) for posterity.

As each of the experiencers in turn told their stories, contactees included, I realized we each had developed our own ways of coping with the intrusions into our lives. I had relied on the insanity fallback; others dealt with the trauma by seeing the aliens as "space brothers"; some concluded they were experiencing a religious phenomenon with the attending angels and devils; still others saw the intrusion as an organized and self-serving exploitation by beings who had learned to manipulate space-time. There were, in fact, more theories than one could shake a laser beam at!

Since others were to speak before me, I took the opportunity to glance over my notes. It struck me then that I would have to say these things out loud! I didn't think I could do that with any semblance of self-control. I fingered Noel's poster which stood on its rolled edge on the floor next to me, realizing I had planned to show the drawing while describing what the figures represented to her. How could I do that?

Suddenly it was my turn. The room seemed very quiet; I could hear a man cough in one of the upper rows; a woman on the panel cleared her throat. I dared a glance up and came face-to-face with the wolves! They were all looking at me! What were they expecting from me? A performance? I hoped not. I would simply read from my notes and pretend there was no one there to hear. I could do this.

I began reading, peering up from my notes occasionally to make sure no one was laughing. It was going fairly well, I thought confidently. Then I reached for Noel's drawing and opened it up for the audience to see, intending to point out specifics as I read Noel's descriptions. I don't now recall what particular word or phrase caused me to break down in front of so many strangers, but break down I did. Unable to maintain my composure, I buried my head in my hands and choked back tears of pure agony. I had never felt so inadequate! My granddaughter was telling me, by her explicit drawings, that she was being taken against her will by beings that defied description—or belief. And I couldn't help her! I couldn't save her from them, couldn't take the memories away or stop it from happening. I was useless to her, as helpless as I had been with my son. Was this how my father had felt?

God! What could I do? What could any of us do?

5. Jamerson

My current therapist wasn't achieving the results we had hoped for, so she suggested I try acupuncture. I was game; I would have tried almost anything to get rid of these headaches. It had worked for my horses, why should I be reluctant to try it?

My first session with Norris Blanks was a real eye-opener. Not only is he an acupuncturist, but he is also a therapist who used hypnosis extensively in his practice. I hit the jackpot. But he had a belief system I was not ready to embrace: He is a New Ager. He believes in the healing power of "the Light" and the "I Am That I Am"; that past and future life experiences impinge on us in the present, and that there is an all powerful spirit to call upon to help us in this life. It was pretty spooky stuff for me, but after all I'd been through, nothing was that foreign. He was not familiar with any of the abduction literature, didn't know about the gray ones, and felt that the majority of attaching entities were of "the Light" and worked for one's highest good. Not quite my opinion, but I was willing to work through this if he was.

We spent several sessions talking and exploring philosophies, usually for two to three hours at a time. He did a type of hypnosis where I relaxed, closed my eyes, listened to his voice, and conjured up images as he directed me. We mainly worked on my headaches, self-esteem, my fear of fear, empowerment and getting my life back in order. Only once did I conjure up a gray one; I made him turn his back and leave me alone! Boy, did I feel powerful!

After a few sessions, Norris asked me if I thought that I had ever made a contract with these energies (that's what he calls the gray ones), permitting them to abduct me. Of course not! I told him I'd heard of other abductees who thought that they had, but I didn't feel that way. He asked if I was willing to look for a contract and if I did make one, would I be willing to break it. I immediately said, "Yes!"

During our next session we talked about the contract and explored the distinct possibility that I may not be willing to break it quite so flippantly. I feel that they may have given me support and possibly love when I needed it. I remember crying myself to sleep at night as a child, feeling my parents didn't love me. Even if the greys caused those feelings, I somehow felt dependent on them. I didn't like feeling that way, but it was there. I hated them for doing that to a defenseless child. So yes, I wanted to know if I made a contract so I could decide what to do about it with more awareness of the consequences.

During the session on July 27, 1993, we talked for about an hour, then did a relaxation session where we worked on fear, and fear of fear. Then we decided to do a hypnosis session. I knew this would be a very different session than the ones I had done with Budd, but I felt comfortable with Norris. Budd Hopkins,[8] as an investigator, was careful not to lead me to any preconceived conclusions. Norris, as a therapist, had no such need. Some of Norris's questions were deliberately leading, and I have no doubt that I confabulated during these sessions. It was hard for me to sort out what I really experienced from what I may have produced to please Norris. In some ways it didn't really matter; this wasn't straight investigation, it was primarily therapy. He never did convert me to the New Age philosophy, yet he helped restore my self-esteem and gave me access to information that helped me cope.

Before hypnosis, we talked about where I imagined my time-line to be; past, present and future. He asked if I could separate myself from the time-line and step out of it. I could. After I was hypnotized, Norris asked me if I had an implant (not a contract!). I said I had an implant, put in the back of my brain.

Transcript of Hypnosis Session with Norris Blanks

Tuesday morning, July 27, 1993

Norris: It is at this point that you have indicated that at some time not of this earth frame there had been an agreement to have an implant inserted in this life. Is this correct?

Anna: Yes.

Norris: Yes. But in this lifetime, you do not believe that the implant is for your highest good?

Anna: Right.

Norris: Were you deceived in the past to have this implant inserted?

Anna: No.

Norris: The agreement was made of your free will?

Anna: I think so.

Norris: Can we journey back to the time when the agreement was made?

Anna: Yes.

Norris: You know you are secure, no harm can come to you. But we will go back and investigate, and find out the beginnings and the origins of this situation. What I would ask you to do now is to move back from your time-line. Now I would like you to move along the time-line either to the future or the past, whenever this event occurred. Do you know whether this has come from a future incarnation or life cycle or whether it has come from the past?

Anna: No.

Norris: What I would like you to indicate with your finger responses, is should we go backwards along the time-line to the past? Should we go forward along the time-line? Okay, we will go forward along the time-line. I want you now to move along the time-line until you are drawn to the point where the agreement for this implant was made. Tell me where you are.

Anna: In a big room.

Norris: Is it night or day? [*After a long pause:*] That's okay. Is it light in the room or dark?

Anna: [*Sigh*] Light.

Norris: Good. Who is in the room with you?

Anna: I see a large head.

Norris: And do you see yourself?

Anna: No.

Norris: But you feel your energy and your presence in this room?

Anna: Yes.

[*Note: I felt like I was a ball of light in the corner of the room.*]

Norris: And is this room a place of instruction or learning or what?

Anna: It's a library.

Norris: Is it a library that has information within it?

Anna: Yes.

Norris: Is this information in book form, or computer form or light form?

Anna: I think there's some books, but they're real old.

Norris: Is it familiar to you?

Anna: Yeah.

Norris: And there's another entity in the room with you?

Anna: Yeah.

Norris: Would you please describe as best you can this entity? You mentioned that there was a large head. Is there any other detail you can add?

Anna: It seems to have stripes on the side of its head, and the front part of the head is very developed.

Norris: What about the eyes?

Anna: They're larger than mine.

Norris: Do they have a color or do they have pupils and irises like we know them or are they all one color?

Anna: I don't know.

Norris: That's okay. Does this entity have a body?

Anna: It has two legs that are thin, but they have muscles on them.

Norris: What is the color of the entity? Does it have a skin color or a covering color?

Anna: Pink.

Norris: Are you able to look into the eyes of this entity quite comfortably?

Anna: All I can see is the side of her head.

Norris: Oh, I see. So you're not facing the entity. What feelings do you have of being in the presence of this entity?

Anna: Respect.

Norris: So you have respect for this entity. Is this occurring within our solar system?

Anna: No.

Norris: It is beyond that. Did you have any idea where this is occurring?

Anna: The red planet.

Norris: By the red planet do you mean possibly Mars?

Anna: No.

Norris: How many light years is it from the earth? Do you have any idea?

Anna: 23 or 27?

Norris: Are you communicating with this being or you're just in its presence?

Anna: I think it's supposed to do something to me, but I don't know what.

Norris: Can you ask it what it's supposed to do?

Anna: I'm supposed to learn something.

Norris: Is it something that you will later use in your earth life?

Anna: Yes. But I'm not supposed to know what it is.

Norris: I understand.

Anna: I don't.

Norris: And so the knowledge will be activated in you at the appropriate time?

Anna: Yes.

Norris: In respect to your earth life in this cycle, what is your mission?

Anna: Change something.

Norris: Do you know what? Is it a structure or a consciousness change?

Anna: I don't know.

Norris: Are there other people that you are associated with here on the earth that are a part of this mission of yours?

Anna: Yes.

Norris: Now these are friends that you habituate with?

Anna: Yes, some I don't know yet, though.

Norris: At this time in 1993, you are not fully aware of your mission?

Anna: Right.

Norris: When do you believe that you will be made fully aware of your mission?

Anna: 1997.

Norris: So what preparation are you going through at the moment? Can you tell me?

Anna: Some sort of metamorphosis. I don't know what that means.

Norris: You said earlier you were unsure that what was happening to you in this life was for your highest good. Do you still believe this to be true?

Anna: Yep.

Norris: Why do you believe that what is happening is not for your highest good?

Anna: They've lied before.

Norris: I understand. So you believe that you may have been deceived. When did they first lie to you, do you remember?

Anna: No, but they hurt me; they told me it wouldn't hurt—a long, long time ago.

Norris: They hurt you physically?

Anna: Yes.

Norris: The people that, or the entities, that you have dealt with, are these representatives of this energy that you are in the room with?

Anna: No, they're somehow different.

Norris: Are they interfering with some other pattern that you have set for yourself?

Anna: I didn't set it.

Norris: If another pattern has been set for you, do you think that the greys are interfering negatively or they are a part of this pattern?

Anna: I don't know.

Norris: Do you wish to break the agreement that you have made?

Anna: Yes.

Norris: Why do you wish to break the agreement?

Anna: Because I don't know what it is.

Norris: Is it wise for you to break the agreement?

Anna: I don't know.

Norris: When you have been involved with these other entities, have you ever felt a sense of love from them?

Anna: No. Duty.

Norris: Are they living beings themselves or are they automaton type beings?

Anna: No, they're living.

Norris: What do you think will happen if you break the contract?

Anna: I don't know, maybe they'll find somebody else.

Norris: What power do you believe you have in this situation?

Anna: Not much. I'm a pawn.

Norris: Are you aware that you may have great guidance systems around you, and other beings that you can call on, who can help you to understand?

Anna: No.

Norris: You're not aware of this, but you feel much more in control of this situation than you did a month ago?

Anna: Yes.

End Transcript

Now I didn't just have the gray ones to worry about, I had dealings with the "Pink Lady" from a red planet as well, an entity that implanted a "thought bomb" in my mind!

I didn't know if any of that was real, although she seemed real. I had accepted that I might have physical implants in my body at various times, as many other abductees had reported, but a mind implant? When Norris asked me what it looked like, all I could see was a small amorphous orange cloud. I now think that it was a memory implant rather than anything physical, that's why I couldn't describe it to him. I feel strongly that I do have knowledge in my head that will be revealed to me in 1997, but I sure would like to know what it is now. I can't quite buy the premise that it was implanted in my brain in the future. I may be willing to believe a lot of things that I never considered possible two years ago, but I hadn't lost all my analytical functioning.

I always feel better after the sessions with Norris. I'm more confident, more relaxed (and tired!), and feel more in control of my destiny. He's really helped me explore my feelings for myself, and my relationships with my family and the aliens. I guess that's the main goal of therapy: Be able to handle your own life independently of the therapist. I'd like to get there soon.

I was coping better, with Norris's help, but all we seemed to discover were more questions, not answers. I'd keep trying.

6. Collings

Fight back how? We tried alarms, sensors, cameras, witnesses—nothing worked! We'd had access to some of the best technology available, yet the shits kept coming! I felt as if we were trying to win a race by running backwards across the start line. I wasn't about to give up, no. That wouldn't accomplish anything. But what had all this technology done for us? There had to be another way!

Anna had read about other abductees who claimed limited success resisting the greys. One method involved chanting selected passages from the Bible; another promoted the use of mental resistance (refuse to go in your mind? Couldn't they continue to take your body?); yet another suggested tying oneself to an immovable object. There was one I found pathetically sad: Kill yourself. If you're dead, they won't want you anymore.

Had these people found relief, though? Well . . . not always. The abductions continued, but according to some, on a less frequent basis. Less frequent than when?

I have a friend, another horseperson and fellow abductee, who is a devout Christian. She believes in God, goes to church regularly, and tries to follow the teachings of her religious faith. During her many years dealing with these abductions, she has steadfastly clung to her beliefs, trying without success to resist them through faith in God. As with Anna and me

—and many more like us—a belief in God, Jesus, the Virgin Mary or the Holy Spirit has not stopped the assaults. Chanting passages from the Bible or praying for relief do not seem to have any affect on these creatures. They have an agenda, a job to do, and although a higher authority may be privy to their plans for us, we apparently are not considered worthy of that knowledge.

It may be (although I doubt it) that these creatures report to the same higher authority as believers here on earth do, and if that is so, what does that tell us about our importance in the scheme of things? In short, if there is a God and He (or She) knows of our predicament (as believers feel is true), then He (or She) has obviously chosen to stay out of it.

I think we are on our own with this one.

Conscious physical resistance has not worked either. One may *think* about clinging to an immovable object, but when *they* come to get you the body is effectively paralyzed and the grip is lost. This method of control works equally well should the victim show any aggressiveness towards them. I know because I've tried. When I was abducted in September of 1992 while on vacation, I was allowed to move in order to finish dressing myself, but as soon as I took a step toward them I was quickly immobilized again. Although this gave me a fleeting sense of power, it was nothing more than wishful thinking.

I had spoken to another abductee (while we were in New York visiting Budd Hopkins) who had actually struck one of the greys. She said the little fellow felt like he was made of papier-mache. But retaliation was swift—and strong. She was quickly knocked down. That, she assured us, was not likely to happen again.

Some diversions had been successful, though. These feeble acts of defiance did not usually stop the abduction, but they could sometimes slow the little buggers down. After one such experience, where they seemed dumbfounded by my polished toenails (asking me how I had injured my feet!), I devised a plan that might confuse them even more. Before going to bed one night, I wrapped each toe in a bandaid—not just your average flesh-colored bandaid, either, but those multi-colored glow-in-the-dark variety that are so popular with children. When I turned out the light, I checked my toes to see if the bandaids really did glow in the dark. Sure enough! It looked like my toes were radioactive! I was so pleased with myself it took me several hours to get to sleep. It was the only time I ever wished for them to make an appearance!

And they did come. And I did go. But when I woke up that morning, all the bandaids were gone! I searched my room from top to bottom, but never did find them. So maybe my defiant gesture didn't change the outcome, but I'd be willing to bet real money that it gave them something to think about.

Anna even suggested that I try dripping red nail polish on my skin to see if that brought a reaction. It couldn't hurt, so I tried it. But nothing changed. I expected by then they must have figured out what I was up to.

Although these little tricks did more to improve my outlook than to change my situation, it wasn't a complete loss. I learned I had not lost my sense of humor after all. I can still imagine those fluorescent bandaids hanging in an exhibition on board some craft, while groups of little gray shits cue up to see this marvelous and mysterious example of human cultural depravity!

And that was the key . . . Humor could be a powerful weapon against fear and oppression. I did not like being a victim. I was tired of it! Maybe I couldn't be in control, but that did not mean I had to meekly succumb, either! Abduction against one's will is surely not a desirable state of affairs, but if I could just find humor in some of it—even at my own expense— maybe life on this plane would be easier. I might actually begin to enjoy things again. That was good advice, and I decided to make a genuine effort to follow it.

7. Jamerson

Are we really being visited by aliens from another planet, or another dimension? I think so; it's real for me. I can no longer hide in the delusion of insanity. I've experienced too much. I've learned too much.

I feel that I have been given an unpleasant task to do: Tell of the impending doom. I don't do it. I wish I could have been given a more amiable message, one of hope, and peace, and love. But that is not to be. When talking with others at work, I find myself curbing the instant mental response, "It doesn't matter." Even if I feel, some days, that there is no use in planning for the future, I have no right to frighten other people by inflicting them with my paranoia. I know the aliens tell lies and use psychological testing to elicit emotional responses, but sometimes I find it hard not to believe them.

Or maybe we are just part of the conditioning process. The casual acceptance of aliens is widespread in the U.S. and abroad. More people than ever believe in the *possibility* of aliens visiting our planet. It's the actuality of it that will be the leap of faith. As more people regain their memories, as they begin to talk more openly about what they have experienced, acceptance will become more reasonable. We are connected to the Earth and to the aliens; what better intermediaries? That assumes some purpose for their revealing themselves. I don't know what that might be. It certainly doesn't seem to be to save us from our own destructive habits.

Their genetic agenda is confusing to me. Everything I read implies that they are developing hybrids. In my own case, I have never knowingly had sex with an alien, although I don't know what types of embryos they may have implanted in my body. I'm convinced that my alien children are genetically fully human, but they have been developed in the laboratories, outside a uterus, and no longer look completely human. If, as they have told me, they are developing beings to colonize other planets, then why do they need me? I'm especially suited to survive on planet Earth. Are there other planets so similar to Earth, and uninhabited, where we can survive? Are we so unique that it is worth all the time and trouble? Why not develop clones that do not require the traumatic collection of sperm and ova? It seems there are always more questions, few answers. I keep looking for patterns, but if they exist, they are obscure. We need more resources devoted to these mysteries. It's time to take this seriously.

I no longer have the need to control the environment or the people around me. I am more accepting of what is, for its own sake. This assimilation was not easy. The grays give me no joy. They stole my childhood by devastating my family relationships, by taking away my memories and supplanting them with others. I hate them for allowing me to believe that my father raped me. How many other children have they done this to? I'm convinced that some of the people who have recalled childhood abuse, especially when the reported incident was never repeated and the accused parent adamantly denies the abuse, have been given screen memories to cover the trauma of alien abuse, not parental abuse. Working with open-minded therapists has finally allowed me to accept what really happened to me. I have come to know that relationships with other people are the most important things in our lives. Everything else is just a way to structure time. Little else really matters.

The past few years have been an awakening experience for me. Not just dealing with the alien interference, although that would have been enough. The process of uncovering hidden memories has forced me to examine the very heart of myself. I'd never have done it willingly; I wasn't that type of person. It's been a journey into the deepest part of myself, a laying bare of who I am, what I think I am, and what is really important to me. I look at each new season, each new vista of this planet I call home, each person I interact with in a different light. Part of me will always question, "Will this be my last spring (sunset, Christmas, lover or horseback ride)?" Another part of me just enjoys the sensations, savoring each new experience as a reflection of truth, not necessarily truth itself.

No matter which interpretation of these strange events in my life is shown to be real, I have learned to accept myself. I like the new me.

8. Collings

Why me? I've asked myself that question countless times. And the answer is always the same: I don't know. I have entertained a number of theories, though. The most credible seems to be that these beings have been abducting generations of families, and may still be doing so. Whether this pattern would stand up to close scrutiny is anybody's guess. By the time I started getting memories, my grandparents were both deceased, so there was no way to verify the odd stories related about them over the years.

My father, fortunately (if that's the right word here), remembered a great deal about his childhood experiences and had documented many of them, but what if he refused to talk about them? He could just as easily have reacted to my inquiries as my mother had, by evading them or leaving the room whenever the subject arose. And what if I hadn't had the courage to confront him? I don't imagine he ever would have broached the subject with me!

There were many strange events during my son's early years that I had conveniently written off as coincidental or just unexplained—until I actually verbalized them. Even after I had memories of being abducted as a small child, I did not want to associate the similarities between my son's night terrors and my own with this phenomenon, because by doing so I could be exposing myself to ridicule. Despite what I said aloud, I really didn't want my son to think I was crazy! When my granddaughter presented her drawing to me, describing these beings and their craft in such vivid detail, I didn't want to accept that either, but in her case my reasons for denial had little to do with my image. I simply couldn't believe these abductions have been going on for four generations! It was easier to accept the notion that our family tree harbored some unidentified genetic defect.

Then other reports surfaced of multiple generations having been abducted. Did this mean that this business had been going on prior to the infamous 1947 purported crash landing of a flying disk? All along I had thought that was when it had started—that flying saucers were unheard of before the early forties, and that abductions were unknown until the Betty and Barney Hill incident in the sixties. Considering the time period, it would be too much to expect that anyone in his right mind would *voluntarily* report being abducted by aliens! Even now, to stick one's neck out by publicly admitting involvement is to chance decapitation.

The populace, as a whole, *is* more accepting than it once was, and this new attitude is evident in almost every aspect of our daily lives. Turn on the TV, and what do you see? Hamburger commercials using a log that suspiciously resembles a UFO, both in appearance and movement; another fast-food establishment uses commercials with varying scenarios involving the landing of UFOs outside a restaurant while patrons go on eating, presumably because the food is so good they cannot be distracted by such a common sight! Weekly programs highlighting sightings and alien abduction reports are more common—and more popular—than ever before. Is this a hint? Or is it only conjecture? Are we being *programmed* for acceptance? If so, by whom and for what purpose?

I have suffered through a roller-coaster ride of emotions in an effort to come to grips with this weirdness. I have denied it outright, accepted it fully, and wavered between the two, but at no time did I consider ignoring it. There have been entire days when I didn't think about it at all, not because I had learned to assimilate—or compartmentalize—but out of pure stubbornness! I wanted to feel in control of my life again; I wanted to know that my actions were the result of personal choice, not alien intervention. Completion of the simplest tasks was an enormous boost to my self-esteem.

The will to survive—and prosper—despite these intrusions, has not been supplanted by the need to reach some conclusion. I have questions, of course—lots of them! I have doubts, too, and suspicions and worries and theories. But what I don't have is my old, safe life. That, clearly, is gone forever. It had only been a veneer after all, so the process of discovering what now lies exposed should be a challenge. Am I up to it? Is anyone? We know more than we did before, but not enough. And there the real challenge lies: Will we recognize and accept understanding when and if it comes?

Again, we are plagued by questions and not enough answers, and speculations do not adequately address the emotional consequences. So many lives have been—and are now—affected by this controversial phenomenon. We can no longer afford the luxury of ignorance. Something is certainly going on here, and as both Anna and I have expressed throughout this book, it is past time for serious examination by the scientific community. We have been told, on a number of occasions, that the abduction phenomenon has proven difficult to explore under scientific guidelines. Why? Because, according to the experts, there is nothing concrete to examine, no physical evidence that would stand up under close inspection.

It's true that this phenomenon, unlike other mysteries, has presented scientists with little in the way of hard evidence, and that the testimony of witnesses also cannot be confirmed (except by other witnesses), but that does not mean it isn't worthy of serious consideration. Human memory is not flawless, but it certainly can be credible! Repressed memories retrieved through hypnosis can be confabulation, but how does that discredit conscious memories evident without the use of hypnosis? It doesn't. And in turn, it also doesn't prove that retrieved memories must be either confabulation or the result of leading by the hypnotist.

It is this human factor that so flusters the scientists. We are not *provable!* We are only human. Maybe it is the very aspect that has so fascinated our visitors.

We *are* unique, yes, but not because we are alone in the universe; we are unique because we crave understanding and knowledge, plan for our future, and embrace the lessons of the past. Once the earth was thought to be the center of the universe; once the world was believed to be flat; once humankind considered space travel impossible. If we have learned anything from our past philosophies, we should have learned that nothing is impossible, nothing is permanent, and truth lies somewhere between interpretation and understanding.

NOTES

Excerpts from Beth Collings and Anna Jamerson, *Connections: Solving Our Alien Abduction Mystery* (Newberg, Ore.: Wild Flower Press, 1996). Reprinted by permission of the authors.

1. These are pseudonyms.

2. The names of all family members and some friends have been changed throughout the course of this book. [Note in original text.]

3. Jamerson and Collings shared a love for horses.

4. Collings and Jamerson referred to the aliens as "gray shits" or "greys" because they recalled the aliens' outer coloring as gray.

5. Two people whom they met after they began to contact UFO-related groups.

6. Or Richard Hall, a UFO investigator whom they learned to trust as they delved into the UFO subculture.

7. Collings's granddaughter Noel drew pictures of the same aliens that Collings encountered, indicating to Collings that Noel, too, was being abducted.

8. Hopkins is a noted UFO investigator. He started the Intruders Foundation, an abduction research group, and is the author of several books about abductions, including *Intruders: The Incredible Visitations at Copley Woods* (New York: Random House, 1987).

FOR FURTHER READING

Adamski, George, *Inside the Flying Saucers* (New York: Warner, 1955). One of the first UFO contactees, Adamski became a well-known advocate for interest in UFOs.

Denzler, Brenda, *The Lure of the Edge: Scientific Passions, Religious Beliefs, and the Pursuit of UFOs* (Berkeley: University of California Press, 2001). A thorough scholarly study of UFO subcultures.

Mutual UFO Network, http://www.mufon.com. The official Website of the Mutual UFO Network (MUFON), one of the major organizations devoted to the study of UFOs through publications and symposia.

Partridge, Christopher, ed., *UFO Religions* (London: Routledge, 2003). A collection of essays, some by major scholars, about many aspects of UFOs and religion.

The Raelian Revolution, http://www.rael.org. The official Website of the Raelian Movement, a major UFO-related religious movement.

Strieber, Whitley, *Communion: A True Story* (New York: Avon, 1987). Strieber is one of the most famous of the recent generation of UFO advocates or abductees.

Part II

New Selves

Chapter 4

Wicca

Wicca, sometimes also called witchcraft or simply "The Craft," is a neo-pagan tradition whose adherents see it as a continuation of a pre-Christian European nature and Goddess spirituality, especially as practiced in the British Isles. Modern Wicca traces its inception to the British folklorist Gerald Gardner, who claimed to have been initiated into a society of Wiccan practitioners, or coven, in the early part of the twentieth century. Gardner (somewhat scandalously) broke the group's tradition of secrecy and detailed his practice and its history in the books *Witchcraft Today* (1954) and *The Meaning of Witchcraft* (1959), which were instrumental in establishing modern Wicca.[1]

Scholars and historians hotly contest whether Gardnerian Wicca or its other modern derivatives do, in fact, represent the revival of an indigenous European practice that remained underground for centuries for fear of persecution during the "Burning Times" from the fifteenth to seventeenth centuries. It is uncertain whether an organized "pagan" or "heathen" religion (both words denote dwellers of the countryside)—as opposed to a localized, shamanic religion focused on natural and ritual healing—ever existed to be resurrected in the twentieth century.[2] Yet to most modern Wiccans this lack of a documented pedigree is irrelevant. Somewhat paradoxically, Wiccan tradition can be created by a practitioner for him- or herself.

As with other neo-pagan faiths, practitioners view Wicca (an Old English word likely meaning "to alter or bend") as a celebration of the power of nature, and especially of the rhythmic cycles of the moon and the seasons. One "attunes" to the spiritual energy underlying the natural world through celebrating important points in the solar cycle called "Sabbats," which include the equinoxes and solstices as well as other important holidays,[3] and "Esbats," periods of ritual efficacy tied to the phases of the moon. Wiccan rituals can be performed with others in a coven, but modern practitioners often work alone as "solitaries." In either case, Wiccans demarcate sacred spaces aligned with the four cardinal directions. They also incorporate the four sacred elements (earth, air, fire, and water) into their rituals with elemental tools (the encircled five-pointed star, or pentacle; the wand; the dagger; and the cup), with the practitioner, priest, or priestess in the center as the fifth element, spirit. Incantations are chanted to invoke the power represented by various gods and goddesses of different religions—all of whom are ultimately considered to be the one Great Goddess: *Gaia,* or "Mother Nature," the Earth as a living entity.[4] In the ritual known as "Drawing Down the Moon," held during the full moon, the power of the Goddess and/or God is invited into the practitioner, making him or her the Goddess or God incarnate. Both solitaries and established covens keep a *Grimoire,* or "Book of Shadows" (or "Secrets"), to record spells, rituals, incantations, and invocations found to be powerful or effective. (Selections found in one Book of Shadows are excerpted below.)

The Wiccan worldview emphasizes the interconnectedness of all living things, not just to show life in its myriad forms the proper respect, but also to use these connections to benefit individual lives through magic or magick. (Most Wiccans prefer the latter, older spelling to distinguish their practice from magic as entertainment). Wiccan rituals and chants are aimed at opening the individual up to the natural, cosmic power flowing through all things, and thereby transforming some aspect of the practitioner's reality—social, sexual, psychological, financial, bodily, and so on. The four elements, besides corresponding to the four cardinal directions, also represent the four essential aspects of the human being—emotion, will, body, and intellect—thereby creating an authentic link between the macrocosm of nature and the microcosm of the person (a concept also central to Chinese religions).

Healing is a common theme in Wiccan rites, as are reincarnation, rebirth, renewal, and the natural cycle of life and death (e.g., the Goddess has three faces or phases: maiden, mother, and crone). To this end, much of Wiccan belief and practice focuses on people's ability to transform themselves into who they "really are," which is, ultimately, divine. Wicca and other neo-pagan faiths are, in this respect, somewhat illustrative of "New Age" religions, despite the fact that their symbols are drawn from an earlier time. However, the focus on individual empowerment or divinity should not obscure Wiccans' underlying belief in the interconnectedness and mutual interdependency of all living things, which is what makes such a reimagining of the self possible. Although Wiccans have generally moved away from the coven model toward that of the solitary practitioner, the ethical ties to other beings—not just humans, but animals and the ecosystem in general—are consistently affirmed. This stance definitively distinguishes Wicca from Satanism, with which it is too frequently conflated.[5]

Indeed, what is in many ways the creed of the Wiccan way of life, the Wiccan Rede, declares: "An [*sic*] it harm none, do as ye will."[6] Here, the dual concerns for others' well-being and one's own freedom are succinctly expressed. These sentiments also evince a strong hope among Wiccans that their practice will help achieve a degree of social justice and planetary healing in a society wracked by capitalistic excesses; the oppression of women, homosexuals, people of color, and non-Christians; and environmental destruction on a global scale. Especially due to the contributions of the authors Starhawk and Zsuzsanne Budapest in the 1970s, most forms of Wicca are staunchly feminist. The focus on the Goddess seeks to rectify centuries of neglect of and violence to women and women's spirituality at the hands of patriarchal religions, particularly Christianity.

The claim to represent pre-Christian ideals itself offers an implicit critique of modern Western society and a chance for those marginalized by it to find the power almost literally "within themselves" to combat it. The spirit of interconnectedness allows even solitary practitioners to feel as though they can reinvent their own small portion of society while they work for the betterment of the whole. Moreover, when Wiccans and other neo-pagans do meet and interact more directly, such as at festivals or even on the Internet, not only do they describe the sense of freedom that comes from finding a society that accepts their "true selves," but they also frequently come to know their fellow practitioners as the supportive family they never had.[7]

Hence, both in solitary and coven practice, the Wiccan seeks to manifest and express a New Self, sometimes symbolized by taking a magical name or identity specific to the worship context. Yet the ability to realize this self is clearly dependent on a New Understanding of the universe (as the Great Goddess) and one's interconnected place in it. Such a new view of the cosmos allows one to see the potential power that lies within, and that one shares with all living beings or even the universe itself. Becoming aware of one's connection to and responsibility for all creatures, however, only throws into stark contrast the damage inflicted on them by most people's current modes of living, economically, religiously, and interpersonally. Wiccan practice and relationships, then, work in both small and large ways to transform one's family history, one's failing society, or even the very planet one lives on into a New Family, a New Society, or a New

World, all free of the oppression, violence, and degradation that plagued the old ones.

Because of the individualistic and anti-authoritarian nature of Wicca, a vast array of materials, old and new, could be considered representative or illustrative of its beliefs and practices—as could none, for that matter. The selections from Eileen Holland and Scott Cunningham below are resource guides geared toward helping the solitary practitioner create and conduct rituals, select invocations to "draw down" the Goddess or God, or work though the steps of a spell or brew. Cunningham's works enjoy more influence and authority in current Wiccan practice, and his presentation of the techniques of creating sacred space, divine invocations, and a solitary dedication (initiation) rite conveys both the practical and emotional sides of the Wiccan ritual experience. On the other hand, the Craft's current eclecticism is usefully represented by Holland, a long-standing Wiccan priestess, who provides a succinct personal overview of the meaning of Wiccan history and practice in the second excerpt, from *The Wicca Handbook*. These selections are preceded by a significant exception to the rule of Wiccan anti-institutionalization: in 1974, the short-lived Council of American Witches convened in Minneapolis and issued "The Principles of Wiccan Belief," whose positions on a number of issues have become widely accepted among practitioners.

"The Principles of Wiccan Belief" (1974)

The Council of American Witches

The Council of American Witches finds it necessary to define modern Witchcraft in terms of the American experience and needs. We are not bound by traditions from other times and other cultures, and owe no allegiance to any person or power greater than the Divinity manifest through our own being. As American Witches, we welcome and respect all life-affirming teachings and traditions, and seek to learn from all and to share our learning within our Council.

It is in this spirit of welcome and cooperation that we adopt these few principles of Wiccan belief. In seeking to be inclusive, we do not wish to open ourselves to the destruction of our group by those on self-serving power trips, or philosophies and practices contradictory to these principles. In seeking to exclude those whose ways are contradictory to ours, we do not want to deny participation with us to any who are sincerely interested in our knowledge and beliefs, regardless of race, color, gender, age, national or cultural origins, or sexual preferences.

We therefore ask only that those who seek to identify with us accept these few basic principles:

1. We practice rites to attune ourselves with the natural rhythm of life forces marked by the phases of the Moon and the seasonal quarters and cross-quarters.

2. We recognize that our intelligence gives us a unique responsibility toward our environment. We seek to live in harmony with Nature, in ecological balance offering fulfillment to life and consciousness within an evolutionary concept.

3. We acknowledge a depth of power far greater than is apparent to the average person. Because it is far greater than ordinary, it is sometimes called "supernatural," but we see it as lying within that which is naturally potential to all.

4. We conceive of the Creative Power in the Universe as manifesting through polarity—as masculine and feminine—and that this same Creative Power lives in all people, and functions through the interaction of the masculine and feminine. We value neither above the other, knowing each to be supportive of the other. We value sexuality as pleasure, as the symbol and embodiment of Life, and as one of the sources of energies used in magickal practice and religious worship.

5. We recognize both outer worlds and inner, or psychological worlds —sometimes known as the Spiritual World, the Collective Unconscious, the Inner Planes, etc.—and we see in the interaction of these two dimensions the basis for paranormal phenomena and magickal exercises. We neglect neither dimension for the other, seeing both as necessary for our fulfillment.

6. We do not recognize any hierarchy, but do honor those who teach, respect those who share their knowledge and wisdom, and acknowledge those who have courageously given of themselves in leadership.

7. We see religion, magick, and wisdom-in-living as being united in the way one views the world and lives within it—a world view and philosophy of life, which we identify as Witchcraft or the Wiccan Way.

8. Calling oneself "witch" does not make a Witch—but neither does heredity itself, or the collecting of titles, degrees, and initiations. A Witch seeks to control the forces within him/herself that make life possible in order to live wisely and well, without harm to others, and in harmony with Nature.

9. We acknowledge that it is the affirmation and fulfillment of life, in a continuation of evolution and development of consciousness, that gives meaning to the Universe we know, and to our personal role within it.

10. Our only animosity toward Christianity, or toward any other religion or philosophy-of-life, is to the extent that its institutions have claimed to be "the one true right and only way" and have sought to deny freedom to others and to suppress other ways of religious practices and belief.

11. As American Witches, we are not threatened by debates on the history of the Craft, the origins of various terms, the legitimacy of various aspects of different traditions. We are concerned with our present, and our future.

12. We do not accept the concept of "absolute evil," nor do we worship any entity known as "Satan" or "the Devil" as defined by Christian Tradition. We do not seek power through the suffering of others, nor do we accept the concept that personal benefits can only be derived by denial to another.

13. We work within Nature for that which is contributory to our health and well-being.

From *The Wicca Handbook*

Eileen Holland

About Wicca

Modern Wicca began in England in 1939, when Gerald Gardner was initiated into a traditional British coven by Dorothy Clutterbuck (Old Dorothy). He later broke the coven's seal of secrecy and published books about the beliefs and practices of British Wiccans, because he feared the religion would die out. This began what continues to be a groundswell of people converting to Wicca.

Debate currently rages over whether Wicca is a new religion, or the oldest of all religions. Some say that Wicca has been practiced continuously in Europe at least since the Ice Age. They cite Paleolithic carvings of female figures, such as the Venus of Willendorf, as evidence of Goddess worship having been the origin of all religions. No, say others, Wicca is a neo-pagan faith, a 20th century construct.

Wicca is actually both, I think, and see no point in debating the issue at all. Modern witches follow in the tradition of our earliest ancestors and are the shamans and healers of the 21st century. We are priests and priestesses of the Great Goddess; we practice the ancient art of sacred magic in the modern world. Certainly witchcraft has changed over the millennia, but we still have much in common with the neolithic practitioner crouched before a fire, crushing herbs for a healing brew. Methods and tools may be different, but the intent is the same: to help and to heal, to honor the Mother in all that we do.

Witchcraft has adapted when necessary—we are only just emerging from the siege mentality that the Burning Times imposed upon us. We are in the process of learning how to live openly as witches again. Witchcraft has also evolved—we no longer slay the sacred king each year to ensure the tribe survives and flourishes. There are no more burnt sacrifices in Wicca, no shedding of animal or human blood to make spells work.

Every Wiccan is a priest or priestess of the Goddess as well as a witch. We serve her in whatever ways we are able to serve, according to our talents, abilities, and personal circumstances. Each Wiccan determines his or her own code of personal conduct and behavior according to the Rede, so you will find Wiccans who are pacifists as well as Wiccans who are professional soldiers, some who are omnivorous and others who are vegans.

Wicca is an Earth religion—an accepting, open-minded faith that celebrates diversity and considers us all to be children of the same Mother. Gender, age, race, sexual orientation, physical status, family background, or ethnic heritage are not important in Wicca. We are male and female, old and young, gay and straight, healthy and disabled, and of all colors. There are no reliable statistics on this, but it seems to me that there are about the same number of male and female Wiccans.

We collect no dues, have no central organization, no governing body, no supreme leader, no great high priestess who speaks for the Goddess. Our temples are gardens and forests, libraries and beaches, mountains and bookstores. Wicca consists simply of its witches and their collective beliefs and practices. It is a voluntary association of individuals who share one faith, but practice it in myriad ways. No one is born Wiccan—not even our children, for we expect them to choose their own spiritual paths when they are old enough to make such choices. There is nothing like a dress code, but many witches wear a pentacle. We have no dietary restrictions, but many witches are vegetarians.

Wicca is an organic religion, one that is evolving and emerging as a worldwide faith. It is growing rapidly, although we neither seek converts [n]or proselytize. This is not a faith that knocks on your door. It is one to which you make your own way. Wicca is a way of life, a belief system that reflects itself in the ways we interact with the world around us. Personal integrity and respect for Mother Nature are important parts of the Wiccan way.

The Wiccan faith has two pillars—the Great Goddess and a poem called "The Wiccan Rede." The first step in becoming a witch is to find your way to the Goddess. The second step is to establish an ethical system in which to use her gift of magic. I am often asked how someone can get involved in the occult without being seduced by its dark side. The answer is that you must have an ethical belief system, one with which you keep faith.

This book [*The Wicca Handbook*] contains everything you need to know to begin to practice magic, but you won't be ready for magic until you have taken those first two crucial steps.

The Great Goddess

Have you ever been jolted from a sound sleep by someone calling your name, then sat up and discovered you were alone? What you heard was the call of the Goddess. She is always there, always with us, always calling, but only some of us can hear her. Those who can are witches, her priests and priestesses.

To be a witch, you have to find your way to the Goddess and establish a relationship with her. There are many ways to do this: studying mythology, spending time with the Moon or the sea, meditating, planting a garden, keeping bees, nurturing a child, taking long walks in the woods, and so forth. She is everywhere; all you have to do is look for her. When you find her, invite her into your life. Offer yourself to her service. Step back and watch the magic begin to flow through you and around you.

The Goddess is the universe itself, not something separate from or superior to it. Creation is the business of the universe, which destroys only to re-create. We personify this as the Great Mother. She is self-created and self-renewing. We share atoms with her, are one small part of the godhead, but we are just one product of her great creative nature. Her variety is infinite, as evinced by snowflakes and fingerprints. She is the yin and yang of being, composed of both female (goddess) and male (god) energy. We worship her by many names: Ishtar, Isis, Shakti, Asherah, Xochiquetzal, Brigit, Pelé, Copper Woman, Lupa, Luna. We also recognize old gods like Pan, Osiris, Tammuz, Jove, Quetzalcoatl, Cernunnos, Mithras, and worship them if we feel moved to do so.

Witches are pagans. We worship many gods and goddesses, but recognize all of them as aspects of the Great Goddess. Some witches worship both a lord and a lady, while others worship only the Goddess. For me, [the Egyptian God and Goddess] Thoth is the lord and Isis is the lady, but choosing what deities to serve, honor, or work with is something each witch decides for herself or himself.

This book [*The Wiccan Handbook*] is full of information about magic, how to cast spells and create them. Don't forget, however, that magic is only one part of Wicca. Witches use magic to improve their lives, but they also use it in service of the Goddess.

From *Wicca: A Guide for the Solitary Practitioner*

Scott Cunningham

Creating Sacred Space

This section consists of arranging the altar (if it isn't a permanent one) and forming the magic circle. . . .

Though many Wiccans place their altars in the center of the area, and indeed in the center of the future magic circle, others do not. Some place it in one of the "corners" of the circle, next to its edge, usually in the North or East. This, they say, makes it easier to move around the circle. I find it to be exactly the opposite. Additionally, it restricts your possible methods of forming the circle.

It doesn't matter which you use, so try both and find out which works the best.

I use two altars. One's permanent, the other erected only for rituals. I always place the altar in the center of the circle, facing North, if only because this is familiar to me. Besides, if I put it at the northern edge of the circle I'd probably kick it over.

Now to the circle, or "sphere of power." You'll find one form of circle casting in *The Standing Stones Book of Shadows* [in *Wicca: A Guide for the Solitary Practitioner*]. There are many other types, and indeed that particular form can't be used in every situation. One of these variants may be more to your liking (or better suited to your ritual space). The first is more heavily dependent upon your visualization and magical abilities than others, for it uses no tools but your mind.

To help your visualization, place a purple cord or some other object(s) on the ground to mark the circle's circumference. Stand before the altar, or in the center of the circle (during outdoor rituals you might not have an altar). Face East or the preferred direction. Build the power within you. When it has reached a fine pitch (you'll know with practice), hold your projective hand palm down, waist level. Point your fingers toward the edge of the future circle.

See and *Feel* the energy flowing out from your fingertips in a stream of vibrating purplish-blue light. Slowly walk the circle, clockwise. Push the power out and form it with your visualization into a circling band of glowing magical light, the exact width of your circle (usually nine feet or less). This circle should hang around you and the altar.

When this band of light is swirling in the air, stretch it with your visualization. See it expanding and increasing in size. Form it into a dome of energy surrounding the ritual area. It should touch the Earth precisely aligned with your cord ring, if any. Now extend this energy down into the Earth until it forms a complete sphere as you stand in its center.

The circle should be a living, glowing reality. Feel its energy. Sense the edge of the circle. Sense the difference in vibration within and without it. Contrary to popular Wiccan teachings, pushing your hand into or walking through a magic sphere will cause no astral damage, any more than will walking through a protective power shield set up around your home. After all, most magic circles are so designed that if you stand near the circle's edge, your head and half your torso extend outside it. Walking through the circle, at most, will give you a jolt of energy. It will also dissipate it. If this happens, simply form it again.

When the circle seems complete and solid around you, break off the flow of energy from your projective hand by turning your palm downward and pulling it back to your body. Shut off the flow. Shake your hand if necessary to break it.

Next, you may wish to invoke the rulers of the four quarters of the circle. There are varied Wiccan teachings and ideas regarding these four rulers. Some link them with the elements; thus the spirit or ruler of the East is related to Air; the South, to Fire; the West, to Water; the North, to Earth.

Then again, some Wiccans don't see them as necessarily elemental in nature, but simply as anciently placed guardians or watchers of the four directions, perhaps created by the goddesses and gods of earlier times.

Still other Wiccans view them as the Mighty Ones, former humans who have spiraled up the incarnational path until they've reached perfection. This allows them to "dwell with the Goddess and God." These Mighty Ones are mythologically linked to the four directions.

Perhaps it's best to get in touch with these energies and discover them for yourself. No matter how you view these rulers, open yourself to them during invocation. Don't just say the words or visualize the colors during the circle casting; invite them to be present. Stretch out with your awareness. *Know* whether they've arrived or not.

Too many Wiccans say the words but don't check their effectiveness. The words are the least important part of a Wiccan ritual, save for their use in promoting ritual consciousness.

Words don't have to be used to invoke the rulers, but they're tools which train the attention, focus our awareness, and stir up the emotions—when properly stated. You can use the invocations in the circle casting section of the Book [of Shadows] or write your own.

To leave the circle during a ritual, cut a doorway. . . . This preserves the flow of energy around the circle save for a small section which you clear. Through this you can pass to the outside world without unduly disturbing the rest of the circle. Just remember to close it after returning.

Another, simpler form of circle construction uses physical activity to raise power, and is easier to do if you're not quite fluent with energy raising. Stand facing North at the edge of the future circle. Turn to the right and walk slowly, marking out the circle's edge with your feet.[8]

As you continue your ritual tread, you may wish to chant Goddess or God names, or perhaps both. You might think of Their presence or simply shift your awareness to the energy that your body is generating. If you've placed the altar to one side of the circle, move a few feet inward as you pass by it.

Continue to move clockwise, but gently increase your pace. The energy will slide off your body and, picked up by your momentum, will be carried around with you in your circular path.

Move faster. Feel the energy flowing within you. You may feel a sensation such as you feel when walking in water—the energy will move with you as you release it. Sense your personal power creating a sphere of energy around the altar. When this is firmly established, invoke the four quarters and the rites can begin.

Both of the above methods are ideal for rituals wherein the magic will take place, but for purely religious rites such constructions of psychic energy are not strictly necessary. Though the circle is thought of as being "between the worlds," and a meeting place with the Goddess and God, we needn't create such psychic temples to commune with the deities of nature, nor do They appear when called like pets. Wiccan ritual is used to expand our awareness of Them, not the other way around.

Therefore, complex circle castings . . . aren't always necessary, especially during outdoor rites where such circles are usually impossible to construct. Fortunately, there are simpler forms which can be used.

An outdoor circle casting may entail nothing more than placing a stick of burning incense at each of the quarters. Start in the North and move clockwise around the circle. Invoke the quarters.

A circle can also be traced in the sand or dirt with a finger, a wand, or the white-handled knife. This is ideal for sea and forest rituals.

Or, you may wish to place objects to mark out the circle's perimeter. Vegetation is particularly appropriate: flowers for spring, pine and holly for winter (see The Herbal Grimoire in *The Standing Stones Book of Shadows* [in *Wicca: A Guide for the Solitary Practitioner*] for other suggestions). A ring of small river-polished stones or quartz crystals are other possibilities.

Some Wiccans pour a small unbroken circle of some substance to define the ritual space. Powdered herbs, flour (as was used in ancient Middle Eastern rituals as well as in contemporary Voodoo rites), crushed colored minerals, sand or salt are poured out while moving clockwise. As mentioned above, a cord can also be laid in a ring.

For more information regarding circle construction, see *The Standing Stones Book of Shadows* [in *Wicca: A Guide for the Solitary Practitioner*].

Invocation

In some ways this is the heart of all Wiccan ritual, and indeed is the only necessary part. Wiccan rites are attunements with the powers that are the Goddess and God; all else is pageantry.[9]

The word "invocation" shouldn't be taken too literally. This usually refers to a spoken prayer or verse, but may also consist of music, dance, gestures, and song.

There are several invocations to the Goddess and God in *The Standing Stones Book of Shadows* [see the last excerpt, below]. Feel free to use them when designing your own rituals, but remember that impromptu invocations are often more effective than the most ancient prayers.

If you do write up your own invocations, you may wish to incorporate a rhyme. Centuries of magical tradition attest to the value of rhyme. It certainly makes invocations that much easier to memorize.

Rhyme also contacts the unconscious or psychic mind. It drowses our societally, materially, and intellectually-based minds and lets us slip into ritual consciousness.

When actually invoking, don't curse if you forget a word, mispronounce something or entirely lose your train of thought. This is quite natural and is usually a manifestation of fatigue, stress or a desire to be word perfect in the circle.

Invocation requires a willingness to open yourself to the Goddess and God. It needn't be a pristine performance. As most rituals begin with invocation, this is in a sense the moment of truth. If the invocation isn't sincere it won't contact the Goddess and God within, and the ritual that follows will be nothing more than form.

Practice invoking the Goddess and God, not only in ritual but daily throughout your life. Remember: Wiccan practice isn't limited to Full Moons or Sabbats—it is a round-the-clock way of life.

In a more metaphysical sense, invocation is a dual-level act. It not only invokes the Goddess and God, it also awakens us (shifts our awareness) to that part of us which is divine—our inviolable, intransmutable essence: our link with the Old Ones.

In other words, when you invoke do so not only to higher forces but also to the deities that dwell within, to that spark of divine energy that exists inside all living creatures.

The powers behind all deities are one. They are resident within all humans. This explains why all religions merge at their cores, and why they work for their respective adherents. If only one correct way of approaching Deity were possible, there would be one religious ideal. This will never happen.

The concept of the Goddess and God dwelling within may seem egotistical (we're all divine!) but only from an unbalanced viewpoint. Yes, when some people grasp this idea they start acting as if they were indeed divine. Seeing the divinity within all other humans helps bring this idea into balance.

While we are, in a sense, immortal (our souls certainly are), we are not *the* Immortal Ones. We're not the universal, timeless, transcendent beings that are revered in all religions.

Call the Goddess and God with love and sincerity, and your rituals should be blessedly successful.

The following self-dedication rite isn't designed to make you a Wicca —that comes with time and devotion (and not through initiation ceremonies). It is, in a mystical sense, a step toward linking your personal energies with those of the goddess and God. It is a truly magical act which, if properly done, can change your life forever.

If you're hesitant, read this book [*Wicca: A Guide for the Solitary Practitioner*] again. You'll know when you're ready.

A Self-Dedication Rite

Prepare yourself by drawing a bath of warm water. Add a tablespoon or so of salt and a few drops of a scented oil such as sandalwood.

If you have no bath, use a shower. Fill a washcloth with salt, add a few drops of essential oil, and rub your body. If you're performing this ritual at the sea or a river, bathe there if you so desire.

As you bathe, prepare for the coming rite. Open your consciousness to higher levels of awareness. Deep breathe. Cleanse your mind as well as your body.

After bathing, dry and dress for the journey. Go to a place in the wild where you feel safe. It should be comfortable spot where you won't be disturbed by others, an area where the powers of the Earth and the elements are evident. It may be a mountain top, a desert canyon or cave, perhaps a dense forest, a rocky outcropping over the sea, a quiet island in the center of a lake. Even a lonely part of a park or garden can be used. Draw on your imagination to find the place.

You need take nothing with you but a vial of richly scented oil. Sandalwood, frankincense, cinnamon or any other scent is fine. When you arrive at the place of dedication, remove your shoes and sit quietly for a few moments. Calm your heart if you've exerted yourself during travel. Breathe deeply to return to normal, and keep your mind free of cluttered thoughts. Open yourself to the natural energies around you.

When you're calm, rise and pivot slowly on one foot, surveying the land around you. You're seeking the ideal spot. Don't try to find it; open your awareness to the place. When you've discovered it (and you'll know when), sit, kneel or lie flat on your back. Place the oil on the Earth beside you. Don't stand—contact the Earth.

Continue deep breathing. Feel the energies around you. Call the Goddess and God in any words you like, or use the following invocations. Memorize these words before the rite so that they'll spill effortlessly from you, or improvise:

> O Mother Goddess,
> O Father God,
> Answer to all mysteries and yet mysteries unanswered;
> In this place of power I open myself
> to Your Essence.
> In this place and in this time I am changed;
> From henceforth I walk the Wiccan path.
> I dedicate myself to you, Mother Goddess and Father God.

(Rest for a moment, silent, still. Then continue:)

> I breathe your energies into my body, commingling, blending,
> mixing them with mine,
> that I may see the divine in nature,
> nature in the divine,
> and divinity within myself and all else.
> O Great Goddess,
> O Great God,
> Make me one with your essence.
> Make me one with your essence.
> Make me one with your essence.

You may feel bursting with power and energy, or calm and at peace. Your mind might be in a whirl. The Earth beneath you may throb and undulate with energy. Wild animals, attracted by the psychic occurrence, might grace you with their presence.

Whatever occurs, *know* that you have opened yourself and that the Goddess and God have heard you. You should feel different inside, at peace or simply powerful.

After the invocation, wet a finger with the oil and mark these two symbols [for Goddess and God] somewhere on your body. . . . It doesn't matter where; you can do this on your chest, forehead, arms, legs, anywhere. As you anoint, visualize these symbols sinking into your flesh, glowing as they enter your body and then dispersing into millions of tiny points of light.

The formal self-dedication is ended. Thank the Goddess and God for their attention. Sit and meditate before leaving the place of dedication.

Once home, celebrate in some special way.

The Standing Stones Book of Shadows

Words to the Wise. . . .

O daughters and sons of the Earth, adore the Goddess and God and be blessed with the fullness of life.

Know that They have brought you to these writings, for herein lie our ways of Wicca, to serve and fulfill the keepers of wisdom, the tenders of the sacred flame of knowledge. Run the rites with love and joy, and the Goddess and God will bless you with all that you need. But those who practice dark magics shall know their greatest wrath.

Remember that you are of the Wicca. No more do you trod the ways of doubt. You walk the path of light, ever climbing from shadow to shadow to the highest realm of existence. But though we're the bearers of truths, others do not wish to share our knowledge, so we run our rites beneath moon filled skies enwrapped in shadows. But we are happy.

Live fully, for that is the purpose of life. Refrain not from earthly existence. From it we grow to learn and understand, until such times that we are reborn to learn more, repeating this cycle 'till we have spiraled up the path of perfection and can finally call the Goddess and God our kin.

Walk the fields and forests; be refreshed by the cool winds and the touch of a nodding flower. The Moon and Sun sing in the ancient wild places: The deserted seashore, the stark desert, the roaring waterfall. We are of the Earth and should revere Her, so do Her honor.

Celebrate the rites on the appropriate days and seasons, and call upon the Goddess and God when the time is meet, but use the Power only when necessary, never for frivolous ends. Know that using the Power for harm is a perversion of Life itself.

But for those who love and magnify love, the richness of life shall be your reward. Nature will celebrate.

So love Goddess and God, and harm none!

Before Time Was

Before time was, there was The One; The One was all, and all was The One.

And the vast expanse known as the universe was The One, all-wise, all-pervading, all-powerful, eternally changing.

And space moved. The One molded energy into twin forms, equal but opposite, fashioning the Goddess and God from The One and of The One.

The Goddess and God stretched and gave thanks to The One, but darkness surrounded them. They were alone, solitary save for The One.

So They formed energy into gasses and gasses into suns and planets and moons; They sprinkled the universe with whirling globes and so all was given shape by the hands of the Goddess and God.

Light arose and the sky was illuminated by a billion suns. And the Goddess and God, satisfied by their works, rejoiced and loved, and were one.

From their union sprang the seeds of all life, and of the human race, so that we might achieve incarnation upon the Earth.

The Goddess chose the Moon as her symbol, and the God the Sun as His Symbol, to remind the inhabitants of Earth of their fashioners.

All are born, live, die and are reborn beneath the Sun and Moon; all things come to pass thereunder, and all occurs with the blessings of the One, as has been the way of existence before time was.

Song of the Goddess (based on an invocation by Morgan[10])

I am the Great Mother worshipped by all creation and existent prior to their consciousness. I am the primal female force, boundless and eternal.

I am the chaste Goddess of the Moon, the Lady of all magic. The winds and moving leaves sing my name. I wear the crescent Moon upon my brow and my feet rest among the starry heavens. I am mysteries yet un-solved, a path newly set upon. I am a field untouched by the plow. Rejoice in me and know the fullness of youth.

I am the blessed Mother, the gracious lady of the harvest. I am clothed with the deep, cool wonder of the Earth and the gold of the fields heavy with grain. By me the tides of the Earth are ruled; all things come to frui-tion according to my season. I am refuge and healing. I am the life-giving Mother, wondrously fertile.

Worship me as the Crone, tender of the unbroken cycle of death and rebirth. I am the wheel, the shadow of the Moon. I rule the tides of women and men and give release and renewal to weary souls. Though the darkness of death is my domain, the joy of birth is my gift.

I am the Goddess of the Moon, the Earth, the Seas. My names and strengths are manifold. I pour forth magic and power, peace and wisdom. I am the eternal Maiden, Mother of all, and Crone of darkness, and I send you blessings of limitless love.

Call of the God

I am the radiant king of the Heavens, flooding the Earth with warmth and encouraging the hidden seed of creation to burst forth into manifes-tation. I lift my shining spear to light the lives of all beings and daily pour forth my gold upon the Earth, putting to flight the powers of darkness.

I am the master of the beasts wild and free. I run with the swift-stag and soar as sacred falcon against the shimmering sky. The ancient woods and wild places emanate my powers, and the birds of the air sing of my sanctity.

I am also the last harvest, offering up grain and fruits beneath the sickle of time so that all may be nourished. For without planting there can be no harvest; without winter, no spring.

Worship me as the thousand-named Sun of creation, the spirit of the horned stag in the wild, the endless harvest. See in the yearly cycle of festi-vals my birth, death and rebirth—and know that such is the destiny of all creation.

I am the spark of life, the radiant Sun, the giver of peace and rest, and I send my rays of blessings to warm the hearts and strengthen the minds of all.

NOTES

Excerpt from Eileen Holland, *The Wicca Handbook* (York Beach, Maine: Red Wheel/Weiser, 2000), 5–8. Used by permission of the publisher.

Excerpts from Scott Cunningham, *Wicca: A Guide for the Solitary Practitioner* (St. Paul, Minn.: Lewellyn, 1998), 89–92, 96–101, 111–12, 113–15. Copyright © 1998. Reprinted by permission of Llewellyn Worldwide, Ltd. PO Box 64383, St. Paul, MN 55164.

1. Margaret Alice Murray's *The Witch-Cult in Western Europe: A Study in Anthropology* (Oxford: Clarendon, 1921), asserted that an organized form of pagan practice had survived in the British Isles. This book may have served as the basis of Gardner's construction of Wiccan religion. Other neo-paganisms focus on Norse, Greek, or Egyptian traditions.

2. For a thorough examination of the controversy, see Margot Adler's comprehensive overview of modern American neo-paganism, *Drawing Down the Moon: Witches, Druids, Goddess-Worshippers, and Other Pagans in America Today*, rev. and expanded ed. (Boston: Beacon, 1986), chap. 4.

3. The most important holidays are Imblog (February 2), Beltane (May 1), Lammas (August 1), and Samhain (Halloween, October 31).

4. One of the first American neo-pagan sects, The Church of All Worlds (CAW), founded by Oberon Zell (now Zell-Ravenheart) and based on a Robert Heinlein novel, espoused worship of the living Earth as Gaia. CAW was especially influential in promulgating a number of the terms and concepts currently used by American neo-pagans, including "neo-pagan."

5. In Satanism, the empowerment of the individual is seen as a means to exercise dominance over others; Satanists view Wiccans as weak and ineffectual.

6. This ethical stance is further reinforced by a belief in the Three-fold Law: whatever you do comes back to you three times over.

7. See Sarah M. Pike, *Earthly Bodies, Magical Selves* (Berkeley: University of California Press, 2001), 29–40; Brenda E. Brasher, *Give Me That Online Religion* (San Francisco: Jossey-Bass, 2001), 85–92.

8. In this hemisphere, most Wiccans move clockwise within the circle, except during some banishing rituals. In Australia and in other parts of the southern hemisphere, circles may be cast counter-clockwise, as this is the apparent direction in which the Sun moves. [Note in original text.]

9. Though it should, of course, promote ritual consciousness. Outdoor rituals rarely need as much invocation because the Wiccans are already surrounded by natural manifestations of the deities. [Note in original text.]

10. My [Scott Cunningham's] first teacher and priestess. She wrote this a decade or so ago. This and the following "Call of the God" aren't necessarily meant to

be spoken in ritual. They can be read for devotional purposes, meditated upon to learn more of the Goddess and God or used in ritual by inserting the words "She" and "He" and making other small changes to agree with these alterations. [Note in original text.]

FOR FURTHER READING

Adler, Margot, *Drawing Down the Moon: Witches, Druids, Goddess-Worshippers, and other Pagans in America Today*, rev. and expanded ed. (Boston: Beacon, 1986). A classic in the study of Wicca and neo-paganism.

Buckland, Raymond, *Buckland's Complete Book of Witchcraft* (St. Paul, Minn.: Llewellyn, 1986). An encyclopedic reference work for all levels of Wiccan practice by one of Gerald Gardner's students.

Clifton, Chas, and Graham Harvey, eds., *The Paganism Reader* (New York: Routledge, 2004). A unique collection of primary materials from the neo-pagan and Wiccan worlds.

Eisler, Riane, *The Chalice and the Blade: Our History, Our Future* (San Francisco: Harper and Row, 1987). A famous study of prehistoric matriarchies that has given supposedly scientific and historical backing to many claims made by those in Wiccan circles.

Eller, Cynthia, *The Myth of Matriarchal History: Why an Invented Past Won't Give Women a Future* (Boston: Beacon, 2000). A scholar looks at the claims made by Wiccans and others regarding myths of a matriarchal prehistory.

Pike, Sarah M., *Earthly Bodies, Magical Selves: Contemporary Pagans and the Search for Community* (Berkeley: University of California Press, 2001). A close look at neo-pagan and Wiccan rituals and worldviews by a noted scholar/participant.

Starhawk, *The Spiral Dance: The Rebirth of the Ancient Religion of the Great Goddess* (San Francisco: Harper and Row, 1979). One of the classic statements of modern goddess worship.

Witchvox, http://www.witchvox.com. An extensive compendium of Wiccan and neo-pagan news, information, and links serving the world community of Wiccans and correcting misinformation about them.

Chapter 5

Soka Gakkai

Soka Gakkai was founded in Japan by Makiguchi Tsunesaburo (1871–1944) with Toda Josei (1900–1951) in 1930 as a lay sect of Nichiren Shoshu, a religious establishment in the Nikko lineage of the Buddhism formulated by the Japanese monk Nichiren (1222–1282) and headquartered at Taiseki-ji temple near Mount Fuji. From the outset, Makiguchi articulated his desire to reform the educational, political, and social status quo in Japanese society, including the leadership of Nichiren Shoshu—a fact reflected in Soka Gakkai's name, which means "value creating society." Makiguchi died in prison after refusing to fold his sect in with other lay Nichiren Shoshu organizations, as ordered by the Japanese government on the eve of World War II.

Toda was also imprisoned, but after the war he reestablished Soka Gakkai with a focus on personal transformation. While primarily concerned with the "human revolution," as Toda named the process of manifesting one's Buddha nature, this movement has always seen the transformation of individuals as the first necessary step in the transformation of a society, and, ultimately, the entire world, into a realm of peace. This concern for bringing about personal, social, and global harmony makes perfect sense in the context of postwar Japan, given the country's firsthand experience of nuclear devastation.

In the 1950s, political parties and reform organizations affiliated with or supporting Soka Gakkai began to have an impact on the Japanese political landscape, riding an anti-corruption, anti–military entanglement platform to become the third largest party in Japan's National Diet since the 1960s.[1] In 1975, Soka Gakkai established a global outreach arm, Soka Gakkai International (SGI), headed by Daisaku Ikeda (b. 1928), who had served as Soka Gakkai's third president for fifteen years. SGI sought to establish a worldwide presence through a promulgation of Nichiren beliefs and practice called *kosen-rufu* (described in the second excerpt below). However, Soka Gakkai's independence and anti-authoritarian stances frequently came into conflict with the Nichiren Shoshu establishment, which led to its 1991 separation from and excommunication by the parent group. Largely due to Ikeda's efforts, Soka Gakkai has continued to thrive since the split and is probably the most widespread of the Japanese "new religions" (*shin-shúkyó*) that emerged in the first half of the twentieth century,[2] with approximately twelve million members in 190 countries and territories.

Soka Gakkai emphasizes the fundamental potential for all human beings to achieve happiness through chanting Nichiren's *daimoku* (invocation), *Nam-myoho-renge-kyo*. This chant is believed to manifest one's dormant Buddha nature or Buddhahood—that is, the "Greater Self," as opposed to the limited, selfish, ego-driven "Lesser Self" most people spend their lives as. *Nam-myoho-renge-kyo* translates as "I devote myself to the Mystic Law of the *Lotus Sutra*," the *Lotus Sutra* being the great text of Buddhist teachings and two chapters of which members of Soka Gakkai read daily (a practice called *gongyo*). The "Mystic Law" denotes the "relationship between the life inherent in the universe and the myriad different ways this life expresses itself"—that is, the means by which cosmic potential can be actualized.[3] Practitioners direct the *daimoku* to a scroll in Chinese and Sanskrit called the Gohonzon, first created by Nichiren in 1279. The Gohonzon scroll contains Nichiren's depiction of the Ceremony in the Air described in chapter 11 of the Lotus Sutra, the "Emergence of the Treasure Tower." Nichiren's signature appears on a mandala (circle representing wholeness and unity) on the scroll together with *Nam-myoho-renge-kyo*, indicating "the oneness of person and Law–that the condition of Buddhahood is a potential within and can be manifested by all people."[4] Soka Gakkai describes the Gohonzon as a mirror that reflects back a person's own Buddhahood in the act of chanting the *daimoku*.

Soka Gakkai envisions the potential of Buddhahood as just one of ten states, or "worlds," that humans can express at any given time, ranging from hell (characterized by suffering and despair, a lack of freedom, and an impulse toward destruction), to anger, to heaven (joy, contentment, fulfillment of desires), to realization, and ultimately to Buddhahood, a state of absolute freedom, compassion, and wisdom. To realize the existence of these states and of one's freedom to rise above the lower, destructive ones represents a New Understanding of the nature of humanity. A New Understanding is also reflected in aspects of the Buddhist worldview that informs Soka Gakkai, especially the Buddha's Four Noble Truths and Eight-fold Path of Liberation. The first step of the Eight-fold Path, in fact, is "Right Understanding" of the truths of the cosmos—that is, of the illusion of reality's permanence, the role of one's own desire and self-deception in creating suffering, the effects of karma, and the process of replacing ignorance with enlightenment.

Following from this new orientation toward reality, Soka Gakkai's practice aims to make Buddhahood—rather than any of the more limited, reactive, and unfulfilling "worlds"—one's primary orientation. The harmonizing effect of the *daimoku*, especially when reflected back by the Gohonzon, allows this true state of being—or, in the language of this reader, the New Self—to emerge in all of one's dealings in life, ultimately effecting a New Society and a New World. The passages excerpted below present the ideals associated with "the human revolution" as articulated, in the first excerpt, by President Ikeda in an essay that appeared in the Manila *Sunday Mirror* on December 12, 1998. The second excerpt, by Richard Causton, former head of SGI-UK and vice-chairman of both SGI and SGI-Europe until his death in 1995, offers a clear look at the process of bringing about such revolution on a world scale, one life at a time.

"Human Revolution"

Daisaku Ikeda

Life is about expressing and developing our individuality as fully as possible—it is about self-realization. This process is what I call "human revolution."

There are many kinds of revolutions—political, economic, industrial, scientific, artistic, and so on. But no matter how external factors change, the world will never get better as long as people remain selfish and apathetic. As John F. Kennedy said, in 1963, "Our problems are manmade—therefore, they can be solved by man. And man can be as big as he wants."

An inner change for the better in a single person is the essential first turn of the wheel in the process of making the human race stronger and wiser. This "human revolution" is, I believe, the most fundamental and most vital of all revolutions. This revolution—an inner process of self-reformation—is completely bloodless and peaceful. In it everyone wins and there are no victims.

Life is a struggle with ourselves; it is a tug-of-war between moving forward and slipping backward, between happiness and misery. We are changing constantly, but the real issue is whether we change for the better or the worse, whether or not we succeed in enlarging our narrow, self-centered focus to take a broader view.

Every day we are faced with countless choices and decisions. We have to decide which path to take in order to feel good about ourselves and become better, more generous-spirited individuals[.] If we just allow ourselves to be ruled by force of habit, the way we've always reacted to a given situation, we will be drawn down the path of least resistance and stop growing as a person.

But if we succeed in challenging ourselves on a fundamental level, we can change from someone who is buffeted about by the environment or the people around us, to someone who can positively influence our situation and surroundings. We actually create the unique shape of our lives by the infinite choices we make each day.

True individuality and character never come to full flower without hard work. I feel it is a mistake to think that who you are right now represents all you are capable of. If you passively decide, "I'm a quiet person, so I'll just go through life being quiet," you won't ever fully realize your unique potential. Without having to change your character completely, you can become a person who, while still basically quiet, will say the right thing at the right time with real conviction. In the same way, a negative tendency toward impatience could be developed into a useful knack for getting things done quickly and efficiently.

But nothing is more immediate, or more difficult, than to confront and transform ourselves. It is always tempting to decide, "That's just the kind of person I am." Unless we challenge this tendency early in life, it will become stronger with age. But the effort is worthwhile in the end, as I believe that nothing produces deeper satisfaction than successfully challenging our own weaknesses. As the Russian author Tolstoy wrote, "Supreme happiness is to find that you are a better person at the end of the year than you were at the beginning."

Human revolution is not something extraordinary, or divorced from our daily lives. It often begins in a small way. Take a man who thinks only of himself, his family and friends. Then, one day, he makes a move to break out of these narrow confines just a little, going out of his way to help a suffering neighbor. This the start of his human revolution.

But this process of human revolution cannot be undertaken alone. It is through our interactions with others that we polish our lives and grow as human beings. In Japan, mountain potatoes known as taros are rough and dirty when harvested, but when put in water and rolled against each other, the skin peels away, leaving the potatoes shining and ready for cooking. The only way to hone and polish our character is through our interactions with others.

By taking action for, and being positively engaged with others, we become better and more disciplined people. But this doesn't mean making others happy while ignoring ourselves or our own happiness. The happiness we create as individuals, and the strong bonds we create with each other, result in the happiness of all mankind.

Transforming our own lives at the most fundamental level actually holds the key to changing society. A deep change in our outlook, the inner reality of our life, produces changes in the external workings of our life, in other people, and our community.

I firmly believe that a great human revolution in just a single individual can help achieve a change in the destiny of a nation and enable a change in all humankind.

The life of Mahatma Gandhi illustrates this point. As a boy he was painfully shy. He was always worried people would make fun of him. Even after passing his exams as a lawyer, he was still timid. When he rose to present the opening arguments in his first court case, his mind went blank from nerves and he had to leave the courtroom.

But a turning point occurred when he was in South Africa, where Indian residents faced severe discrimination. Gandhi was riding in a first-class carriage on a train, when he was ordered to move to the freight car. He refused, and was eventually forced off the train. In the waiting area at the station, Gandhi stayed awake all night, debating whether he should return to India or endure the hardship of taking a stand and fighting for human rights. He finally realized that it would be cowardice to run from his fears and disregard people being discriminated against as he had been.

From that moment, Gandhi squarely faced and challenged his timid nature, determined to challenge injustice. And his inner change sparked one of the greatest developments of the twentieth century—the movement for social change through non-violence.

Every single person has tremendous potential which is largely untapped. Through the hard work of our human revolution, this potential can be revealed and we can establish an independent, unconquerable sense of self. We can deal creatively with any situation that life has to offer. This open-ended process enables us to keep growing and developing throughout our lives, and beyond. We will never meet a deadlock in our eternal journey of self-realization.

From *The Buddha in Daily Life: An Introduction to the Buddhism of Nichiren Daishonin*

Richard Causton

Practice

As we have seen, the practice of Nichiren Daishonin's [an honorific title meaning "Great Sage"] Buddhism falls into two parts: practice for oneself and practice for others.

Strictly speaking, we cannot compartmentalize our practice in this way as we are each inseparable from our own unique environment. Thus, as we gain benefits from our practice, so we quite naturally began to benefit others. For example, if someone who has always lacked money changes this aspect of his karma, he will no longer rely on his friends or family for support and so will cause those people less worry. Conversely, through teaching others about *Nam-myoho-renge-kyo* we can help them to change those areas of their karma which cause them to suffer, and so we gain the benefit of seeing them become happy too. In the same way, we need to study not only to understand how Buddhist concepts apply to our own lives, but also to explain Buddhism effectively to others who wish to learn about it. Indeed, study for the sake of intellectual, theoretical satisfaction has no place whatsoever in Nichiren Daishonin's Buddhism.

Practice for Oneself

Bearing these points in mind how, first, does one "practice for oneself"? The most basic practice of the Daishonin's Buddhism is to chant *Nam-myoho-renge-kyo*. If you want to chant, all you have to do is sit or kneel upright, with your hands together and eyes open, and simply repeat this phrase out loud over and over again in a rhythmical manner, with a clear and relaxed voice. In pronouncing *Nam-myoho-renge-kyo,* all the vowels are short and each syllable is pronounced separately, thus: Nam-myoho-renge-kyo, *Myo* and *kyo* are both spoken as one syllable—m'yo, k'yo (this latter as in *Tokyo*)—and the *n* and *g* in *renge* are both hard, as in Be*n* and *g*et. If you do not have a Gohonzon you will find it easier when you start chanting to face a blank wall, as this will help your mind to cease wandering and concentrate on the sound of chanting. The speed and volume at which you chant are not important (except you should not upset your neighbours): what does matter is the rhythm and pronunciation of your *daimoku* (each *Nam-myoho-renge-kyo*), the firmness of the vibrations of your voice and the sincerity with which you chant.

Sincerity may be the last thing you think you are experiencing when you begin to chant, as it is not unusual for people to feel a little foolish or embarrassed at first. After all, this action is probably one that is completely outside the range of your previous experience and you may even wonder, at first, quite why you are behaving in this apparently bizarre manner, or what your friends would say if they saw you. Sincerity in this context, however, ultimately means the strength of your desire to put Buddhism to the test, so if you chant with the attitude of "Single-mindedly yearning to see the Buddha," any feelings of embarrassment will quickly evaporate as you begin to experience your own Buddhahood for the first time.

When and where you chant are entirely up to you, although obviously it is better to choose a time and place that allows you to concentrate. How long you should chant is again your decision, although, as already mentioned, Nichiren Daishonin encourages us to chant to our "heart's content"; this can vary according to our specific needs and the demands of our daily schedules. It is best, however, to establish a regular and consistent practice in which at first we chant for, say, ten minutes each morning and evening, as this matches the basic daily rhythm of our lives. As you begin to experience the effect of chanting you might quite naturally want to increase the amount of chanting you do; or at times—during a crisis, for example—you may be encouraged to do more chanting by other people. This is because they know from experience that, at such times, one needs to be able to draw hard on the qualities of Buddhahood that extra *daimoku* gives one. Once again, though, just how much effort you put into your practice is ultimately determined by no one but you.

People often worry about what they should be thinking when they chant, but there are no hard and fast rules on this score. Generally, it is a good idea when you begin each chanting session to try to concentrate on establishing a precise and clear rhythm and to listen to the sound of your *daimoku*. Then, quite naturally, any problems you may be facing, or your current preoccupations or desires, will probably come into your mind as prayers, to be bathed, as it were, in your own intuitive Buddha wisdom. Gradually, as you repeat this process, you will find that the decisions you start to make (not while you are chanting, but in your daily life) will be based more and more on this wisdom—an expression of your true self— and you will begin to orientate your life towards the kind of happy future you begin to realize could be yours. Chanting, however, does not always work in exactly this way. For example, through chanting at times you will be able to re-inspire yourself with the courage and confidence to keep battling when things look black; at other times you will be able suddenly to see a solution in what seemed like a hopeless situation; or at times you may simply be able to keep fatigue at bay to finish an urgent task. In short, chanting *Nam-myoho-renge-kyo* to the Gohonzon is designed for any problem or circumstance, no matter how insignificant it might seem, like getting up on time; or however overwhelming or awesome, such as the problem of world peace. Finally, in the same way as when we began, we should listen to our voice chanting during the last few moments of our *daimoku* when, quite naturally, we can feel joy rising up within us; indeed, ideally we should continue to chant until we feel this joy welling up from deep within our lives.

In order to see for ourselves that there is no limit to what we can chant for, we are encouraged to set specific goals when we practise, in any area of our lives that is causing us to suffer. Naturally, these goals are as varied as the people who set them—a job; somewhere better to live; more money; overcoming an illness; a better relationship and so on—and although they can often be quite self-centred when we start to chant, they mark an important initial step in proving to ourselves that the practice works. Once we have gained this proof, so our practice tends increasingly to turn outwards, towards practising for the happiness of other people or overcoming our own weaknesses or failings. But whatever form our desires take, the most important thing to remember is to chant regularly and wholeheartedly so that we can steadily build up the inner strength—the life-force—we need to overcome any obstacle to happiness that life might throw at us, at any time, on any day. . . .

The Power of the Negative Force of Life

An important thing to remember when you chant is that, every time you do so, you are engaged in a battle to overcome the negative and destructive influences that exist within your life. These influences, which are quite natural and inherent in every aspect of life, are called in Buddhism by a variety of names—fundamental darkness, illusions, devils and demons, obstacles—and can appear either as internal forces, such as laziness, fears and doubts, or as external opposition, such as the ridicule or criticism of your Buddhist practice by other people. However this negativity manifests itself, it will always touch on your own, unique areas of weakness—your personal Achilles heel—and so always work to weaken your faith and stop you revealing your Buddhahood. In other words, because you are making the supreme good cause for your happiness by starting to practise, it is perfectly natural that the negativity within and around you will try to stop you from doing so. As Nichiren Daishonin explains:

> The doctrine of *ichinen sanzen*[5] revealed in the fifth volume of the *Maka Shikan* is especially profound. If you propagate it, devils will arise without fail. Were it not for these there would be no way of knowing that this is the true teaching. One passage from the same volume reads, "As practice progresses and understanding grows, the three devils and four obstacles[6] emerge, vying with one another to interfere. . . . You should neither be influenced nor frightened by them. If you fall under their influence you will be led into the paths of evil. If you are frightened by them, you will be prevented from practising true Buddhism." This quotation not only applies to Nichiren but also is the guide for his disciples.

Therefore, it is only by continually challenging and overcoming this negative force, both within yourself and in your environment, through chanting *Nam-myoho-renge-kyo,* that you can become truly happy because, at root, it is this very negativity which restricts your life and makes you suffer. On the other hand, as Nichiren Daishonin points out, if we never had anything to fight there would be no way of seeing for ourselves just how effective this practice is: as he says in another writing, "Only by defeating a powerful enemy can one prove his own strength." Fundamentally, "the powerful enemy" is nothing other than our own illusions and our "strength," simply our Buddhahood. To practise Nichiren Daishonin's

Buddhism is therefore to engage in a battle for your own lasting happiness
—a battle between the Buddha, the creative force of life, and the "devil,"
its destructive opponent. Buddhism teaches that it is the eternal struggle
between these two opposing forces which creates the very energy of life
itself. Thus, even the "devils" have an important function in life and must
therefore exist innately within us all.

This point is clearly illustrated in the experience of Marina Cantacu-
zino, the development of whose practice is by no means unusual. She
started to chant very soon after learning about *Nam-myoho-renge-kyo*, but
it was only after practising for some eighteen months that she began to
feel as if she was doing it from her own desire, rather than out of a sense
of obligation of some kind. As she says, "I realized that just because my
feelings towards the practice had often been negative, full of criticism,
doubt and fear, this did not mean that the cause was to be found in the
practice itself. My attitude was just a symptom of my own negativity
which had always held me back and came from the very depths of my
being."

Marina had started chanting when she was in America with her husband, Dan, visiting his brother who had been practising strongly for about
three years, "At that point I felt very relaxed about it," she says. "Everyone
seemed friendly and the philosophy made sense. I was just a visitor and
I enjoyed being an onlooker. I wanted it to stay that way." When they
returned to England, though, they both joined their local SGI-UK group
and began attending meetings regularly; at this time the first wave of negativity hit Marina; "It was all right as long as we were visitors but, as soon
as we became official group members, as it were, the panic set in. I didn't
want to commit myself. I wanted to remain on the fringe of things."

Matters got so bad that she used to dread answering the phone in case
it was someone asking her to go to a meeting. When she did go, it was not
because she wanted to but because she feared some kind of retribution if
she failed to turn up. But even when she did attend, Marina still suffered:
"At district meetings I hated most of all the introductions because I felt all
I could say with honesty was my name and where I lived; unlike everyone
else I could not claim that chanting *Nam-myoho-renge-kyo* had changed
my life. I can see now that everything about my practice was faint-hearted,
so how could I possibly have expected to feel the change inside which I so
desired?" She would often leave meetings feeling not only depressed, but
filled with a kind of fear—as she puts it, "a fear of the unknown, of feeling
out of place and out of touch. I felt I was unlike everyone else there."

Despite everything, however, Marina continued to practise with the result that she was slowly able to get to the root of why she felt as she did. She explains: "I think a lot of my negativity towards the practice was due to a kind of cultural allegiance. I felt by embracing Buddhism I was rejecting my past; having been raised as a Catholic and having always been very close to my mother, it also felt like a rejection of her." In addition, she worried that by joining an organization she would, as she puts it, lose her "edge." She says, "I thought SGI-UK would make me speak and act like everyone else and rob me of my identity. I did not realize then that *Nam-myoho-renge-kyo* is not a path but is life itself which includes all things and all different kinds of people. It includes my individuality, my political beliefs and even my Christian upbringing."

Another way in which Marina's negativity towards Buddhism expressed itself was in her attitude to it when with friends and family. As she explains, "Because I lacked self-confidence I often worried about what others thought. In the past, my moods, my happiness, my self-respect (or lack of it) were all determined by what others had said or done to me. So I became what you could call a 'closet chanter.' I never chanted when I was staying in other people's houses and I avoided talking about it to people I thought would be sceptical or think me peculiar. Occasionally, out of a sense of duty, I forced myself to talk to others about Buddhism, but it was always disastrous because it did not come from the heart. I said what I felt I was supposed to say because, in an awful kind of way, I felt I had to apologize for what might appear to be the eccentricities of the practice and justify my involvement with it."

Needless to say, just before receiving her Gohonzon, Marina went through terrible doubts. "I felt completely trapped," she says, "and the goodwill of everyone in my district only made me feel more pressurized. Of course, I had a perfect right to say 'No,' but somehow I knew that to say 'No' to the Gohonzon would be a backward step, leaving me in a position of deadlock and unable to change the things in my life which I did not like. In the end I adopted a 'Well, why not?' attitude, and told myself that I'd return it within a year if nothing good had happened." But even after receiving the Gohonzon, at first Marina could not bring herself to accept the fact that she was actually practising Buddhism, even going so far as to disguise the area where her Gohonzon was enshrined when friends came round, afraid that it looked too "religious."

After a year with the Gohonzon, however, her basic attitude had changed. Now she says, "Because I am more sure I am doing the right thing, I leave everything as it is and I don't mind what people say. A few people still think it's weird or freakish, but whereas in the past this would have immediately weakened my belief and made me think they had a point, now it does not in any way undermine my faith, but just makes me all the more determined to prove the power of the practice through my own life. I can see that my old attitude was once again a reflection of my tendency to sway with the wind, believe whoever happened to be talking at the time and never stick to my own conviction." Summing up, Marina realizes that learning to "stand alone"—that is, establishing a solid practice through overcoming some problems or area of weaknesses within oneself—is only the first step towards a completely fulfilled existence. As she says, "I don't necessarily have all the answers now, but I do feel completely confident in my practice. I can say with truth that I do it because I want to do it, because it has enabled me to understand why I am like I am, and how I can get rid of the negativity and fear in my life which had plagued me for so long."

Everyone who chants continues to battle with the negative side of life, though as their faith grows they become swifter and more skilled in taking control of it. Likewise, those who decide at some point to challenge the influence of this negativity are able, like Marina, to come to a much higher condition of life as a result. This is exactly what the process of "human revolution" is all about—turning the "poison" of one's negativity into the "elixir" of enlightenment. Nevertheless, since it is an essential component of life as a whole, the dark side of life never completely disappears, but is always present in some form—to keep us on our toes, as it were. Even so, after some years of chanting, the negativity which those who practise have to contend with may often not be so much their own but someone else's, or that expressed collectively in society as a whole. Indeed, it is because we cannot be truly happy in an unhappy and negative world that, from the very outset of our practice, we are taught Nichiren Daishonin's emphasis on practice for others as being of equal importance as practice for oneself.

Practice for Others

If the ultimate aim of "practice for oneself" is our individual "human revolution"—conquering the negative aspects of our character and developing wisdom, courage, compassion and joy—the ultimate aim of "practice for others" is *kosen-rufu*. *Kosen-rufu* literally means to "widely declare and spread"; in other words, to propagate this Buddhism throughout the world.

Nowadays, in the West at least, there is a certain amount of suspicion towards any sort of religious proselytism, especially when it concerns so-called "new religions." Undoubtedly, this suspicion is well founded, for there are numerous instances of gullible people being tricked out of their money by religious charlatans, or even out of their lives, as demonstrated by the case of Jim Jones and the mass suicide at Peoples Temple in Guyana in 1978. Nichiren Daishonin's Buddhism, however, opens one's eyes to the vulnerability of people in this respect because, traditionally, religious teachings have so often placed emphases on self-sacrifice as a virtue. Jim Jones and his flock were an extreme example of the effect of such teachings.

In the practice of Nichiren Daishonin's Buddhism there is no such thing as self-sacrifice, since practice involves enlightenment to the universal law of cause and effect. Thus, one discovers that "practice for others," based on the profound compassion of *jihi*—the desire to help others overcome their sufferings and gain lasting happiness through practising this Buddhism—is in fact the most pure and noble of all causes. This reaps the most pure and noble of all rewards: the purification of one's own unhappy karma, entirely through one's own efforts. A follower of Nichiren Daishonin's Buddhism might well decide to live amongst the poor, for example, not in order to share their poverty but to help them to become "rich," both in spirit and in satisfying their daily material needs.

Viewed from this perspective, *kosen-rufu* might be described as the cumulative effect of many individuals freely deciding to undertake their own human revolution. Moreover, the international movement for *kosen-rufu* is in strict accordance with the Buddha's will. For example, in the *Yakuo* (twenty-third) chapter of the Lotus Sutra, Shakyamuni[7] states: "In the fifth 500 years after my death, accomplish worldwide *kosen-rufu* and never allow its flow to cease."

In the broadest sense, then, practice for others consists of any action one takes that leads another person, either directly or indirectly, towards his or her own eventual enlightenment. This is called *shakubuku*. The most direct *shakubuku*, of course, is to tell others about chanting *Nam-myoho-renge-kyo* and explain the Buddhist view of life. While some people are willing to try chanting simply because they are told about it in this way, others are more sceptical. Generally speaking, these people will begin to practise only because, over a period of time, they come to respect someone they know who is chanting and trust him or her as a person of good sense, warmth and understanding. Indeed, there are numerous cases of people starting to practise only many years after just learning about *Nam-myoho-renge-kyo* but who, during the whole of that period, have nevertheless been keeping a watchful eye on their friend, relation, colleague or neighbour who does chant. From this it follows that showing proof of the benefits of practising this Buddhism, particularly in the form of our own human revolution, in itself constitutes *shakubuku* when it gradually convinces others of the power of *Nam-myoho-renge-kyo*.

From this it can be clearly understood that Nichiren Daishonin's Buddhism sees *kosen-rufu* as coming about by entirely natural, peaceful methods. Essentially, this means that others are persuaded to practise this Buddhism only when they become convinced by one or more of the three proofs mentioned in the Introduction [of *The Buddha in Daily Life*]. That is to say, through *documentary* proof—the written evidence that all Buddhist teachings lead to the Lotus Sutra and from there to *Nam-myoho-renge-kyo* and the Gohonzon—people will realize that Nichiren Daishonin's Buddhism represents the correct and orthodox Buddhist teachings for this age and for all types of people, whatever their backgrounds. Through *theoretical* proof—learning about the profound principles of Buddhism—people will gradually come to understand that *Nam-myoho-renge-kyo* perfectly elucidates the mysteries of life and death. Most importantly, through *actual* proof—witnessing the change in those who practise —more and more people will come to see how chanting this phrase can radically alter a person's life for the better. In other words, just as scientific discoveries may initially shake the way ordinary people look at the world, but are gradually accepted because they can be proved empirically, so, in time, will Nichiren Daishonin's Buddhism be accepted as a matter of common sense simply because so many people will have proved it for themselves. Nichiren Daishonin's followers consequently feel no need to coerce others into practising this Buddhism or to be intolerant of those who practise other religions and philosophies. . . .

Fundamentally, members of the SGI believe that a lasting world peace will be established only when enough people—ordinary, down-to-earth people like those whose experiences you have read in the course of this book [*The Buddha in Daily Life*]—learn to live their daily lives according to the profound philosophy of Nichiren Daishonin's Buddhism; a philosophy which, while respecting the fundamental dignity of all life, is powerful enough to release in ordinary people the strength with which to overcome their sufferings, and flexible enough to allow everyone to express and develop their own individuality.

It would be a mistake to suppose that the achievement of *kosen-rufu* implies that everyone must practise this Buddhism for world peace to come about—indeed, those who practise this Buddhism recognize that such a thing will probably never happen. What they do foresee, is the existence of a large minority of people who chant *Nam-myoho-renge-kyo*, supported by another large group—possibly even the majority—who, while they may not practise themselves, will be broadly in agreement with the aims and philosophy of Nichiren Daishonin's Buddhism. Together, these two groups will then have enough power to influence positively the course of world affairs away from war and destructive conflict, despite the lack of cooperation from a third, uncaring group, who will be either directly opposed to, or simply uninterested in, the spread of this Buddhism or any form of religion, for that matter.

Kosen-rufu is not limited just to eradicating conflict in the international arena, though. Rather, as can be seen in the experiences related earlier, since the practice of this Buddhism gives back to ordinary people an increasing measure of control over their own lives and environment, the effect of a great many people practising in any society will be seen throughout that society: in a lower crime rate, for example, a lower incidence of drug and alcohol abuse, a lower divorce rate, a stronger economy and higher standards of living, generally better health, a greater life expectancy and so on. For just as a climate of fear, apathy, hopelessness and depression can be created by a small but energetic minority—witness the activities of various terrorist groups in Northern Ireland, for example —so an atmosphere of creativity and vitality can be generated by a minority who are inspired and sustained by more positive and humane goals. Moreover, when that minority base their actions on the inexhaustible life-force, courage, wisdom and compassion they draw from their own lives through chanting to the Gohonzon, in time they will quite naturally gain the trust and respect of others around them. The effect of *kosen-rufu* in society is described in poetic terms by Nichiren Daishonin in the following passage:

The time will come when all people,[8] including those of Learning, Realization and Bodhisattva, will enter on the path to Buddhahood, and the Mystic Law alone will flourish throughout the land. In that time, because all people chant *Nam-myoho-renge-kyo* together, the wind will not beleaguer the branches or boughs, nor will the rain fall hard enough to break a clod. The world will become as it was in the ages of Fu Hsi and Neng Shun[9] in ancient China. Disasters will be driven from the land and the people will be rid of misfortune. They will also learn the art of living long, fulfilling lives.

This is not merely wishful thinking on the part of Nichiren Daishonin but is, rather, a vision of the future based on a clear and profound understanding of cause and effect, specifically the effect of many people chanting *Nam-myoho-renge-kyo*. It is also worth recalling in this context that, of all the world's major religions, only Nichiren Daishonin's Buddhism foresees the human race developing to a point where it can learn to overcome the many problems which it has created and now confront it, rather than perishing in the flames of some mythical Armageddon.

NOTES

Daisaku Ikeda, "Human Revolution" (1998). Reprinted by permission of Soka Gakkai.

Excerpts from Richard Causton, *The Buddha in Daily Life: An Introduction to the Buddhism of Nichiren Daishonin* (London: Rider, 1995), 246–48, 252–61. Reprinted by permission of SGI–UK and The Random House Group, Ltd.

1. Anson Shupe, "Soka Gakkai and the Slippery Slope from Militancy to Accommodation," in *Religion and Society in Modern Japan: Selected Readings*, ed. Mark R. Mullins, Shimazono Susumu, and Paul L. Swanson (Berkeley, Calif.: Asian Humanities Press, 1993), pp. 233–34.

2. These "new religions" are frequently distinguished from the "new, new religions" (*shin-shin-shūkyō*) that came to prominence in Japan in the 1970s and 1980s.

3. Richard Causton, *The Buddha in Daily Life: An Introduction to the Buddhism of Nichiren Daishonin* (London: Rider, 1995), 101–2.

4. "What is the Buddhism of Nichiren?" on the Soka Gakkai International–USA Website, http://www.sgi-usa.org/buddhism/bofnd.html#gohonzon.

5. Here indicates *Nam-myoho-renge-kyo*. Nichiren uses this term to emphasize the direct relationship between his Buddhism and T'ien-t'ai's. [Note in original text. T'ien-t'ai was the sixth-century Buddhist priest and "Great Teacher" who systematized the various schools of Chinese Buddhism.]

6. A categorization of the various obstacles and hindrances which trouble one's practice of Buddhism, such as doubt, fear, sickness, opposition from one's family and so forth. Also called *sansho shima*. [Note in original text.]

7. *Shakyamuni,* or "Shakya sage," refers to the Buddha, Siddhartha Guatama (c. 563–483 B.C.E.), a member of the Shakya clan.

8. Not everyone living, but, rather, people in all conditions of life, i.e. the Ten Worlds. [Note in original text.]

9. Legendary kings who reigned over ideal societies in ancient China. [Note in original text.]

FOR FURTHER READING

Hammond, Phillip E., and David W. Machacek, *Soka Gakkai in America: Accommodation and Conversion* (New York: Oxford University Press, 1999). A noteworthy sociological study of Soka Gakkai.

Hochswender, Woody, Greg Martin, and Ted Morino, *The Buddha in Your Mirror: Practical Buddhism and the Search for the Self* (Santa Monica, Calif.: Middleway, 2001). A presentation of Soka Gakkai Buddhism for an American audience.

Hurst, Jane D., *Nichiren Shoshu Buddhism and the Soka Gakkai in America: The Ethos of a New Religious Movement* (New York: Garland, 1992). The author has studied Soka Gakkai since 1972.

Ikeda, Daisaku, *Complete Works* (Tokyo: Seikyo Press, 1968). The early writings of Daisaku Ikeda, concerned especially with Japanese political and religious reform through the "human revolution" and the prospects for world peace.

Krieger, David, and Daisaku Ikeda, *Choose Hope: Your Role in Waging Peace in the Nuclear Age,* trans. Richard L. Gage (Santa Monica, Calif.: Middleway, 2002). A dialogue between SGI President Ikeda and the founder of the Nuclear Age Peace Foundation.

Soka Gakkai International, http://www.sgi.org. The official SGI Website.

Soka Gakkai International–USA, http://www.sgi-usa.org. The official SGI-USA Website.

Part III

New Families

Chapter 6

The Unification Church

The Holy Spirit Association for the Unification of World Christianity (HSA-UWC), or the Unification Church, was founded by Korean-born Sun Myung Moon (b. 1920). Members of the Unification Church, or Unificationists (also popularly called Moonies), believe that Moon and his wife, Dr. Hak Ja Han Moon (b. 1943), are the True Parents, that their children are without sin, and that they have established the True Family. All couples who go through the Blessing (marriage) ceremony are grafted onto this True Family. These couples are expected to have children, who will also be sinless. Thus God's universal law, or the Divine Principle, will finally be observed by a perfected humanity on the earth, fulfilling both God and His creation. Because family is central to its thought, the Unification Church is the NRM that most easily fits into the category of New Family as used in this volume.

Although the Unification Church insists that its purpose is to unite all Christians, many of its concepts either echo or derive directly from non-Christian religious systems prevalent for centuries on the Korean peninsula. Like most Koreans of his generation, Moon was raised in a Confucian family that took a shamanistic worldview for granted and also incorporated Buddhist rituals and principles. When he was ten years old, his family converted to Christianity. In 1936, he claimed to receive a vision of Jesus Christ, who asked Moon to complete Jesus' mission to establish the kingdom of God on earth. In later years, Moon had spiritual encounters with the Buddha, Muhammad, and other religious founders and prophets. These encounters may reflect the influence of Korean folk shamanism, with its emphasis on communicating with the dead. Similarly, the emphasis on family (see below) arguably reflects a Confucian focus on the family as basic to a harmonious society. Even the idea of an all-pervading Principle, so fundamental to Unification thinking, resembles Confucian teaching about a cosmic Principle that maintains balance and harmony in the world. Buddhist influences include the Unification notion of paradise, which resembles the Pure Land of certain Buddhist sects. And the Unification notion of continuous revelation bears more than a passing resemblance to Mahayana Buddhism's insistence that the Buddha revealed many of his teachings only when his listeners were ready for them.

As a young man, Moon studied electrical engineering in Japan, but he eventually returned to Korea. After World War II he began his own church in Pyongyang, in modern-day North Korea, but was persecuted and imprisoned several times by the Communists. After being freed from prison by Allied forces in 1950, Moon moved to Pusan, South Korea, where he continued to have trances and visions and communicate with spirits. Moon also set about revising traditional Christian doctrines, teaching that a messiah called the Lord of the Second Advent would come to earth to complete Jesus' mission. In 1954, Moon founded the Unification Church in Seoul. He married but eventually separated from his first wife before marrying Hak Ja Han in 1960. In 1957, *Divine Principle*, a collection of many of Moon's teachings, formulated since 1945 and recorded by his followers, was first published. Although this book is regarded as the Unification Church's sacred text, Unificationists also assume that revelation is ongoing. Thus, *Divine Principle* does not contain all of the messages that God has revealed or will reveal to Moon, and his subsequent sermons and teachings are also considered authoritative.

One of the Unification Church's early converts was Young Oon Kim (1915–1989), a seminary-trained Methodist leader who also received visions. Kim moved to Oregon in 1959 and started the first group of Unificationists in the United States. Later she became a prolific writer and noted theologian for the Unification Church. In the early years Unificationists in the United States were few in number and were largely condemned as heretical by those Christian clergy who noticed them. Kim's group later moved to San Francisco, and other groups arose elsewhere as Unificationist missionaries from Asia proselytized among Americans.

By the late 1960s and early 1970s, the Unification Church was among the "cults" attracting negative attention from concerned parents, ministers, and the news media in the United States. Unificationists recruited many white, middle-class, college-aged youth, who gave up their families and lifestyles to live communally, devoting long hours to selling flowers and copies of *Divine Principle* on street corners to raise money. Alarmed relatives and friends feared that the Unification recruits were being "brainwashed," although the techniques used for recruitment and retention did not differ radically from those of other organizations, secular or religious, that also had absolutist goals.

Moon sponsored a dizzying array of subsidiary organizations to promote the causes he deemed most crucial to his mission. These included the International Cultural Foundation; the International Religious Foundation; the Inter-Religious Federation for World Peace; the World Media Association; the Professors World Peace Academy; the Collegiate Association for the Research of the Principle; the Unification Theological Seminary in Barrytown, New York; the *Washington Times* newspaper; the International Conference on the Unity of the Sciences; the Assembly of the World's Religions; and the Family Federation for World Peace and Unification. All of these organizations were intended to further peace, democracy, and religious toleration in the world, goals that Unificationists saw as necessary (although not sufficient) to move human society toward a perfect world. Skeptics and critics of the Unification Church were suspicious of these multiple organizational expressions of the Unification cause, raising questions about Moon's funding and intentions. Moon himself attracted considerable public attention and scorn. He called for renewal among Christians in the United States, but most Christians objected to many Unification doctrines. He supported President Richard Nixon in 1974, after the Watergate cover-up came to light. And Moon was convicted of income tax evasion in 1982 and served an eighteen-month prison sentence.

The story of the Unification Church has thus contained both growth and expansion, on the one hand, and controversy and conflict with other institutions and movements on the other. By the late 1980s and 1990s, thousands of Americans, Europeans, Japanese, and Koreans had joined the Unification Church. In the West, however, many thousands more had left. Those who stayed in the church married and raised children, many of whom are now entering adulthood. As an NRM, the Unification Church has successfully weathered decades of growth and decline, success and disappointment. As of this writing, Moon is in his eighties. After he dies, the future of the Unification Church, despite its significant assets, institutional bases, and theological development, will be somewhat uncertain.

Unification theology is complex and multifaceted. *Divine Principle* is not an easy book for someone unfamiliar with Unification teachings to comprehend. Its language is rooted in an evolving theological tradition grounded in Moon's continuous revelations and the interpretations of a growing number of Unification thinkers. According to *Divine Principle,* God has qualities of both sexes, and creation is infused with male and female principles that complement one another, much like yin and yang in Taoist thought. The term "relationship" probably best describes the basic structure of the cosmos in Unification thought. All things relate to one another. What is most important to understand about God's nature is that God loves and wants an object for that love. Without an object, God's love cannot be satisfied.

God made Adam and Eve to become True Parents, and thus perfected objects of His love. As spouses they would have a relationship with one another that was mutual, a relationship with God that would place them in a subordinate position, and a relationship with their children that would place them in a dominant position. Thus would be established the "four position foundation": husband, wife, God, and child (see "The Purpose of Creation," below). The first humans could only reach this ideal situation, however, by passing through three stages of development, or the Three Blessings. First they must perfect their character. Then they must create a family. And finally they must become dominant over creation.

Adam and Eve never achieved the First Blessing, of perfecting their character, because Lucifer, an angel appointed by God to watch over them, was jealous that they were receiving God's love. So Lucifer tempted Eve to have an emotional relationship with him, and she in turn convinced Adam to have a sexual relationship with her. This, according to Unification thought, was the Fall, in which humanity became sinful and passed that sinfulness to future generations. Had Adam and Eve obeyed God and not misused God's love, all would have developed according to God's plan, and God's law, the Divine Principle, would have been fully realized on earth.

To restart the process toward perfection, God has sent messiahs to earth who could restore the true state of humanity's relationship with God. Before that can happen, however, humans must perform good deeds that cancel the bad effects of sin. Unificationists call this "indemnity." Showing love and devotion to one's fellow humans, especially within families, helps pay this indemnity.

Jesus was a messiah. When he was born, the indemnity had been paid to the point where the world could have been restored. Jesus should have married and begotten perfect children. However, before he could fulfill this mission, John the Baptist, who initially proclaimed Jesus' messiahship, failed to support Jesus. The Jews lost hope in Jesus, which ultimately led to his crucifixion. Jesus' death and resurrection provided future generations with spiritual salvation. Nonetheless, complete restoration required a physical messiah, the Lord of the Second Advent.

Unificationists believe that the present era is the appointed time for this Lord to appear. Like certain times in ancient history when the potential for restoration was great, so today good and evil are separated. Moon saw this battle between good and evil being played out in the Cold War between non-Communist and Communist states. But the balance between the satanic and the godly can only be tipped in favor of the latter when the messiah appears to teach the truth of God's love. Unificationists believe that this messiah—who is coming for all humanity, not just Christians— was born in the East, in a place where many religions have existed, in a nation where good and evil have been in dramatic conflict, and in a nation that paid a national indemnity in human suffering. All signs point to Korea as the birthplace of the messiah of this age. *Divine Principle* does not identify Moon as the messiah, but in 1992 Moon admitted that he was that messiah, the Lord of the Second Advent.

As noted earlier, Unificationists believe that Moon and Hak Ja Han are the True Parents whose own children are sinless, and by blessing the marriages of couples, Moon and Hak Ja Han thus insure that children from those marriages are sinless. Although the men and women in these marriages are not perfected themselves, the True Parents can cancel that effect in the Blessing ceremony. Moon has become world-famous for presiding over Blessing ceremonies—usually called "mass weddings" in the media— involving thousands of couples. Preceding these ceremonies are Holy Wine ceremonies in which the True Parents purify the lineage of the couples to be married.

The Blessing restores the four position foundation essential to the kingdom of God on earth. The Unification Church sees marriage and family as necessary to bring perfection to the world. More than any other NRM in this volume, New Family is at the very core of Unification theology. Through the New Family, a New World of perfected humans, related in multiple directions, will enjoy and return God's love perpetually.

In the first excerpt that follows, taken from *Exposition of the Divine Principle,* the centrality of Adam and Eve's marriage and family in Unification thought is apparent. God intended them to perfect their character (the First Blessing), then marry and bear children (the Second Blessing), then assume dominion over all creation (the Third Blessing). They would then become the ideal objects of God's love and joy, in an unending four position foundation. They would reflect God's internal nature and external form—that is, the ideal and the expression of that ideal. And humans are the highest form of God's creation, embodying in themselves all the internal designs and external manifestions of those designs found in nature.

The second excerpt is taken from a collection of essays published by the Unification Theological Seminary. A Unification couple, Hugh and Nora Spurgin, provide a vivid, first-person account of the actual experiences of an American Unification couple, indicating the tensions as well as delights in living the Unification life. Although the essay was published more than twenty years ago, and some aspects of Unification community and belief are different today, the essay still conveys much of the reality of living a Unificationist marriage in today's world.

"The Purpose of Creation"

From *Exposition of the Divine Principle*

3.1 The Purpose of the Creation of the Universe

It is recorded in the Bible that after God completed each day of creation, He saw that it was good.[1] This suggests that God wanted His creations to be object partners embodying goodness that He might take delight in them. How can the creation give God the greatest joy?

God created human beings as the final step in creating the universe. He created them in His image, in the likeness of His internal nature and external form, and gave them sensibility to all feelings and emotions because it was His intention to share joy with them. After their creation, God blessed Adam and Eve:

> Be fruitful and multiply, and fill the earth and subdue it; and have dominion over the fish of the sea and over the birds of the air and over every living thing that moves upon the earth.—*Gen. 1:28*

These are the *three great blessings:* to be fruitful (mature and ready to bear fruit), multiply and have dominion over the creation. Had Adam and Eve obeyed this divine mandate and built the Kingdom of Heaven, there is no doubt that God would have felt the greatest joy as His sons and daughters rejoiced in the world of His ideal.[2]

How can God's three great blessings be fulfilled? They can be realized only when the four position foundation, which is the fundamental foundation of creation, has been established. The three great blessings are fulfilled when the whole creation, including human beings, completes the four position foundation with God as the center. This is the Kingdom of Heaven, where ultimate goodness is realized and God feels the greatest joy. This is, in fact, the very purpose for which God created the universe.

The ultimate purpose of the universe, with human beings at its center, is to return joy to God. All entities have dual purposes. As was explained earlier, every entity has dual centers of movement, one of internal nature and another of external form. These centers pursue corresponding purposes—for the sake of the whole and for the sake of the individual—whose relationship is the same as that between internal nature and external form. These dual purposes relate to each other as cause and result, internal and external, subject partner and object partner. In God's ideal, there cannot be any individual purpose which does not support the whole purpose, nor can there be any whole purpose that does not guarantee the interests of the individual. The infinite variety of beings in the universe form one vast organic body interwoven by these dual purposes.

3.2 Good Object Partners for the Joy of God

To understand more precisely the issues concerning God's purpose of creation, let us first examine how joy is produced. Joy is not produced by an individual alone. Joy arises when we have an object partner in which our internal nature and external form are reflected and developed. Our object partner helps us to feel our own internal nature and external form through the stimulation it gives. This object partner may be intangible or it may be substantial. For example, an artists's object partner may be an ideal in his mind, or the finished painting or sculpture which substantiates that idea. When he visualizes his idea or beholds his work, he is stimulated to feel his own internal nature and external form reflected in it and feels joy and satisfaction. When his idea alone is the object partner, it is not as stimulating, nor is the joy that it brings as profound as that from a finished work. This nature of human beings originates in God's nature. In like manner, God feels the fullness of joy when He is stimulated by His substantial object partners to feel His original internal nature and original external form through them.

It was explained earlier that when the Kingdom of Heaven is realized— through the fulfillment of the three great blessings and the establishment of the four position foundation—it becomes the good object partner that gives joy to God. Let us investigate how the Kingdom becomes God's good object partner.

The key to God's first blessing is the perfection of individual character. An individual's mind and body are discrete projections and object partners of God's dual characteristics. In order for an individual to perfect his character, he must form a four position foundation within himself whereby his mind and body become one through give and take action with God as their center. Such individuals become the temples of God,[3] achieve complete oneness with Him,[4] and acquire a divine nature. They experience the Heart of God as if it were their own. Hence, they understand His Will and live fully attuned to it. When a person abides in the state of individual perfection, he lives as the substantial object partner to his mind. Because the center of his mind is God, he also lives as the substantial object partner to God. Both the mind and God rejoice as they experience their internal nature and external form through the stimulation which their object partners give them. Accordingly, when people realize God's first blessing, they become God's beloved who inspire Him with joy. Sharing all the feelings of God as their own, they would never commit any sinful acts that would cause God grief. This means they would never fall.

God's second blessing was to be fulfilled by Adam and Eve after they had achieved individual perfection as object partners to God, each manifesting an aspect of God's dual characteristics. In order to construct the four position foundation in their family, Adam and Eve should have joined in loving oneness as husband and wife and raised children. This would have been the fulfillment of the second blessing. A family or society that has formed the four position foundation in line with God's ideal is patterned after the image of a perfect individual. It thus becomes the substantial object partner to the individual who lives in oneness with God, and consequently, it also becomes the substantial object partner to God. The individual feels joy, and likewise God feels joy, when each perceives in this family or community the manifestation of his own internal nature and external form. When God's second blessing is fulfilled, this family or community also becomes a good object partner giving joy to God.

Before we examine how a person upon attaining the third blessing establishes a good object partner giving joy to God, we must first investigate the relationship between human beings and the creation from the viewpoint of internal nature and external form.

Prior to creating human beings, God created the natural world by expressing partial reflections of the internal nature and external form He had conceived for human beings. Consequently, a human being contains within himself the sum total of the essences of all things. This is the reason he is called the microcosm of the cosmos.

When God created living things, He began with creatures of a lower order. Over the course of time, He created animals of a higher order with more complex biological functions, culminating with human beings at the highest level. Therefore, human beings contain all the elements, structures and qualities found in animals. For example, human vocal cords are so versatile that they can imitate virtually any animal sound. Because the human body contains all the beautiful curves and lines of the creation, an artist hones his skills by drawing nude models.

Although human beings and plants have different structures and functions, they are similar in that they both are composed of cells. All the elements, structures and characteristics of plants can be found in human beings. For example, a plant's leaf corresponds to the human lung in appearance and function. As leaves absorb carbon dioxide from the atmosphere, the human lung absorbs oxygen. Branches and stems of plants correspond to the human circulatory system, which distributes nourishment to the entire body; the xylem and phloem correspond to human arteries and veins. The roots of a plant correspond to the human stomach and intestines, which absorb nutrients.

Human beings were fashioned from clay, water and air; consequently they contain elements of the mineral kingdom. Moreover, the earth displays a similarity to the structure of the human body: the earth's crust is covered with plants, its underground waterways exist inside the substrata, and beneath it all lies a molten core surrounded by a rocky mantle. This resembles the structure of the human body, which has skin covered with hair, blood vessels running inside the musculature, and marrow lying deeper still within the bones.

The meaning of God's third blessing is the perfection of a human being's dominion over the natural world. To fulfill this blessing, the four position foundation of dominion must be established centered on God. Human beings and the natural world, which are the substantial object partners of God at the level of image and symbol respectively, must share love and beauty to become completely one.[5]

The natural world is an object partner which exhibits human internal nature and external form in diverse ways. Hence, ideal human beings receive stimulation from the world of nature. Sensing their own internal nature and external form displayed throughout the creation, they feel immense joy. God also delights when He experiences the stimulation of His original internal nature and original external form from the universe; this is possible when it becomes His third object partner through the harmonious union of human beings and the natural world. Therefore, when human beings realize God's third blessing, the entire universe becomes yet another good object partner giving joy to God. Had God's purpose of creation been realized in this way, an ideal world without even a trace of sin would have been established on the earth. We call this world the Kingdom of Heaven on earth. When life in the Kingdom of Heaven on earth comes to a close, people are to enter the spirit world and naturally enjoy eternal life in the Kingdom of Heaven there.

Based on the discussion thus far, we can understand that the Kingdom of Heaven resembles a person who has achieved individual perfection, taking after God's original internal nature and external form. In an individual, the mind's command is transmitted to the whole body through the central nervous system, causing the body to act with one purpose. Likewise, in the Kingdom of Heaven, God's direction will be conveyed to all His children through the True Parents of humankind, guiding everyone to live as one.

"Blessed Marriage in the Unification Church: Sacramental Ideals and Their Application to Daily Marital Life"

Hugh and Nora Spurgin

Families today are in crisis, in part because for many marriage has become merely a secular contractual arrangement which can be terminated at will. In contrast, the Unification Church seeks to revive such traditional values as premarital chastity, fidelity, and parental heart, while simultaneously introducing some novel religious concepts and practices. Unification though affirms a moral code and belief system which stress both nuclear and extended families as a channel through which the spirit of God can work. The Movement highlights the spiritual depths of love, marriage, and parenthood. For Church members, God is experienced as a full and essential Partner in the give-and-take inherent within familial relationships.

The Blessing

What Does It Mean?

The doctrines of marriage and the family are fundamental to Unification thought and lifestyle, and cannot be understood apart from their religious context. They are the central focus which unites the Church's ideal with everyday experience. In the Unification Church the most sacred rituals are the engagement and wedding ceremonies, referred to as "the Blessing." For the faithful, the Blessing connotes far more than a ceremony. It is one of the few Unification sacramental liturgies and includes practices similar in form to communion, baptism, penance, matrimony, and other traditional Christian sacraments. It is a moment of encounter with God, of rebirth. Ideally the Blessing provides us with moral assurance and spiritual benefits.

One does not automatically become spiritually mature. The ideal needs to be actualized experientially. Thus, the Blessing is said to be "conditional" (i.e., dependent upon human fulfillment). Blessed couples are those who have received the Blessing, including the responsibilities, commitments, opportunities, and promises implied. Blessed couples perceive themselves as in the process of becoming the "true" or ideal people that God desires. "Blessed" marriage is a special holy marriage through which one attains a new position before God. We will explain more about the theological meaning of this, but first let us mention our own introduction to the Unification Church.

Personal Experiences

In this paper we will give some personal experiences as a "Blessed" couple, as well as a general understanding of marriage in the Unification Church. We were married in 1970 in the wedding of 777 couples performed in Seoul, Korea, by Rev. Sun Myung Moon. We had joined the church independently of one another, almost four years earlier for Nora, and two years earlier for Hugh, and had both lived in the National Headquarters center in Washington, D.C., in the late 1960s.

Nora joined the Church while working on a master's degree in social work at New York University. Her interest in studying the extent to which religious systems change people's basic values (for a master's thesis) led her to two young women who were teaching the Divine Principle (Rev. Moon's teachings) which she studied and eventually decided to adopt. Upon graduation Nora moved to D.C. in order to work and train in the headquarters center and continued to work professionally as a therapist.

In 1968 Hugh obtained a master's degree in public administration from Syracuse University and went to Washington to work as a management analyst with the Department of Navy. One month after arriving in D.C. he met the Church. Agnostic and interested in politics, he was attracted to the answers the Divine Principle provided to his questions and the social breadth of the church's world view. (Nora taught him part of the Church's teachings.) Hugh continued to work for the U.S. government. Over the next two years both studied, taught, worked, witnessed, prayed and worshipped together.

In America the movement at that time was small and the feeling was somewhat like that of the early disciples of Jesus. There was a strong sense of purpose, of being "chosen" to help bring the kingdom of Heaven on earth. Our lifestyle was very simple. We worked at jobs to support ourselves and our spiritual efforts.

Later on we will share our personal experience of our matching, Blessing, and subsequent marriage. However, let us explain some of the ideological underpinnings of the faith, attitudes and practices which are so much a part of our lives.

The Theology of the Blessing

The Blessing is at the ethical and theological center of Unification lifestyle and thought. Ethically it is essential because the daily life, practices, and attitudes of Unification members, single as well as married, revolve around it. Single members look forward to the moment when they will receive the Blessing, thereby entering a new stage in their spiritual growth. They are eager for the arrival of the day when they will be wed, hopefully, to their ideal complement, an eternal spouse. From a Moonie perspective, although a single member works, fundraises, witnesses, studies, and preaches, those tasks are secondary to what is happening internally to prepare him or her for the Blessing. Presumably Blessed members are even more aware of both the benefits and the struggles inherent within the concept and experience of being Blessed, since the Blessing forms an integral part of their lives. To be a sacrificial, exemplary couple is neither easy nor trite.

Theologically the Blessing is central because marriage and the family are among the most basic of concepts within Unification thought and tradition. This statement is supported by an understanding of the following basic doctrines of the Unification Church: (a) God exists and is the origin and pattern for all human life, values, emotions, and institutions; (b) the internal and external traits of humans reflect the characteristics of God their creator; (c) God is the origin of the two genders, male and female. Though a man has elements of femininity, essentially he is a male; though a woman has elements of masculinity, essentially she is a female; (d) God's ideal since the beginning of time was for love, families, spouses, parents, children, and people in general to be "true people (according to their original nature),"[6] but because of the fall of man, such ideals have yet to be realized; (e) ultimately every person who is living, has ever lived, or will ever live, will eventually be able to become a true person able to love others and the creation with the same quality of love as God; (f) the central and most fundamental social institution is the family centered on God; God did not make the individual completely, emotionally self-sufficient; people need people; everyone needs someone to fully love and with whom to share; (g) though capable of reaching individual maturity alone, and thus able to achieve a certain degree of fulfillment, each person is designed to form a larger unit with his complement. To fully reflect God's nature (which is both masculine and feminine), and fulfill one's own emotional needs to a higher degree, there is a need to experience being a spouse and raising children; and (h) only with Christ's second coming and the beginning of a new age, can the eschatological hopes and goals discussed here be fully achieved.

Like all aspects of life, marriage and children are gifts from God. They are blessings that are possible only because God created and continues to sustain the world. According to the Biblical account in Genesis, marriage and progeny are God's second great blessing to Adam and Eve. In total there were three blessings given to them by God. The first blessing, to be fruitful, meant that each individual was to be responsible for perfecting his or her character by developing a relationship with God. The second blessing, to multiply and fill the earth, meant to achieve perfection on a social level, to create an ideal family and community. The third blessing, to have dominion over creation, indicated that all people should (on the foundation of the first two blessings) exercise a dominion of love over the natural world. The first blessing concerns individual maturity; the second, social development; and the third, ascendancy over creation. As part of the second blessing, the family occupies a central position between the other two blessings. It is a connecting link between the individual and the world.

Chosen Families

Adam and Eve—the Original Family

God did not intend Adam and Eve to marry, according to Rev. Moon, until they had become mature, until they could stand as true husband and wife. Otherwise they could never be true parents to their children. Adam and Eve were allowed the opportunity, and given the responsibility, to participate in creation of their own characters. They were to keep God's commandments, especially the commandment not to eat the fruit (interpreted by Rev. Moon to mean not to live a married life without an indication from God that they had reached the appropriate level of spiritual maturity). By remaining obedient, they would have become co-creators with God. If they had developed their own spirits, God would have taken it as a condition for their participating in the creation of the entire world. This would have then entitled them to dominion over the natural world.

Unfortunately, Adam and Eve had a premature, unprincipled sexual relationship. They failed to obtain God's approval. Their marriage was never blessed.[7] History has been, Unification thought teaches, a continual attempt by the Creator to find couples who meet spiritual requirements to be blessed. God's desire has always been to have an ideal couple on earth. He wants a couple who can show others the appropriate pattern of God-centered love and marriage needed to create an ideal family. Unfortunately most relationships are self-centered and less than loving. God's plan, then, would be for a Blessed couple and family, to serve as a nucleus, and to extend that paradigm to all those willing and able to meet the qualifications for a blessed marriage and family. Thus a new dispensational family would be established, centered upon the highest of spiritual ideals.

The Restored Family and Its Messianic Role

As Unificationists, we believe that nearly 2,000 years ago, Jesus came as the Messiah to establish on earth an ideal family, community, nation, and world, which he called the kingdom of Heaven on earth. He was able to achieve complete perfection only on an individual level before being crucified. Humanity was not yet ready to accept the perfect love and truth which he brought. He achieved spiritual, but not physical, salvation. He was unable, at that time, to substantialize in the social order God's ideal for humanity. Such a realization awaits the second coming of Christ. Jesus was always single; he had no natural family which could serve as an example to others; he had no progeny; hence he could provide no example for husband-wife/parent-child relationships.[8] . . .

God continued preparing the world for that messianic family to which other families could be spiritually "grafted" and thus restored to God's original intention. For us, that time is now—and Rev. and Mrs. Moon are the central family through whom we as followers can find new meaning for marriage and family life.

Extending the Restored Family

As Unificationists we skip the current practice of romantic courtship, trusting choice of a spouse to our spiritual leader, Rev. Moon. We can say that a Unification Blessed marriage begins with the matching, and members consider it a privilege to be matched and subsequently Blessed, even though arranged marriages are foreign to much of contemporary culture.

Built into the faith of a member is a sincere trust in Rev. Moon as a vessel through whom Divine guidance is given. There is a great deal of idealism and high expectation among single members. Thus, we have confidence in the method and in the specific choice of the matching process. Nevertheless, emotions are very real and (regardless of the ideal) there is the reality of facing a real person complete with liabilities as well as assets, weaknesses in addition to strengths. This is the person one must decide whether to accept "for better or for worse," not only "until death do us part," but for eternity! Existentially it is a moment laden with great emotion. For some the path is simple and clear: acceptance is absolute. God's decision, as revealed through the founder of the Church, is their choice. They have no other personal preference. For others, there is great caution and consideration before the couple makes a decision to accept or reject the suggestion of Rev. Moon.

It is through a matching process in which Rev. Moon selects spouses that the marriages of most Unification couples are arranged. Occasionally there are recommendations by a major Church leader. Such was the case for us. In 1970, when we were matched, Rev. Moon was not in America, making our engagement somewhat different. The Korean missionaries working in America discussed potential candidates with Rev. Moon, then returned to America to talk with each individual about the matches they had discussed with Rev. Moon. Because the person Rev. Moon had suggested for Nora had left the Church, Nora was asked by Dr. Young Oon Kim if there was someone she would like Rev. Moon to consider. After prayerful consideration, she said Hugh. Recalling her reasoning, Nora declared, "I knew we were very different and he was younger than I, but I always felt good being around him and things always went well when we worked together. However, I had no idea how he felt about me as a wife rather than a co-worker. I was worried he would think I was too old for him." (Nora is six and a half years older than Hugh.)

Hugh recalls, "I was surprised when Dr. Kim asked me who I would like to marry. Although I had often felt drawn toward Nora, I tried hard to focus on doing the work and will of God and not to have romantic feelings for her. However, because Dr. Kim asked my preference I told her Nora. Though we had never talked about it, I thought it was a great match. I called her to let her know I also had talked with Dr. Kim, and was baffled when she hesitated about getting married. When I told her I'd always cared about her even though I had never revealed it, she immediately changed and became excited about going to Korea for the wedding." Nora later said she was worried Dr. Kim would pressure Hugh and wanted to know what he really felt. Our pictures were sent to Rev. Moon who then approved the match. In more recent engagements, Rev. Moon has been personally present, choosing men and women who then consulted privately with each other, returning to give their acceptance or rejection of the match. But in those early days, he only came to America for brief visits.

The Ceremonies

After the matching, a holy wine ceremony is conducted to formalize the engagement. Externally, it may resemble a eucharistic service, but it has a different meaning. During that ceremony, we believe, new life is given by God through Rev. and Mrs. Moon to each couple. At that point the commitment is binding and eternal. Through the taking of the wine and participation in the ceremony, sins are forgiven and rebirth occurs. The couple is then offered to God as newly recreated beings, pure and free of past sins. In the same position, theoretically, as the newly created Adam and Eve (i.e., undefiled by original sin), they become a replacement before God for their "fallen" ancestors. Part of a new spiritual lineage, they have the potential to become parents of offspring freed from sins of the past. The taking of the wine is a symbol of new life flowing into the body. Externally the couple is recognized as a married couple, internally they are viewed as new citizens of the kingdom of God.

For the wine ceremony to be efficacious, several elements are needed: a mediator, holy wine, and an eligible couple. As mediators, between God and man, Rev. and Mrs. Moon are believed to bring the blessing of forgiveness to fallen people and lift them up in the sight of God so that they can be accepted as new citizens in the kingdom. One might liken it to receiving citizenship in a nation which is not one's native land. The holy wine is a symbol of new life. The newly engaged couple stand in the position to restore God's lost children; from their descendants a new order of heavenly children will populate the world.

The final step in transmission of the Blessing is the public wedding. Though externally resembling other services, there are elements which are different. A distinguishing feature is its size; usually a large number of couples are married simultaneously. Although some individuals have been wed in small, private ceremonies, most Unificationists were married *en masse*. Since their paradigmatic marriage in 1960, Rev. and Mrs. Moon have officiated at many weddings, including eight mass weddings: 36 couples in 1961, 72 couples in 1961, 124 in 1963, 430 in 1968, 777 in 1970, 1,800 in 1975, and 2,075 and 5,837 in 1982. (In addition, there were small, private weddings, including Blessings in America of 35 couples in 1976 and of 74 in 1977.)

With the Blessing ceremony, Unification couples are married, ready to begin the responsibilities of married life and parenthood. However, there is one more specific requirement before family life begins. To make a spiritual foundation for the family, a 40-day period of sexual abstinence is observed before consummating the marriage. This is a period of prayer and preparation. Since the wedding is a mass wedding (not individualized according to personal situations) depending on each couple's situation there may be even longer periods of separation before the couple is ready to begin the marriage. For instance, couples may be asked to complete a certain mission or meet some spiritual requirement before starting a family.

The Making of a Unification Marriage

Attitudes toward Marriage

As Blessed couples we believe that a perfect marriage is made, rather than found; a perfect spouse grows, rather than appears. As single people, we are taught that it is one's spiritual responsibility to "perfect oneself" while on earth, where opportunity is provided for the working out of kinks, irregularities, and "less than desirable traits" in one's personality. Perfection is viewed as the maturing and fulfilling of one's potential, and should not be confused with robot-like sameness. Single members with idiosyncrasies and personality difficulties are often advised to work out their problems prior to marriage, since problems may intensify in the intimacy and constancy of the marital relationship. In fact, group and communal-style living is believed helpful in polishing off rough edges and in expanding one's ability to love, thus preparing the single person for potentially successful marriage.

Beyond the sacramental value of the Blessing, married life is considered a further opportunity to perfect oneself. Whereas a solitary person can keep greater distance between himself and others (able to hide his real self and problems), a spouse and parent is constantly challenged to grow and change. To many Church members this is a challenge sought and valued. Marriage is approached and nourished in the Unification Church in the above context, thus making it a part of a couple's spiritual responsibility in life to work out a good relationship, coming before God together as a new creation which transcends the sum total of the two individuals.

One may ask what makes Unification marriages different, apart from the arrangement and the scale of the wedding. We would be foolish to imply that there are no problems—Unification couples are real people. Coming from all sorts of backgrounds and experiences, our common faith is a great source of strength, yet we also go through crises and tests of faith, and couples sometimes feel they have irreconcilable differences. Practically speaking, we have the same struggles other couples have—personality conflicts, financial problems, child-rearing problems, etc.

A New Value System

Although our day-to-day married life may look very similar to that of others, from our training in the Divine Principle we have gained several valuable elements.

One attitude learned is the value of fidelity. Spiritual meaning is given to the maintenance of faithfulness; therefore, a trusting relationship usually can exist. A blessed wife of eleven years, Anne Edwards, gives this advice: "Be faithful. Be determined to be committed to God, the True Parents, and your mate forever. He or she will feel this and reward you with gratitude and a similar fidelity. Once you make this commitment with mind and heart, you are free. With the secure center of commitment and fidelity, we can go anywhere in the garden of marriage without fear of loss."[9] This fidelity is essential for the spiritual and emotional growth of the children as well.

Secondly, our common faith gives strength and meaning to everything the Unification family is and does. Parents and children have a framework around which to judge right from wrong, and into which fit the pieces of life into a larger perspective. We develop our own Sunday School curriculum and give our children religious training which we hope will help them to understand the beauty and mystery of the spiritual side of life, as well as give them a well-rounded sense of who they are, and a practical guide for living a life of goodness and success. Our experience has been that children are very naturally religious and understand theological concepts far better than one would anticipate. We were surprised to overhear our four and five year old children discussing whether God is inside or outside the world and asking whether God had a Mommy and a Daddy.

Thirdly, as Unificationists, we have been taught not to fear struggle. The difficulties in life are there to be overcome—not avoided. Problems in marriage are viewed as presenting a challenge for growth. Rev. Moon often stresses learning to embrace an ever-widening circle of people. To be able to love ever more deeply is considered one of the greatest goals in life. It is with this attitude that many couples enter into interracial, intercultural marriages. Rev. Moon once said that a black mother looking into her child's blue eyes cannot help lose feelings of racial resentment.

Fourthly, there is the support of others who share the same belief system. In the Church we have a tradition of trinities of couples. Although not yet well developed in America, the ideal is that three couples care for each other in such a way that they will be willing to live as an extended family—taking responsibility to help one another in time of need, praying together, and raising children in the enriched atmosphere of a large number of role-models. Korean couples who have employed this system tell of the moral, financial, and emotional support they have received from other families of their trinity at such a time as the death of a spouse. Japanese couples explain how they share apartment buildings and work out cooperative baby-sitting arrangements. In all situations, the three couples serve each other so that all can make some contribution to the larger mission.

Until recently, many of the couples in America have continued to be part of the center life, living communally and often serving in a capacity of house-parents to single members. However, with the recent Blessing of many more couples, many are moving into homes and apartments and becoming vital parts of the community. This new providential era of home church[10] will probably change the structure and methods of the church, as well as its image. In one sense, the church will be far less visible. Rev. Moon has often said that his desire is not to build big churches—or even a new church at all—but to bring truth and rebirth to humanity— no matter what the external structure.

The Demands of a Family

The lifestyle of Unification members in America has been primarily a communal, celibate style seemingly more appropriate for young, single members. With the introduction of a small number of Blessed marriages (only twenty couples in the U.S. until 1975) to the Church community, couples often served as leaders or parent figures to the "Family" of single members congregated in a local center—a role which recognized and allowed for the nuclear family to exist and grow within the core lifestyle of the Church. The role had dignity and provided a means of support for the family in the midst of the larger extended Family. However, as new, larger groups of couples joined the ranks and began to have children, the Church had also begun broadening and differentiating, and this earlier role could not easily be applied. For instance, a larger number of couples in a center must have the opportunity to grow and expand their nuclear families; they can no longer fit the style of the single members.

The increase in the number of couples and in the size of their families, compounded by the growth of Church business enterprises and other activities, is in the process of changing the lifestyle. For some this change has not been easily made. Couples have found themselves concerned with caring for and supporting a growing family, while simultaneously in the midst of a transition in their occupational role as Unification leaders or members. The life of faith is no longer the simple total involvement and communal lifestyle that was possible for single people. Sometimes the heart is torn between one's love for one's spouse and children and the sacrifices made in the religious life. This is the painful experience of many Unification parents who have gone to the mission field to do evangelical work (for months or even years), leaving their dear ones in the care of others. Some, with absolute faith, have made many sacrifices for the sake of God's Providence, including temporarily working apart from spouses and children. However, for others, the desire to provide the best of everything in a material sense may introduce a new conflict into a seemingly absolute faith. This, we feel, is one of the areas of greatest potential conflict for Unification couples.[11] It is not easy to maintain the same level of commitment after being married. Many Unification couples have done so, but not without much personal and familial sacrifice.

The Interim Ethic: the Process of Restoration

At this point it seems appropriate to express something about the difference between our ideals and everyday reality. Most Unification members are idealistic people; therefore, every discrepancy between ideal and practice is painful, and is difficult to explain without an in-depth study of the role that *restoration* plays in the Divine Principle. This aspect of our belief system is among the most misunderstood in sociological circles. . . . The "real world" is the world as we know it. It is composed of contemporary social institutions, personality theories, even religions. The "ideal world" . . . is the world we are striving to attain. It is the ideal taught in the Divine Principle. The core of this world is the God-centered family, out of which a God-centered society with God-centered institution is envisioned to grow. How do we get from . . . [the "real world" to the "ideal world"]? By the path of Restoration! It is deeply religious and requires faith and sacrifice. It necessitates a self-denying interim ethic. . . . [Essential to this is] the re-birth experience—the stripping down of the trappings of the old world, the shedding of everything which, though good in itself, may hinder the process. One could liken it to the Biblical reference to a "camel going through the eye of a needle."

Unlike a single born-again experience, we see marriage (indeed, the religious life in general) as a lifetime process which begins when a person first hears the Divine Principle and joins the church. Often the life seems spartan to others; certainly it is sacrificial. But there is also the gradual rebuilding of a fuller life. In the ideal world—the kingdom of heaven—we believe that all institutions and levels of society, as well the individual, will be restored. Until that time we are in the process of becoming restored. We believe that as more individuals are restored, the path broadens and individual maturation becomes shorter and easier.

For the early Blessed couples it was painful to pioneer the path. We made, and still make, many personal and collective sacrifices. Careers, ties with parents and friends, time with children, ambition, wealth, and leisure are often sacrificed. Our lives are not our own, but are viewed as being for the sake of others, which requires broadening the path—with the hope that the Kingdom can come in the next generation. Our tears, and the tears of our children, are the most precious gift we can offer humanity. For us the deepest pain comes, not in the making of the offering, but in being misunderstood. Knowing the ideal for which we are striving makes every deviation from that more intense. We are not zombies without feeling, nor do we lack desire, at times, for easier ways of life. But, we believe that we are paying a redemptive price for humankind which will allow God a working base from which to bring the Kingdom of Heaven on earth.

Conclusion

One point that stands out is the strong emphasis in the Unification Church on faith and spirituality. It is something which transcends, but is present in, daily human relationships. The challenges of life are given meaning and are experienced from the perspective of one's total life of faith as growth-producing. We, as a couple, have chosen this course for ourselves and our family because we believe that we are living at a turning point in history. We believe that because of God's blessing, our children are born into this new providential era and a new lineage. Unlike us, they are free from original sin and the need to go through such a difficult restoration process. Of course, they also are responsible for their own spiritual growth and are affected by the influences (both good and evil) of their environment.

Our desire to have the optimum situation in which to raise our children, and at the same time participate in the restoration, is often a source of tension and conflict. It is here that couples sometimes face a crisis of faith and marital conflict. A personal example would be fitting here. We discussed our answers to a questionnaire Nora had prepared for Unification couples. One question dealt with the tension between commitment to one's family and commitment to the Church which is the foundation of that marriage and family.[12] One possible response read: "In a situation where my spouse is having a struggle of faith, I would continue my commitment to the church even though my spouse could not continue in the church." Nora was somewhat surprised that (as a third choice) Hugh chose this doctrinal answer, rather than another response which stated: "Our marriage and family ties are very strong, and if in conflict with church responsibilities, we have chosen or would choose to protect the family bond and have a less demanding relationship with the church." Hugh was surprised that Nora, if faced with no alternative but a choice between him and the Church would choose to stay with him in order to keep the family intact, even if it meant externally leaving the Church community. Of course, the question is hypothetical; neither knows what his or her choice would be if such a situation were to arise. Fortunately, although some tension is always present between these two priorities, few couples have been faced with such an extreme choice. Based on our contact with other couples, we feel that most of them strongly value their family, as we do, and would go to great lengths to keep it intact. Our responses may reflect the tendency for each individual to apply in his own way the two great commandments, to love God with all one's heart and to love one's neighbor (especially one's children and spouse) as oneself. These are the marriage of the vertical and horizontal; the two are inseparable.

NOTES

"The Purpose Of Creation," chapter 1, section 3 of *Exposition of the Divine Principle* (New York: The Holy Spirit Association for the Unification of World Christianity, 1996), 32–36. Reprinted by permission.

Excerpt from Hugh and Nora Spurgin, "Blessed Marriage in the Unification Church: Sacramental Ideals and Their Application to Daily Marital Life," in *The Family and the Unification Church,* ed. Gene G. James (Barrytown, N.Y.: Unification Theological Seminary, 1983), 121–37. Reprinted by permission.

1. Gen. 1:4–31 [Note in original text.]

2. The excerpt below by Hugh Spurgin and Nora Spurgin explains these three blessings in a more contemporary American idiom.

3. 1 Cor. 3:16 [Note in original text.]

4. John 14:20 [Note in original text.]

5. Cf. Creation 5.2.3 [Note in original text. This section of *Divine Principle* explains "the realm of direct dominion," in which humans enjoy God's love directly and perfectly.]

6. "True" is a favorite word of Unificationists. In this context it means to be ideal, perfect and mature. [Note in original text.]

7. Sex is not itself sinful, since God intended man and woman to procreate, but only within the confines of a God-centered and sanctioned, marital relationship. [Note in original text.]

8. He had no bride who could represent (in addition to his mother) the feminine aspects of the Creator. [Note in original text.]

9. Anne Edwards, "Marriage, some practical concepts," *The Blessing Quarterly*, Vol. 1, no. 2. (Summer 1977): 61. [Note in original text.]

10. "Home church" is the name given to the concept of making one's home in the community a central, spiritual hub. [Note in original text.]

11. It might also be noted that some other religious communities have avoided this problem by banning marriage and remaining celibate. [Note in original text.]

12. The question and possible responses were as follows: Blessed marriage and families are a fundamental and external bond of great spiritual significance, according to the Divine Principle. Also, our affiliation with, and contribution to the church, are of great spiritual value. These two commitments are not always equal in strength. Please check the phrase or phrases which best describe your feelings. If you check several, rate them 1, 2, 3, etc.

We are confident and secure in our marriage and are willing to make the sacrifices which may be required for the higher purpose.

Our marriage and family ties are very strong, and if in conflict with church responsibilities, we have chosen or would choose to protect the family bond and have a less demanding relationship with the church.

When conflicts come up between church commitment and my family, I usually choose or would choose to sacrifice my family even though my spouse would find this very difficult to live with.

In a situation where my spouse is having a struggle of faith, I would continue my commitment to the church even though my spouse could not continue in the church. [Note in original text.]

FOR FURTHER READING

Barker, Eileen, *The Making of a Moonie* (New York: Basil Blackwell, 1984). One of the earliest and most reliable studies of the Unification Church by a non-Unificationist scholar.

Chryssides, George D., *Advent of Sun Myung Moon: The Origins, Beliefs and Practices of the Unification Church* (Houndmills, U.K.: Macmillan, 1991). An excellent scholarly study of the Unification Church.

Durst, Mose, *To Bigotry, No Sanction: Reverend Sun Myung Moon and the Unification Church* (Chicago: Regnery Gateway, 1984). An account of the Unification Church in the United States by an early convert.

Mickler, Michael L., and Michael Inglis, *40 Years in America: An Intimate History of the Unification Movement, 1959–1999* (New York: Holy Spirit Association Publications, 2000). A recent historical study of the Unification Church by Unificationist historians.

Moon, Rev. Sun Myung, *Exposition of the Divine Principle* (New York: The Holy Spirit Association for the Unification of World Christianity, 1996). The core text for the Unification Church, written by its founder.

The Unification Church, http://www.tongil.org. The official Website of The Holy Spirit Association for the Unification of World Christianity (HAS-UWC), or the Unification Church.

Chapter 7

The Family / Children of God

The group once known as the Children of God (COG), a name that ceased to be used after 1978, and now called The Family International (hereafter, The Family) was founded by David Brandt Berg (1919–1994), also known by followers as Father David, Mo, Moses, and Moses David. The son of a Protestant evangelical itinerant minister, Berg was ordained in the Christian and Missionary Alliance denomination. He married, started a family, and for many years devoted his life to the evangelical ministry. By the late 1960s, Berg was in Huntington Beach, California, ministering to hippies. The efforts of his "Teens for Christ," who appealed to the hippies by dressing like them and identifying with their subculture, attracted many new followers—most of them white, middle-class youths—who in turn became proselytizers for the group. One of these early members was Karen Zerby, later called Maria. She and Berg formed a sexual relationship, and she eventually became his second wife and, after his death, co-leader of the organization.

Berg preached against the System, his name for the social, economic, cultural, and religious mainstream in the United States. The Family, by contrast, was the Revolution that stood against the System. Berg's opposition to the prevailing ethos of the day would characterize The Family throughout its history. Berg preached that the end times were near, when Christ would return to earth to initiate the final phase of history. He insisted on aggressive evangelization tactics aimed at saving as many people as possible through a personal relationship with Jesus Christ. Although these ideas were consistent with much of Protestant evangelicalism, Berg's later sexual experimentation and communal living arrangements were not.

Berg and his group left California and relocated to Canada, where he told followers about revelations supposedly given to him about new sexual practices to be followed by movement members. During their subsequent travels they also recruited more members. By the early 1970s, the patterns of life for The Family were established. Members were assigned to communal group homes, initially called "Colonies" and then, after 1978, "Homes." Members devoted as much time as possible to witnessing to others for Christ, through various techniques such as "litnessing," or distributing literature produced by the movement. Another witnessing technique was Flirty Fishing, or FFing, the practice by which (mostly female) members of the movement targeted (mostly male) likely converts, sharing love and sometimes sexual intercourse with them as a means of recruitment (see "Fishers of Men," below). In addition to FFing, Berg preached that sexual relationships among members, whether married or not, were permissible as long as their encounters did not harm others with emotional ties to the partners (see "Sex and the Law of Love," below). Indeed, Berg regarded monogamous marriage as symptomatic of all that was wrong with the System, and he did not hesitate to place love of God above love within a committed marriage as conventionally conceived (see "One Wife," below). These ideas led to the formation of alternative family relationships that differed significantly from the nuclear family arrangements accepted as normative in American society. Family members, then, lived communally, engaged in sexual practices across marital boundaries, and when applicable used sex as a recruiting tool.

By the 1970s, concerned parents of members had formed "Free Our Children from the Children of God," or FREECOG. They employed famed deprogrammer Ted Patrick to rescue their adult children from The Family and reverse the effects of Family indoctrination. Some individuals did respond to this process, becoming ardent critics of The Family. But Family membership continued to increase. Colonies were established outside the United States, in South America, Australia, New Zealand, Japan, Europe, and India. As Family members moved onto the international scene, the group's composition diversified and white, middle-class young adults became less predominant.

Berg elevated his status to End Time Prophet, and his circulars to Colonies, the "Mo Letters," provided regular and copious advice about all manner of things relevant to Colony life and Family theology. By the late 1970s, some of the group's leaders began to question Berg's charismatic identity, and the movement saw significant defections. Also, some members did not agree with the more liberal sexual practices observed within the movement. But sexual exploration continued into the early 1980s and sometimes included relationships between children, or between children and adults, which led to a series of confrontations with legal authorities over possible child abuse. Sexual experimentation with children was probably never as widespread as Family critics maintained, but eventually the movement altered its teaching in this regard and today provides for strict control of and care for children in its Homes (see "Responsibilities of the Charter Home: Regarding Children and Parents," below).

In the 1980s, members were encouraged to move to Homes outside of Europe and North America to avoid the expected nuclear holocaust that would accompany the end times. Also, as Family children—many born as a result of sexual liaisons that occurred when FFing was practiced on a large scale—grew into adolescence, Teen Training Camps were established to help socialize pre-adolescents and teenagers. During the 1980s, the leaders in daily contact with Berg evolved into World Services, the leadership component of The Family. Reports of harsh leadership at the local level led World Services to produce literature urging local leaders to moderate their style. This trend occurred simultaneously with moderation of earlier sexual practices. FFing was abolished in 1987, and stricter guidelines were enforced regarding sexual activity involving children and teenagers.

After Berg's death in 1994, Peter Amsterdam and Maria became co-leaders of The Family. In the last decade or so, The Family has undertaken three initiatives, all of which indicate a healthy organization that will probably last into the foreseeable future. The first was the publication in 1995 of The Love Charter, which provides rules and guidelines for all aspects of Family life. This document stipulates what kinds of sexual contact are permissible and directs Homes to follow "democratic participation and decision making."[1] The second undertaking in recent years was the provision for varying levels of membership. The most committed are Charter Members, who accept all of Berg's prophecies, as well as those from Maria and Peter, as divinely inspired. Fellow Members do not follow Family rules as intensely and might, for example, engage in sexual intercourse with outsiders, something not allowed among Charter Members. Outside Members do not live in Homes but support Family ministries through donations or by subscribing to Family periodicals. The third way that The Family has adapted for long-term growth is by establishing boards that have specific functions, such as missionary outreach, education of children, and public relations. This constitutes a "corporate model of organizational decision-making and control under the centralized authority and direction of Maria and Peter and their World Service advisors."[2]

As its name implies, The Family has, according to the typology of this reader, centered its theology, communal structure, and individual practice around the New Family ideal. Each member's identity and status are based upon his or her place in a larger communal structure that is understood to be both the key to individual salvation (New Understanding and New Self) and the vessel in which members will ride out the storm of the coming end times, which will usher in a New World. The New Family of this NRM, however, is characterized by sexual practices and norms regarded as scandalous by other evangelical Protestant Christians. The following excerpts highlight these aspects of the movement. The first, taken from a recent pamphlet outlining Family teachings regarding women, justifies the witnessing technique of FFing, placing it within a biblical frame of reference. The second excerpt, from a "Mo Letter" dating from the early 1970s, gives us an indication of the early movement's radical departure from accepted marital practice. The third excerpt is a more recent attempt to justify retrospectively previous Family teaching on sexuality through an evangelical reading of the New Testament emphasis on love. The final excerpt, taken from *The Love Charter,* shows the recent organizational efforts to regulate family life in Homes, especially where children are concerned. This excerpt indicates how far The Family has come in eradicating past excesses and mistakes as it seeks to maintain a stable Home environment for future generations.

From *Women in The Family*

Paul and Nora Williams

"Fishers of Men"—Matthew 4:19

Jesus called to His disciples, some of whom were fishermen, saying, "Come, follow Me, and I will make you fishers of men." This challenge meant that if they would leave their nets and follow Him, they would learn to bring people to Jesus. Instead of fish, they would "catch" men for the Kingdom of God.

In the late '70s, a new and different method of "fishing for men" was revealed to David.[3]

Having traveled a lot in his former years to promote Gospel shows for television, David knew firsthand the deep agony of loneliness that so many men and women endure when their jobs separate them from the arms and beds of loved ones. Then, too, so many people who do find sex may not receive the deep and reassuring love they need.

One typically chilly London evening, David and Maria[4] encountered a lonely businessman named Arthur at a ballroom studio. David suggested that Maria dance with Arthur and encourage him.

As David watched Maria warmly interacting with and witnessing to the tall man with the lonely eyes, he wondered just how far a Christian can go to show God's Love to those in need. Here was a man in obvious need of love, reassurance and sex. Can a Christian even go to bed with someone in order to show God's Love for that person?

The Bible says that if we see a brother or sister without food, and only say nice things to them and send them on their way without food, we have done nothing. (See James 2:15–17.) Of course, it is one thing to give a hungry person food, but could that same principle be applied to needs for love and sex?

And even if one did have the faith to share one's own wife or husband to satisfy another person's sexual needs, could they endure the inner hurt and fear of losing the one dearest to them? Would God be pleased with such sacrifices? After much thought and prayer, David decided that the answer had to be yes.

What better way to show them the Love of God than to do your best to supply their desperately hungry needs for love, fellowship, companionship, mental and spiritual communication and physical needs such as food, clothing, shelter, warmth, affection, a tender loving kiss, a soft warm embrace, the healing touch of your loving hands, the comforting feeling of your body next to theirs—and yes, even sex if need be![5]

So began the ministry of "Flirty Fishing" (FFing), as David dubbed it, and it didn't take long for this unorthodox approach to evangelism to hit the news worldwide. FFing proved to be tremendously fruitful. FFing was effectively used as an outreach ministry in The Family for close to ten years. Over 100,000 people were won to Jesus because of the sacrificial love of Family men and women who laid down their lives and their wives to prove the Lord's Love.[6]

The personal cost was very great. Although some mistakes were made along the way, those souls won to God's Kingdom are truly eternal and well worth the sacrifices made for their sakes.

We do not consider it wrong that the Lord used the beauty, love and charm of the missionary women in The Family through this ministry to set men free, give them the Gospel and to show them God's Love, even at great personal sacrifice. What many of our women chose to do was done out of love and to win eternal souls for the Kingdom of God. There was nothing degrading or sinful about it. The motivation for Flirty Fishing was not money or power, unlike what happens in society at large today where the beauty of women is used by advertisers to sell all manner of goods, and to seduce the masses for material gain.

In 1987, The Family discontinued FFing to emphasize other means of ministering the Word of God to others, as well as to take advantage of opportunities to reach more people than the very personalized ministry of FFing allowed. At that time as well, the plague of AIDS had just begun its rampage through the world, which seemed to us another clear indication that it was time to stop the FFing ministry. We believe the principles behind the FFing ministry remain sound, even though we no longer allow any sexual involvement with those outside our communities.

From "One Wife"

Moses David

Sections 1–4

1. GOD WILL HAVE NO OTHER GODS BEFORE HIM, NOT EVEN THE SANC-TITY OF THE MARRIAGE GOD! The System proclaims and brags about the sanctity of the home and marriage, and marriage being the building block of the home and family, and yet the way they live belies the whole hypocrisy of their lying self-righteousness. They only promote marriage on the surface: "Oh, you're not married?—You don't have a marriage license?—You're just living together?"—But it's perfectly all right for them to have licenses and then still be running around with other people! *God is the*

God of marriage, too, and the main thing is to be married to Him and His Work, and when a marriage is not according to His Will, He doesn't hesitate to break it up and form other unions to further His work!

2. THE FAMILY MARRIAGE, THE SPIRITUAL REALITY BEHIND SO CALLED GROUP MARRIAGE, IS THAT OF PUTTING THE LARGER FAMILY, THE WHOLE FAMILY, FIRST, even above the last remaining vestige of private property, your husband or your wife! That's why Paul says, *"nevertheless,"*[7] to avoid *fornication* (or going wild with too much liberty), let every one have his own husband or wife. You can see a lot of situations Paul was running into which the weaker brethren just couldn't handle.

3. WHAT THE WORLD THINKS ARE OUR WEAKNESSES ARE ACTUALLY OUR STRENGTHS. *We do not minimise the marriage ties, as such. We just consider our ties to the Lord and the larger Family greater* and *more* important. —And when the *private* marriage ties interfere with *our Family* and *God* ties, they can be readily abandoned for the glory of God and the good of *The* Family! We are not forsaking the marital unit. —We are adopting a greater and more important and far larger concept of marriage: The *totality* of the *Bride* and her marriage to *the Bridegroom* is *The* Family! We are adopting the *larger* Family as *The* Family unit: The Family of *God* and *His* Bride and Children!

4. WHAT DOES "UNIT" MEAN?—SOMETHING THAT IS UNITED!—Something that is *one!* So that, even if *God has to break up these little private twosomes in order to make us conscious of the greater unit* of *The* Family, He will do it! If He can trust you with the private unit for the Glory of God, He will do it. But if you put that privacy first before the Whole Family Unit, God will blow on it and destroy it if He has to!—And it's happened before in the Revolution!

Sections 15–16

15. THROUGH THE EXPERIENCES WE ARE GOING THROUGH, GOD IS TRYING TO SHOW US HE WILL NOT FIT IN SECOND PLACE! *He will not have any other gods before Him!* If He allows you any nice cosy little *private* relationship, you can be very thankful for it! It is, in a sense, a *privilege,* a

special little dispensation of grace to feel that only *two* of you belong to each other in *particular*. But he will *only* allow that provided you make it very clear to *each other* and the *Lord* and the *others* in the Revolution that you belong to *God most of all*, and your private relationship doesn't interfere with your *work* and your relationship with the *Lord!*

16. IF YOU ARE ALLOWED ANY PERSONAL PRIVATE RELATIONSHIP WITH ANY PARTICULAR INDIVIDUAL CALLED "MARRIAGE," *it can only be tolerated provided it does not interfere with your marriage to God and your relationship with the rest of God's Wife—the Body, His total Bride!* They say that the Bible doesn't teach *plural marriage,* but one of the greatest examples of all is the marriage of *God Himself* to *His plural Bride* composed of *many* members, *all* of whom are nevertheless *One* Bride!

Sections 20–23

20. GOD BREAKS UP MARRIAGES IN ORDER THAT HE MIGHT JOIN EACH OF THE PARTIES TOGETHER TO HIMSELF. He rips off wives, husband [*sic*] or children to make up His Bride if the rest of their family refuses to follow! He is the worst "ripper-offer" of all! God is the greatest Destroyer of home and family of anybody! God does more to break up marriages than anybody! If they won't *both* put Him and *His* larger Family *first,* He will just take the *one* that *is willing* and let the *other* one go! Maybe we're learning something about marriage and its *un*importance!

21. WE ARE REVOLUTIONARY! If the church has *over*emphasised marriage, we are going to the opposite extreme of *under*emphasising and almost *belittling* marriage, and not even hesitating to *destroy marriages that don't glorify God and put Him and His Work first!* What *God* has put together don't let man put asunder: But how many has God actually put together? If *God* didn't put them together, He won't hesitate to break them up for *His* Glory and the welfare of *His Family!*

22. DON'T FORGET THIS MEANS YOUR CHILDREN, ALSO! *Special favouritism and partiality—that is selfish private property interest!* If you love your flesh-and-blood children more than you love *God's* children of *God's* Family, then you really haven't come to the realisation of what God's Family is

all about! If you're kinder to your own flesh-and-blood children and give them things you don't give the others, or see that they have more comfort than the other children, then you are being *partial* and *selfish* and *private!* With your selfishness and lack of sacrificiality you are striking at the very foundation of God's Family, and that kind of selfishness will destroy and undermine the unity of *The* Family as a *whole.*

23. IN OTHER WORDS, PARTIALITY TOWARD YOUR OWN WIFE OR HUS-BAND OR CHILDREN STRIKES AT THE VERY FOUNDATION OF COMMU-NAL LIVING—*against the unity and supremacy of God's Family* and its *oneness* and *wholeness!* What you're doing when you do that is whittling away and chopping off little chips and bits of *The* Family to separate them in *spirit,* and even sometimes in actually [*sic*], from the *rest* of *The* Family, just because they're *"yours"!*

From "The Family's Foundation: God's Law of Love"

The Family

The Lord's Law of Love

Jesus summarized the Law of Love in general terms in the above passage.[8] He expressed it again in His famous "Golden Rule": "So in everything, do to others what you would have them do to you, for this sums up the Law and the Prophets" (Matthew 7:12, NIV). Saint Paul echoed this when he said: "All the Law is fulfilled in one word, even in this: You shall love your neighbor as yourself" (Galatians 5:14). These biblical passages encapsulate the essence of all of God's laws and should guide all our actions and inter-actions with others. This is a belief that we in *The Family* hold in common with millions of other Christians around the world.

However, what distinguishes us from many other Christians is our firm understanding, from these passages and other scriptures, that loving God first and foremost and loving others is the ultimate fulfillment and com-pletion of Biblical law, including the Ten Commandments. Because, if we as Christians love the Lord with all our heart, soul and mind, and if we love others as we love ourselves, we will by nature fulfill the spirit of these other laws. For example, we won't put other gods before Him or take His name in vain. To love our neighbor as ourselves precludes murdering, stealing, lying to our neighbor, or coveting what he or she has. The motivation for Christians to obey these commandments is not out of fear of divine judgment, but rather because they are compelled to exhibit godly love and consideration for their neighbor. We refrain from such activities because doing so would not be in accordance with God's Law of Love.

We therefore hold as a basic tenet that if a person's actions are motivated by unselfish, sacrificial love—the love of God for our fellow man— and are not intentionally hurtful to others, such actions are in accordance with Scripture and are thus lawful in the eyes of God. "The fruit of the Spirit is love; . . . against such there is no law" (Galatians 5:22, 23).

Through the Lord's salvation and His Law of Love, Christians are released from the hundreds of rules under the Mosaic laws in the Old Testament and are no longer required to observe them. *Family* members do practice some aspects of the Mosaic Law out of common sense and as a part of love. For example, we refrain from eating unclean foods or engaging in unhealthy habits, such as smoking or over consumption of alcohol or food, because to do so would hinder our ministry to others.

The Law of Love Is a Stricter Code

In some ways, God's Law of Love is a stricter code of ethics than the old Mosaic Laws. The Ten Commandments stated that man was expected to act justly and righteously in order to avoid Hell and attain salvation. Under Jesus' Law of Love, much more is required of humankind—love and mercy. You do not attain salvation by "being good," but rather by inviting Jesus Christ to come and live in your heart, take over your life, and therefore let Him love others through you. "Not by works of righteousness which we have done, but according to His mercy He saved us" (Titus 3:5). "For by grace you have been saved through faith, and that not of yourselves; it is the gift of God, not of works, lest anyone should boast" (Ephesians 2:8–9).

This godly love is a much higher ideal to aspire to than mere religious righteousness. In the Mosaic Law, there was little forgiveness or mercy. It was "an eye for an eye and a tooth for a tooth" (Exodus 21:24; Leviticus

24:20). Jesus, to the contrary, said, "Do unto others what you want them to do unto you" (Matthew 7:12). Jesus even went so far as to say that we should love our enemies, pray for them and forgive them! (Matthew 5:38–44.) This ultimate application of the Law of Love renders it much greater and more profound than the old Mosaic Law.

In fact, Jesus' law is so much more difficult to keep that it's humanly impossible. This prompted Jesus to tell His disciples, "Without Me, you can do nothing" (John 15:5). But the Bible also tells us "we can do all things through Christ who strengthens us" (Philippians 4:13). Our founder, David Brandt Berg (1919–1994), in referring to this principle, wrote:

Jesus' law is much stricter [than the Mosaic Law], much more difficult to keep—in fact, impossible. If the old law was impossible, Jesus' law is even more impossible! . . . You can't possibly keep His Law of Love unless you're saved and you have Jesus in your heart, the Spirit of God's love within you, to give you the power and the strength to love others more than you love yourself." (ML #1968:35,36).

It's no easy task to live Jesus' commandments of love. To love the Lord with all our heart, soul and mind, to love others as ourselves, and to give our lives to others through daily loving sacrifice requires a life of self-sacrifice. To have this kind of love is only possible through the supernatural love of God.

The *Family's* governing Charter[9] summarizes this principle in its reference to the Law of Love, in stating that Family members are responsible to:

Endeavor to live by the principles of the Law of Love: To love, care for and interact lovingly and harmoniously with all members of the Home [community] in which they reside, and with Family members at large.

This clause in the Charter is one of the most important, as it sets the tone for all that is to follow. . . . Unselfish love—the love that puts the needs of others before our own, the great love that lays down its life for others, the Love of God in our hearts—that is the heart and soul of this Charter. ("Responsibilities of Individual Members")

Sex and the Law of Love

Jesus' Law of Love can also be applied to our sexual interaction with others. Although Christian scholars throughout history have explored this subject, applying the sexual aspect of the Law of Love sets *The Family* apart from mainstream Christian theology.[10]

Our founder, David Brandt Berg, further explored the theme that sexuality is not inherently evil in the eyes of God, and that loving heterosexual relations between consenting adults, even outside of marriage, are permissible as long as others immediately affected by these actions are not hurt. God created human sexuality, and *The Family* believes that our love for each other is an expression or illustration of God's love for us. As such, we consider sexual relations between consenting adults, which are carried out in love for one another, to be lawful in God's eyes.

It is our understanding of Scripture that Mosaic prohibitions and traditions in this regard no longer apply to God's children, who operate under Jesus' Law of Love. "Love does no harm to a neighbor; therefore love is the fulfillment of the law" (Romans 13:10). Consequently, *Family* adults, whether single or married, are free to partake of loving sexual relationships with other consenting *Family* members who are of age, provided their actions are done in love and with the agreement of others concerned.

We regard sex as a basic need, though the need for sex varies greatly from individual to individual. Married *Family* members, if they choose, interact sexually with singles within *The Family* because "the love of Christ constrains them"[11] to help their brother or sister in need, those who do not have a companion. Such giving is regarded as a sacrifice and is respected in *The Family* as being evidence of unselfish love. This ensures that everyone's sexual needs are being provided for in a clean, healthy, safe and loving environment. Married *Family* members also interact sexually with other married members, if they so choose.

Sexual sharing between Family members, whether single or married, with those other than their mates, does not have to be a "sacrifice" per se to be within the guidelines of the Law of Love. Members can partake in such sexual sharing to bring greater unity or additional pleasure and variety into their lives.

What About Adultery?

In presenting our views on the acceptability of sexual relations between consenting adults regardless of their marital status under the Law of Love, the question inevitably arises, "But what about adultery?"

In support of the view that such relations would be adulterous, some invoke the biblical story of the woman who was caught in the act of committing adultery and brought before the religious leaders to be stoned.

These leaders took her to Jesus and asked Him: "Teacher, this woman was caught in the act of adultery. In the Law, Moses commanded us to stone such women. Now what do You say?" Jesus responded, "If any one of you is without sin, let him be the first to throw a stone at her." Convinced by their own consciences, one by one her accusers left. Jesus ultimately told the woman, "Go and sin no more" (John 8:3–11, NIV).

The accepted interpretation of this is that since Jesus commanded her to sin no more, that He was in effect saying that adultery was a sin. We agree that it *was* a sin for her because she was under the Mosaic Law, and also because Jesus' fulfillment of the Law by His death on the cross had not yet been accomplished. Even so, the Lord forgave her for her sin, saying, "Neither do I condemn you" (John 8:11). However, the New Testament makes it clear that as Christians saved by grace, we are no longer bound by the Mosaic Law. If we are acting in accordance with the guidelines and restrictions of the Law of Love in that "love does *no* harm to a neighbor" (Romans 13:10), then there is no sin.

In stating our beliefs above, it is not our intent to assert that adultery no longer exists in the world today, or that all Christians must preach and practice the sexual aspects of the Law of Love. We acknowledge that the world is rife with adultery. For a sexual act of this nature to not be adultery, the act has to fall within the guidelines of God's Law of Love that have been stated above, and one must have received Jesus' freedom from the Mosaic Law by accepting His gift of salvation through grace.

Many spouses in secular society engage in extramarital affairs, contrary to the desires or knowledge of their spouse. These trysts result in broken trust and hurt feelings, and often destabilize marriages and result in broken families. Such behavior would be unacceptable in our fellowship, as it violates the basic principle of the Law of Love. Stepping outside of the stipulated boundaries of the Law of Love would contravene *The Family's Charter of Responsibilities and Rights*.[12] Although we are not bound by the Mosaic Law, our sexual interaction with others must be carried out in love and must not hurt others. If the guidelines for married members—having the willing consent of their spouse, hurting no one and doing all things in love—are not followed, then such behavior would be considered a sin.

From "Responsibilities of the Charter Home: Regarding Children and Parents"

The Family

Since the children and parents have certain individual rights granted them under the Charter, it becomes the *Home's responsibility* to work toward fulfilling those rights.

The Charter Home:

A. Shall have regard to the welfare of and allocate sufficient time for the spiritual, emotional, intellectual and physical development of its resident children, and provide resources, materials and personnel to fulfill these responsibilities.

Our children are a precious gift from the Lord and we must do all we can to ensure that they are well cared-for in every possible way. While it is *ultimately* the parents' responsibility to make sure their children develop properly, the Home's population is collectively responsible for the same. It is the Home's responsibility to schedule the time, and provide the resources and personnel, to provide the means for its children's spiritual, intellectual, emotional and physical development.

Obviously, a Home can only provide personnel as available within the Home. If they don't have enough Home members to help properly care for and teach their children, they should try to get extra personnel, or hire a tutor. If their schedule doesn't allow for enough Word[13] or school time, then they should revamp their schedule. If they don't have enough resources and materials for their education, then they should likewise pray, discuss and attempt to find ways to get whatever is needed. . . .

Once we establish that these children belong to all of us and God holds us all responsible, regardless of who physically bore them, we'll have a little more to work with, a few more people to work with, and we won't be giving all the responsibility—physical, intellectual and spiritual—to only the flesh parents. Even the System knows they have to share the responsibility of their children with the churches and the schools (ML #2670:15).

When it comes to our children, whether they have one parent or two, if they have a need, it's the job of all of us to be burdened and desperate about that need. These are our children, and we need to pray fervently for God's supernatural love that will help us to love them as we do our own natural children. We need to pray for them as we pray for our own, and be as desperate for solutions to their problems as we are for our own (ML #2953:4).

B. Provides, by whatever means, an adequate education for its resident children by allotting sufficient time, opportunity and educational materials for them to become competent in a manner appropriate to their age, ability and aptitude in the skills of reading, language arts, mathematics, social studies, science, practical-life skills and other curricular subjects.

. . . children are entitled to an adequate education; thus the Home is responsible to provide it by whatever means is available to them. Generally Homes will home school their children, which we have found to be the best method for schooling. However, there may be situations where it's not possible to do so, or the Home doesn't feel it has qualified personnel, in which case the parents and the Home could decide to get a private tutor or place the children in an outside secular or religious school. The decision to do so belongs to the parents, but the Home must be in agreement. . . . If the Home is not in agreement, the parents, of course, can use their *Right of Mobility* to remedy the situation.

We're for the most part trying to encourage them that they can teach their own children, have their own childcare workers and their own teachers if possible. If not, they can send them to the local System [school] if they have to! (ML #332B:80).

C. Allocates sufficient time for the keeping of the educational records of the resident children.

D. Keeps parents informed, on a regular basis, of the spiritual, physical and educational well being of their children under the age of 18 residing in it, regardless of the residence of the children's parents.
1. For resident parents, "regular basis" is determined by a simple majority of the Home.
2. For non-resident parents, "regular basis" is not less than once during every three-month period.

E. Allocates sufficient time for resident parents and children to have time together. . . .

F. Allocates sufficient time for the children to regularly engage in witnessing activities. . . .

G. Supplies sufficient assistance to resident parents in the physical and spiritual care and education of resident children. A two-thirds majority determines "Sufficient assistance."

> We're the only way He has of training and shepherding and parenting them. He's expecting us to do a good job of it, and He's holding us *all* responsible for the children He's given us. Each one of us is going to have to give an account to God for what we've done with our children. Have we played our part—no matter how large or small—faithfully, diligently, lovingly and responsibly? Have we done our best to help our children? (ML #2670:31).

H. Agrees together upon a discipline standard for its resident children that operates within the bounds of, and in accordance with, the *Child Discipline Rules,* page 247.

I. Supplies to its children a current address and/or telephone number of their non-resident parent(s).

J. Recognizes that a single parent faces the challenge of raising his or her children without the assistance of a spouse, and therefore may need additional assistance in supplying the physical, spiritual, emotional, educational, economic and disciplinary care of their children. Having recognized this fact, the Home endeavors to supply, to the best of its ability, additional assistance and to take into account the special challenges single parents face.

> . . . our single parents are faced with more difficulties in raising their children than couples are. Added to this, they can sometimes be tempted to feel that they and their children are a burden to the Home. With the enactment of this Charter, many single parents may fear that they will be voted out of, or not be accepted into Homes, because they may be considered a weight to the Home.

Many single parents already feel that they must almost do "double duty" by working extra hard in order to prove to the Home that they are a blessing. This, coupled with the fact that they must be both mother and father to their children, can be very taxing on them.

We must all recognize the difficulties and challenges that our single parents face and do all we can to help. We should put ourselves in their shoes and try to be loving and understanding of their and their children's needs, and our love should be "in deed and in truth" (1 John 3:18). We need to "bear one another's burdens" (Galatians 6:2).

Members of the Home individually and collectively are responsible to help supply the single parents in the Home with additional help in the care and raising of their children. *All* of the children in *your* Home are *your* children, because they are Family children. Every child needs a daddy and mommy, and if they don't have one, the Home and its members are responsible to help provide their needs. They might want to arrange for the single parent to team up with another single or a couple in a parenting teamwork so the single parent would have regular help with and counsel about their children.

Our Homes need to take into account that our single parents face a special challenge in the care of their children, and if any of our single parents are not able to carry the same weight in a Home as a married couple, or single person without children, the Home should be loving, compassionate and understanding.

In our society it is easier for a woman with children to live separately from her husband because she has the assistance of the Colony in the care of both herself and her children if the Colony so agrees. Even a man with children separated from his wife will receive assistance in the care of his children in our Colonies if the Colonies so agree (ML #359:15).

[Jesus,] do help us all to cooperate and do all we can to be unselfish and loving and kind and helpful to our young parents and their children. (Maria: And to our older single parents, Lord.) Yes, and to our older single parents who are usually women with children. Help us all to be more kind, unselfish, considerate and helpful, and the single men to help the single mothers and really be good fathers! (ML #2582:21).

NOTES

Excerpt from Paul and Nora Williams, *Women in The Family* (Zurich: The Family, 1996). Reprinted by permission of The Family International.

Excerpt from Moses David, "One Wife," October 28, 1972 Gp No. 249 (The Children of God, 1972). Reprinted by permission of The Family International.

Excerpt from "The Family's Foundation: God's Law of Love" (Zurich: The Family, 1993–2000). Reprinted by permission The Family International.

Excerpt from "Responsibilities of the Charter Home: Regarding Children and Parents," in *The Love Charter* (Zurich: The Family, 1998). Reprinted by permission of The Family International.

1. These three initiatives are discussed in Gordon Shepherd and Gary Shepherd, "The Family in Transition: The Moral Career of a New Religious Movement," paper presented at the 2002 CESNUR International Conference, Salt Lake City and Provo, Utah, June 20–23, 2002 (quotation from p. 4).

2. Ibid., 8.

3. David Berg, the founder of the Children of God.

4. Karen Zerby (Maria) was Berg's second wife and became one of The Family's co-leaders after Berg's death.

5. ML #501:50; 4/76. [Note in original text. "ML" refers to the Mo Letters, the correspondence between Berg and the Children of God that began in 1969.]

6. See "Flirty Fishing—The Inside Story"—a series of testimonies of lives changed through FFing. [Note in original text.]

7. Probably in reference to 1 Corinthians 7:2: "Nevertheless, to avoid fornication, let every man have his own wife, and let every woman have her own husband" (KJV).

8. Matthew 22:35–40.

9. Our Family Charter is comprised of two main components, the "Charter of Responsibilities and Rights" and the "Fundamental Family Rules." These outline the most important principles, goals and beliefs of our movement and codify its method of government. [Note in original text.]

10. For further information, please write us for copies of "Christianity and Sex"—parts 1 and 2, in the Family's *Christian Digest* series. [Note in original text.]

11. 2 Corinthians 5:14.

12. See the Sex and Affection rules in our *Charter of Responsibilities and Rights* for details on our *Family* rules and policies about implementing the Law of Love among our members. [Note in original text.]

13. A reference to the Bible, or to Family materials specifically designed for children.

FOR FURTHER READING

Chancellor, James D., *Life in the Family: An Oral History of the Children of God* (Syracuse, N.Y.: Syracuse University Press, 2000). The standard scholarly history of The Family, based on extensive interviews with members.

The Family: Making a Difference, http://www.thefamily.org. The official Website of The Family, also known as the Children of God.

Lewis, James R., and J. Gordon Melton, eds., *Sex, Slander, and Salvation: Investigating the Family / Children of God* (Stanford, Calif.: Center for Academic Publications, 1994). A collection of essays by scholars on controversial aspects of The Family.

Williams, Miriam, *Heaven's Harlots: My Fifteen Years as a Sacred Prostitute in the Children of God Cult* (New York: William Morrow, 1998). An ex-member tells of her experiences in The Family.

World Services, *The History of the Family* (Zurich: World Services, 1995). The official account of The Family.

Chapter 8

Santería

Santería is the popular name for one of many orally based religious traditions of the African diaspora in the Americas. It is also called Lucumí, from the Yoruba for "friend," and the *orisha* (deity, guardian angel) religion. Other religions of the African diaspora include Candomblé in Brazil and Vodou in Haiti. Santería originated among Afro-Cubans, most of whom were descendents of Yoruba people from urban centers in western Africa (specifically, modern-day Nigeria) who were enslaved in the eighteenth and nineteenth centuries and shipped to Cuba to work on sugar plantations. The first practitioners of Santería combined traditional Yoruba beliefs and practices with the Roman Catholicism of Spanish Cuban culture, and later with the Spiritist tradition of Allan Kardec (1804–1869), which emphasized communication with the dead. Kardec, a French occultist, published many books about the spirits that were translated into Spanish and disseminated in the Americas. Afro-Cuban practitioners of Santería met in secret to avoid the attention of the Spanish authorities. Although slaves were permitted to retain their African beliefs, they were told that God sanctioned Spanish Catholic rule, and the Church assumed that eventually those of African descent would convert to Catholicism. Santería indicates that the conversion process was never complete. Free people of color, especially in Cuban cities, formed *cabildos* (social clubs) based largely on tribal affiliations, and it was among these groups that Santería first arose.

Santeros (feminine form, *santeras*), as practitioners and priests of Santería are called, believe that the original source of all life, the energy that maintains all things in balance and harmony, is *ashé*. Western notions of good and evil find little purchase here. *Santeros* recognize situations in which a lack of harmony needs to be corrected, but absolute evil is foreign to the worldview of Santería. *Ashé* finds expression in the high god of Santería, Olodumare, from whom all *orishas* are descended. Olodumare does not interact directly with human beings, but he is behind and within all interactions between humanity and the *orishas*.

The *orishas*, most of which are derived from Yoruba culture and history, are the various manifestations of *ashé*, and thus of Olodumare. A diverse group of multidimensional deities, they represent all aspects of the universe. Their powers are limited, but they nonetheless exercise great influence over human affairs, often acting as guardian angels. Typically, the multiple dimensions of an *orisha* will include an identification with the Virgin Mary or with a particular Roman Catholic saint. Although these identifications helped early *santeros* survive in Cuba by masking their religion under a veneer of Catholic piety, they also represent a genuinely syncretistic strategy that is consistent with Santería notions of the multiple manifestations of each *orisha*.

An extensive body of folklore and legend called the *patakís* tells stories about various *orishas*. These texts provide the narrative grounding for each individual's appropriation of an *orisha* and especially for the outcome of divination. For example, Obatalá is the creator *orisha*, sometimes described as Olodumare's son on earth. He can manifest in many forms, from the aggressive warrior Ayáguna to the weak old man Oshalufon. He has also been identified with the Virgin Mary and may take feminine forms. Elegba or Eleggua is the *orisha* who watches the earth for Olodumare. Elegba links humanity with Olodumare, knows the destiny of each human being before birth, and has a childlike disposition that comes out in his many ways of testing an individual's faith. Ogun is the *orisha* of war and iron. He blesses many professions and crafts, from hunting to warfare, surgery to blacksmithing. His Roman Catholic manifestation is St. Peter. Oshun or Ochun is the *orisha* of rivers. She has a sensual and hedonistic nature, capable of more caprice than all the other *orishas*. She controls the flow of blood in the body and is associated with the heart. She is manifested in the Catholic domain as Our Lady of Charity. Shangó is the *orisha* of thunder and fire, his sign the double-headed ax. Shangó, like Ogun, is associated with war. He is Olodumare's avenger, punishing those who upset the balance of *ashé*. *Patakís* relate his amorousness and virility, of which he is boastfully proud. Yemayá is the *orisha* of the sea. She oversees fertility and reproduction. In one legend she gave birth to Elegba, Ogun, Oshun, and other *orishas*. Like the ocean, she can be calm in one situation, yet as destructive as tidal waves in another.

In sum, *orishas* are diverse, multidimensional, and represent all aspects of the universe. They are the manifestations of *ashé*, and thus Olodumare, in many forms. Their powers are limited, but they nonetheless exercise great influence over human affairs. In the Santería cosmos, the next level of entities below the *orishas* are the ancestors. Some ancestors eventually become *orishas*, but most reincarnate into the human sphere. As ancestors, however, they watch over their earthly families, and if properly respected in ritual, they can be a great help to *santeros*. At the lowest level of power, below humans, are plants and inanimate objects, which in their own ways contain *ashé* and thus contribute to the universal drive toward harmony and balance.

Santería is a religion that is primarily enacted through ritual, although the *patakís* referred to above are also important. In rituals, *santeros* experience many things: solutions to immediate problems, rites of passage to the next level of participation in Santería, closer identification with specific *orishas* with whom they are destined to be linked throughout their lives. Divination is an important aspect of Santería ritual life, and one to which *santeros* often turn when they cannot solve a problem by other means. At the simplest level, divination can be accomplished by reading the arrangements of coconut pieces (*obi*) after they have been thrown. More complex forms of divination have also developed, such as using brightly colored sea shells (*dilogun*). The toughest problems are referred to a *babalawo*, a specialist who is trained to decipher the secret nature of situations and relationships through a complex divination process called Ifá. This is the highest level of human initiation, and *babalawos* are treated with great respect within Santería communities.

Another ritual form involves sacrificing food. Each *orisha* is associated with specific foods, vegetable or animal. Offerings made to *orishas* seal their commitment to help a human initiate with a specific problem. In Hialeah, Florida, in the 1990s, the city government passed ordinances forbidding the killing and torturing of animals. These ordinances were aimed at local *santeros* who had sacrificed animals. In the Supreme Court case that resulted, the *santeros* won, and Hialeah had to overturn its ordinances. Nonetheless, animal sacrifice remains one of the most controversial aspects of Santería today, especially in the United States.

Following the Communist takeover of Cuba in 1959, many *santeros* fled to the United States. What had been a traditional religion, deeply rooted in Cuban history, became an NRM in the American context and served as a cultural and political marker for Afro-Cubans intent on maintaining symbolic (and literal) ties to Cuba. Today Santería has become an international NRM, with practitioners in many countries besides the United States and Cuba. This internationalization of the movement has led to ritual and doctrinal diversity, so that the description of Santería given here merely serves as a general introduction based on the most traditional beliefs and practices. In the United States, *santeros* include African Americans, white Americans, Americans from various Caribbean islands, and others. As the movement has diversified, Santería's Spiritist component, also called Espiritismo, has become increasingly important.

In its American context, Santería has served the same subversive function that it originally served in Cuba: to enable those with little social and political power, or those who perceive themselves to be deprived in some manner, not only to survive, but also to thrive in hopes of a better future for themselves and their progeny. Furthermore, Santería offers a profoundly communal way of achieving this goal, and it is for this reason that we have included it in the New Family category in this volume.

The family emphasis probably evolved early in Santería's history, during slave times, when Africans brought to Cuba were separated permanently from their families and had to form new familial bonds in order to survive the harsh conditions of slavery. It continues today, wherever Santería spreads. The *santero* is surrounded by and enmeshed in familial relationships with a host of other entities: *orishas,* ancestors, fellow initiates, priests and priestesses, and parental figures—both human and nonhuman. Within Santería communities, each individual is assigned a godmother and godfather who shepherd the *santero* through initiations and through life in general. In addition, each individual is destined to be guided by two *orishas* who act as both guardian angels and spiritual "parents." Initiates are possessed by guardian *orishas* in trance states that, to the untrained observer, may seem bizarre and frightening. For *santeros,* however, such experiences are both natural and essential if one is to progress in this life.

Not surprisingly, the author of the book from which the following excerpts are taken, an Afro–Puerto Rican woman named Marta Morena Vega who grew up in the United States, discovered her Santería family as she immersed herself in the world of Santería. Vega, founder of the famous Caribbean Cultural Center in New York City, had been an educator and advocate for Puerto Rican culture when she recalled certain powerful memories of her family's past, especially of her *abuela* (grandmother), who had a Santería altar in her home. After an eventful adulthood that had included marriage, children, a graduate degree, teaching, and the founding of the Caribbean Cultural Center, as well as the deaths of her mother and grandmother, Vega decided to embrace the religious and cultural heritage of her people (for Santería had spread to Puerto

Rico) more deeply. The book that is excerpted here is Vega's account of her personal transformation.

In the first excerpt, Vega and an old friend, Javier, attend a Santería ceremony in Cuba during which Vega is overwhelmed when her deceased mother communicates with her. In the next excerpt, Vega learns from her godmother, Zenaida, about the *orisha* guardian angels who will guide her. In the third excerpt, we are introduced to Vega's godfather, Elpidio. In the fourth excerpt, Vega hears the testimony of an elderly *santero* whose guardian is Shangó. In the fifth and sixth excerpts, Vega tells of her own initiation, culminating in the advice given to her by one of her guardian *orishas,* Ellegua, through a priestly diviner named El Chino.

From *The Altar of My Soul: The Living Traditions of Santería*

Marta Morena Vega

I was still curious to learn more about the practices of Espiritismo and Santería, so I accompanied Javier as he made preparations for his ceremony. I was invited to attend a *misa* [séance], a spiritual session that would inform his guardian angels of his upcoming Ifá initiation ceremony. I found myself sitting in a room filled with spiritualists and initiates of the Santería religion. The apartment belonged to the spiritual medium Olga Serrano; it was located between Animas and Trocadero in Old Havana. Olga was a long-trusted friend of Javier's family, and he had asked her to arrange the *misa.* Her home was decorated in shades of yellow—the colors of her *orisha,* Ochun. Olga's living room felt as if it were filled with sunlight and bright golden sunflowers.

Surrounded by the familiar scents of Florida water, sandalwood incense, and cigar smoke, I thought of Abuela and of my mother, who always dabbed her forehead with Florida water when she had a headache or felt pain in her chest. It had been twenty years since Abuela had died, and fifteen years since my mother had passed. Looking around the room, I noticed familiar images that also reminded me of my childhood. A portrait of Saint Michael, the archangel, was placed behind the entrance door. She had installed a small shelf. On it she placed a horseshoe alongside a glass of water and a piece of hard bread. On a small table toward the back of the room, Olga had a large statue of El Kongo, similar to the one on my *abuela*'s altar. The smell of tuberoses permeated the room and mixed with the poignant smell of sandalwood incense.

Olga's altar to Ochun was in a small room next to the living room where the *misa* was to begin. The altar, covered in yellow lace cloth, had two peacock-feather fans and a vase filled with sunflowers next to the image of La Caridad del Cobre, the Catholic image that served to hide the Yoruba goddess during enslavement and continues to be identified with the African divinity. Ochun, the *orisha* of sweet water, love, beauty, and fertility, exudes happiness and gaiety surrounded by her favorite color, yellow. High on a stool covered with satin brocade cloth was a covered yellow porcelain bowl that held the sacred water stones of Ochun. On the floor was a small brass bell resting on a straw mat, which initiates were to ring when they asked Orisha Ochun for her blessings.

After embracing Olga, the initiates took turns gathering in the room, prostrating themselves before the altar and ringing the bell to ask Ochun for her blessings. Then they returned to the main room to greet friends and to introduce themselves to unfamiliar members of the gathering. I was struck by the congeniality and familial feeling of this bustling group. Dressed in white, proudly wearing their beaded necklaces, old and young seemed strengthened by the ancient wisdom they possessed.

Elder men and women in their late eighties were given special attention, in honor of their long years of initiation and profound knowledge. Their cottony white hair, gray-aged eyes, and tissue—thin black skin made them appear deceptively fragile, while at the same time they seemed to glow with clarity of mind and confidence. These unassuming elders projected an aura of serenity and coolness that was reminiscent of my grandmother and my mother.

Throughout my travels I met with elders much like these in Brazil, Haiti, Trinidad and Tobago, New Orleans, Puerto Rico, Santo Domingo, and in other countries throughout the world. They have developed an inner power and strength that quietly blankets their environment with a special, magical aura of peace. This desired quality acquired over time requires that initiates set aside a period of time to meditate and acknowledge the *orisha* that resides within—the Orí—who represents our destiny.

With tremendous pride, Javier introduced me to the Iyalorisha Mina, a longtime friend of his deceased mother. She was a thin old woman, bent with age from many years of harsh work. Ma Mina herself had been initiated by a once-enslaved African woman who taught her the ancient secrets of the African *orisha* initiation. Javier explained that she spoke Yoruba and had initiated more than fifty people into the religion.

Wearing a long white dress, her head covered with a kerchief trimmed in nine colors. Ma Mina gently held my hands. She slowly looked up, gazed intently into my eyes, and said, "The spirits of my ancestors have been good to me. Oyá, the *orisha* that claimed me, has guided me since I was ten years old. *Orisha* is love, *orisha* is health and family; do not be afraid to learn about your ancestors, because in knowing them you learn about yourself." Thanking her, I gingerly took my seat, trying to comprehend why she had directed this message to me. I wondered if she knew something I did not.

The *espiritista* Olga began the *misa* with a series of Catholic prayers from *The Collection of Selected Prayers* by Allan Kardec, a nineteenth-century French educator and philosopher well regarded in the spiritualist community. A short, husky woman with curly black hair and cashew smooth skin, Olga exuded cheer and friendship. Olga was a *santera* as well as an *espiritista*. She was initiated into the Santería religion and was a medium who could be possessed by spirits of the ancestors. She explained that Ochun saved her life when complications arose during the birth of her first child. She praised and loved her *orisha*; however, her true gift was as an *espiritista*. When she sat down in front of the group, all chatter quickly ceased. Silence fell over the room as she started the session.

Softly, the twenty-five people present began to pray with Olga and joined in the songs to attract the spirits. The room was soon filled with a thick, gray-blue haze as most participants leisurely smoked their cigars. One by one, participants went before the *bóveda*, scooped up perfumed water and flower petals from the white enamel basin on the floor, and cleansed their auras with this Florida water mixture while the others began reciting prayers. The pleasant murmuring of the prayers lulled me into a pleasant tranquillity. When everyone was seated, the songs started. Then, suddenly, my soul stood on edge as I again heard the songs calling the spirits. It was the same beautiful song that I had heard for the first time during my mother's illness.

Congo de Guinea soy.
Buenas noches, criollo,
Congo de Guinea soy.
Buenas noches, criollos,

Yo dejo mi hueso allá.
Yo vengo a
hacer caridad.
Yo dejo mi hueso allá
Yo vengo a
hacer caridad.
Si la luz redentora te
llama, buen ser.
Y te llama con amor a
la tierra.
Yo quisiera ver a ese ser,
Cantándole gloria al
Divino Manuel.
Oye, buen ser.
Avanza y ven,
Que el coro te llama
Y te dice, ven.

I am a Congo from Africa.
Good evening, creoles,
I am a Congo from Africa.
Good evening, creoles,
I left my bones there.
I have come to perform a
good deed.
I left my bones there.
I have come to perform a
good deed.
If the redeeming light calls
you, good spirit.
And it calls you with love
to Earth.
I want to see that spirit,
Singing gloriously to the
divine saint Manuel.
Listen, good spirit.
Hurry and come,
The chorus is calling you
Asking you to come.

When I looked up at Olga, she had gone into a trance, swaying gently back and forth on her chair. She tossed her head back, massaged the left side of her chest with her right hand, and started foaming at the mouth. From a low hum, she began to moan loudly.

Suddenly, her short body grew lean and tall. I was shocked. Without a word being spoken, I somehow knew my mother was present in that room. And her spirit began to speak through Olga.

"Marta, I am glad that I am finally able to speak to you. I have waited a long time for this moment. The time has come for you to assume your spiritual responsibility and open your heart to the *orishas*. My beloved family is being destroyed because I refused to follow the calling of the spirits. You must assume your spiritual calling. Open your heart and let the spirits and the *orishas* guide you. Always remember that I am by your side."

The *misa* began my spiritual journey into the teaching of the spirits and Santería. My memory of the first encounter with my mother's spirit deepened with time, and the lessons she shared became clearer as I learned more about the power of the spirit world. I have learned, for example, that spiritual energy can be inherited; therefore, it is important that we learn as much as possible about our ancestral history. I also learned not to dwell in the past. In order to heal, it was necessary to accept and leave the pain behind me. The deep love I held for my childhood family was to be cherished forever; however, I had to accept that it no longer existed in the same form. It was necessary for me to help re-create a new, healthy family that would assist in healing and nurturing the future generations that would be born into our family.

The need to move on, to re-create and transform our reality, does not disrespect our past but rather honors it. Too many of our people have suffered and withstood pain so we could inherit their spiritual guidance and create a better world for our children. Every time we allow negative energy to interrupt us or distract us from a positive path, we dishonor our ancestors and the sacred powers. To grow spiritually, we must work with our guardian angels to build positive, functional lives. Part of the process is understanding the dynamic and ever-changing forces in our lives. Change is a symbolic form of dying; it is the elimination of the dysfunctional parts of our lives through acceptance. Acceptance spawns invigorating ideas that encourage new behavioral patterns, creating an environment of spiritual renewal. Renewal requires letting go of unnecessary grief so that space is free for nurturing new, exhilarating thoughts.

Mother's spirit helped me to understand that sometimes we must experience physical pain to appreciate better and make full use of the limited gift of life we have on Earth. She explained it is through identifying our guardian angels that we learn to better comprehend our behavior.

Before I was initiated into Santería, my godmother, Zenaida, held a *misa* to identify my spirit guides. When I asked why this was necessary, my godmother explained, "We all have spirits who protect and guide us. They present themselves to the living in many forms. Sometimes you hear an invisible inner voice guiding you; other times an intuitive feeling protects you from harm. There are times when you are alone in a room and feel that someone is there. In spiritual sessions, *misas*, the spirits have the opportunity to speak through a medium and give direct advice to the living. Spirits that are enlightened led a healthy life on Earth. These are spirits that are honored by the family and friends and through prayers and rituals; these spirits gain enlightenment and are in turn helpful to the living. Those spirits who have led unhealthy lives often have family and friends who ignore them in their prayers and do not place candles in their honor. These spirits are confused and afflicted in the afterlife. They bring chaos into the lives of the living.

"Each of your guardian angels, *cuadro espiritual,* is made known to you in a special *misa.* If one of your spirits was a professor in life, in the afterlife that spirit will help you with your studies. It could be that one of your spirits was initiated into the Santería religion. That spirit will encourage and help initiate you into the religion and share the knowledge that it possesses with you. Perhaps one of your guardian angels was an artist, and now the spirit is sharing this talent with you. We will determine this in the *misa.*"

My godmother urged me to do my part to create a positive spiritual future for my family by nurturing my guardian angels while on Earth. She told me that we must all live actively, fulfilling our earthly and spiritual obligations, because this is what prepares us for our afterlife. Like the spirits, we have many roads that we travel simultaneously, and these paths eventually converge into the totality of our complex identities.

Sitting around the kitchen table drinking coffee, listening to the teachings of Elpidio and Zenaida, I felt as if I were back in my home in El Barrio, and I easily entered into a casual conversation. Javier, amused by the meandering way his godfather dispensed his wisdom, remained quiet. "My daughter, today you witnessed the power of the spirit world. You mother's spirit touched you. It is ultimately your decision if you accept her guidance. As you are a studious person, I know you want a precise account of what occurred." Trying to find the right words, Elpidio hesitated, then cautiously said, "You want an analytical explanation that makes scientific sense. This is not possible. When you live with the spirits, when you embrace *orisha* and feel it work, then you know they exist."

He explained that spirit visitations are generally made by family members and close friends. Elpidio further explained that spirit-time spans generations. Therefore, possession by spirits who lived long ago is a common occurrence. When I asked how the *orishas* differ from the spirits, he smiled and said, "Think of them as spirits that reached the highest level of evolution and were transformed into the forces of nature. They are the elements that give us life. They are nature itself."

Inspired by his explanation, Zenaida said, "The paths of the spirits and *orishas* require lifelong study, dedication, and commitment. When you are claimed by the spirits and *orishas,* you are destined for a divine journey filled with spiritual responsibilities. Today was just the beginning."

Continuing his orientation session with me, Elpidio said that we are all born with guardian angels and *orishas.* "It is our task in life to connect both to our spirits and to nature's energy forces in order to have health, happiness, and prosperity in our lives."

Zenaida added pensively, "When the soul and body are healthy and your state of mind is positive, everything is possible; nothing can stop you."

I was gradually coming to understand that when the spirits and *orishas* claim you, it is a blessing that brings significant responsibilities. Both Zenaida and Elpidio assured me that there was nothing to fear. It was their belief that a positive religious journey opened up pathways to new knowledge that helped the seeker find prosperity on Earth and in the spirit world.

Elpidio and Zenaida's love of Espiritismo and Santería was evident in their dedication to protect and pass on the religion through both their natural and religious families. Throughout the day, people came seeking advice and guidance from both of them. Their home was a meeting place and a temple, a crossroads for Santería worshipers, who ranged from teachers and artists to government workers and community folk. I could feel the apartment vibrating with *aché,* facilitating conversations among divergent groups, providing direction and information that could assist initiates in finding out about future rituals and social events.

Elpidio would generally sit in the back bedroom with his godsons, discussing at length the complex and profound meaning of the *odus* and *patakís*, the literary poems of Ifá. He explained that it is the responsibility of the Ifá priest to study each of the sixteen major *odus* and their meanings, in order to develop the skills necessary to help solve the problems of clients. He explained that the patterns represented by the *odus* allow the diviner to identify the *pataki* that will provide a solution to the practitioner's problem. He also confided that while it is important for the priest to have an engaging and tender manner in order to put his clients at ease, ultimately it is the success of his predictions that makes people return for advice. Elpidio's manner was usually very soothing; however, I noticed that when the situation required his admonishing a client for not following Orula's instructions, he did not hesitate to show great strength and determination. I was discovering that the philosophy embodied in the legends of the *orishas* remained central to the religion. In my later travels to Brazil, I found that diviners there also hold an esteemed position in the religious community. Unlike in Cuba, women in Brazil are prominent members of the circle of diviners. Casting cowry shells and *obí*, four coconut pieces, women in Brazil are equal in skill to their male counterparts.

According to historians, the Portuguese in Brazil feared the power of the *babalawos* among enslaved Africans, and they hunted the holy men down and killed them. Priestesses in Brazil rose to fill the void. When I visited the Yoruba sacred city of Ile Ife, Nigeria, in 1981, I learned that unlike the Cuban religious system, women were allowed to initiate in the Ifá system once they had completed menopause. Observing Zenaida as she assisted Elpidio in his preparations, it was evident that she had mastered the meaning of the patterns. . . . Her eyes sparkled with understanding, as she silently formed the names of the *odus* that appeared on the divining tray—the *opon* Ifá. For me, the varying ways that practices have survived in the Americas reflects the strength of the *orishas* to adapt to the conditions they found in each country.

Other times, Elpidio would show his godsons how to consult with the divining chain for a client. As the elder, he would watch as his godsons divined and provided the advice that was dictated by the symbols of the *odu* and accompanying poems. Always pushing the boundaries of his godson's studies, Elpidio would then add poems and possibilities for interpretations they had not considered. A loving father and mentor, he made certain that all of his students continued to think and expand their information base. Elpidio constantly indicated to us that Santería is a religion that requires study.

"The more we learn, the more we understand what we need to know," was Elpidio's mantra. His favorite way of stressing the point was to say, "No one knows what is at the bottom of the ocean—Yemayá is the only one who knows what is in her house. It is up to us to discover what secrets she holds, if she allows us to. All the *orishas* have a wealth of information to offer us, and we can figure it out only when we dedicate ourselves to studying."

Often, he would show us his library of books and endless files of stories he had accumulated over the years, all neatly catalogued according to the symbols of divination. Since he had godchildren and friends spread throughout the world, Elpidio constantly received books and research papers that further expanded his studies. When he locked himself in the back room, everyone knew to remain quiet and respect his study time.

In the living room, Zenaida would generally gather with women friends as they cleaned the rice and black beans and seasoned the meat for ceremonial feasts. In the kitchen, men and women gathered to prepare objects that were needed for rituals. Sometimes *elekes* [beads] were strung; other times they made raffia curtains to cover the entrance of a ceremonial room. . . .

"I was a weak, sickly, skinny child, given to blackouts. My parents took me to see doctors and specialists to find out the cause of my weak condition. My parents were not Santería practitioners, nor did they attend ceremonies. They were faithful Catholics.

"One day, our next-door neighbors held a ceremony for Shangó. The drummers were playing the *batá* drums with so much power that the walls by my bed vibrated. The rhythm of the drums and Shangó put me into possession. Shangó took me into the ceremony, saying that I must initiate immediately in order to save my life. He wanted to cure my sickness.

"Friends at the ceremony told my parents of Shangó's message. Desperately concerned about my worsening health, they decided to follow Shangó's instructions. My parents arranged immediately to have our neighbors perform the initiation ceremony. Shangó kept his promise; he cured me during the first week of my initiation. The blackouts stopped, food remained in my stomach, and soon I regained my strength. Let me tell you, by the end of the week I had gained five pounds. When I was presented to the community at the coming-out ceremony, *el día del medio,* everyone was amazed at my healthy, robust appearance. *Maferefun Shangó,* praise be to Shangó. To this day, my *orisha* has kept his word.

"In life, Shangó was a king of the city of Oyo," Guillermo told me. "Shangó was born a warrior, and that is why he carries the *oché,* the double-headed ax, on his head. Shangó is amiable, loves to dance, and is the owner of the *batá* drums. He celebrates life to the fullest and, therefore, does not want to know of suffering or death. He controls fire and manifests in nature through thunder and lightning. One of the powers of Shangó that is not often spoken of is his generosity. When his children are in trouble, he comes to the their rescue." As I listened to Guillermo that day, it occurred to me that *patakís* are a way of establishing a common set of values, and a code of ethical behavior for the international community of initiates. Through these stories, issues that most of us face on a daily basis are addressed and resolved. The *orishas'* escapades are very human and provide ways of addressing interpersonal relationships.

Our time with Guillermo was part of a centuries-old process of sharing and building community. He knew that Zenaida would bring only visitors that she deemed worthy of his knowledge and time. As it came time to leave, Guillermo reminded us, "*Orisha* is love, faith, and commitment." Zenaida told him we were going to meet with Panchita. As Guillermo escorted us to the door, he waved good-bye and told us to give Panchita his regards. . . .

Since I was considered a child, Zenaida and Virginia [Zenaida's godmother] dressed me for my public presentation. The dress slipped smoothly over my body. My crown felt heavy on my newly shaved head. Bracelets identifying the *orishas* I had received were placed on my arms. The metal bracelets chimed gently as I moved around the room trying to adjust the layers of crinoline that held up the bell-like shirt of my dress. Zenaida and Virginia were my eyes since I was not allowed to look into a mirror. They fussed over me, making certain I looked perfect.

Zenaida called in Laura [Vega's sister], who was waiting to see me. As she carefully pulled back the curtain and entered, I could see the sign of relief in her eyes. Laura had not seen me since her arrival in Cuba and had been unaware of the lengthy religious ceremonies I would undergo. She was understandably frightened and apprehensive as she watched the activities from afar. As she was the only member of my family able to attend my initiation, I was grateful for her courage in supporting my decision to initiate.

"You look absolutely beautiful," were her first words as she marveled in amazement at my appearance. "It is unfortunate that the rest of the family is not here to witness this important step in your life," Laura continued, as she walked around, admiring the dress.

"That is why it is so important that you are here," Zenaida remarked as she fussed with the crown on my head. "There is at least one who is the eyes for the whole family."

"How do you feel?" Laura asked.

Trying to find the right words, all I could say was, "Renewed."

When we were ready to leave the room, Zenaida placed a white *iroke* [fly whisk] in one of my hands and a white lace fan in the other. Pleased with my appearance, they were ready to present me to the religious community.

They escorted me to the front room, where I saw an elaborately decorated altar in honor of Obatalá. Constructed in the corner of the room and draped in the ceremonial cloths lent by the elders, the throne was magnificent. Like a nineteenth-century parasol, it was covered with lace, intricately embroidered materials, and decorative doves, creating an environment of dignity and elegance. The artist who had constructed the throne had created roselike swirls from lace cloth, letting streamers of white satin ribbon erupt from the center. In place of the porcelain bowl with the sacred stones at the center of the altar, I would sit on a stool covered with white satin cloth, in my ritual dress, and the altar would become my throne. The throne radiated pride and pulsated with an energy that engulfed the room.

Zenaida and Virginia helped position me on the stool, spreading the skirt of my dress and placing my hands in a comfortable position to hold the *iroke* and fan for the long celebration. "Remember, my daughter, Obatalá is a king, and you are his daughter. You are royal and reflect his *aché*," Zenaida whispered as she arranged my dress. I felt magical.

The room was filled with well-wishers. The elders who had spent the night were the first to acknowledge my initiation. Family and godchildren of Zenaida, Elpidio, and Virginia had arrived, lending a festival atmosphere. I was reminded of my childhood Christmas celebrations in El Barrio when everyone assembled to enjoy one another's company; the rhythmic voices were the music, and their laughter the instruments. So it was with this gathering. Although there was no music, the chattering voices were like the flow of a dance beat. The saucy smell of hot food filled the air as the clatter of dishes joined in the escalating noise of the room.

Well-wishers graciously blessed me, as five *iyawos* [novices] sat on the floor surrounding me. The others entertained themselves with the most recent gossip, while the *iyawos* and I talked about our initiation.

Sonia, a middle-aged mother of three who had initiated four months before, began the conversation, saying, "Electrical currents were running through my body as I sat on the throne. I was in a dream world. When my husband saw me on the throne, he cried with happiness, telling me I looked more beautiful than on our wedding day."

Then Tina, a small, perky teenager, joined in the conversation. Speaking with a nervous giggle, she said, "I initiated six months ago. When I sat on the throne dressed in the ritual dress of Yemayá, I felt like a queen. I didn't want to take off the dress at the end of the day."

Mario, a strong mulatto man in his thirties, smiled and thought carefully before he shared his experience. "I am a father of two children and have a wonderful, devoted wife. Before initiation I was always in nightclubs, had many women, and didn't attend to my family. Going home drunk one night, I was hit by a car and hospitalized with a broken leg. The doctors thought they might have to amputate my leg. I asked a *babalawo* friend of mine to divine for me to see if there was anything that the *orishas* could do. Oggun stood up for me in a divination session and said he would repair my leg, but I must initiate soon after leaving the hospital. He also said that I must change my life and take care of my family. Oggun has tested me this year. I avoided getting into fights. I've been faithful to the rules of the religion. I get home early, don't drink, and have not gone to nightclubs. My home life is wonderful, and it has been a very peaceful year," he said with a smile.

Virginia was right; I would never forget this moment. I felt spiritually engulfed by my ancestral lineage, family, and community. Like the others, I did not want the day to end. That evening, I was escorted back to my room by my godmothers.

Visitors came all during the week, sharing their memories of initiation. The feeling of rebirth I was experiencing and the sense of being guided onto an enlightened path were reaffirmed in the stories they told. During my week's stay, Zenaida took every opportunity to share information with me, and she gathered material for me to study when I arrived home, including a series of mimeographed pamphlets developed by initiates.

Although I missed my family, it felt wonderful to have this glorious time to revel in my thoughts and surrender the responsibility of making decisions. My godmothers cared for me completely during this first week. I lived in a small space on the floor, sleeping, eating, and studying, and I was able to think and examine the meaning of my initiation and how my life would change. I did not worry about daily chores like selecting clothing, fixing my hair, preparing food, finding shoes, or looking in the mirror to check my appearance. During this week the responsibilities of taking my children to school, getting to work on time, writing proposals for funding deadlines, and cleaning the house were not a problem. My former life seemed to be eons away. . . .

The next morning was similar to the previous one. After I showered, Virginia prepared breakfast and accompanied me, while Zenaida and Elpidio prepared for the divination session of initiation on the day of *itá* [a divination for the initiate], *El Dia de Itá*. Virginia warned me that it would be a long session, but a rewarding one. Each of the *orishas* I received would reveal their names through the cowry shells of the *oriate* [the priest who presides at the initiation ceremony], the *santero* diviner, and my future would be determined by my *orishas* through the pattern of the shells.

We entered the room of initiation, where tureens containing the sacred stones of the *orishas* born on the day of my initiation lined the walls. The *oriate* sat on a straw mat on the floor. On a low stool next to him sat Justina, who was to record in a book the names of each of my *orishas*, their prophesies, my new African name, and the names of the witnesses present.

Virginia explained that special care is always taken to make certain that these readings are conducted by expert *oriates*, because this reading would establish the foundation of special rules that would guide my life. Virginia cautioned that when I received the book, the *libreta*, it would be a detailed record of the way I must behave the rest of my life.

"It is your personal bible, your detailed horoscope," she added, trying to explain the profundity of my *itá*.

A tall, thin Asian man nicknamed El Chino welcomed me into the room. In a scene that reminded me of the photographs I had seen of the Afro-Asian visual artist Wilfredo Lam, El Chino was surrounded by the elder *santeros* and *santeras*. I sat on a low stool facing him, with my bare feet placed on the straw mat. When he began to move the sixteen cowry shells in his delicate hands, everyone stopped talking and focused their attention on him. El Chino began sprinkling drops of cool water on the ground, reciting the prayers calling the ancestors and then Ellegua to guide his hands.

Acknowledging all the *santeros* and *santeras* in the room, he then turned to me and asked, "Do you understand the significance of the *itá?*"

"Yes," I responded. "My *orishas* will talk to me through the cowries. I will be told how best to guide my life, things I should do and things I shouldn't do. What to eat for my health and which foods will be harmful to me."

Satisfied with my response, El Chino continued with the reading. Casting the *dilogun,* cowries, on the straw mat, he carefully studied the patterns. The patterns of the *dilogun* kept changing as he gathered them in his hands and gently let them fall again. The pleasant rustle of the cowries in his hands was the only sound in the room. With measured words he began to speak.

"Ellegua says to be cautious with your business negotiations. Read everything three times before signing any papers. Try to finalize your business negotiations during the day when the sun is bright. Ellegua says that when the time comes, he will bring many godchildren to your door. You will be very surprised at the large *orisha* house you will have." El Chino ended by saying, "Your Ellegua wants to be surrounded by toys, and he promises to care for you as long as you care for him.

"Oyá says to organize yourself totally. In your home, job, and social life, you must place everything where it belongs. She warns that your lack of organization will one day publicly embarrass you. Oyá says you should dress in white as much as possible. She wants you to place a tiger skin over your Shangó. Oyá tells you not to eat fried food. She says fried food is not good for your digestive system." With a shy smile that revealed his sparkling gold tooth, he said, "You enjoy fried food?"

"Yes." I nodded.

"Well, Oyá is telling you to stop immediately," he said gently. "Ochun is saying that many people talk about you. Whether it is good or bad do not worry. This is good for you; it means that people have to think about you. You are not invisible to the world. Ochun tells you that once you have made a decision, stick to it. She tells you to beware of where you eat. Your food must not be of the extremities of the animal. No tail, feet, or head. Do you understand?"

"Yes, I don't eat those parts anyway," I responded.

"Ochun is telling you not to start," El Chino murmured. "Yemayá tells you to honor your spirits; they will bring you health. When you have problems, go to the sea and tell Yemayá your problems. She will listen and help you to solve them. Yemayá tells you to make certain that you repair anything that is broken in your home. If it cannot be fixed, throw it out. Yemayá says to document everything you do; you will find out one day how important your notes will be.

"Shangó says that you must live your life without desperation. You must be calm in the face of adversity. Always leave with plenty of time to get to your location. He doesn't want you to rush anywhere; it is with calculated calm that things will come your way." El Chino then added, "When you leave a place, never return immediately. Walk around the block, come back the next day. Avoid making hasty decisions.

"Obatalá wants you to be very respectful of children. Children will bring you joy and all that you desire. Embrace your children and yourself every day. Remember that Obatalá's domain is all that is white in the body. Go for checkups regularly, especially your eyes and teeth. Obatalá says that he wants you to give a *tambor* for the spirits of your mother and grandmother, because they are very close to you and are pleased with this important step you have taken."

Casting the shells, he determined that the road of my *orisha* was Obatalá. He said, "Obatalá Ayáguna, the young warrior, is your *orisha*. He is like Shangó, but younger and more daring. Ayáguna will protect you in times of crisis."

Without commenting, I realized that Yemayá's prophecy was already occurring; my dreams were predicting and confirming events before they happened. I had already known that Ayáguna would claim me.

"Do you have any questions?" El Chino asked tenderly as he looked from me to my godmothers. Then he asked Zenaida, "What name do you want to give your daughter?"

"*Adufora*," she said.

Casting the shells, he said, "Obatalá accepts."

As he gathered his divination objects, El Chino advised, "Make certain that you follow the instructions of your *orishas* for life; in helping yourself, you also protect your family. Having these sacred powers in your possession will radiate in everything you do. I wish you the very best," and then went to embrace Zenaida and Virginia.

"My daughter, the *orishas* have spoken clearly," said Zenaida. "It is your responsibility to follow what has been said."

NOTES

Excerpts from Marta Morena Vega, *The Altar of My Soul: The Living Traditions of Santeria* (New York: One World / Ballantine, 2000). Reprinted by permission of the author.

FOR FURTHER READING

Bascom, William, ed., *Sixteen Cowries: Yoruba Divination from Africa to the New World* (Bloomington: Indiana University Press, 1980). A collection of Santería stories and legends compiled by a noted scholar of the movement.

Mason, Michael Atwood, *Living Santería: Rituals and Experiences in an Afro-Cuban Religion* (Washington, D.C.: Smithsonian Institution Press, 2002). A study of Santería that blends scholarly discussion with personal account by an initiate.

Murphy, Joseph, *Working the Spirit: Ceremonies of the African Diaspora* (Boston: Beacon, 1994). An excellent scholarly treatment of Santería and other religions of the African diaspora in the Americas.

Santeria, http://sparta.rice.edu/~maryc/Santeria. A scholarly Website with reliable information about Santería.

Part IV

New Societies

Chapter 9

The Rastafarians

The roots of the Rastafarians, who emerged in Jamaica in the 1930s, run deep not only in that country's colonial history, but, as they see it, in the lost history of the once great African people themselves. Jamaica had been home to more than 700,000 slaves. Even after the end of the slave trade in 1838, its population was largely rural and destitute. A large-scale urban migration between 1920 and 1960 to Kingston, the capital, did not improve the average Jamaican's socioeconomic status; in fact, the dire conditions in the city exacerbated their frustrations and brought them into more direct conflict with their white overseers' legal and educational systems.

The early Rastafarians were strongly influenced by Marcus Garvey (1887–1940), a Jamaican-born black nationalist leader whose Universal Negro Improvement Association (UNIA) advocated for the return of all peoples of African descent to Africa—and specifically to Ethiopia, which was understood to be the site of the original, and superior, human civilization and hence home to all black men and women now scattered by the diaspora of slavery. The key theme of return to a homeland after liberation from slavery echoed loudly in the ears of a people who, in many parts of the world, had not only been enslaved, but also immersed by Christian missionaries in the freedom narrative of the Jews. Garvey's movement was primarily political, but it inspired a number of religious figures, including Alexander Bedward (1840?–1930) and Robert Athlyi Rogers (d. 1931), to designate Ethiopia not only as the true homeland of the black race, but also as Zion, the "True Israel." (Rogers's 1924 rereading of Garvey's program as sacred revelation, *The Holy Piby,* is excerpted below.) This convergence of religious and political symbolism effectively identified all blacks as both Ethiopians and Jews. Drawing on the role of Ethiopia in the Old Testament (see, e.g., Psalm 68), these theologians adopted an alternative biblical narrative according to which the Queen of Sheba (i.e., Ethiopia) has a son by King Solomon of Israel. The Queen returns to her homeland not only with her boy, David, who is recognized as a prophet and a king like his father and grandfather—King David, his namesake and Israel's ideal king—but also with the Ark of the Covenant, hence establishing Ethiopia as Zion, the Seat of Jah (the shorter form of the name Jehovah or Yahweh), with all descendants of Ethiopia—that is, all blacks—as members of its royal family. A portion of this narrative is reprinted below from *The Kebra Nagast*, known as the "lost Bible of the Blackman."

In 1929, Garvey held a UNIA Convention in Jamaica, and soon a Garveyite-Athlyi (Gaathlyi) church had been established there. The following year, Ras Tafari Makonnen (1892–1975) was crowned emperor of Ethiopia as Haile Selassie I ("Power of the Trinity") and given the messianic titles "King of Kings, Lord of Lords, Conquering Lion of the Tribe of Judah, Elect of God, and Light of the World." Hence, the stage was set to read this event as a divine signal for black repatriation. Selassie came to be seen as God incarnate, the Black Christ, appearing on earth for the fourth time (after Moses, Elijah, and Jesus Christ) to bring his children home and wreak vengeance on their white oppressors, in the model of the avenging Christ of the Book of Revelation. (This image is also reinforced by the description of the conquering divine figure with "hair like wool" in Daniel 7:9.) The white-dominated systems of government, police, education, and religion—that is, the institutions of British rule, which lasted until 1962—became known collectively as "Babylon," alluding to the wicked Gentile empire that destroyed the royal line of David and Solomon in ancient Jerusalem, sending the Jews into exile. "Babylon" also returns in the New Testament Book of Revelation to identify the oppressive empire persecuting the righteous in the end times. In fact, in a parallel to the theodicy (theory of suffering) that emerged among Jews to explain their exile in Babylon, Rastafarians believe that the black peoples also disobeyed God and hence were exiled from Ethiopia, handed over to the whites to be enslaved. The Rastafarians' appropriation of these biblical symbols neatly combines both the Jewish and Christian narratives of oppression and ultimate justice into one, underscoring their view that biblical history is really black history, much of which has been distorted by whites to justify their dominance. Rastafarians insist, however, that only they have the key to interpretation that will show what the Bible truly means.

Those who saw Selassie as the living God incarnate ushering in the new age of his Kingdom on Earth believed that they, like their God, would not die. When Emperor Selassie visited Jamaica on April 21, 1966, the date quickly became an official Rastafarian holy day, as did his birthday and date of coronation. These dates are celebrated with parties called *Nya-bingis,* or *bingis* for short; part ritual dance, part spontaneous drum-and-chant session, and part anticolonial political performance, they bring Rastafarian religious and political expression together at their peaks. However, the Emperor's removal by a coup in 1974 and, immeasurably more so, his death in 1975 predicated some serious theological reinterpretation. Most Rastafarians have since understood that Jah simply left his incarnate form at that time and continues to be with each individual as an eternal presence.

The first Jamaican to proclaim the divinity of Haile Selassie, Leonard Howell (1898–1981), tied this belief to Garvey's strident anti-colonial, pro-African stance. In fact, Howell is widely regarded as the founder of the Rastafarian religion proper (which, obviously, borrows Selassie's precoronation name as its own), and his "Six Principles" to a great (if not overt) extent define the movement to this day:

1. Hatred of the White race;
2. The complete superiority of the Black race;
3. Revenge on Whites for their wickedness;
4. The negation, persecution, and humiliation of the government and legal bodies of Jamaica;
5. Preparation to go back to Africa; and
6. Acknowledging Emperor Haile Selassie as the Supreme Being and only ruler of Black people.

Unsurprisingly, Howell's stances drew negative attention from the British authorities in Jamaica, and he was arrested for sedition. While in jail, Howell borrowed heavily (most would say plagiarized) from Rogers's *The Holy Piby* and Rev. Fitz Balintine Pettersburgh's *Royal Parchment Scroll of Black Supremacy* to write the religious text *The Promised Key.* Upon his release, he founded a secluded Rastafarian commune in the Jamaican hills. The Pinnacle, as it was called, fostered a number of the practices that make the group distinctive, both in Jamaica and elsewhere. Members stopped combing their hair, forming "dreadlocks," long mats that are both symbolic of the mane of the Lion of Judah and evocative of the biblical hero Samson. Dreadlocks represent a direct affront to the white social order; a short-haired white or black "baldhead" is seen as having acquiesced to the corrupt world. Pinnacle members also farmed *ganja,* or

marijuana, which became a quintessential part of "reasonings," the Rastafarian name for sacred discussions of politics, religion, and events of the
day. In this ritual setting, ganja not only acts as a mellowing or meditative agent, but is also thought to open up one's true self—a cosmic consciousness that is a part of Jah Himself. It is also seen as the "herb" given
the divine stamp of approval in the Bible (see Genesis 3:18; Proverbs
15:17). However, outsiders might warily note that ganja's only practical
effect may be temporarily to enhance individual and communal self-
esteem and provide a brief respite from the often devastating conditions
of daily existence.

While Rastafarianism as a whole has no overarching structure or organizational leader (even Haile Selassie himself was not a member), the
Pinnacle legacy established a strict, patriarchal, theocratic, "Zionic" social
order of its own among members. This order is largely based on certain
Old Testament regulations, as befits Rastafarians' self-identity as the true
inheritors of Israel's covenant with God. Nowhere is this more clear than
in the taboos against women, or the "sistren," who are to defer to all men
of any age. Rastafarian men believe that women take a man's spiritual
essence during sexual intercourse. They also believe that women can con-
taminate them with dangerous powers during their monthly periods;
hence, women are not allowed to cook during these times. Today, however,
women are pushing for their own liberation and equality within Rastafarianism, with slow but measurable success. The Old Testament influence is
also found in the Rastafarian men's refusal, like many Orthodox Jews, to
cut their hair or beards (see Leviticus 21:5) and in certain dietary restrictions. Pork is strictly prohibited, alcohol and tobacco use is discouraged,
and vegetarianism is promoted. One recent trend promotes a diet based
on *Ital* foods, said to be purer and better for one's vital essence, or "Ital."
On the other hand, Rastafarian communities also centrally value mutual
assistance, collective ownership, nonviolence, and antimaterialism, forms
of resistance ritually vocalized as "chanting down Babylon."

In fact, Rastafarian beliefs and practices are to a large degree actualized
in language. The use of the word "I" and its combination with other words
to make new ones is the essence, as it were, of the famous Rastafarian dia-
lect known as Dread Talk. "I" is that aspect of oneself that is also divine,
part of the incarnate Jah, Haile Selassie I (hence, they say, the "I" at the end
of his name). In that manner, all Rastafarians are also unified with each
other; "I" overcomes all separation between members. We is expressed "I

and I" and is indicative of a special consciousness or connection with Jah and the "I's" around you. You becomes "the I." Other words are reimagined, too: eternal is "Iternal"; creator is "Ireator"; and divine is "Ivine"; not to mention "Ises" (praises or prayers), "Ithiopia," and "forIver," seen in the prayer "Ises unto the Most High—Haile I Sellassie I," below. To feel good, especially on ganja, is to be "Iru." Rastafarian wordplay is expressed in countless other ways as well: politics is referred to as "politricks," oppression is "downpression," and understanding is "overstanding."

The Rastafarians' sense of spiritual play and political justice gained a worldwide audience with the explosion of reggae music on the world scene in 1970s, led by songwriter and musician Bob Marley (1945–1981). Robert Nesta Marley was born into the rural poverty that had originally given birth to the Rastafari movement, but both as a child and an adult experienced the slums, oppression, and racism of Kingston. Like his wife, Rita, and his bandmates, the Wailers, he accepted the Rastafari message after Haile Selassie's visit to Jamaica in 1966 (though Marley himself was in the United States at the time of the visit), becoming a member of the more progressive Twelve Tribes of Israel sect. All his life Marley had been immersed in the Bible, Jamaican folklore, and then the vision of an incarnate Black God calling his people back to Africa, and his music is steeped in all of these influences. While non-Rastafarians are rightly captivated by the feel-good messages of love and the sinewy melodies, beats, and bass lines, the unflinching political message is loud and clear, especially in songs such as "Crazy Baldheads," "Babylon System," "Exodus," "Natty Dread," "Duppy Conqueror," "Jump Nyabingi," "Jah Lives" (written after the death of Haile Selassie), and the traditional "Rastaman Chant," whose lyrics, adapted from *The Holy Piby,* are reprinted below. Marley's popularity around the world, and especially in America, also spurred a fascination with Rastafarian culture, although all too often it has been reduced to dreadlocks and ganja. Be that as it may, as Afrocentric as Rastafarianism is, whites are not excluded from joining. Individual whites are not evil in themselves (just the "Babylon system" they perpetrate), and like blacks, they only need a spiritual awakening of their own divine I to Jah's power and the rightness of His prescribed lifestyle. Converts are often called "manifests," in light of their own personal manifestation of the divine.

The central vision of a global, holy New Society for the black race, regrouped as a nation in "Zion" (an idealized, heavenly Ethiopia), figures prominently in the excerpts below. But equally clear is how thoroughly the

Rastafarian individual is reborn in the divine I—a New Self who is a God-man and King-man with a cosmic, interconnected "I-and-I" conscious-ness. Furthermore, the communal living of the "bredren" and the "sistren" —that is, the "Ithren"—and its assurances of reciprocity and caretaking demonstrate just how much of a New Family each of the various sects and communes provides for its members. Yet underpinning all of these ele-ments is the messianic/millenarian hope for a reign of peace on earth, once all the Children of Ethiopia are brought home to Zion to reclaim their rightful place over a New World devoid of the racial strife caused by the wicked white race. To this end, some believe the whites will wipe themselves off the face of the planet with nuclear weapons.

While reading the excerpts below, it is important to keep in mind just how little of the Rastafari tradition depends on the written word. Rastafar-ians live in a world of orality, as suggested by their wordplay and echoed in the texts reproduced below, as well as in reggae music in general. Both *The Kebra Nagast* ("Glory of the Kings" in Amharic, the national language of Ethiopia, thought by Rastafarians to be the original human language) and *The Holy Piby* rework the narrative and legal traditions of the Bible. The former, said to have originated in Ethiopia in the sixth century c.e. and been compiled by the Coptic church,[1] explains how Ethiopia came to be favored by God over the Israelites because of the establishment of the Ark of the Covenant and the Solomonic line of succession there, and also because they did not reject the incarnation of Jah as Jesus. *The Holy Piby* parallels the visionary callings of Old Testament prophets and apocalyptic seers and concludes with a list of Holy Commandments, several of which allude to the Ten Commandments. It must also be recalled that while these texts clearly influenced the rise of the Rastafarians, they were not specifi-cally produced by the movement; however, much in them is also found in the sacred practice and daily life of Rastafarians. For example, in addition to adhering to the aspects of the Israelite Levitical code advocated in *The Kebra Nagast*, Rastafarians' "livity" (sacred lifestyle) also reflects the text's emphasis on compassion, nonviolence, and rejection of materialism. In addition, language from the *Piby*, including "The Shepherd's Prayer," has been incorporated into daily prayers as well as reggae lyrics. (The prayer of praises to Haile Selassie, itself underscoring many Rastafarian social con-cerns, that opens the edition of *The Holy Piby* used here is also included.) With Bob Marley's popularity continuing long after his death in 1981, *The Holy Piby* and other proclamations of Rastafarian wisdom are sure to remain influential far beyond the small population of actual adherents.

From *The Kebra Nagast: The Lost Bible of Rastafarian Wisdom and Faith from Ethiopia and Jamaica*

Gerald Hausman, editor

After he slept, there appeared to King Solomon a dazzling vision. He saw a brilliant Sun come down from heaven and shed a great splendor over Israel. There it stayed for a time, but suddenly withdrew itself and flew away to the country of Ethiopia, where it shone brightly forever. Solomon waited to see if the brilliance would come back to Israel but it did not return. Then, while he waited, a light rose up in the heavens and another Sun came down in the country of Judah, and it sent forth light which was much stronger than before.

Now Israel, because of the flame of that Sun, refused to walk in the light thereof. And that Sun paid no heed to Israel and the Israelites hated Him, and it became impossible that peace should exist between them and the Sun. And they raised their hands against Him with staves and knives, and they wished to extinguish that Sun. Thus they cast darkness upon the whole world. And earthquakes came and thick darkness. They had destroyed His light and they set a guard over His tomb wherein they had cast Him. And He came forth where they did not look for Him, and illumined the whole world. Those places most bathed in His light were the First Sea, the Last Sea, Ethiopia, and Rom [*sic*]. And He paid no heed, no heed whatsoever to Israel, and he ascended his former throne.

When Solomon the King saw this vision he became disturbed. His understanding went away and he woke with a troubled mind.

The Queen [of Ethiopia (Shebah)] said to Solomon, "Let me depart to my own country." Solomon gave her camels and wagons and had them laden with beautiful things. He also gave her a vessel wherein one could traverse the sea, and a vessel wherein one could traverse the wind—these Solomon made by the wisdom which God gave him.

And when [Solomon's and the Queen's son] David saw the Lady Zion,[2] he proclaimed, "Wherever you go, salvation shall be in the house and in the field. Salvation shall be in the palace and the lowly hollow. Salvation shall be on the sea and on the desert sand. Salvation shall be in the high mountains and near hills. Salvation shall be in the heavens and on the earth. Salvation shall be on firm ground and in the empty abyss. Salvation shall be in death and in life, and it shall be in thy coming and thy going forth, and it shall cover our children and our tribe. Salvation shall be in the country and in the city, and shall touch both king and beggar, fruit and plant, man and beast, bird and creeping thing. And from this time forward, our Lady shall guide us, teach us, and give us understanding and wisdom, so that we may learn to praise each day, every day, every night, every hour, and all the length of time. "Rise up Zion, give us strength, our Queen, for you are the habitation of the God of Heaven." Thus spoke David the King, the son of Solomon, King of Israel. For the spirit of prophecy descended upon him. And he knew not what he said. And everyone who listened marveled and said, "This son of a prophet has now become one himself."

Then, early in the morning, the wagons rose up and resumed their journey as before; and the people sang songs to Zion, and as the people of Egypt bade them farewell, they passed before them like shadows. And the people of Ethiopia took their flutes, horns, and drums, and the noise of their instruments smashed the idols of Egypt. These were in the forms of men, dogs, and cats. And the idols fell off their pedestals and so broke into pieces. Figures of birds made of gold and silver fell down and were broken.

And the people came to the sea of Eritrea, the Red Sea, and when the holy Zion crossed over, the sea received them, and its waves were as whitecapped mountains which were split asunder, and the sea roared as the loudest of lions and made a noise like the winter thunder of Damascus. And the sea worshipped Zion. But while its billows grew into mountains, the wagons of Ethiopia were raised above the waves, and the sound of the breaking sea mingled with the sounds of the people's horns and drums. And whales and fishes came forth and worshipped Zion. And birds flapped through the froth, and there was joy in the sea of Eritrea.

And they arrived opposite Mount Sinai and remained there while the angels sang. The children of the earth raised their voices in song and psalm and their tambourines made joyful noise. Then they loaded their wagons and rose up and journeyed until they came to the country of Ethiopia. And as they traveled, Zion sent forth a light like that of the sun and it penetrated the darkness.

When Zadok the Priest returned to Solomon the King, he found him sorrowful. And the king told him, "When the Queen of the South came here I had a night vision. It seemed as if I were standing in the chamber of Jerusalem. And the sun came down from heaven to the land of Judah and lighted it up with great splendor. And having tarried a time it went down and lighted up the country of Ethiopia, and it did not return to the land of Judah. And again the sun came down from heaven to the country of Judah and it lighted it up more brilliantly then before. But the Israelites paid no heed to it and they even wished to extinguish its light and now it rose below the earth in an unexpected place. And it illumined the country of Ethiopia."

Zadok the Priest then answered the King, saying, "Oh my Lord, Why did not you tell me this before? Something has happened to our Holy Lady, the heavenly Zion. Truly, I fear it."

And the king said, "Our wisdom is forgotten and our understanding is lost. The sun that appeared to me long ago when I slept with the Queen of Ethiopia was surely the symbol of the Holy Zion."

"The splendid covering that was lying upon Zion, I took it off," said Zadok. "But I did not trouble myself to look under the two coverings that remained."

"Go quickly and look at our Lady," said the King. "Examine her closely."

Zadok the Priest took the keys and opened the house of the sanctuary, but there he found nothing except the wooden boards which Azarayas had put there. These resembled the sides of the pedestal of Zion, but when Zadok saw them he fell forward on his face and dropped into a coma.

Now it came to pass that when David the son of Solomon returned with the Ark of the Covenant, he met his mother Makeda and she granted that he should be King of Ethiopia. She saw that he was his father's son, and she spoke then of the great wisdom she had learned from the King.

"Wisdom," she said. "I have drunk from her but have not fallen. Because of her I have dived down into the great sea and have seized in her depths a pearl whereby I am rich. I went down like an iron anchor and I found a lamp which burned in the dark water. And I came up to breathe the air of understanding. I went to sleep in the depths of the sea and lay becalmed as upon my own bed wherein I dreamed a dream. And it seemed to me that there was a star in my womb, and I marvelled at it, and I laid hold upon it and made it strong in the splendor of the sun. I went into the deep well of knowledge and drew for myself the water of wisdom. I went into the blaze of the sun, and I made a shield for myself cast from my understanding. And my confidence is not for myself only but for all of those who travel in the footprints of wisdom, for the Kingdom of Ethiopia and all the nations around us."

And the Queen said to her son, "Speak to me of what you know."

And Azarayas, the son of Zadok the Priest, spoke for King David when he said, "We see that the country of Ethiopia is better than the country of Judah.

"Your waters are good and are given without payment, the air is fine without fans, and the wild honey is as plentiful as the dust of the market-place.

"You are black of face and God is the light in your heart, therefore nothing can do you harm. You do not touch meat that dies of itself, nor blood, nor the bodies torn by wild animals.[3]

"But now you must hearken to God, the holy one of Israel, and do this good pleasure, for he has rejected our nation and has chosen you. Hearken well unto his command which I will now declare to you.

"Let no one overcome another by violence. Take no possession of your neighbor. You shall not revile each other, not oppress each other, and you shall not quarrel amongst yourselves. And if, by chance, an animal belonging to your neighbor should come to you, then make it go back to him. And if a man is carrying a heavy load, you should not pass on your way until you have helped him to lift it up or lighten it for him, for he is your brother.

"You shall not turn aside the rights of those who are unfortunate. You shall not take bribes to turn aside the right and bear false witness. You must remember to treat all creatures both wild and domestic with kindness, so that your days may be long upon the earth. And when you shall harvest, you shall not take all, but will leave something for the stranger in your city. And you shall not work with impurity, nor judge with partiality, nor deal with one another oppressively. For the law of God has commanded that there will be a curse on the worker of evil. And over and above all of these things you shall worship no other gods. Blessed are those who listen to the voice of God and obey his commandments, and blessed are those who turn aside from those who do evil. Blessed is the one who gives up his possessions unselfishly and who teaches others to do so as well.

"And this is what you shall eat: Every creature with a cleft hoof and the creatures that chew the cud. And those which you shall not eat among those so mentioned are the camel and the hare.

"The pig you shall not eat, for the hoof is cleft, but they do not chew the cud.

"Whatever is in the water with fins and scales, you shall eat.

"Whatever is unclean, that which lives in the shell, you shall not eat.

"Among birds, you may eat everything that is clean; but those that are unclean, those that eat meat themselves, you shall not eat.

"You shall not eat things that fly and spring and have six feet, namely grasshoppers and locusts.

"Now these things we have declared to you, so that you may be blessed in your country, which God has given you because of the heavenly Zion. Because of Her you have been chosen and blessed. He will bless the fruit of your land and He will multiply your cattle and He will protect them in everything wherein they are to be protected.

"And as for you, My Lady, Makeda, your wisdom is good, and it surpasses the wisdom of men. There is none that can be compared with you, not only in the intuition of women, but the understanding of your heart is deeper than that of men. And there is no one who compares to you in the abundance of understanding except my Lord, Solomon.

"For you have drawn the Tabernacle of the Law of God,[4] overthrown the house of idols, cleansed what was unclean among your people, and driven away from them that which God would not bless."

So ended the speech of Azarayas to Queen Makeda.

And Azarayas said, "Bring here the trumpets and let us go to Zion, for there we will make a new kingdom for our lord David."

Then he took the oil of sovereignty and anointed David. And they blew horns, pipes, and trumpets, and beat drums, and there was singing and dancing, and the people were glad of heart. And all of the men and women of Ethiopia were present, the small and the great, and those to whom glory was given in that sunlit land.

So in this way the kingdom of David, the son of Solomon, was renewed in Mount Makeda, in the House of Zion, where the Law was established for the first time by the King of Ethiopia, and where it flourished because of the devoutness of the people.

And the people of Ethiopia prospered because of their belief in the Lord; and when the Pearl, the Son of the Lord, was born, He wrought many signs and wonders.

He raised the dead and healed the sick, and He made the eyes of the blind see again.

And He performed miracles which were written down, and miracles which were not recorded, and therefore miracles which no one knows.

But the wicked of Israel thought He was a man and they were envious of Him, and they decided to kill him. Yet as we know, He was only a man so that the people might see Him. For when the Pearl passed into His mother, He was not visible, but He became so only because mortal man had need of Him, and had to see Him as other men are seen.

And the people of Ethiopia were loved by God because the Savior of the World, His Son, was beloved by them. And in the time when He was reborn to redeem Adam, they believed the signs and wonders that He wrought, though the people of Israel did not believe them. And for this reason God has deeply loved the people of Ethiopia.

From *The Holy Piby: The Blackman's Bible*

Robert Athlyi Rogers

The Second Book of Athlyi Called Aggregation

Chapter 1: Heaven Grieved

For as much as the children of Ethiopia, God's favorite people of old, have turned away from his divine Majesty, neglecting life economic, believing they could on spiritual wings fly to the kingdom of God, consequently became a dependent for the welfare of others.

Therefore the whole heaven was grieved and there was a great lamentation in the Kingdom of God. Ethiopian mothers whose bodies have been dead for a thousand years, weeping for their suffering generations and shall not be comforted [*sic*].

And behold two angels of the Lord resembling two saints of Ethiopia appeared before Athlyi and he inquired of them what is the cry?

And they answered him saying, Ethiopian mothers who have been dead a thousand years pleading before Elijah for the redemption of suffering Ethiopia and her posterities who by the feet of the nations are trodden.

ETHIOPIA ANOINTED

And when the two messengers of the Lord were midways they cried out unto the earth saying, blessed be thou Ethiopia for this day thou art anointed, thou art blest with a blessing, be ye forever united and stand up, let the world know your God.

And when the two angels of the Lord neared the multitude the whole host roared with a thunder of joy that shook the earth like a mighty earthquake.

And it came to pass that an angel robed in four colors came forward to receive them and the whole celestial multitude stood and quietly formed an aisle.

And when the two messengers appeared before the heavenly host they bowed to the multitude and turned themselves around and bowed also to the earth.

Then came forward the mighty Angel robed in four colors and placed a gold ring upon their heads, and came forward also two mothers of Ethiopia, each with a star in their right hand, and pinned them on the left breast of the two messengers of the Lord.

And it came to pass that heaven and earth shook three times and the two angels marched up the aisle and joined with the multitude.

REJOICING IN HEAVEN

There was great rejoicing in Heaven and singing hosanna to Elijah; praise ye Douglas;[5] blessed be thou Ethiopia forever and forever; the people at the end of the known world, and world unknown, shall look for the coming of thy children with food and rainment [*sic*].[6]

And when the two angels had joined the multitude and the mighty angel had finished his performance the said angel who was robed in colors turned to the heavenly host and said:

"Mothers of Ethiopia, the convention has triumphed, your sorrows have brought joy to Ethiopia, your tears have anointed her soil with a blessing, your cries have awakened her children throughout the earth, yea in the corners of the unknown world are they aroused, and is [*sic*] prophesying, saying prepare ye the way for a redeemer."

Chapter 3: God's Holy Law to the Children of Ethiopia

Great and manifold are the blessings bestowed upon us the oppressed children of Ethiopia, by His Divine Majesty, Lord God Almighty, King of all mercies, when by his most holy command His divine highness, Christ, Prince of the Heavenly Kingdom, descended and anointed us that we may be prepared to receive these noble men, servants of God and redeemers of Ethiopia's posterities. His honor, Marcus Garvey and colleague, his holiness the shepherd Athlyi, supreme minister of God's Holy Law to the children of Ethiopia, may we show gratitude to our God by being submissive to his teachings through these his humble servants, and submitting ourselves in obedience to his Holy Law that we a suffering people may reap the fruit thereof.

When as it was the intention of others to keep us forever in darkness, by our faithfulness to the Law we shall in time prove to the nations that God has not forsaken Ethiopia.

THE HOLY COMMANDMENTS

I. Love ye one another, O children of Ethiopia, for by no other way can ye love the Lord your God.

II. Be thou industrious, thrifty and fruitful, O offsprings [sic] of Ethiopia, for by no other way can ye show gratitude to the Lord your God, for the many blessing he has bestowed upon earth free to all mankind.

III. Be ye concretize[d] [sic] and ever united, for by the power of unity ye shall demand respect of the nations.

IV. Work ye willingly with all thy heart with all thy soul and with all thy strength[7] to relieve suffering and oppressed humanity, for by no other way can ye render integral service to the Lord your God.

V. Be thou clean and pleasant, O generation of Ethiopia, for thou art anointed, moreover the angels of the Lord dwelleth with thee.

VI. Be thou punctual, honest and truthful that ye gain favor in the sight of the Lord your God, and that your pathway be prosperous.

VII. Let no people take away that which the Lord thy God giveth thee, for the Lord shall inquire of it and if ye shall say some one hath taken it, ye shall in no wise escape punishment, for he that dieth in retreat of his enemy the Lord shall not hold him guiltless, but a people who dieth in pursuit of their enemy for the protection of that which the Lord God giveth them, shall receive a reward in the kingdom of their Father.

VIII. Thou shalt first bind up the wound of thy brother and correct the mistakes in thine own household before ye can see the sore on the body of your friend, or the error in the household of your neighbour.

IX. O generation of Ethiopia, shed not the blood of thine own for the welfare of others for such is the pathway to destruction and contempt.

X. Be ye not contented in the vineyard or household of others, for ye know not the day or the hour when denial shall appear, prepare ye rather for yourselves a foundation, for by no other way can man manifest love for the offsprings [sic] of the womb.

XI. Athlyi, Athlyi, thou shepherd of the holy law and of the children of Ethiopia, establish ye upon the Law a Holy temple for the Lord according to thy name and there shall all the children of Ethiopia worship the Lord their God, and there shall the apostles of the shepherd administer the law and receive pledges thereto and concretize [*sic*] within the Law. Verily he that is concretized within the Law shall be a follower and a defender thereof, more-over the generations born of him that is concretize within the law are also of the law.

XII. O generation of Ethiopia, thou shalt have no other God but the Creator of Heaven and Earth and the things thereof. Sing ye praises and shout Hosanna to the Lord your God, while for a foundation ye sacrifice on earth for His Divine Majesty the Lord our Lord in six days created the heaven and earth and rested the seventh; ye also shall hallow the seventh day, for it is blessed by the Lord, therefore on this day thou shall do no manner of work or any within thy gates.

RASTAFARIAN PRAYER, BASED ON *THE HOLY PIBY*'S
"THE SHEPHERD'S PRAYER"

Prince and princesses shall come out of Ithiopia
Ithiopians shall stretch forth their hands Unto JAH
Oh thou JAH of Ithiopia
Thy Ivine Majesty,
Thy spirit come into our hearts and
bless us, Lead us,
Teach us to love, Teach us to forgive
Teach us love, loyalty on earth as
It is in Zion.
Endow us with thy wise mind,
knowledge and overstanding,
to do thy will
Thy blessing to I-n-I
That the hungry be fed
The naked clothed
The sick nourished
The Aged protected, and
The infants cared for.

Iliver I-n-I from all evil
When our enemies are passed and decay,
In the depths of the earth,
In the depths of the sea, or
In the belly of a beast.

Oh JAH
Give I-n-I a place in thy everloving
Kingman, Forevermore.[8]

ISES (PRAYERS) UNTO THE MOST HIGH—
HALIE I SELLASSIE I [SIC]

For if one day its [sic] coffee
   The next day may be tea
but if there is nothing at all,
ALMIGHTY, I-n-I will still give thanks to
     Thee;

For the Court-House and Judges have
set their hearts against the children
   of the Most High, and
   no Justice can come
   from unholy men;

The Police and warders have all
taken an oath of allegiance to
   persecute I-n-I.

The Politicians have pledged
Loyalty to the whoredom, babylon queen,
   and so pass laws to suppress the
   children of the Most High.

False Leaders of the earth, have
taken council against Haile Sellassie I and against
   I-n-I His anointed saying
   Let us break their bands asunder
   and cast away their chords from us.

But the ALMIGHTY saw it all
   and transformed them into faggots, whores
   and vipers with maggots eating-out their
   brains, and JAH have crowned I-n-I,
     The Prince of Peace
     The Rose of Sharon
     Wonderful, Mighty and
Blessed children, to dwell within the Garden of

Zion, where the Lion and the Calf
Dwell together.

Where International Morality
   has prevailed
where I-n-I never cease the chant and
Glorious things are written.

   HOSANNA
   HOSANNA

Blessed is the King of Ithiopia
Blessed is he who trodeth in this dispension [*sic*][9]
knowing that he is and forIver will be
   The ALMIGHTY—JAH RASTAFARI[10]

"Rastaman Chant"

Traditional, recorded by Bob Marley and the Wailers on the album *Burnin'*
(1973).

I hear the words of the rasta man say
Babylon your throne gone down, gone down
Babylon your throne gone down

Said, I hear the words of the higher man say
Babylon your throne gone down, gone down
Babylon your throne gone down

And I hear the angel with the seven seals
Babylon your throne's gone down, gone down
Babylon your throne gone down

I say fly away home to zion, fly away home
I say fly away to zion, fly away home
One bright morning when my work is over
Man will fly away home

One bright morning when my work is over
Man will fly away home
One bright morning when my work is over
Man will fly away home

I say fly away home to zion, fly away home
I say fly away to zion, fly away home
One bright morning when my work is over
Man will fly away home

NOTES

Excerpts from Gerald Hausman, ed., *The Kebra Nagast: The Lost Bible of Rastafarian Wisdom and Faith from Ethiopia and Jamaica* (New York: Saint Martin's Press, 1997), 93–94, 111–14, 144–49. Reprinted by permission of St. Martin's Press.

Excerpts from Robert Athlyi Rogers, *The Holy Piby: The Blackman's Bible* (originally published 1924; reprint, Chicago: Research Associates, School Times Publications / Frontline Distribution, 2000), 25, 27–29, 35–38. Reprinted by permission of Miguel Lorne Publishers.

1. Gerald Hausman, "Editor's Note," in *The Kebra Nagast: The Lost Bible of Rastafarian Wisdom and Faith from Ethiopia and Jamaica* (New York: St. Martin's Press, 1997), 15.
2. The Ark of the Covenant, surreptitiously taken by David from the Temple in Jerusalem with the aid of Azarayas, the son of the High Priest.
3. This comes from the Jewish kosher laws found in the Book of Leviticus, as does most of the last portion of the excerpt.
4. The Ark of the Covenant.
5. The mighty angel robed in four colors.
6. Probably "raiment," clothing.
7. Paraphrasing the Jewish creedal statement, the *Sh'ma*: "You shall love the Lord your God with all your heart and with all your soul and with all your might" (Deuteronomy 6:5).
8. Quoted by Ras Michael (Miguel) Lorne, introduction to *The Holy Piby* (Chicago: Research Associates, School Times Publications / Frontline Distribution, 2000), 10–11.
9. Probably "dispansion," meaning "dispersal," referring to the African diaspora.
10. "Ises Prayer," in *The Holy Piby*, 10–11.

FOR FURTHER READING

Babatunji, Ayotunde Amtac, *Prophet on Reggae Mountain: Meditations of Ras Shabaka Maasai, Prophet of Jah Rastafari* (Rochester, N.Y.: Garvey-Tubman-Nanny-Nzinga Press, 1994). First person reflections from a Rastafarian prophet.

Chevannes, Barry, *Rastafari: Roots and Ideology* (Syracuse, N.Y.: Syracuse University Press, 1994). A study by a noted scholar of Rastafarianism.

Edmonds, Ennis Barrington, *Rastafari: From Outcasts to Culture Bearers* (New York: Oxford University Press, 2002). A history of Rastafarianism that focuses on internal developments within the movement as it evolved.

King, Stephen A., et al., *Reggae, Rastafari, and the Rhetoric of Social Control* (Jackson: University Press of Mississippi, 2003). A scholarly appraisal of reggae music in the context of Rastafarianism.

Murrell, N. Samuel, William D. Spencer, and Adrian Anthony McFarlane, eds., *Chanting Down Babylon: The Rastafari Reader* (Philadelphia: Temple University Press, 1998). A collection of scholarly essays on a variety of aspects of Rastafarianism.

Chapter 10

The Nation of Islam

Although some African Muslims were brought to the Americas during the era of European colonization, Islam was not significantly represented among slave populations in North or South America. In the early 1900s, however, Islam emerged in the African American community in association with various forms of black nationalism. African American spokespersons had been calling for a return to Africa, either literally or symbolically or both, since the 1800s. Some freed slaves did cross the Atlantic to settle in western Africa, where they established the country of Liberia. For others, however, Africa came to be seen as a state of mind, a place of origin as well as a symbol of hope.

Africa was central to Marcus Garvey (1887–1940), perhaps the most influential black nationalist leader in the United States in the first half of the twentieth century. The Jamaican-born Garvey entered the United States in 1916 and eventually formed the Universal Negro Improvement Association (UNIA), a popular, black-supported movement for social, economic, cultural, and religious uplift. Garvey's message of black pride and return to Africa appealed to many poor urban blacks in cities of the American Northeast and upper Midwest, like New York, Boston, Philadelphia, Detroit, and Chicago. In the early 1900s, African Americans migrated in massive numbers from the American South to these Northern cities in search of employment and to escape the racism of Southern society. Garvey's UNIA was the kind of organization that they needed. Virtually all subsequent leaders of African American Muslim movements were influenced by, if not directly enrolled as members in, Garvey's UNIA. Garvey started the Black Star Line in 1919 as a shipping concern for transporting African Americans to Africa. He also established black-owned and -operated businesses, schools, and other social institutions. In these ways the UNIA attempted to create a viable social, economic, and cultural world for African Americans living in a society dominated by whites. The Black Star Line failed, however, and Garvey was imprisoned for mail fraud. He was released and deported to Jamaica in 1927, after which his movement declined in the United States. But Garvey and the work of the UNIA inspired many African Americans to continue black nationalist activities.

Muslim symbols and ideas were woven into various UNIA themes, as were critiques of white-dominated Christianity. Garvey and others argued that God and Jesus were black. Garvey wanted a black civil religion that would draw on the religious aspirations of African Americans but free them from centuries of religious indoctrination under white enslavement. These themes were picked up by various early black Muslim groups. The most significant of these, before the Nation of Islam, was the Moorish Science Temple, established in 1913 by Noble Drew Ali (1886–1929). Born Timothy Drew, Ali created a black organization that shifted African American identity from race to ethnicity, telling his followers that they were not Negroes, but Moors from Morocco, and that their lineage was noble. Ali claimed to be a prophet sent by Allah, the Arabic term for God, to rescue African Americans from their mental blindness. Members of the Moorish Science Temple adopted Islamicized names to designate their rediscovered, true identities. Ali established Moorish Science centers in various Northern cities, and the movement survives to the present.

The most well-known African American Muslim movement, however, has undoubtedly been the Nation of Islam (NOI), founded by a mysterious figure named Wallace D. Fard or W. Fard Muhammad. His racial and ethnic identity remain uncertain, although he was thought to be an Arab by the African Americans to whom he sold silks and other Middle Eastern products door-to-door in the poor Detroit neighborhood of Paradise Valley. Beginning in 1930, Fard established a loose movement composed of poor urban blacks in Detroit, encouraging them to assume Muslim customs and names and to reject Christianity, which he associated with both white-imposed slavery in the past and white-sanctioned social, legal, and cultural restrictions placed upon African Americans in the present. The first NOI temple resulted from meetings Fard held in rented public halls. Eventually the NOI would establish temples in many Northern cities with significant African American populations.

Whether the NOI would have become the most famous and influential African American Muslim movement under Fard's leadership alone remains a matter of speculation. That it did so is largely due to the efforts of Elijah Muhammad (1897–1975). Born Elijah Poole in Sandersville, Georgia, Elijah Muhammad, like so many African Americans who responded to advocates of black nationalism and Islam in the early twentieth century,

had migrated to the urban North in search of a better life. He was influenced by Garvey's teachings, but by 1930 no significant leader had
emerged among African Americans to take Garvey's place. Elijah Muhammad supposedly recognized Fard's true identity right away: Fard
was Allah. NOI theology teaches that Fard was born in Mecca and that
his racial composition was half black and half white, so that he could
reach blacks with his message but move about easily in a white-dominated
society.

The version of Islam taught by Fard and Elijah Muhammad, who succeeded him as leader of the NOI, would not have been recognized as such
by Sunni or Shi'a Muslims. Early NOI members (also called Black Muslims) were taught that they were the Original People who had lived in
Arabia centuries ago. God was not an invisible spirit, but was initially a
self-created black man who had always existed. This man created black
people, who established an advanced and peaceful civilization. However,
the seeds of this divine civilization's destruction came from within. The
God-as-black-man made the Original People with both positive and negative qualities. The negative was dramatically shown when, in the distant
past, an evil black scientist tried to destroy this civilization by boring a
hole in the earth and setting off an explosive device that spun a piece of
the planet into space. This became the moon. So God-as-black-man hid
himself from the Original People and established a plan for their perfection. One of the Original People, a brilliant scientist named Yakub, began
a series of cloning experiments on the island of Patmos that eventually led
to the creation of human beings with white (Caucasian) skin color (see
"Truths to Set You Free," below). Yakub distilled negativity out of blackness by displacing it into white human beings. In NOI mythology, whites
are thus understood to be evil by nature. The earliest generations of these
evil whites were Jews, led by Moses. Later they populated Europe, and then
the Americas. Modern-day African Americans, on the other hand, are
descended from the Original People. But they were enslaved by whites,
and according to NOI teaching must awaken to their true identity, throw
off the shackles of white rule, and reestablish the harmonious society of
the Original People. This is to be accomplished by establishing NOI temples; cultivating highly ethical behavior among NOI members; and creating black-owned and -operated businesses, farms, and schools. These
developments are all part of the divine plan to perfect the Original People.
But in order to achieve their true perfection, they must first overcome the
negative effects of evil in the world, embodied in whites.

Fard was arrested and forced to leave Detroit. According to official NOI history, he mysteriously disappeared in 1934 while in Chicago. Elijah Muhammad became the NOI prophet, with headquarters in Chicago, and declared Fard's divinity. Until his death in 1975, Elijah Muhammad preached to African Americans about the need for black-only territory, black pride, and Islam as the means of achieving black perfection. He organized men into the Fruit of Islam, a kind of bodyguard and paramilitary arm of the NOI, and established women's auxiliaries and boys' and girls' groups. Ideally, children were to be educated in NOI schools. Temples were led by ministers who worked to propagate the NOI message in African American urban communities. Elijah Muhammad, like other African American Muslim figures, was observed by the FBI, especially in the early 1940s, on suspicion of being anti-American, and was imprisoned from 1942 to 1946.

The NOI entered a new period of growth in the 1950s, especially after Malcolm X (1925–1965) became the most important advocate of NOI theology. Born Malcolm Little, he endured racist discrimination in Michigan, where he spent his childhood. As a young man he moved to Boston, where he engaged in criminal acts that eventually led to his imprisonment in Norfolk, Michigan, in 1946. While he was in jail, members of his family told him about Elijah Muhammad, and Malcolm began corresponding with the NOI leader. According to the *Autobiography of Malcolm X* (1964), Elijah Muhammad's encouragement and NOI teachings revolutionized Malcolm X's thinking. Upon his release from prison, Malcolm X began working full-time for NOI, and by the 1960s he was the group's best-known public advocate. He has often been depicted as the black foil to Martin Luther King, Jr., the Christian minister and universally accepted leader and visionary of the civil rights movement. Malcolm X advocated black nationalism, black separatism, and Muslim concepts and practices, in contrast to King's Protestant Christian, nonviolent approach to the racial problems of American society. In their later years, both figures moved ideologically toward one another in important respects, but Malcolm X's public career was cut short when he was assassinated in 1965. By that time, disillusioned with certain discrepancies in Elijah Muhammad's behavior and ministry, Malcolm X had separated from the NOI and supported racial cooperation, as well as a more orthodox Muslim lifestyle, due in large measure to the effects of his travels in the Middle East, where he witnessed more traditional Muslim practices of toleration, especially while he was on pilgrimage to Mecca.

After Elijah Muhammad's death, his son Wallace D. Muhammad (b. 1933) succeeded him and began to shift the NOI toward mainstream Islam as practiced by millions of Sunni Muslims around the world. He changed the organization's name to the American Muslim Mission and taught followers to conform to traditional Muslim teachings. Since 1985, individual mosques (formerly temples) have existed independently of one another, and Wallace D. Muhammad has become a prominent Muslim leader in the United States.

Others in the NOI could not accept these changes, wishing instead to retain the organizational, theological, and cultural roots of the NOI from Elijah Muhammad's era. Under Louis Farrakhan (born Louis Walcott in 1933), a revived Nation of Islam was formed in 1978. With Farrakhan as its new prophet, this group sees Elijah Muhammad as the messiah, saying that he only appeared to die in 1975 but is in fact alive. Farrakhan reports that he had a vision in 1985 in which he was lifted into a massive spaceship and city in the heavens called the Mother Plane, from which God was influencing human life on earth. Farrakhan believes that at a divinely appointed time evil white domination will end and African Americans will realize their full potential as Original People. But Farrakhan holds out hope for some whites, arguing that their evil is psychological and can thus be changed. Farrakhan has led the NOI toward more conventional Muslim practices while retaining basic NOI teachings. He supported Jesse Jackson's campaign for president in 1984, during which he made anti-Semitic remarks that attracted considerable attention and added to increasing strain between the Jewish and African American communities in the United States. In 1995 the NOI under Farrakhan sponsored the Million Man March in Washington, D.C., designed to highlight ethical and spiritual behavior on the part of African American men and to encourage them to support their families and communities and help eradicate persistent problems such as poverty, drug abuse, crime, and fragile families.

The heart of NOI teaching is an insistence on the New Self: African Americans should realize that they are not just descendants of African slaves brought to the Americas, but in fact descendants of the divine Original People. Until they achieve this realization, God will delay their collective perfection. Arguably this is not a "new" self-identification, but rather a call to recover a very old, indeed original, one. However, calling contemporary individuals back to some timeless truth or identity is a common theme among NRMs and, indeed, among religions worldwide. African Americans are called by NOI to adopt a New Self, replacing the identity that their families, ancestors, and churches taught them. The ultimate goal is a New Society, perfected in all particulars. But this New Society can only materialize if New Selves acknowledge their true identity and work to make all Original People cognizant of their past and their destiny.

In the excerpts that follow, this image of the New Self is explored through the published writings of key NOI leaders Elijah Muhammad and Malcolm X. The first excerpt, taken from one of Elijah Muhammad's speeches, tells the creation myth of the NOI. The second excerpt, from Malcolm X's *Autobiography*, recounts his time in prison and dawning realization that Elijah Muhammad's message would become his own. The Yakub story is recounted in this context. The third and final excerpt, also from the *Autobiography*, relates Malcolm X's early involvement in the NOI, during which time he came to recognize other African Americans as fellow Original People and sensed the urgency of proclaiming this truth to any who would listen.

From *Message to the Blackman in America*

Elijah Muhammad

Chapter 107: Truths to Set You Free

What should you know, what should you do, and what is your place in this change of worlds, governments and people? You have the best offer; better than that of any other human beings who have ever lived.

You have been taught for the past 34 years from the mouth of Almighty God, Allah, through his Messenger that you are the first and the last and that you have been loose in what He (Allah) calls a wilderness—a place of sin and evil doings opposed to a civilization of righteousness and the doings of good. For the past 400 years you have been robbed completely of the knowledge of self and kind and of Almighty god—the Creator and Maker of the heavens and the earth. We are the direct descendants of God, while those who have mistreated us and still do are the direct offspring of a rebellious scientist of God.

A scientist who grafted and made the white man an enemy to us. From the rebellious spirit of their creator, they have deceived, murdered and ruled the righteous, who are of the original Black Nation of the earth. This has been made very clear. Being born and nursed by the enemy of righteousness, you have fallen in love with them.

The history of the life of your fathers reveals an evil, murderous condition that they had to undergo. The treatment you are receiving now and have received should bear enough witness to the truth. Your love for this unalike people and their wealth which they have robbed you of and the majority of your people now makes you want to be one of them and desire to intermarry with such people, while history has recorded them as burning your actual living flesh at the stake out of the law of justice.

We live in a government that has always yielded and sided with the murderers and those who slay us and our people at home and abroad—anywhere the black man may be on the earth. You should realize that your black brother is your black brother wherever he is on the face of the earth. Look at your brother in Africa who has been dominated by the Europeans and other white races of the earth. He is fighting for a chance to shake off the shackles of the open enemies, while you here in America profess to be their friends. Are not you ashamed of yourselves, seeking love and intermarriage with them?

Your brother is trying to regain the power of his own country. You are playing the part of a hypocrite to yourself and your kind—wherever they live—by appealing to the murderers to accept you as one of them, as their sons-in-law. What a fool you are making of yourself without the knowledge of self and the time in which you are living.

This is the time that justice has come to you to settle the injustice done to you by your enemies and separate you from such evil people and give you a place somewhere on this earth that you can call your own. But you do not want a place of your own; you want to continue to live in a place with the murderers and crushers. What a silly people you are.

At the same time, he is shooting and killing you in the open eyes of the world, showing that he is your worst enemy and hated you from the very beginning and will always hate you as long as he is a human being made in nature which he is.

The Prophets were, unable from Moses to Muhammad, to reform him into a God-like person to deal justly. He cannot be reformed unless you graft him back into that which he was grafted from. As Jesus said to Nicodemus, "By no means can you see the kingdom of heaven unless you be born again." This refers to the whole Caucasian race. They must be born again. Not just a change, but a change in the very nature of them.

You are lying at their gates and foot steps begging, fighting and bleeding and falling from their blows and gunshots. You are trying to get them to accept you as their equal and as a free person. There is no way that you can settle the price of justice between you and your open enemy but by your entire submission of will to Allah who came in the person of Master Fard Muhammad; come follow me, your brother Elijah Muhammad.

From *The Autobiography of Malcolm X*

Malcolm X and Alex Haley

"The true knowledge," reconstructed much more briefly than I received it, was that history had been "whitened" in the white man's history books, and that the black man had been "brainwashed for hundreds of years." Original Man was black, in the continent called Africa where the human race had emerged on the planet Earth.

The black man, original man, built great empires and civilizations and cultures while the white man was still living on all fours in caves. "The devil white man," down through history, out of his devilish nature, had pillaged, murdered, raped, and exploited every race of man not white.

Human history's greatest crime was the traffic in black flesh when the devil white man went into Africa and murdered and kidnapped to bring to the West in chains, in slave ships, millions of black men, women, and children, who were worked and beaten and tortured as slaves.

The devil white man cut these black people off from all knowledge of their own kind, and cut them off from any knowledge of their own language, religion, and past culture, until the black man in America was the earth's only race of people who had absolutely no knowledge of his true identity.

In one generation, the black slave women in America had been raped by the slavemaster white man until there had begun to emerge a home-made, handmade, brainwashed race that was no longer even of its true color, that no longer even knew its true family names. The slavemaster forced his family name upon this rape-mixed race, which the slavemaster began to call "the Negro."

This "Negro" was taught of his native Africa that it was peopled by heathen, black savages, swinging like monkeys from trees. This "Negro" accepted this along with every other teaching of the slavemaster that was designed to make him accept and obey and worship the white man.

And where the religion of every other people on earth taught its believers of a God with whom they could identify, a God who at least looked like one of their own kind, the slavemaster injected his Christian religion into this "Negro." This "Negro" was taught to worship an alien God having the same blond hair, pale skin, and blue eyes as the slavemaster.

This religion taught the "Negro" that black was a curse. It taught him to hate everything black, including himself. It taught him that everything white was good, to be admired, respected, and loved. It brainwashed this "Negro" to think he was superior if his complexion showed more of the white pollution of the slavemaster. This white man's Christian religion further deceived and brainwashed this "Negro" to always turn the other cheek, and grin, and scrape, and bow, and be humble, and to sing, and to pray, and to take whatever was dished out by the devilish white man; and to look for his pie in the sky, and for his heaven in the hereafter, while right here on earth the slavemaster white man enjoyed *his* heaven.

Many a time, I have looked back, trying to assess, just for myself, my first reactions to all this. Every instinct of the ghetto jungle streets, every hustling fox and criminal wolf instinct in me, which would have scoffed at and rejected anything else, was struck numb. It was as though all of that life merely was back there, without any remaining effect, or influence. I remember how, some time later, reading the Bible in the Norfolk Prison Colony library, I came upon, then I read, over and over, how Paul on the road to Damascus, upon hearing the voice of Christ, was so smitten that he was knocked off his horse, in a daze. I do not now, and I did not then, liken myself to Paul. But I do understand his experience.

I have since learned—helping me to understand what then began to happen within me—that the truth can be quickly received, or received at all, only by the sinner who knows and admits that he is guilty of having sinned much. Stated another way: only guilt admitted accepts truth. The Bible again: the one people whom Jesus could not help were the Pharisees; they didn't feel they needed any help.

The very enormity of my previous life's guilt prepared me to accept the truth.

Not for weeks yet would I deal with the direct, personal application to myself, as a black man, of the truth. It still was like a blinding light.

Reginald [Malcolm's brother] left Boston and went back to Detroit. I would sit in my room and stare. At the dining-room table, I would hardly eat, only drink the water. I nearly starved. Fellow inmates, concerned, and guards, apprehensive, asked what was wrong with me. It was suggested that I visit the doctor, and I didn't. The doctor, advised, visited me. I don't know what his diagnosis was, probably that I was working on some act.

I was going through the hardest thing, also the greatest thing, for any human being to do; to accept that which is already within you, and around you.

I learned later that my brothers and sisters in Detroit put together the money for my sister Hilda to come and visit me. She told me that when the Honorable Elijah Muhammad was in Detroit, he would stay as a guest at my brother Wilfred's home, which was on McKay Street. Hilda kept urging me to write to Mr. Muhammad. He understood what it was to be in the white man's prison, she said, because he, himself, had not long before gotten out of the federal prison at Milan, Michigan, where he had served five years for evading the draft.

Hilda said that the Honorable Elijah Muhammad came to Detroit to reorganize his Temple Number One, which had become disorganized during his prison time; but he lived in Chicago, where he was organizing and building his Temple Number Two.

It was Hilda who said to me, "Would you like to hear how the white man came to this planet Earth?"

And she told me that key lesson of Mr. Elijah Muhammad's teachings, which I later learned was the demonology that every religion has, called "Yacub's History." Elijah Muhammad teaches his followers that, first, the moon separated from the Earth. Then, the first humans, Original Man, were a black people. They founded the Holy City Mecca.

Among this black race were twenty-four wise scientists. One of the scientists, at odds with the rest, created the especially strong black tribe of Shabazz, from which America's Negroes, so-called, descend.

About sixty-six hundred years ago, when seventy per cent of the people were satisfied, and thirty per cent were dissatisfied, among the dissatisfied was born a "Mr. Yacub." He was born to create trouble, to break the peace, and to kill. His head was unusually large. When he was four years old, he began school. At the age of eighteen, Yacub had finished all of his nation's colleges and universities. He was known as "the big-head scientist." Among many other things, he had learned how to breed races scientifically.

This big-head scientist, Mr. Yacub, began preaching in the streets of Mecca, making such hosts of converts that the authorities, increasingly concerned, finally exiled him with 59,999 followers to the island of Patmos—described in the Bible as the island where John received the message contained in Revelations in the New Testament.

Though he was a black man, Mr. Yacub, embittered toward Allah now, decided as revenge to create upon the Earth a devil race—a bleached out, white race of people.

From his studies, the big-head scientist knew that black men contained two germs, black and brown. He knew that the brown germ stayed dormant as, being the lighter of the two germs, it was the weaker. Mr. Yacub, to upset the law of nature, conceived the idea of employing what we today know as the recessive genes structure, to separate from each other the two germs, black and brown, and then grafting the brown germ to progressively lighter, weaker stages. The human resulting, he knew, would be, as they became lighter, and weaker, progressively also more susceptible to wickedness and evil. And in this way finally he would achieve the intended bleached-out white race of devils.

He knew that it would take him several total color-change stages to get from black to white. Mr. Yacub began his work by setting up a eugenics law on the island of Patmos.

Among Mr. Yacub's 59,999 all-black followers, every third or so child that was born would show some trace of brown. As these became adult only brown and brown, or black and brown, were permitted to marry. As their children were born, Mr. Yacub's law dictated that, if a black child, the attending nurse, or midwife, should stick a needle into its brain and give the body to cremators. The mothers were told it had been an "angel baby," which had gone to heaven, to prepare a place for her.

But a brown child's mother was told to take very good care of it.

Others, assistants, were trained by Mr. Yacub to continue his objective. Mr. Yacub, when he died on the island at the age of one hundred and fifty-two, had left laws, and rules, for them to follow. According to the teachings of Mr. Elijah Muhammad, Mr. Yacub, except in his mind, never saw the bleached out devil race that his procedures and laws and rules created.

A two-hundred-year span was needed to eliminate on the island of Patmos all of the black people—until only brown people remained.

The next two hundred years were needed to create from the brown race the red race—with no more browns left on the island.

In another two hundred years, from the red race was created the yellow race.

Two hundred years later—the white race had at last been created.

On the island of Patmos was nothing but these blond, pale-skinned, cold-blue-eyed devils-savages, nude and shameless; hairy, like animals, they walked on all fours and they lived in trees.

Six hundred more years passed before this race of people returned to the mainland, among the natural black people.

Mr. Elijah Muhammad teaches his followers that within six months time, through telling lies that set the black men fighting among each other, this devil race had turned what had been a peaceful heaven on earth into a hell torn by quarreling and fighting.

But finally the original black people recognized that their sudden troubles stemmed from this devil white race that Mr. Yacub had made. They rounded them up, put them in chains. With little aprons to cover their nakedness, this devil race was marched off across the Arabian desert to the caves of Europe.

The lambskin and the cable-tow used in Masonry today are symbolic of how the nakedness of the white man was covered when he was chained and driven across the hot sand.

Mr. Elijah Muhammad further teaches that the white devil in Europe's caves was savage. The animals tried to kill him. He climbed trees outside his cave, made clubs, trying to protect his family from the wild beasts outside trying to get in.

When this devil race had spent two thousand years in the caves, Allah raised up Moses to civilize them, and bring them out of the caves. It was written that this devil white race would rule the world for six thousand years.

The Books of Moses are missing. That's why it is not known that he was in the caves.

When Moses arrived, the first of these devils to accept his teachings, the first he led out, were those we call today the Jews.

According to the teachings of this "Yacub's History," when the Bible says "Moses lifted up the serpent in the wilderness," that serpent is symbolic of the devil white race Moses lifted up out of the caves of Europe, teaching them civilization.

It was written that after Yacub's bleached white race had ruled the world for six thousand years—down to our time—the black original race would give birth to one whose wisdom, knowledge, and power would be infinite.

It was written that some of the original black people should be brought as slaves to North America—to learn to better understand, at first hand, the white devil's true nature, in modern times.

Elijah Muhammad teaches that the greatest and mightiest God who appeared on the earth was Master W. D. Fard. He came from the East to the West, appearing in North America at a time when the history and the prophecy that is written was coming to realization, as the non-white people all over the world began to rise, and as the devil white civilization, condemned by Allah, was, through its devilish nature, destroying itself.

Master W. D. Fard was half black and half white. He was made in this way to enable him to be accepted by the black people in America, and to lead them, while at the same time he was enabled to move undiscovered among white people, so that he could understand and judge the enemy of the blacks.

Master W. D. Fard, in 1931, posing as a seller of silks, met, in Detroit, Michigan, Elijah Muhammad. Master W. D. Fard gave to Elijah Muhammad Allah's message, and Allah's divine guidance, to save the Lost-Found Nation of Islam, the so-called Negroes, here in "this wilderness of North America."

When my sister, Hilda, had finished telling me this "Yacub's History," she left. I don't know if I was able to open my mouth and say good-bye.

I was to learn later that Elijah Muhammad's tales, like this one of "Yacub," infuriated the Muslims of the East. While at Mecca, I reminded them that it was their fault, since they themselves hadn't done enough to make real Islam known in the West. Their silence left a vacuum into which any religious faker could step and mislead our people.

Wednesdays, Fridays, and Sundays were the meeting days of the relatively small Detroit Temple Number One. Near the temple, which actually was a storefront, were three hog-slaughtering pens. The squealing of hogs being slaughtered filtered into our Wednesday and Friday meetings. I'm describing the condition that we Muslims were in back in the early 1950's.

The address of Temple Number One was 1470 Frederick Street, I think. The first Temple to be formed, back in 1931, by Master W. D. Fard, was formed in Detroit, Michigan. I never had seen any Christian-believing Negroes conduct themselves like the Muslims, the individuals and the families alike. The men were quietly, tastefully dressed. The women wore ankle-length gowns, no makeup, and scarves covered their heads. The neat children were mannerly not only to adults but to other children as well.

I had never dreamed of anything like that atmosphere among black people who had learned to be proud they were black, who had learned to love other black people instead of being jealous and suspicious. I thrilled to how we Muslim men used both hands to grasp a black brother's both hands, voicing and smiling our happiness to meet him again. The Muslim sisters, both married and single, were given an honor and respect that I'd never seen black men give to their women, and it felt wonderful to me. The salutations which we all exchanged were warm, filled with mutual respect and dignity: "Brother". . . "Sister" . . . "Ma'am" . . . "Sir." Even children speaking to other children used these terms. Beautiful!

Lemuel Hassan then was the Minister at Temple Number One. "As-Salaikum," he greeted us. "Wa-Salaikum," we returned. Minister Lemuel stood before us, near a blackboard. The blackboard had fixed upon it in permanent paint, on one side, the United States flag and under it the words "Slavery, Suffering and Death," then the word "Christianity" alongside the sign of the Cross. Beneath the Cross was a painting of a black man hanged from a tree. On the other side was painted what we were taught was the Muslim flag, the crescent and star on a red background with the words "Islam: Freedom, Justice, Equality," and beneath that "Which One Will Survive the War of Armageddon?"

For more than an hour, Minister Lemuel lectured about Elijah Muhammad's teachings. I sat raptly absorbing Minister Lemuel's every syllable and gesture. Frequently, he graphically illustrated points by chalking key words or phrases on the blackboard.

I thought it was outrageous that our small temple still had some empty seats. I complained to my brother Wilfred that there should be no empty seats, with the surrounding streets full of our brainwashed black brothers and sisters, drinking, cursing, fighting, dancing, carousing, and using dope —the very things that Mr. Muhammad taught were helping the black man to stay under the heel of the white man here in America.

From what I could gather, the recruitment attitude at the temple seemed to me to amount to a self-defeating waiting view . . . an assumption that Allah would bring us more Muslims. I felt that Allah would be more inclined to help those who helped themselves. I had lived for years in ghetto streets; I knew the Negroes in those streets. Harlem or Detroit were no different. I said I disagreed, that I thought we should go out into the streets and get more Muslims into the fold. All of my life, as you know, I had been an activist, I had been impatient. My brother Wilfred counseled me to keep patience. And for me to be patient was made easier by the fact that I could anticipate soon seeing and perhaps meeting the man who was called "The Messenger," Elijah Muhammad himself.

Today, I have appointments with world-famous personages, including some heads of nations. But I looked forward to the Sunday before Labor Day in 1952 with an eagerness never since duplicated. Detroit Temple Number One Muslims were going in a motor caravan—I think about ten automobiles—to visit Chicago Temple Number Two, to hear Elijah Muhammad.

Not since childhood had I been so excited as when we drove in Wilfred's car. At great Muslim rallies since then I have seen, and heard, and felt ten thousand black people applauding and cheering. But on that Sunday afternoon when our two little temples assembled, perhaps only two hundred Muslims, the Chicagoans welcoming and greeting us Detroiters, I experienced tinglings up my spine as I've never had seen.

I was totally unprepared for the Messenger Elijah Muhammad's physical impact upon my emotions. From the rear of Temple Number Two, he came toward the platform. The small, sensitive, gentle, brown face that I had studied on photographs, until I had dreamed about it, was fixed straight ahead as the Messenger strode, encircled by the marching, strapping Fruit of Islam guards. The Messenger, compared to them, seemed fragile, almost tiny. He and the Fruit of Islam were dressed in dark suits, white shirts, and bow ties. The Messenger wore a gold-embroidered fez.

I stared at the great man who had taken the time to write to me when I was a convict whom he knew nothing about. He was the man whom I had been told had spent years of his life in suffering and sacrifice to lead us, the black people, because he loved us so much. And then, hearing his voice, I sat leaning forward, riveted upon his words. (I try to reconstruct what Elijah Muhammad said from having since heard him speak hundreds of times.)

"I have not stopped one day for the past twenty-one years. I have been standing, preaching to you throughout those past twenty-one years, while I was free, and even while I was in bondage. I spent three and one-half years in the federal penitentiary, and also over a year in the city jail for teaching this truth. I was also deprived of a father's love for his family for seven long years while I was running from hypocrites and other enemies of this word and revelation of God—which will give life to you, and put you on the same level with all other civilized and independent nations and peoples of this planet earth . . ."

Elijah Muhammad spoke of how in this wilderness of North America, for centuries the "blue-eyed devil white man" had brainwashed the "so-called Negro." He told us how, as one result, the black man in America was "mentally, morally and spiritually dead." Elijah Muhammad spoke of how black man was Original Man, who had been kidnapped from his homeland and stripped of his language, his culture, his family structure, his family name, until the black man in America did not even realize who he was.

He told us, and showed us, how his teachings of the true knowledge of ourselves would lift up the black man from the bottom of the white man's society and place the black man where he had begun, at the top of civilization.

Concluding, pausing for breath, he called my name.

It was like an electrical shock. Not looking at me directly, he asked me to stand.

He told them that I was just out of prison. He said how "strong" I had been while in prison. "Every day," he said, "for years, Brother Malcolm has written a letter from prison to me. And I have written to him as often as I could."

Standing there, feeling the eyes of the two hundred Muslims upon me, I heard him make a parable about me.

When God bragged about how faithful Job was, said Elijah Muhammad, the devil said only God's hedge around Job kept Job so faithful. "Remove that protective hedge," the devil told God, "and I will make Job curse you to your face."

The devil could claim that, hedged in prison, I had just used Islam, Mr. Muhammad said. But the devil would say that now, out of prison, I would return to my drinking, smoking, dope, and life of crime.

"Well, now, our good brother Malcolm's hedge is removed and we will see how he does," Mr. Muhammad said. "I believe that he is going to remain faithful."

And Allah blessed me to remain true, firm and strong in my faith in Islam, despite many severe trials to my faith. And even when events produced a crisis between Elijah Muhammad and me, I told him at the beginning of the crisis, with all the sincerity I had in me, that I still believed in him more strongly than he believed in himself.

NOTES

Excerpt from Elijah Muhammad, *Message to the Blackman in America* (originally published 1965; reprint, Norfolk, Va.: United Brothers Communications Systems, 1992), 244–46. Reprinted by permission of the Copyright Clearance Center, Inc.

Excerpts from Malcolm X and Alex Haley, *The Autobiography of Malcolm X* (New York: Grove Press, 1965), 162–68, 194–98. Copyright © 1964 by Alex Haley and Malcolm X. Copyright © 1965 by Alex Haley and Betty Shabazz. Used by permission of Random House, Inc.

FOR FURTHER READING

Clegg, Claude Andrew, III, *An Original Man: The Life and Times of Elijah Muhammad* (New York: St Martin's Press, 1997). The standard biography of Elijah Muhammad.

DeCaro, Louis Anthony, Jr., *On the Side of My People: A Religious Life of Malcolm X* (New York: New York University Press, 1995); and *Malcolm and the Cross: The Nation of Islam, Malcolm X, and Christianity* (New York: New York University Press, 1998). A two-volume biography of Malcolm X that focuses on the religious dimensions of his life.

The Final Call, http://www.finalcall.com. The online edition of the official newspaper of the Nation of Islam.

Gardell, Mattias, *In the Name of Elijah Muhammad: Louis Farrakhan and the Nation of Islam* (Durham, N.C.: Duke University Press, 1996). To date, the most in-depth study of the history and theology of the Nation of Islam available.

Lincoln, C. Eric, *The Black Muslims in America*, 3d ed. (1961; reprint, Grand Rapids, Mich.: William B. Eerdmans, 1994). The first book-length study of Nation of Islam that brought the movement widespread public attention.

Nation of Islam, http://www.noi.org. The official Website of the NOI.

Tate, Sonsryea, *Growing Up in the Nation of Islam* (San Francisco: Harper, 1997). A first-person account by a woman who grew up in the Nation of Islam.

Turner, Richard Brent, *Islam in the African-American Experience* (Bloomington: Indiana University Press, 1997). Places the Nation of Islam within the larger context of Islam in its many forms in African American communities.

Chapter 11

Peoples Temple

Peoples Temple originated in the outreach ministry of pastor Jim Jones (1931–1978). Jones felt the injustice of racism acutely growing up in a part of Indiana with a strong Ku Klux Klan presence, and he became a Methodist pastor in 1953. Yet because he saw the communal living arrangement of the early apostles described in Acts 4:32–35, or "apostolic socialism," as a model for achieving a raceless, classless society in the United States, and because of his struggles to integrate his Methodist congregation, in 1956 Pastor Jones founded the Pentecostal congregation that would become known as Peoples Temple Full Gospel Church, and then simply Peoples Temple. By 1964 Jones and Peoples Temple were officially affiliated with the Disciples of Christ and soon after moved to Ukiah, California; before long, Jones also had churches in Los Angeles and San Francisco. In these urban locations especially, the congregation's clear affirmation of racial acceptance and religious brotherhood swelled its rolls with people of all colors and socioeconomic backgrounds.

Over the course of most of his ministry, Jones's commitment to ending racism and achieving social justice was unquestioned and virtually unequaled. He and his wife, Marceline, adopted several children of different races. He was appointed the head of the Commission on Human Rights in Indianapolis and chair of the San Francisco Housing Authority. The San Francisco church opened health clinics, soup kitchens, drug treatment facilities, and day care centers to assist people, mostly minorities, struggling against the strictures of American society. He received major humanitarian awards in 1976 and 1977 and was named by *Religion in Life* magazine one of the top one hundred clergymen in the United States.

Clearly, Jones's earliest and most pressing concern for his Christian organizations was combating the evils of racism and economic disparity in the United States. Underlying this was a socialist critique of American wealth, media, and occasionally politics, though he was also known to be shrewd and pragmatic when it came to working within the system. Ironically, this critique ultimately emphasized the false and exploitive nature of traditional Christianity itself, as reflected in his 1974 "Political and Religious Lecture," and the unreliability of the King James Bible, implied in his criticism of Scripture in the 1976 Philadelphia sermon, both excerpted below. However, as is also evident from the 1974 lecture, Jones increasingly came to regard himself, not as a mere mortal, but as God. Jones did not see himself as the Christian God, however, but rather the incarnation of the "spirit of socialism," the embodiment of the "Christ Principle," and the Prophet who would lead the charge against an inhumane world.

Jones's characteristic paranoia and feelings of isolation combined with his self-appointed charge to defend righteousness against an unjust society to fuel an increasingly apocalyptic worldview. The now-infamous Jonestown settlement in Guyana, South America, began as an agricultural commune, a utopian "Promised Land" in the jungle to offer refuge from "Babylon," as Jones portrayed the United States. As lawsuits, government inquiries, and unflattering media portrayals—often triggered by ex-members—began to mount in the United States, most of the group, including Jones himself, departed for the relative peace and safety of Jonestown in 1977. The apocalyptic element of the Peoples Temple worldview, rooted as much in the group's socialist as in its Christian origins, was confirmed as external crises escalated. Jones felt that both nuclear war and a fascist takeover of the United States were imminent. Indeed, the site in Guyana (like the earlier one in Ukiah) was specifically chosen for its relative safety in the event of a nuclear war.

Accounts by members, ex-members, and the families of the victims at Jonestown all illustrate that what made this movement cohere through all of its trials was its underlying family structure, especially the identification of Jones as "Father" or "Dad." As he proclaims in the "Sermon in Philadelphia" excerpted below, Jones wanted to "adopt" his followers as their "natural" or "earthly" father. Jones promised protection and, ultimately, salvation for his entire "family," a commitment that he affirmed repeatedly in a variety of ways. For one, much of a Peoples Temple service (especially if visitors were present) consisted of testimonials to Jones's healing powers and ethereal knowledge. These were often accompanied by a demonstration: sucking out cancers, curing ulcers, revealing information about people's private lives and then prophesying about their future. The message was that Jones knows about you, cares about you, and can help you in ways that no one else, including the Christian God and American society, can or will.

However, the very intimacy of this "idealized" family setting paved the way for the abuses inflicted by Jones on his congregation at all levels. "Catharsis sessions" held members up for extensive emotional and physical abuse. Any criticism of Jones among members was reported and publicly exposed. Despite its efforts to eliminate racial inequity in the world, Peoples Temple fell short of this goal in its own organizational structure, as almost no high-level positions were held by nonwhites, despite the fact that African Americans made up the majority of the community. Jones also focused increasingly on sex as a matter of control—on who wanted to have sex with him and who didn't, and on which community members were having sex with each other. He initiated or at least insinuated homosexual encounters between members and, often, with himself. Ultimately, it was the dissonance between the lofty ideals espoused by Peoples Temple and Jones's gross abuses of power that caused many members to leave in the years before the move to Guyana. Most stayed with the group, however, rationalizing their allegiance to Jones as part of the sacrifice necessary to advance "the Cause" of a perfect society, free of racism and economic want. Ultimately, Jones began to ask congregants if they were willing to die for this Cause.

Those who left for Jonestown did so willingly, by and large. It was a chance for a new life, building a society from scratch based on the ideals of apostolic socialism. But the group's problems followed them to their new home. At the urging of Concerned Relatives, a group of families with members in Peoples Temple, California congressman Leo Ryan traveled to Jonestown on a fact-finding mission, accompanied by family members and reporters. On November 18, 1978, as Congressman Ryan was preparing to leave, he assured Jones that he saw no evidence that the pastor was using force or "brainwashing" against his followers, but he was going to take with him several residents who wished to leave. Someone wielded a knife at the exiting party but did not injure anyone. Soon after, however, Ryan and four others were shot to death as they tried to board their plane. Seeing that the group would no longer be able to keep at bay the forces that sought to destroy it, Jones led his followers in one final "White Night," a ritual preparation for "revolutionary suicide"[1] that they had routinely practiced. In all, 918 people, including Jones, died, mainly by the self-inflicted cyanide poisoning, though some had been shot or had their throats slit.

Undoubtedly, Peoples Temple was a New Society movement at its core, as its ideal of transforming racist and capitalist America into a utopia of tolerance and economic balance never wavered. However, what made this group function so effectively in its struggles both within and outside of the United States was its explicit New Family element. The testimonials of Jonestown residents found on what became known as the "Death Tape," recorded during the mass suicide, make clear that they regarded Jones as their "Dad" and trusted him to do what was best for the group as the society they so despised closed in on them. And yet the suicide was also conceived of as an escape from this old, corrupt world to a New World of peace in death, sometimes described by Jones simply as the "next plane" of existence. That the struggle for justice had transcended particular political and social forms and had taken on global, even cosmic dimensions, is echoed throughout member Richard Tropp's suicide letter (excerpted below), as are Christian apocalyptic tropes from the crucifixion ("It is finished") to the Book of Revelation ("Let the books be opened.")

The first four selections are from transcripts of tapes and interviews with Jim Jones made by Fielding McGehee III, brother-in-law of two victims at Jonestown, Carolyn Layton and Annie Moore. In the first excerpt, a radio interview, Jones discusses the impact his congregation has had on the community of Ukiah concerning the racial issue. Next, the sermon from 1974 illustrates Jones's rhetoric at its most extreme—that there is no God, that he never believed in God, that the spirit of socialism is God, and that Jones himself is God. In the 1976 sermon, Jones preaches against being caught up in the literalism of Scripture ("the letter killeth") and then emphasizes his role as fatherly—and godly—protector. The "Death Tape" selection is from the recording made during the White Night suicides/murders. The last excerpt is the suicide note left by Jonestown member Richard Tropp. Some notes and language in these selections not affecting their meaning have been edited for readability. All materials were made available courtesy of the Jonestown Institute.

Interview on Ukiah Radio Station, May 10 or 11, 1973

Jim Jones

Jim Jones: We came here with the *hope* that California—having Indians here, all racial groups, a pretty cosmopolitan mixture—that we could have some peace. And I'd lived in the inner city, being a governmental employee, as well as a pastor. We had a ghetto church that served two thousand free meals to the *poorest* of people for thirteen long years. And you might say we were tired from the battle, and my children—I felt like I somewhat had placed them on the altar of community *service.* So some of us, the principal leaders, decided we would like to relocate, and establish our church here, not [sic] proselytize, no one in this community can ever say we've rapped on a door or gone house-to-house trying to win anyone. People who've come to our church have come from the desperate world of drugs, and they've been rehabilitated, a hundred and forty. Our people don't use drugs even, or alcohol or tobacco. We've been told repeatedly from the law enforcement up and down this state, that once a person unites with our church, they've never had any trouble with the law thereafter. We're a *law*-abiding people.

If this world was made up of as *good* a people as we are, there'd be peace. There would be no alienation. We're inclusive, we have Jewish, we have Christians of all varieties, we do have blacks. Another fear is, of course, I hear constantly, one of the local pastors who has been very supportive said, "Jim," he said, "it all boils down to one thing. The *fear* of the unknown, that every black person they see they think is a member of your church, and indeed, I see a lot of black people in the community that *I* do not know." Actually, the Redwood Valley church is *ninety percent* Caucasian. We have *very* few black people who have settled [sic] this area. Our black people in San Francisco who have jobs that—that far surpass anything they could get here, and there is no *intention* of moving blacks in, but the reason they don't *want* to move in, certainly they have the right to live here if they choose, but as this pastor said, a great deal of this is a fear, he said, it all boils down to that race question, that there—there's just a fear that we're going to be *blanketed* with hundreds of black people, and I think we have four black business people here, and I *think* about twenty-five black residents. Now that's not hardly a threat to the community—but it's the unknown again. I understood one person who's an executive in the lumber industry. He said, they used to tell our lumbering industry, they were going to bring in [*deliberate tone*] five thousand blacks, and that rumor has passed through down the years, and I—I *really* believe in being objective, and I don't think there's any subjective thing in this, that *much* of this is this fear, because we are inclusive, that we're going to somehow bring in hundreds and hundreds of black people, which we would not do to the black people [*short laugh*] in the first place, and we certainly wouldn't to the *economic* picture. We have enough of a depressed economic problem, and *our* people are gainfully employed. It's been hard to *get* jobs. We [don't] have a person that's a shirker in our *midst*. We're good workers, hard workers, and so our employers tell us, we do a good job, but *jobs* are not that plentiful, so we have no intention of moving people in here.

Interviewer: From what you're saying, however, it seems quite clear, that at the *root* of your controversy, your difficulty seems to be the racial issue.

Jones: I'm afraid so. I'd *hoped* America had grown up in these years of violence that we've seen where a number of leaders have been—civil rights leaders have been killed, and there's been question that even maybe President [John] Kennedy was killed because of that, that he was a man of peace. I would *hope* that this had gotten through. And indeed, to pastor in churches here, it *has*. . . .

Interviewer: Will you give some indication of the size of the membership of your church?

Jones: I—to be accurate, I couldn't—it's a growing church, particularly in the metropolitan area. We have a *vast* membership in Los Angeles, about two thousand here, I suppose three thousand in San Francisco, four thousand in Los Angeles. We're an *active* church. We take care of our own people in the tradition of the scripture that says, take care *first* of the household of faith. And we believe that the church, if it would do this more, there would be less danger of the increasing tentacles of big government and bureaucracy. This frightens us. Now some people think of us as a, I think again, a conspiratorial communistic group. We've had people call up, "Commie lover, we're gonna kill you," this, that, and the other. If there were any more anti-bureaucratic or big government or imperialistic, communistic, fascistic group than ours, I don't know how it could be. Now indeed, we're utopianist, in the terms of the acts of the Apostles, where, when they received their baptism of the Holy Spirit of their ineffable union with Christ, they shared and shared in every way, but again, we don't [*unintelligible word*] people not transferring properties to us, they're not *willing* us anything, we take offerings in routine ways, we have projects, like every other church, and—instead of *taking* from our people, we give *far* more than we take. But being that we are united and very supportive of each other, that—that *attracts* certainly in this day of alienation.

Political and Religious Lecture, October 15, 1974

Jim Jones

I'm reading to you from the paper, they don't want you really to *know* it, but they know that you won't–the average American won't *read* this, because [the] average person's in church tonight, *praying,* on their knees, talking to a fairy godmother, *a holy spirit,* a goblin, a ghost, a *spook.* Most people will not *read* what's even in the paper so they can even give you a little bit of the truth. One hundred million persons will starve to death *this* year. And you believe in a God? You must be an idiot. You believe in any god other than what you can see in the spirit of socialism, that I happen to be at this moment in time and space incarnated, you *must* be an idiot. Anyone that can believe that there's a loving God and allow one hundred million people—that is *half* the population of the United States—is going [*sic*] to die before Christmas, half—and I don't mean in the United States, but they're plenty of 'em dying right here, too, of starvation every day. But one hundred million people are going to die across this world, then *you* have believed in a loving God—*how* you can believe in a loving God is a *reflection* on your own intelligence.

All right, because let me tell you, nobody helped me. That's what bothers me with some people. *Nobody* helped me. I came out of all kind of miracles happening to me. When I touch myself, I *heal* myself. When I touch myself, I got up when no one *would* help me. When I wanted to get something done, I *got it done.* When I wanted to create a church in a year in Indianapolis, the folk could tell you, in one year, it looked im—virtually impossibility [*sic*], I had a *great* synagogue and a food commissary program and I got it paid for one day, just one day before the day I prophesied it'd be done. Everything I've ever set my mind to do, I've been able to get done, but I have *never* believed in any loving God. . . .

This sermon is a [*struggles for words*] a *seminar.* And if you get this sermon, we wouldn't have so much trouble to do or to go through. But when I say Goddamnit it, I guess I can damn it, because I'm God. . . . [*shouts*] I'll quit church, I hope you do, by dammit. If you don't like the truth, that's what you need to do. If you don't want to help us fight for what's right, if you're here because of that stupid carryover religion, if you've still got that falseness that we have been using to try to build a better world, if you're still caught up in religion, by dammit, we'd be better off without you anyway.

Sermon in Philadelphia, 1976

Jim Jones

Hey! And I said, you've touched the ark. It's no longer a wooden box, it's no longer a paper Bible. Jeremiah said, get rid of the paper box, the talisman, the ark of the covenant, and I said get a–rid of the letter, 'cause the letter killeth. I've told you, as I did in the day of Jesus, go out without purse or scripture. Don't go out with anything but the Living Word. [You] Say, "I don't have it." Well, then, get around me. You'll get it. You'll get it. [*voice rises*] I'll make you fishers of men. I'll give you power. I'll cause you to go forth and lay hands on all these—these oppressive devils, all these oppressive spirits that've held us down in racism. You get around me, and I will send you out [*cries out*] in my name, and you will set the people free. [*applause*]

[*calm*] Think I can't do it? I've done it, as I said, I've sent them to all of our churches, and I sit at home, writing letters, and told them who to call out, and who to take out of wheelchairs, though I'd be four thousand miles away, I would tell them what to do, because [*voice rises*] I'm on the scene. I said, I am that I am² has come. The very same Jesus, and the very same God. . . .

Peace. I only came for the few that are chosen, that'll serve, that'll be liberators, that've chosen not to be waited upon but to come to serve. As Jesus said, I have come to serve and not to be served. I've come to lose my life, and then find it. But you, the one to keep your life, you're gonna lose it anyway. [*low tone*] All right, all right, all right. Now, have I got your ears open? I hope so. 'Cause they're coming. I've prophesied the date, the month, the hour and the year. We were led to a mountain, and we said an enemy would die under the shadow of that mountain of protection. We've got a mountain that goes to the depth of the earth, and there's no end to it. You can't find the end to it, and only we have found it. And I was led three thousand miles to find it, and I found it. And it's got enough room for you and everybody else, and they're coming. [*voice rises*] You say, I don't need it. God's coming. Did he come—I looked at that newspaper— [Philadelphia civil rights leader] George Wiley, out there, he fell out of his boat, and the poor [*unintelligible word*] the scar on the little boy, you say a Skygod, He's got all power, Skygod's everywhere, Skygod sees everything, Skygod knows everything, Skygod can do anything, but that little—that man fell off the boat yesterday, and his little boy—think what's on his conscience. That father said [*breathless*], "Son, please help me. Hurry." And the son threw a rope, but it was too late. George Ri—Wiley went down beneath the water. [*voice rises in ministerial cadence*] I don't claim to be any Skygod, but I claim that if you'll let me be your natural father, if you'll let me adopt you as an earthly father, I will save you. I've not had one have an accident, but that's not what I'm trying to promise, I'm promising that if you go to jail, I'll go to jail. If they come after you, they have to come after me. If they hurt you, they'll have to hurt me. [*in full throat*] That's what I promise.

The "Death Tape," November 18, 1978

Woman 10: [*joyous*] I just want to say something for everyone that I see that is standing around and/or crying. This is nothing to cry about. This is something we could all rejoice about. We could be happy about this. They always told us that we could cry when you're coming into this world. So when we're leaving, and we're gonna leave it peaceful, I think we should be —we should be happy about this. I was just thinking about Jim Jones. He just has suffered and suffered and suffered. We have the honor guard, and we don't even have a chance to [*unintelligible word*] got here. I want to give him one more chance. There's just one more thing I want to say. That's few that's gone, but many more here. That's not all of us. That's not all yet. That's just a few that have died. I tried to get to the one that—there's a kid over there. I'm looking at so many people crying. I wish you would not cry. And just thank Father. I been here about— [*sustained applause*]

I've been here ah—one year and nine months. And I never felt better in my life. Not in San Francisco, but until I came to Jonestown. I had a very good life. I had a beautiful life. And I don't see nothing that I could be sorry about. We should be happy. At least I am. That's all I'm gonna say. [*applause, music*]

Woman 11: [*weepy*] —good to be alive today. I just like to thank Dad, 'cause he was the only one that stood up for me when I needed him. And thank you, Dad.

Woman 12: I'm glad you're my brothers and sisters, and I'm glad to be here. Okay.

Jones: Please. For God's sake, let's get on with it. We've lived—we've lived as no other people have lived and loved. We've had as much of this world as you're gonna get. Let's just be done with it. Let's be done with the agony of it. [*applause*]

It's far, far harder to have to walk through every day, die slowly—and from the time you're a child 'til the time you get gray, you're dying.

Dishonest, and I'm sure that they'll pay for it. They'll pay for it. This is a revolutionary suicide. This is not a self-destructive suicide. So they'll pay for this. They brought this upon us. And they'll pay for that. I leave that destiny to them.

Who wants to go with their child has a right to go with their child. I think it's humane. I want to go—I want to see you go, though. They can take me and do what they want—whatever they want to do. I want to see you go. I don't want to see you go through this hell no more. No more, no more, no more. We're trying. If everybody will relax. The best thing you do is to relax, and you will have no problem. You'll have no problem with this thing, if you just relax.

Man 4: [*unintelligible phrase*]—a great deal because it's Jim Jones. And the way the children are laying there now, I'd rather see them lay like that than to see them have to die like the Jews did, which was pitiful anyhow. And I'd just like to—to thank Dad for giving us life and also death. And I appreciate the fact of the way our children are going. Because, like Dad said, when they come in, what they're gonna do to our children—they're gonna massacre our children. And also the ones that they take captured, they're gonna just let them grow up and be dummies like they want them to be. And not grow up to be a socialist like the one and only Jim Jones. So I'd like to thank Dad for the opportunity for letting Jonestown be, not what it could be, [*emphatic*] but what Jonestown is. Thank you, Dad.

*

Jones: —taking us through all these anguish years. They took us and put us in chains and that's nothing. This business—that business—there's no comparison to that, to this. They've robbed us of our land, and they've taken us and driven us and we tried to find ourselves. We tried to find a new beginning. But it's too late. You can't separate yourself from your brother and your sister. No way I'm going to do it. I refuse. I don't know who fired the shot. I don't know who killed the congressman. But as far as I am concerned, I killed him. You understand what I'm saying? I killed him. He had no business coming. I told him not to come.

Woman 13: Right, right. [*music and crying*]

Jones: [*pleading*] I, with respect, die with a degree of dignity. Lay down your life with dignity. Don't lay down with tears and agony. There's nothing to death. It's like Mac [Temple leader Jim McElvane] said, it's just stepping over into another plane. Don't be this way. Stop this hysterics. This is not the way for people who are Socialists or Communists to die. No way for us to die. We must die with some dignity. We must die with some dignity. We will have no choice. Now we have some choice. Do you think they're gonna stand—allow this to be done and allow us to get by with this? You must be insane. Look children, it's just something to put you to rest.

Man 5: —hate and treachery. I think you—you people out here should think about how your relatives were and be glad about, that the children are being laid to rest. And all I'd like to say is that I thank Dad for making me strong to stand with it all and make me ready for it. Thank you.

Jones: All they're doing is—All they do is taking a drink. They take it to go to sleep. That's what death is, sleep. I'm tired of it all.

Woman 15: Everything we could have ever done, most loving thing all of us could have done, and it's been a pleasure walking with all of you in this revolutionary struggle. No other way I would rather go [*sic*] to give my life for socialism, communism, and I thank Dad very, very much.

Woman 16: Right. Yes. Dad's love and nursing, goodness and kindness, and he bring[s] us to this land of freedom. His love—his mother was the advance—the advance guard for socialism. And his love and his principles [*unintelligible*] will go on forever unto the fields of—

Jones: Where's the vat, the vat, the vat? Where's the vat with the Green C on it? Bring the vat with the Green C in. Please? Bring it here so the adults can begin.

Woman 16: Go on unto the Zion, and thank you, Dad.

Jones: Don't fail to follow my advice. You'll be sorry. You'll be sorry. [*tape edit*]—if we do it, than that they do it. Have trust. You have to step across.

We used to think this world was—this world was not our home—well, it sure isn't—we were saying—it sure wasn't. He doesn't want to tell me. All he's doing—if they will tell 'em—assure these kids. Can't some people assure these children of the relaxation of stepping over to the next plane? They set an example for others. We said—one thousand people who said, we don't like the way the world is. Take some. Take our life from us. We laid it down. We got tired. We didn't commit suicide, we committed an act of revolutionary suicide protesting the conditions of an inhumane world.

Suicide Note

Richard Tropp

Nov. 18, 1977 [sic]—*The Last Day of Peoples Temple*

To Whomever Finds This Note

Collect all the tapes, all the writing, all the history. The story of this movement, this action, must be examined over and over. It must be understood in all of its incredible dimensions. Words fail. We have pledged our lives to this great cause. We are proud to have something to die for. We do not fear death. We hope that the world will someday realize the ideals of brotherhood, justice and equality that Jim Jones has lived and died for. We have all chosen to die for this cause. We know there is no way that we can avoid misinterpretation. But Jim Jones and this movement were born too soon. The world was not ready to let us live.

I am sorry there is no eloquence as I write these final words. We are resolved, but grieved that we cannot make the truth of our witness clear.

This is the last day of our lives. May the world find a way to a new birth of social justice. If there is any way that our lives and the life of Jim Jones can ever help that take place, we will not have lived in [vain].

Jim Jones did not order anyone to attack or kill anyone. It was done by individuals who had too much of seeing people try to destroy this movement, Jim Jones. Their actions have left us no alternative, and rather than see this cause decimated, we have chosen to give our lives. We are proud of that choice.

Please try to understand. Look at *all.* Look at all in perspective. Look at Jonestown, see what we have tried to do—This was a monument to *life,* to the [re]newal of the human spirit, broken by capitalism, by a system of exploitation & injustice. Look at all that was built by a beleaguered people. We did not want this kind of ending—we wanted to live, to shine, to bring light to a world that is dying for a little bit of love. To those left behind of our loved ones, many of whom will not understand, who never knew this truth, *grieve not,* we are grateful for this opportunity to bear witness—a bitter witness—history has chosen our destiny in spite of our own desire to forge our own. We were at a cross-purpose with history. But we are calm in this hour of our collective leave-taking. As I write these words people are silently amassed, taking a quick potion, inducing sleep, *relief.* We are a long-suffering people. Many of us are weary with a long search, a long struggle—going back not only in our own lifetime, but a long painful heritage.

(*Please* see the histories of our people that are in a building called teachers resource center.)

Many of us are now dead. Each moment, another passes over to a peace. We are begging only for some understanding. It will take more than small minds, reporters [*sic*] minds, to fathom these events. Something must come of this. Beyond all the circumstances surrounding the immediate event, someone can perhaps find the symbolic, the eternal in this moment—the meaning of a people, a struggle—I wish I had time to put it all together, that I had done it. I did not do it. I failed to write the book. Someone else, others will have to do this. Please study this movement, from the very origins of Jim Jones in the rural poverty of Indiana, out from the heart of the America that he later was to stand against for its betrayal of its ideals.

These are a beautiful people, a brave people, not afraid.

There is quiet as we leave this world. The sky is gray. People file [*illegible word*] slowly and take the somewhat bitter drink. Many more must drink. Our destiny. It is sad that we could not let our light shine in truth, unclouded by the demons of accident, circumstance, miscalculation, error that was not our intent, beyond our intent.

I hope that someone writes this whole story. It is not "news." It is more. We merge with millions of others, we are subsumed in the archetype.

People hugging each other, embracing, we are hurrying—we do not want to be captured. We want to bear witness *at once.*

We did not want it this way. All was going well as Ryan completed [his] first day here. Then a man tried to attack him, unsuccessfully at some time, several set out into jungle wanting to overtake Ryan, [his] aide, and others who left with him. They did, and several [were] killed. When we heard this, we had no choice.

We *would be taken.* We have to go as one, we want to live as Peoples Temple, or end it. We have chosen. *It is finished.* [*emphatic underline, with flourish*]

Hugging & kissing & tears & silence & joy in a long line.

Touches and whispered words as this silent line passes. Determination, purpose. A proud people. Only last night, their voices raised in unison, a voice of *affirmation* and today, a different sort of affirmation, a different dimension of that same victory of the human *spirit.*

A tiny kitten sits next to me. Watching. A dog barks. The birds gather on the telephone wires. Let all the story of this People[s] Temple be told. *Let all the books be opened.* This sight . . . O terrible victory. How bitter that we did not, could not, that Jim Jones was crushed by a world that he didn't make—how great the victory.

If nobody understands, it matters not. I am ready to die now. Darkness settles over Jonestown on its last day on earth.

NOTES

Excerpt from interview with Jim Jones on Ukiah radio station, May 10 or 11, 1973, reprinted courtesy of the Jonestown Institute.

Excerpt from Political and Religious Lecture, October 15, 1974, reprinted courtesy of the Jonestown Institute.

Excerpt from Sermon in Philadelphia, 1976, reprinted courtesy of the Jonestown Institute.

Excerpt from the "Death Tape," November 18, 1978, reprinted courtesy of the Jonestown Institute.

Suicide Note by Richard Tropp, November 18, 1978, reprinted courtesy of the Jonestown Institute.

1. A phrase borrowed from Black Panther co-founder Huey Newton.
2. The translation of the Hebrew name for God, Yahweh, from Exodus 3:14.

FOR FURTHER READING

Hall, John R., *Gone from the Promised Land: Jonestown in American Cultural History* (New Brunswick, N.J.: Transaction, 1987). An assessment of Peoples Temple and Jonestown by a well-known scholar of the movement.

The Jonestown Institute, http://jonestown.sdsu.edu. This Website provides "Alternative Considerations of Jonestown and Peoples Temple," updated information on Jonestown-related activities, and memorials to those who died at Jonestown.

Maaga, Mary McCormick, *Hearing the Voices of Jonestown: Putting a Human Face on an American Tragedy* (Syracuse, N.Y.: Syracuse University Press, 1998). This study emphasizes gender and power in the Peoples Temple story.

Mills, Jeannie, *Six Years with God: Life Inside Reverend Jim Jones's Peoples Temple* (New York: A & W, 1979). A remarkably evenhanded account of the Peoples Temple movement from an ex-member.

Moore, Rebecca, *A Sympathetic History of Jonestown: The Moore Family Involvement in Peoples Temple*, Studies in Religion and Society, vol. 14 (Lewiston, N.Y.: Edwin Mellen Press, 1985). An engaging narrative of one scholar's struggle to come to grips with the consequences of losing family members at Jonestown.

Part V

New Worlds

Chapter 12

The Adventist Tradition

Quite possibly the largest NRM America has ever produced came about as the result of the two-year self-conducted Bible study of a farmer from upstate New York. William Miller (1782–1849) set out in 1816 to see if an exhaustive, line-by-line study of Scripture could harmonize any of the Bible's apparent contradictions. By 1818, not only was he satisfied with the Bible's perfect reliability, but his study of the apocalyptic books of Daniel and Revelation convinced him that events described in these ancient prophecies also depicted the historical augurs of the Endtimes. Daniel, in particular, presented a timeline of the Advent, the events leading up to the final days of this world—in Christian terms, the Second Coming (also called the *Parousia*) of Christ prior to his millennial reign, the thousand years of peace mentioned in Revelation 20. Miller realized that if one of these prophetic occurrences could be associated definitively with a specific episode in history, then one could map out the rest of history and determine when, exactly, the Second Coming should happen.

Miller's religious understanding developed simultaneously with the Protestant revivalism of the Second Great Awakening of the American Northeast. In this worldview, there was only one candidate for the "abomination of desolation" portrayed in Daniel 8: the Catholic Church. Marking the date of the "Papal abomination" at 538 C.E., when the Bishop of Rome first asserted control over the Christian church as Pope, Miller determined other events before and after that along a timeline made up the 2,300 prophetic "days" of Daniel 18:14. Relying on a traditional form of biblical interpretation that takes one day in prophecy as equal to one year in history, Miller declared that this "abomination" was "taken away" when Napoleon's forces banished Pope Pius VI after seizing Rome in 1798. By Miller's calculations, as shown in the first excerpt below, the Second Coming would occur forty-five years later—that is, in 1843.

Miller was initially uneasy about sharing his conclusions with others. American culture was largely postmillennial, meaning that the time leading up to the Second Coming was viewed as a period of human social, moral, and spiritual perfection. Miller's vision, however, was decidedly premillennial, suggesting a long period of decline, war, and apostasy before the world would be saved and transformed by Christ and the Host of Heaven.[1] In 1831, he began to deliver sermons laying out his case. There was an immediate response, and the shy, reticent New Englander suddenly found himself in demand to spread the word of the imminent return of Jesus Christ in church after church. Fortunately for Miller, his message caught the ear of a Boston minister, Joseph Himes, who organized Miller's and others' appearances and began to publish a periodical called Signs of the Times (which the Seventh-day Adventists [SDAs] still publish today).

As the predicted date for the Second Coming approached—further determined to be sometime between March 21, 1843, and March 21, 1844 —the Millerite movement spread across the United States, attracting an estimated 50,000 or more adherents. When Christ failed to appear during the predicted time, the date was adjusted to October 22, reflecting the date of Yom Kippur thought to have been set by the scripturally conservative Karaite Jews, and the ensuing intensity reached a fever pitch. Once again, however, there was no Second Coming, and most Millerites saw their greatest hopes solidly dashed, an event that has come to be known as "The Great Disappointment," after which most of Miller's followers abandoned such prophecy altogether. Miller himself died five years later, still expecting the End.

Some of the faithful, however, made another readjustment, just as they had with the first failed date. The change this time was spatial, not temporal: they asserted that Christ had left one chamber of the heavenly Holy of Holies, the inner sanctum of the eternal Temple of which he was High Priest, and entered another, to cleanse it before his return to earth in judgment. That is, the Millerites had the date right, just not the event, and therefore the Advent was still imminent. In December 1844, a seventeen-year-old Millerite named Ellen Harmon (1827–1915)—who would later marry and be known as Ellen G. White—began to have spontaneous visions about the perseverance of the Adventists (as the Millerites came to be known) and her prophetic role as their messenger. Many Adventists, White included, also began celebrating a seventh-day (Saturday) Sabbath, following the Millerite and Adventist leader Joseph Bates, who saw the Catholic Church's Sunday Sabbath as a usurpation of the Fourth Commandment and a matter of great cosmic injustice. By 1860, these believers, led in no small part by White's "Spirit of Prophecy" and revelation of "the new light" for her times, organized as the Seventh-day Adventists (SDAs).

In the course of her life, White experienced more than a thousand visions and published fifty-four books from the hundreds of thousands of handwritten pages that detailed them. She saw herself as a messenger of God, though she insisted that her prophecies were ancillary to Scripture. (This position has not always been held by the SDA Church itself, which generally has seen the Bible, too, as divinely inspired, not literally dictated.) White remained greatly concerned about the failure of Christ to appear upon the earth, and she came to believe that if the original Millerites had remained true to their convictions and continued to spread the word, the groundwork would have been laid and the *Parousia* would have taken place. As the delay in Christ's return grew, White attributed it to at least two additional reasons: the lax moral character of most Christians, including Adventists; and the incomplete work of evangelism to all nations. Thus, the Endtimes were postponed so the SDAs could continue to work to improve the world—a striking shift from a premillennial to a postmillennial position.

Over time, White's prophecies came to serve this end, as well as the expansion and institutionalization of the SDA organization. In 1863, she had a vision that prompted a comprehensive ministry for bodily health. SDAs began promoting vegetarianism and temperance in all things, especially alcohol and tobacco, elements that remain cornerstones of SDA living today, and founded sanitariums, hospitals, and medical schools. White later promulgated a far-reaching philosophy of Christian education, leading to the establishment of SDA schools and colleges around the country.

The easing of eschatological expectations was the result, not just of the delay in Christ's return, but also of the fact that many of the "signs of the times" that once seemed to point to its immediacy were no longer present. Chief among these were the attempts to pass Sunday "blue laws" in the United States, legally establishing Sunday as the nation's Sabbath. The SDAs saw this push in Congress both as a violation of the Fourth Commandment and as the work of an unholy alliance among the Catholic Church, "apostate" Protestants, and the U.S. government. White had deemed this conflation of church and state a clear sign that the Endtimes vision of Revelation 13 was coming true, with the Catholic Church as the First Beast and the federal government as the Second. Ultimately, before the *Parousia*, she predicted that the U.S. government, its power usurped by

the Catholic Church, would persecute the "remnant" of true Christian be-
lievers, the SDAs. She published her Endtimes scenario in 1888 in *The
Great Controversy Between Christ and Satan* (republished as *America in
Prophecy* and excerpted below).[2]

But such dire events never transpired; in fact, over time Congress and
the federal judiciary continued to protect not just religious liberty but also
the separation of church and state, of which SDAs have been vigilant de-
fenders. Moreover, as the Church's schools and hospitals thrived, it was in
the SDA's interest to accommodate, even cooperate with, the larger society
in some ways. SDA colleges became accredited, seminaries disregarded
Miller's and White's "proof-texting" (i.e., the use of scriptural references to
give a specific theological position the authority of revealed "truth") interpretation of the Bible for the higher criticism of modern biblical scholarship, and hospitals merged with secular and even Catholic ones. Although
the SDA Church continued to see "signs of the times" in the two world
wars, John F. Kennedy's election as the first Catholic president, and the
sexual revolution—and although, on the 150th anniversary of the Great
Disappointment in 1994, it affirmed its ongoing expectation of Christ's
imminent return—the importance of eschatology has clearly receded. In
no small part due to this ability to adapt to changing circumstances, the
SDA Church had, by the latter half of the twentieth century, become a
mainstream Christian denomination, with more than ten million members in two hundred countries worldwide, and had emerged as the majority faith in many developing countries.

This shift in emphasis, however, traded tensions with the surrounding
world for tensions with the SDA's own past. As early as the mid-1930s, a
sect of SDAs saw the group's acculturation as an "apostasy" that left no
one to preach the imminent Second Coming—a situation Ellen White had
also warned would signal the Endtimes. This sect's leader, Victor Houteff,
was ousted by the Church and moved with his followers, known as Davidian Adventists, to Waco, Texas, where he established a religious community called Mt. Carmel. After Houteff's death in 1955, his widow, Florence,
moved the community to a new property outside of Waco, and it was here,
in 1981, that another disaffected Seventh-day Adventist named Vernon
Howell (1959–1993) came to join a group of like-minded believers, now
known as the Branch Davidians, with a sense of their role in the coming
Endtimes.[3]

Howell claimed to have received revelations that he was the seventh
angel mentioned in Revelation 10:7. In 1985, on a trip to Israel, he had a

vision of a heavenly ascent in which his messianic role was revealed. Taking as his model Cyrus (or Koresh, in Hebrew) the Persian, who in Isaiah 45 is portrayed as the liberator of the Jews from their Babylonian oppressors, he adopted the name Koresh as well as the quintessentially messianic David. He established himself as not only the group's leader, but also as the individual whose family and community would lead the world as the Elders of Zion after Armageddon and Christ's Second Coming. This world-transforming event was expected in 1995, following a war between the Branch Davidians and "Babylon," the U.S. government. Tragically, the end came sooner than expected, as Koresh and seventy-three of his followers died on April 19, 1993, in the fire that ended a fifty-one-day siege of Mt. Carmel by agents from the Federal Bureau of Investigation and the Bureau of Alcohol, Tobacco, and Firearms.

The three selections below—from Miller, White, and David Thibodeau, a Branch Davidian who survived the siege at Mt. Carmel—emphasize the interpretive relationship between the Christian Scriptures and the unfolding of history. While Miller demonstrates the correspondence between the visions of Daniel and the events of the Napoleonic Wars, White compares the disappointment of the Millerites after 1844 to that of the Apostles following the Crucifixion and indicates that, like Christ's Messianism, the Millerite prophecy had been fulfilled, just not in the way its adherents expected it. White then emphasizes the proper stance toward interpretation in the "latter days" as a bulwark against the skepticism, secularism, and false teachers—both professorial and ecclesiastical—of the age. Miller's approach to Scripture, which required an openness to the guidance of the Holy Spirit while comparing passage against passage to reveal the true meaning, is reflected in White's admonitions, as is his sense that the imminent end of the age is coded in the texts themselves.

The excerpt from David Thibodeau's memoir of his time at Mt. Carmel, *A Place Called Waco,* also shows that David Koresh's means of interpreting the Scriptures—if not his personal, charismatic style—is completely continuous with that of Miller and White. (In fact, White, like Koresh, believed that she and Miller were among the angelic messengers mentioned in the Book of Revelation.) All three of these phases of the Adventist movement clearly focus on the immediacy of a New World, brought about in the manner depicted in the Book of Revelation. The traditional apocalyptic emphases on the "hidden" knowledge of the end, and on the ability to read the signs of Scriptural prophecy in history that reveal that knowledge, underscore a New Understanding of cosmic justice, human history, and the ultimate dispensation of God's will on earth that such groups offer. But a statement to Thibodeau by a Branch Davidian at the very beginning of his association with the group suggests another element of the bonds formed by those who wait for the end together: a New Family. "Mount Carmel is the one true, stable family I've ever really had," he said. "And that's David's doing. He's been more of a loving father to me than any man I've ever known."[4] In fact, as seen in Thibodeau's selection below, Koresh believed that it was specifically *his family*, his children fathered with the women of the group, who would establish the heavenly Zion on earth, the perfect New Society of Christ's Millennial Reign. Much of the excerpt from Thibodeau's book intimates the very personal connection that Koresh's followers could feel with him, even as they may have had serious doubts about where their leader was, in fact, leading them.

From *Evidence from Scripture and History of the Second Coming of Christ about the Year 1843: Exhibited in a Course of Lectures*

William Miller

DANIEL xii. 8. *"And I heard, but I understood not: then said I, O my Lord, what shall be the end of these things?"*

. . . But God is now trying his people, he is now giving them a great rule to know their love for his word. If the word of God is to them foolishness, and they take more delight in the popular writers of the day, they may depend upon it they are stumbling at that stumbling stone. But the Angel tells us that many shall be purified and made white. This was good news to Daniel, and ought to be so to us, for it is the declaration of God through the medium of Gabriel his messenger. "And from the time that the daily sacrifice shall be taken away, and the abomination that maketh desolate set up, there shall be a thousand two hundred and ninety days. Blessed is he that waiteth, and cometh to the thousand three hundred and five and thirty days: but go thou thy way till the end be, for thou shalt rest, and stand in thy lot at the end of the days" [Daniel 12:11–13]. Now Daniel had all he could ask for, now he could understand the time and the length, and part of every division which the Angel had given him in his instruction, so far as to fill up his vision of 2300 years (as we shall call them, having proved in a former lecture that they ought to be so reckoned and have been so fulfilled). He has now learned that to begin and reckon back from the resurrection which he well knew would be 1810 years after Christ's crucifixion, he might find out when the daily sacrifice abomination would be taken away. Therefore take 1335 years from 1810 years would leave 475 years; and he could reckon from the end of the 70 weeks or 490 years to the end of Pagan Rome, would be 475, from thence to the time he should stand in his lot would be 1335 years. Then by adding 490 [to] 475 [to] 1335 would make the sum total of his whole vision 2300 years. And now let us suppose he wished to know when the abomination of desolation would end, and when it would begin. He has only to take his number one thousand two hundred and ninety, as given him by his angel, from his 1335, thus, 1335–1290 = 45 and he finds that 45 years before the resurrection, the little horn would lose his civil power. Now let him take his time, times and a half, and add say 1260 years to 45 years, and he will find that the little horn begun his reign 1305 years before the resurrection, and 30 years after the daily sacrifice abomination was taken away. And now he is prepared to give his vision and the instruction of the Angel all their proper bearings, and prove it thus:—

1st. The seventy weeks or 490 years to the crucifixion of Christ, 490 [years.]

From crucifixion, to taking away daily abomination, 475 [years.]

From taking away Pagan rites, to the setting up abomination of desolation, 30 [years.]

From setting up Papal power, (time, times and an half,) to the end of his civil reign, 1260 [years.]

From the taking away the Papal civil rule, to the resurrection, 45 [years.]

Now add these together and you will have the whole 2300 years of Daniel's vision. Do you not, kind hearer, see by this mode, and by these last numbers given him, Daniel could learn every part and division of the whole history down to the time when he should stand in his lot. But now, for your instruction, we will suppose Daniel understood our mode of reckoning time, he might have given it to us in this way, "The 70 weeks or 490 years will be accomplished, A.D. 33. The Pagan abomination will be taken away 475 years afterwards, which will be A.D. 508. The Papal abomination will be set up 30 years after, A.D. 538, and will continue 1260 years, A.D. 1798. After this 45 years, I shall stand in my lot, and all that come forth to this resurrection will be blessed, A.D. 1843, "Blessed is he that waiteth and cometh to the thousand three hundred and five and thirty days." Rev. xx. 6. "Blessed and holy is he that hath part in the first resurrection."

From *America in Prophecy*

Ellen G. White

The earnest sincere believers [in William Miller's prophecy] had given up all for Christ, and had shared His presence as never before. They had, as they believed, given their last warning to the world, and, expecting soon to be received into the society of their divine Master and the heavenly angels, they had, to a great extent, withdrawn from the society of those who did not receive the message. With intense desire they had prayed, "Come, Lord Jesus. And come quickly." But He had not come. And now to take up again the heavy burden of life's cares and perplexities, and to endure the taunts and sneers of a scoffing world, was a terrible trial of faith and patience.

Yet this disappointment was not so great as was that experienced by the disciples at the time of Christ's first advent. When Jesus rode triumphantly into Jerusalem. His followers believed that He was about to ascend the throne of David, and deliver Israel from her oppressors. With high hopes and joyful anticipations they vied with one another in showing honor to their King. Many spread their outer garments as a carpet in His path, or strewed before Him the leafy branches of the palm. In their enthusiastic joy they united in the glad acclaim, "Hosanna to the Son of David!" When the Pharisees, disturbed and angered by this outburst of rejoicing, wished Jesus to rebuke His disciples, He replied, "If these should hold their peace, the stones would immediately cry out." Luke 19:40. Prophecy must be fulfilled. The disciples were accomplishing the purpose of God; yet they were doomed to a bitter disappointment. But a few days had passed ere they witnessed the Savior's agonizing death, and laid Him in the tomb. Their expectations had not been realized in a single particular, and their hopes died with Jesus. Not till their Lord had come forth triumphant from the grave could they perceive that all had been foretold by prophecy, and "that Christ must needs have suffered, and risen again from the dead." Acts 17:3.

Five hundred years before, the Lord had declared by the prophet Zechariah, "Rejoice greatly, O daughter of Zion; shout, O daughter of Jerusalem. Behold, thy King cometh unto thee. He is just, and having salvation; lowly, and riding upon an ass, and upon a colt the foal of an ass." Zechariah 9:9. Had the disciples realized that Christ was going to judgment and to death, they could not have fulfilled this prophecy.

In like manner, Miller and his associates fulfilled prophecy, and gave a message which Inspiration had foretold should be given to the world, but which they could not have given had they fully understood the prophecies pointing out their disappointment, and presenting another message to be preached to all nations before the Lord should come. The first and second angels' messages were given at the right time, and accomplished the work which God designed to accomplish by them.

The world had been looking on, expecting that if the time passed and Christ did not appear, the whole system of Adventism would be given up. But while many, under strong temptation, yielded their faith, there were some who stood firm. The fruits of the advent movement, the spirit of humility and heart-searching, of renouncing of the world, and reformation of life, which had attended the work, testified that it was of God. They dared not deny that the power of the Holy Spirit had witnessed to the preaching of the second advent, and they could detect no error in their reckoning of the prophetic periods. The ablest of their opponents had not succeeded in overthrowing their system of prophetic interpretation. They could not consent, without Bible evidence, to renounce positions which had been reached through earnest, prayerful study of the Scriptures, by minds enlightened by the Spirit of God, and hearts burning with its living power; positions which had withstood the most searching criticisms and the most bitter opposition of popular religious teachers and worldly-wise men, and which had stood firm against the combined forces of learning and eloquence, and the taunts and revilings alike of the honorable and the base.

True, there had been a failure as to the expected event, but even this could not shake their faith in the word of God. When Jonah proclaimed in the streets of Nineveh within forty days the city would be overthrown, the Lord accepted the humiliation of the Ninevites, and extended their period of probation; yet the message of Jonah was sent of God, and Nineveh was tested according to His will. Adventists believed that in like manner God had led them to give the warning of the judgment. "It has," they declared, "tested the hearts of all who heard it, and awakened a love for the Lord's appearing; or it has called forth a hatred more or less perceivable, but known to God, of His coming. It has drawn a line, . . . so that those who will examine their own hearts, may know on which side of it they would have been found, had the Lord then come—whether they would have exclaimed, 'Lo! this is our God, we have waited for Him, and He will save us;' or whether they would have called to the rocks and mountains to fall on them to hide them from the face of Him that sitteth on the throne, and from the wrath of the Lamb. God thus, as we believe, has tested His people, has tried their faith, has proved them, and seen whether they would shrink, in the hour of trial, from the position in which He might see fit to place them; and whether they would relinquish this world and rely with implicit confidence in the word of God." —*The Advent Herald and Signs of the Times Reporter,* vol. 8, no. 14 (Nov. 13, 1844).

It is the first and highest duty of every rational being to learn from the Scriptures what is truth, and then to walk in the light, and encourage others to follow his example. We should day by day study the Bible diligently, weighing every thought, and comparing scripture with scripture. With divine help, we are to form our opinions for ourselves, as we are to answer for ourselves before God.

The truths most plainly revealed in the Bible have been involved in doubt and darkness by learned men, who, with a pretense of great wisdom, teach that the Scriptures have a mystical, a secret, spiritual meaning not apparent in the language employed. These men are false teachers. It was to such a class that Jesus declared, "Ye know not the Scriptures, neither the power of God." Mark 12:24. The language of the Bible should be explained according to its obvious meaning, unless a symbol or figure is employed. Christ has given the promise, "If any man will do His will, he shall know of the doctrine." John 7:17. If men would but take the Bible as it reads, if there were no false teachers to mislead and confuse their minds, a work would be accomplished that would make angels glad, and that would bring into the fold of Christ thousands upon thousands who are now wandering in error.

We should exert all the powers of the mind in the study of the Scriptures, and should task the understanding to comprehend, as far as mortals can, the deep things of God; yet we must not forget that the docility and submission of a child is the true spirit of the learner. Scriptural difficulties can never be mastered by the same methods that are employed in grappling with philosophical problems. We should not engage in the study of the Bible with that self-reliance with which so many enter the domains of science, but with a prayerful dependence upon God, and a sincere desire to learn His will. We must come with a humble and teachable spirit to obtain knowledge from the great I AM. Otherwise, evil angels will so blind our minds and harden our hearts that we shall not be impressed by the truth. . . .

We are living in the most solemn period of this world's history. The destiny of earth's teeming multitudes is about to be decided. Our own future well-being and also the salvation of other souls, depends upon the course which we now pursue. We need to be guided by the Spirit of truth. Every follower of Christ should earnestly inquire, "Lord, what wilt Thou have me to do?" We need to humble ourselves before the Lord, with fasting and prayer, and to meditate much upon His word, especially upon the scenes of the judgment. We should now seek a deep and living experience in the things of God. We have not a moment to lose. Events of vital importance are taking place around us; we are on Satan's enchanted ground. Sleep not, sentinels of God; the foe is lurking near, ready at any moment, should you become lax and drowsy, to spring upon you and make you his prey.

Many are deceived as to their true condition before God. They congratulate themselves upon the wrong acts which they do not commit, and forget to enumerate the good and noble deeds which God requires of them, but which they have neglected to perform. It is not enough that they are trees in the garden of God. They are to answer His expectation by bearing fruit. He holds them accountable for their failure to accomplish all the good which they could have done, through His grace strengthening them. In the books of heaven they are registered as cumberers of the ground. Yet the case of even this class is not utterly hopeless. With those who have slighted God's mercy and abused His grace, the heart of long-suffering love yet pleads. "Wherefore He saith, Awake, thou that sleepest, and arise from the dead, and Christ shall give thee light. See then that ye walk circumspectly, . . . redeeming the time, because the days are evil." Ephesians 5:14–16.

When the testing time shall come, those who have made God's word their rule of life will be revealed. In summer there is no noticeable difference between evergreens and other trees; but when the blasts of winter come, the evergreens remain unchanged, while other trees are stripped of their foliage. So the false-hearted professor may not now be distinguished from the real Christian, but the time is just upon us when the difference will be apparent. Let opposition arise, let bigotry and intolerance again bear sway, let persecution be kindled, and the half-hearted and hypocritical will waver and yield the faith; but the true Christian will stand firm as a rock, his faith stronger, his hope brighter, than in days of prosperity.

From *A Place Called Waco: A Survivor's Story*

David Thibodeau and Leon Whiteson

David [Koresh]'s essential message derived from his vision that the entire Bible, from Genesis to Revelation, was an integrated, coded narrative describing humanity's spiritual history. He claimed he'd been given the key to unlocking this coded story, thereby making the events prophesied in Scripture about the end of human history actually happen.

"I've been sent to explain the Scriptures," he said.

David believed he was the incarnation of the sacrificed Lamb spoken of in Revelation—*the Lamb that was slain to receive power*—who took the mysterious book from God's hand and proceeded to unlock the Seven Seals described in Revelation, one by one. He made clear that he was not a resurrected Jesus but an "anointed one," a Hebrew term referring to the biblical ceremony in which oil is poured over the head of a priest or king.

David said he followed Jesus and his predecessor, Melchizedek, a priest who was a contemporary of Abraham, *made like unto the Son of God*. David argued that, since the messianic Melchizedek had lived 2,000 years before Jesus, another prophet could appear 2,000 years after. . . .

The text of Revelation is filled with amazing figures out of some biblical *Star Wars* epic. There are seven-headed beasts, winged creatures with faces of lions, calves, eagles, and human beings, a false horned prophet, Satan in the form of a dragon, a harlot on beastback, one woman drunk with the blood of saints, another covered in a garment of stars. Frogs come out of the dragon's mouth and angels hurl millstones big enough to destroy a mighty city.

What kind of mind could dream up such an incredible scenario? I wondered. Either a genius or a loony. And what kind of man must David be if he could claim to have the key to unraveling these magnificent obscurities? Either inspired or nuts. . . .

David's study sessions, held before a large crowd under the airless chapel's open-raftered ceiling, often ran on for twelve hours at a stretch.

As a teacher, David's style was all his own. He was not charismatic in the manner of a Jim Jones or some television preachers. Neither was he formal or dignified, like a robed priest or a rabbi in his prayer shawl. In fact, his whole style was a kind of debunking of such expectations. He spoke fluently but he was never preachy, which for me would've been an instant turnoff.

In his teaching mode, David Koresh was a Texas good ol' boy transformed by the spirit. He shuffled up to the podium in jeans and T-shirt, wearing sneakers, sometimes still sweaty from jogging or biking, other times with mechanic's grease on his fingers or streaking his cheeks, hurrying in from the auto shop where he loved to tinker. Much of the time he hadn't even bothered to shave, signaling to us that studying the Scripture was just part of everyday life, not something removed from the mundane but woven into its texture.

When he began to speak his voice was low, casual, almost chatty. One of his favorite similes was comparing the puzzle of Scripture to the workings of a car engine. "To fire it up, get the wheels moving, you have to have the plugs, pistons, gears, transmission, and all operating in sync, otherwise all you have is a junker. Our souls are junkers, stuck in neutral, until we get our spirits in sync."

Holding the Bible pressed to his brow, he said: "I have these pictures in my head. Most people see this book as two pieces of leather with pages in between. I hold the book to my head and see it instantaneously, panoramically, all the events happening now. The written Word of God and the Mind of God are harmonized in my brain, and all I can do is show it to you." This notion that he was living in a movie that had begun thousands of years ago, way back in the origins of the human imagination, caught my fancy. If it were true, what an experience it must be!

David spoke of being "in the message" or "coming into the message." When he read Scripture it was as if he were actually there taking part in the events, striding back and forth, gesturing expressively. If God was cursing his flock, David's voice would rise dramatically. As he warmed up he took fire, his wiry, six-foot frame twisting with the intensity of his deliverance, his glasses smudged with the heat of his feelings, his words stuttering as his larynx struggled to keep pace with his racing brain. But he was no hellfire Pentecostal minister. When he spoke of the grace of God his voice was loving and compassionate: Altogether, his stamina was amazing; he could talk for up to twenty or thirty hours at a stretch, barely pausing to sip a glass of water while his listeners took notes and the kids played at their parents' feet.

At times, though, his metaphors could be downright disgusting, like his comparison of sin with a sticky booger hanging on your finger. "You're pickin' away, and it gets on your other finger, even when you're goin' fifty down the road and you're tryin' to flick it off." We chuckled at these images, sometimes with embarrassment, but they caught our attention.

He disarmed doubters by jokingly dismissing the Bible as "just a game the Jews made up." Scripture, he told us, was a way to escape "the guy in the mirror. We want to go from here to a place of freedom where we're no longer in bondage to the flesh, our stupidity, our vanity." He likened the prophets to a bunch of journalists "giving you a hot scoop on the future." He compared the biblical texts he quoted to a series of movie previews, "fast, action-packed pictures to grab your eye." Other times, describing God's harsh judgments, he commented: "the Lord is beating some butt, right?" He was always honest with us about the consequences of his theology. "It ain't going to be pretty," he warned.

There were moments when David seemed exhausted by his own intensities. "I'm tired of giving Bible studies to you guys," he'd say wearily. "Leave me be." Occasionally he dozed off from exhaustion in the middle of a study. When that happened, people just sat and waited, often for an hour or more, for him to wake and pick up the thread of his discourse exactly where he'd left off.

Sometimes he'd deliberately provoke us, to jar us out of a trance. "You know, I hate black people," he said once, out of the blue. I cringed reflexively. The crowd, which was around one-third black, was shocked. You could cut the hush with an axe. "And I hate yellow people," David went on after a pause. "And I hate white people. The People I value are people of light."

Suddenly, the audience let out a huge sigh of collective relief. "Are you people of light?" David challenged harshly, and the brief moment of complacency evaporated. Listening to him, I ran through a whole catalogue of emotions, from fascination to frustration. Sometimes the study really took off like a good jam session, David and the crowd right there in the groove, flying on the wings of his words. Then there seemed to be a powerful energy in the room, everyone attuned to the same soul rhythms. David was inspired, feeding off the power of the response, like I would when the riffs were rolling. On other occasions, exhausted by his energy I fell asleep or left the room to stretch my legs, so choked by all the talk I just had to go outside and kick the dirt for the hell of it.

"How long is this going to friggin' go on?" I cried out one time when I was outside and was startled to hear Steve [Schneider] chuckling behind me. I challenged him: "How do you go through this, sitting still for hours on end, living in this hellhole?" He laughed grimly. "You wouldn't believe the things I've been through to be here." There was an edge of resentment in his voice, and he broke off abruptly, afraid of seeming disloyal.

That night I had a surprising dream. In the dream, Michele Jones[5] and I were down by the lake at night. I knew I wasn't supposed to have this assignation, but the warm black night and the big Texas moon, the crickets and the fireflies, softened my guilt. I was about to kiss Michele when, looking over my shoulder, I saw David watching us, smiling knowingly.

I woke up abruptly. *What does that mean?* I wondered. *Am I already trapped here? Is there no way of getting away from this guy?*

Though I was strongly drawn to David and fascinated by his ideas, I often had difficulty believing everything he said. I didn't doubt that he believed, but my natural skepticism got in the way of my own credulity.

For example, I had a hard time with David's account of his vision on Mount Zion, received during his second visit to Israel, in 1985. He said that Russian cosmonauts had reported the presence of seven angelic beings flying toward earth with wings the size of jumbo jets!

"Okay, so what happened was, while I was standing on Mount Zion," he said, "I met up with these angels, these presences made of pure light. They were warriors surrounding the Merkabah, the heavenly throne, riding on fiery horses, armed with flaming swords. They only allow those who can reveal the Seals into the higher realm, into those innumerable worlds that exist alongside our own.

"I was taken up past Orion, to meet God. He spoke to me, and I saw that he was made of unblemished flesh. In a flash I received a complete key to the Scriptures, how the puzzle fitted together. I knew then it was my destiny to unlock the Seals and open the way for our community."

[Branch Davidian] Clive Doyle told me that David's visionary experience in Jerusalem was so concentrated and so charged he could barely stutter afterward. "As he described it, the way he saw the Bible was like a video, and at first he couldn't speak as fast as he could see it. He told us that he would bring us the Seventh Angel's message, predicting that the End Time would happen in 1995, ten years after that amazing moment on Mount Zion. He was truly inspired."

After this, David began to speak of the "Cyrus message." Cyrus is the anointed king mentioned in Isaiah 45. *And I will give thee the treasures of darkness, and the hidden riches of secret places.* In this view, the people living at Mount Carmel were the "wave sheaf," the core group leading the way for the 144,000 souls chosen to follow, and David was the Lamb who would open the Seals.

As David's grasp of his role in the fulfillment of prophecy evolved, he had a further series of revelations. One of the most important and startling of these was his "New Light"[6] experience during the summer of 1989, in which he foresaw the crucial role of sex and procreation in what he called the coming New World Order—a phrase later echoed by President George Bush around the time of the 1991 Gulf War.

The New Light revelation was so radical it shocked some of his people and shook their faith. Simply put, it mandated celibacy for everyone except David. Single men in the community had to give up sex. Married men, such as Steve Schneider and Livingston Fagan, had to separate from their wives and cease making love altogether. Sex was a distraction, David told his people, an untamed power seducing the spirit away from its focus. Only David was given the right to procreate with any of the women, married or single, to generate the inner circle of children who would rule the coming kingdom to be established in Israel.

In David's spiritual logic, he saw himself assuming the burden of sexuality for the entire community, both male and female. The children David would have with these women, married and single, ranging in ages from twelve to forty, would represent the most sacred core of the community. "They are our hope and our future," he said simply.

David's children were intended to be the twenty-four wise ones or Elders surrounding the divine throne, as described in Revelation 4, *clothed in white raiment; and they had on their heads crowns of gold.* These Elders would rule the earthly kingdom to be set up in Israel in the last days, as Isaiah predicted. In Psalm 45, the Messiah fathers children meant to be princes under the Lamb. It was a bold, astounding, even incredible notion; but, for David, it was crucial to his entire belief in his calling.

"It was a tough thing to sell," David admitted. "Some of the guys and some of the women chomped at the bit. But I told them Jesus himself spoke about becoming celibate for the kingdom's sake, and most finally accepted the New Light."

"You mean—?" I began, slowly grasping the implications of this notion.

"Yes," David cut in bluntly. "If you join us, you'll have to be celibate. Can you cut it, a randy guy like you?"

"No way," I retorted instantly. Then, considering it, I modified this reaction. "I'd have to think about it, you know? I mean, if it's part of the deal, if I understand its purpose in the whole scheme. . . ."

"It's a toughie," David conceded, "but I hope you will come to understand its purpose. Some of the people didn't, like Marc Breault, the man who was then closest to my heart. He'd just married this girl, Elizabeth, and couldn't give her up. They left us."

In Marc Breault, David had his Judas—a favorite disciple who abandoned and betrayed him. Whenever he spoke of Breault, a veil of baffled sadness fell over his face.

David met Marc in early 1986 through Perry Jones, who'd struck up a conversation with him in a bookstore in Southern California. Again the common bond was music, and Marc joined the band, playing the keyboards. Born in Hawaii, he was a computer whiz and had a master's degree in religious studies from a Seventh-day Adventist college.

"He was bright as a penny, like a brother to me," David said. "I trusted him with my life."

Along with Steve Schneider, whom Marc had recruited, he was David's most loyal and articulate ally. But he broke away a year or so before I first met up with David. As an apostate, he became David's bitter and vindictive enemy. Hiding out in Australia, he hired a detective to investigate Mount Carmel and "expose" the community. Later, Marc played a diabolical role in provoking the government's assault on Mount Carmel.[7]

One of the appealing things about David was that when he wasn't giving a study period he became just one of the guys. He liked to hang out with other musicians when he was relaxing, and after a particularly intense Bible session he'd come down off the podium and invite a bunch of us to go into town, "kick back, swallow some suds, play some tunes." On these occasions David, Jamie, Mike Schroeder, and I piled into the Camaro and headed for town, to the Chelsea Street Pub, a popular west Waco eatery.

While downing a few beers, we mingled with the crowd and chatted to the band playing in the din.

During our expeditions among the Wacoans, David was like a chameleon. He had many different modes, telling strangers what he sensed they needed to hear. His manner was easy, his twang broader, and people opened up to him. When he was around there was a quiet energy in the room. But it was clear that those who decided to hate David really loathed him. Within minutes of walking into a bar or after talking to him for a short while, some men and women became his immediate adversaries. When that happened, he'd simply walk away, deflecting confrontation. Or he'd buy the person a beer and say, "Well, let's just be best enemies, okay?"

Once or twice during these bar busts we took over the stage to bang out a couple of songs, me on the drums, David singing and plucking a borrowed guitar. We did hard rock, no religion, just the music I grew up with, like Peter Frampton and Ted Nugent. In a way that maybe only fellow musicians can truly understand, by performing together I recognized that David had an intuitive understanding of where I was at and what I yearned to be.

Despite his easy ways, I couldn't avoid the slow realization that there appeared to be a very dark side to David's "truth." It seemed that he expected to be destroyed, along with anyone who followed him. The possibility that the forces loose in the world would reject and kill him was always on David's mind; and if the world rejected his message, his death was inevitable and terrible. *For wherever the carcass is, there eagles will be gathered together,* he quoted [Matthew 24:28]. "I am the one whose body will be mutilated and left to rot in the open field." As he explained it, the opening of the Fifth Seal includes the prediction that the community will suffer a violent death. *I saw under the altar the souls of them that were slain for the word of God,* Revelation writes, portraying a terrible confrontation between the temporal powers and the Lamb, between "Babylon" and the "Peculiar People," like the Mount Carmel community. In the pivotal events of the Sixth Seal, Mount Carmel and society at large would be hit by terrifying natural disasters. "I knew then that we had to live through the 'little season' spoken of in Revelation Five, before being killed," David said. "It's a hard fate, but inevitable, and somehow magnificent."

His words scared me. I simultaneously absorbed them and buried them in my subconscious: This cataclysmic scenario was too tough to swallow whole. My old habit was to live day by day, chewing on morsels of experience and information as they came. Like many of the people at Mount

Carmel, and maybe David himself, I kind of hoped the prophecies would be modified somehow, and his followers wouldn't have to suffer the total annihilation predicted in Scripture. But the words of Revelation 6:12, that on the opening of the Sixth Seal, *there was a great earthquake; and the sun became black as sackcloth, and the moon became as blood,* echoed in my mind. In other words, the place was primed for martyrdom.

David represented himself as the intercessor between humanity and a wrathful deity. Sometimes he compared himself to Noah, warning of the flood to come and being scoffed at by everyone except his own family.

When David spoke like that my nape hairs prickled and my palms got clammy. Was I really ready to accept an inevitable, possibly violent death? Was what I was learning from David really worth such a risk? These questions hovered in the air, never really answered until the final period of the siege of Mount Carmel.

NOTES

Excerpts from *Evidence from Scripture and History of the Second Coming of Christ about the Year 1843: Exhibited in a Course of Lectures,* by William Miller (Troy, N.Y.: Kemble & Hooper, 1836), 76–80, 81–83, 87.

Excerpts from Ellen G. White, *America in Prophecy* (Jemison, Ala.: Inspiration Books East, 1988), 381–84, 577–78, 579–80. Originally published as *The Great Controversy Between Christ and Satan,* 1888. Reprinted by permission of Inspiration Books East, Inc.

Excerpt from David Thibodeau and Leon Whiteson, *A Place Called Waco: A Survivor's Story* (New York: PublicAffairs, 1999), 47–48, 49–57. Reprinted by permission of the Copyright Clearance Center, Inc.

1. In fact, Miller's view of historical periods as corresponding to times of prophetic significance places him firmly in premillennialist dispensationalism, popularized in the nineteenth century by Charles Nelson Darby and the Plymouth Brethren denomination. See also the selection from Charles Taze Russell's *Millennial Dawn* in the next chapter.

2. In the 1980s, evidence emerged that White had relied heavily on others' work, even to the point of plagiarism, but it has not affected the regard with which the SDA Church holds her or her writings.

3. The word Branch was added to the group's name by Ben and Lois Roden in the 1960s; Ben saw himself as the "anointed branch" of Zechariah 3:8 and 6:12, as well as the "vine of many branches" of John 15:1–3, a role traditionally understood to be Christ's.

4. David Thibodeau and Leon Whiteson, *A Place Called Waco: A Survivor's Story* (New York: PublicAffairs, 1999), 27.

5. Koresh's Mount Carmel wife.

6. Alluding to Ellen White's phrase for a progressive revelation in accordance with the times at hand.

7. Breault and his wife became leading activists against Koresh and his hold over the Branch Davidians, feeding the media and the American government a view of Koresh as the most stereotypically pathological "cult leader" imaginable.

FOR FURTHER READING

Barkun, Michael, *Crucible of the Millennium: The Burned-over District of New York in the 1840s* (Syracuse, N.Y.: Syracuse University Press, 1986). A classic study of the context for William Miller's ministry.

Doan, Ruth Alden, *The Miller Heresy, Millennialism, and American Culture* (Philadelphia: Temple University Press, 1987). A rich cultural history of the rise of the Millerite movement.

Numbers, Ronald L., and Jonathan M. Butler, eds., *The Disappointed: Millerism and Millenarianism in the Nineteenth Century* (Knoxville: University of Tennessee Press, 1993). An important collection of scholarly articles about Seventh-day Adventism.

Numbers, Ronald, and Janet S. Numbers, *Prophetess of Health: Ellen G. White and the Origins of Seventh-day Adventist Health Reform* (Knoxville: University of Tennessee Press, 1992). A noted biography of the founder of Seventh-day Adventism.

Seventh-day Adventist Church, http://www.adventist.org. The official Website of the Seventh-day Adventist Church.

Tabor, James D., and Eugene V. Gallagher, *Why Waco? Cults and the Battle for Religious Freedom in America* (Berkeley: University of California Press, 1995). One of the best scholarly appraisals of the Branch Davidians available. Tabor was one of the biblical scholars who spoke with David Koresh before the Mt. Carmel community was destroyed.

Wright, Stuart, ed., *Armageddon in Waco: Critical Perspectives on the Branch Davidian Conflict* (Chicago: University of Chicago Press, 1995). An excellent collection of scholarly essays about the Branch Davidians and Waco.

Chapter 13

Jehovah's Witnesses

The legacy of William Miller's form of biblical interpretation is found not only in the Adventist tradition (discussed in the previous chapter), but also in the beliefs and lifestyle of the Jehovah's Witnesses. However, whereas the apocalyptic fervor of the Seventh-day Adventists largely receded during the lifetime of their prophetess, Ellen G. White, Jehovah's Witnesses continue to be resolutely committed to spreading the imperative knowledge of the imminent end to human society in the coming war of Armageddon. In the course of their history, the Witnesses have set, reinterpreted, and revised a number of dates for these apocalyptic events, especially Christ's Second Coming, or *Parousia* (understood in its literal Greek sense of "presence," rather than "coming," as it is translated in the King James Bible), including 1914, 1918, 1925, and 1975. The Witnesses' organizational, theological, and evangelical systems, intricately intertwined as they are, have been remarkably adept at keeping individuals "in the Truth" following the disappointment of failed prophecy.

Jehovah's Witnesses owe their distinctive worldview and lifestyle almost exclusively to two men: Charles Taze Russell (1852–1916) and Joseph Franklin Rutherford (1869–1942). Russell, a Pittsburgh businessman who was raised a Presbyterian, increasingly became disillusioned both with certain established Christian doctrines—especially the belief that a good and powerful God would inflict eternal suffering on human beings in Hell—and with the failings of human systems of thought and governance. Russell attended a meeting of Seventh-day Adventists in 1870, which sparked an intense period of Bible study and interpretation, culminating in his establishment of what became the Watch Tower Bible and Tract Society. This religious organization and publication clearinghouse soon became international in scope, publishing magazines, tracts, pamphlets, and books, including Russell's own multivolume commentary on biblical prophecy, *Studies in the Scriptures*.

While Russell adamantly resisted establishing a sectarian denomination, calling his followers "Bible Students," his publications uniformly served to define and disseminate his distinctive views, most of which reflected his strict reliance on the Bible as the literal Word of God and his rejection of all other forms of authority in the world. Russell rejected not only human governments, but also Christian churches (especially Roman Catholicism), which were collectively designated as the evil "Babylon the Great" of the Book of Revelation. According to Russell, God had placed all of the current world, religious and secular, under the rule of Satan as a test for humanity.

In keeping with his unflinching stance against any theological innovations developed in the course of Catholic or Protestant history, Russell rejected the concept of the Trinity as unscriptural. (Jehovah's Witnesses teach that God created Jesus, as "Christ," and anointed him to be His redeeming messenger, and hence Jesus and God are neither the same nor equal.) Russell also came to assert that Christ's *Parousia* would initially be invisible and would mark the beginning of the "great harvest" of the 144,000 elect believers of Revelation 7 and 14, also called the "little flock" and "Bride" or "Body" of Christ," who would rule with God in Heaven. (See the first selection below, from Russell's *Millennial Dawn*, and the third selection, from Jehovah's Witness tract literature.) The true Christian church needed to witness God's plan to all who would listen, offering them the opportunity to survive the Endtimes and even be raptured to Heaven preceding them. In the meantime, its members would need to purify their own moral character in preparation for the New Millennium. According to calculations of biblical prophecy not unlike those of William Miller, Russell discerned that the invisible return of Christ would occur in 1874, while his reign as King of God's government on earth would commence in 1914.[1]

When 1914 brought World War I rather than Armageddon, Russell revised his predictions. Given the global tumult, he foresaw an end to the war by apocalyptic means in 1918. Russell would not live to see this date fail also, and the work of preparing a corrupt world for God's impending judgment fell to Rutherford, his successor as president of the Watch Tower Society. Rutherford reinterpreted 1914 as the date of the invisible *Parousia* and seized on 1925 as the year of Armageddon, which became the focus of a book and missionary campaign called *Millions Now Living Will Never Die*. After 1925, despite a third prophetic failure among the faithful in eleven years,[2] Rutherford, by sheer force of personality, began to consolidate his power and mold the teaching, beliefs, and practices of the group to suit his own disposition. The two most notable and visible changes, undoubtedly, were the declaration of a new name for the Bible Students, "Jehovah's Witnesses"[3] (based, among other passages, on Isaiah 43:10–12 and the "faithful witness" of Revelation 1:5 and 3:14), and, reflecting this new name, a dedicated emphasis on door-to-door evangelism. Less visibly, but no less notably, was his explicit refashioning of the Society into a theocracy, with Rutherford, as president, at the head.

Under Rutherford, the Jehovah's Witnesses set themselves apart from the world even more radically, spiritually and morally, if not physically, than they had under Russell. Many of the group's distinguishing features were instituted during his time and reflected his outwardly severe and disciplined demeanor. As the last excerpt below, from *Knowledge That Leads to Eternal Life*, indicates, Christian celebrations such as Christmas and Easter are decried as pagan in origin, and even personal celebrations such as birthdays are linked to godless people. One celebration is allowed —the annual "Lord's Evening Meal," during which those who are moved to claim a place among the heavenly 144,000 partake of communion. Rutherford also instituted a medical prohibition against receiving blood transfusions, linking it to the Kosher laws against eating blood in the Book of Leviticus and the entreaty in Acts 15:28–29 that Gentile Christians abstain from certain impure practices in lieu of circumcision. His experience of being imprisoned in the United States for sedition during World War I, as well as the persecution of Jehovah's Witnesses in Nazi Germany in the 1930s, steeled Rutherford's resolve against acknowledging any symbols of secular governmental authority, such as saluting the flag, serving in the armed forces, voting, or jury duty. For Jehovah's Witnesses, then as now, there is only one government worthy of serving—the kingdom of God, already invisibly present on the earth.

Central control of the Watchtower Society during this time came to rest in its Governing Body in Brooklyn, New York. Only this group, identified as the "faithful and discreet servant" of Matthew 24:45–47 and the earthly representative of the heavenly 144,000, can decipher the Bible's true meaning in the "New Light" revealed in these Last Days. The Governing Body's unquestioned authority means that there is next to no tolerance for dissent, innovation, or even personal spiritual reflection or Bible study. Witness Bible study and evangelical training are based on official materials provided by the Governing Body, including the biweekly publications *The Watchtower* and *Awake!*, and are always done with others at five weekly meetings at a member's house or the local "Kingdom Hall," the Witnesses' unadorned, functional gathering place. The Governing Body appoints an overseer for each congregation, and ultimately both communal and personal lives—including sexual practices, use of intoxicants and stimulants (though alcohol in moderation is allowed), and association with "Babylon"—are strictly regulated from the top. Those who fail to abide by the Society's moral standards or theological precepts risk being ousted, or "disfellowshipped."

This puritanical stance is entirely consistent with the apocalyptic morality as manifested in other times and places, but for the Witnesses it must also be viewed in the context of their evangelism. The fact that Witnesses are compelled to proselytize to nonbelievers, literally to the ends of the earth, before the Messianic age can commence, demands that they be constantly immersed in the world they reject so thoroughly. The strict moral standards, therefore, maintain a spiritual separation from "Babylon" when a physical one would not serve the ultimate goal of the group, namely, to gather as many men and women as possible into the "great multitude" of Revelation 7:9. These believers, in addition to the 144,000 elect who go to heaven, will be saved from Armageddon and enjoy eternal life on earth as perfect subjects of God's Kingdom (a concept also introduced to the Society under Rutherford).

Witnesses' missionary commitment can vary from a few hours a week for part-time "publishers" to more than a hundred hours a month for dedicated full-time "pioneers." *The Watchtower* and *Awake!*, as well as tracts, books, and the Witnesses' own *New World Translation of the Holy Scriptures*, aid in the promulgation of their worldview. Edenic illustrations (such as the one described in the second selection, below), typically depicting people of all races and nations living in joy and harmony, make vivid the promise of the future. In fact, Witness literature continually emphasizes the happiness to be derived from godly living, both in this world and the next. This appeal appears to be genuinely effective, as the Society claims more than five million members in about 232 countries and continues to grow.

There is nothing metaphorical about the anticipated New World for Jehovah's Witnesses. In fact, the phrase "New World" is used incessantly and prominently in their literature to describe the coming transformation of the earth. Yet, as illustrated in the tract below, "Life in a Peaceful New World," inextricably bound to their conception of the New World is a New Society under Christ's heavenly rule, which will eradicate all human governments—and other churches—once the world is sufficiently prepared. (One semi-authorized history of the Witnesses, by Marley Cole, is subtitled *The New World Society.*) A New Family element is evidenced not only by its emphasis on family unity and marital purity, but also by the appellations "brother" and "sister" used among Witnesses. Finally, there are decidedly *not* New Selves engendered among Jehovah's Witnesses; the rigid organizational structure that oversees communal scriptural study, enforces conformity in evangelistic practice, and dictates norms of personal behavior (including the exclusion, as much as possible, of nonbelievers in one's social life), strongly mitigates against exhibiting any distinctive individual identity. The selections below—one from *Millennial Dawn*, the first volume of Russell's *Studies in the Scriptures* series; two from Witness tract literature (also found on its Website); and one from *Knowledge That Leads to Everlasting Life*, a guide to moral living in a world deceived by Satan—all emphasize the continuity and centrality of the apocalyptic message, especially, in the contemporary pieces, as an appeal to those not "in the Truth" to find their way before it is too late.

From *Millennial Dawn*, vol. 1: *The Plan of the Ages*

Charles Taze Russell

Some expect an actual coming and presence of the Lord, but *set the time* of the event a long way off, claiming that through the efforts of the Church in its present condition the world must be converted, and thus the Millennial age be introduced. They claim that when the world has been converted, and Satan bound, and the knowledge of the Lord caused to fill the whole earth, and when the nations learn war no more, then the work of the Church in her present condition will be ended; and that when she has accomplished this great and difficult task, the Lord will come to wind up earthly affairs, reward believers and condemn sinners.

Some scriptures, taken disconnectedly, seem to favor this view; but when God's Word and plan are viewed as a whole, these will all be found to favor the opposite view, viz.: that Christ comes before the conversion of the world, and reigns for the purpose of converting the world; that the Church is now being tried, and that the reward promised the overcomers is that after being glorified they shall share with the Lord Jesus in that reign, which is God's appointed means of blessing the world and causing the knowledge of the Lord to come to every creature. Such are the Lord's special promises:—"To him that overcometh will I grant to sit with me in my throne." (Rev. 3:21.) "And they lived and reigned with Christ a thousand years."—Rev. 20:4.

There are two texts chiefly relied upon by those who claim that the lord will not come until after the Millennium, to which we would here call attention. One is, "This gospel of the Kingdom shall be preached in all the world for a witness unto all nations; and then shall the end come." (Matt. 24:14.) They claim this as having reference to the conversion of the world before the end of the Gospel age. But *witnessing* to the world does not imply the conversion of the world. The text says nothing about how the testimony will be received. This witness has already been given. In 1861 the reports of the Bible Societies showed that the Gospel had been published in every language of earth, though not all of earth's millions had received it. No, not one half of the fourteen hundred millions living have ever heard the name of Jesus. Yet the condition of the text is fulfilled: the gospel has been preached in all the world for a *witness*—to every *nation*.

The Apostle (Acts 15:14) tells that the *main object* of the gospel in the present age is "to take out a people" for Christ's name—the overcoming Church, which, at his second advent, will be united to him and receive his name. The witnessing to the world during this age is a secondary object. . . .

A further examination of God's revealed plans will give a broader view of the object of both the first and second advents; and we should remember that both events stand related as parts of one plan. The specific work of the first advent was to *redeem* men; and that of the second is to *restore*, and bless, and liberate the redeemed. Having given his life a ransom for all, our Savior ascended to present that sacrifice to the Father, thus making reconciliation for man's iniquity. He tarries and permits "the prince of this world" to continue the rule of evil, until after the selection of "the Bride, the Lamb's wife," who, to be accounted *worthy* of such honor, must overcome the influences of the present evil world. Then the work of giving to the world of mankind the great blessings secured to them by his sacrifice will be due to commence, and he will come forth to bless all the families of the earth.

True, the restoring and blessing could have commenced at once, when the ransom price was paid by the Redeemer, and then the coming of Messiah would have been but one event, the reign and blessing beginning at once, as the apostles at first expected. (Acts 1:6.) But God had provided "some better thing for us"—the Christian Church (Heb. 11:40); hence it is in our interest that the reign of Christ is separated from the sufferings of the Head by these eighteen centuries.

This period between the first and second advents, between the ransom of all and the blessing of all, is for the trial and selection of the Church, which is the body of Christ; otherwise there would have been only the one advent, and the work which will be done during the period of his second presence, in the Millennium, would have followed the resurrection of Jesus. Or, instead of saying that the work of the second advent would have followed at once the work of the first, let us say rather that had Jehovah not purposed the selection of the "little flock," "the body of Christ," the first advent would not have taken place when it did, but would have occurred at the time of the second advent, and there would have been but the one. For God has evidently designed the *permission* of evil for six thousand years, as well as that the cleansing and restitution of all shall be accomplished during the seventh thousand.

Thus seen, the coming of Jesus, as the sacrifice and ransom of sinners, was just long enough in advance of the blessing and restoring time to allow for the selection of his "little flock" of "joint-heirs." This will account to some for the apparent delay on God's part in giving the blessings promised, and provided for, in the ransom. The blessings will come in due time, as at first planned, though, for a glorious purpose, the price was paid longer beforehand than men would have expected.

The Apostle informs us that Jesus has been absent from earth—in the heaven—during all the intervening time from his ascension to the beginning of the times of restitution, or the Millennial age—"whom the heaven must retain *until* the times of restitution of all things," etc. (Acts 3:21.) Since the Scriptures thus teach that the object of our Lord's second advent is the restitution of all things, and that at the time of his appearing the nations are so far from being converted as to be angry (Rev. 11:18) and in opposition, it must be admitted either that the Church will fail to accomplish her mission, and that the plan of God will be thus far frustrated, or else, as we claim and have shown, that the conversion of the world in the present age was not expected of the Church, but that her mission has been to preach the Gospel in all the world *for a witness,* and to prepare herself under divine direction for her great future work. God has not yet by any means exhausted his power for the world's conversion. Nay, more: he has not yet *even attempted* the world's conversion.

This may seem a strange statement to some, but let such reflect that if God has attempted such a work he has signally failed; for, as we have seen, only a small fraction of earth's billions have ever intelligently heard of the *only name* whereby they must be saved. We have only forcibly stated the views and teachings of some of the leading sects—Baptists, Presbyterians and others—viz., that God is electing or selecting out of the world a "little flock," a Church. They believe that God will do no more than choose this Church, while we find the Scriptures teaching a further step in the divine plan—a RESTITUTION for the world, to be accomplished through the elect Church, when completed and glorified. The "little flock," the overcomers, of this Gospel age, are only the body of "The Seed" in or by whom all the families of the earth are to be blessed.

From Jehovah's Witness Tract Literature

Life in a Peaceful New World

When you look at the scene on this tract [image of a woman and child petting a wild bear, as an antelope looks on from in front of a house; it is accompanied by the caption "The righteous themselves will possess the earth and they will reside forever upon it."—Psalm 37:29], what feelings do you have? Does not your heart yearn for the peace, happiness, and prosperity seen there? Surely it does. But is it just a dream, or fantasy, to believe these conditions will ever exist on earth?

Most people probably think so. Today's realities are war, crime, hunger, sickness, aging—to mention just a few. Yet there is reason for hope. Looking to the future, the Bible tells of a "new heavens and a new earth that we are awaiting according to [God's] promise, and in these righteousness is to dwell."—2 Peter 3:13; Isaiah 65:17.

These "new heavens" and "new earth," according to the Bible, are not a new material heavens or new literal earth. The physical earth and heavens were made perfect, and the Bible shows they will remain forever. (Psalm 89:36, 37; 104:5) The "new earth" will be a righteous society of people living on earth, and the "new heavens" will be a perfect heavenly kingdom, or government, that will rule over this earthly society of people. But is it realistic to believe that "a new earth," or glorious new world, is possible?

Well, consider the fact that such ideal conditions were part of God's original purpose for this earth. He placed the first human couple in the earthly Paradise of Eden and gave them a marvelous assignment: "Be fruitful and become many and fill the earth and subdue it." (Genesis 1:28) Yes, God's purpose was for them to have children and eventually to spread their Paradise over all the earth. Although they later chose to disobey God, thus proving to be unfit to live forever, God's original purpose did not change. And it must be fulfilled in a new world!—Isaiah 55:11.

In fact, when you pray the Lord's Prayer, or the Our Father, asking for God's Kingdom to come, you are praying for his heavenly government to rid the earth of wickedness and to rule over this new world. (Matthew 6:9, 10) And we can be confident that God will answer that prayer, since his Word promises: "The righteous themselves will possess the earth, and they will reside forever upon it."—Psalm 37:29.

Life in God's New World

God's Kingdom will bring earthly benefits beyond compare, accomplishing everything good that God originally purposed for his people to enjoy on earth. Hatreds and prejudices will cease to exist, and eventually everyone on earth will be a true friend of everyone else. In the Bible, God promises that he will "make wars to cease to the extremity of the earth." "Nation will not lift up sword against nation, neither will they learn war anymore."—Psalm 46:9; Isaiah 2:4.

The whole earth will eventually be brought to a gardenlike paradise state. The Bible says: "The wilderness and the waterless region will exult, and the desert plain will be joyful and blossom as the saffron. . . . For in the wilderness waters will have burst out, and torrents in the desert plain. And the heat–parched ground will have become as a reedy pool, and the thirsty ground as springs of water."—Isaiah 35:1, 6, 7.

There will be every reason to be happy in the Paradise earth. Never again will people hunger for lack of food. "The earth itself will certainly give its produce," the Bible says. (Psalm 67:6; 72:16) All will enjoy the fruits of their own labor, as our Creator promises: "They will certainly plant vineyards and eat their fruitage . . . they will not plant and someone else do the eating."—Isaiah 65:21, 22.

In God's new world, no longer will people be crammed into huge apartment buildings or run–down slums, for God has purposed: "They will certainly build houses and have occupancy. . . . They will not build and someone else have occupancy." The Bible also promises: "They will not toil for nothing." (Isaiah 65:21–23) Thus people will have productive, satisfying work. Life will not be boring.

In time, God's Kingdom will even restore the peaceful relations that existed in the garden of Eden between animals, and between animals and humans. The Bible says: "The wolf will actually reside for a while with the male lamb, and with the kid the leopard itself will lie down, and the calf and the maned young lion and the well-fed animal all together; and a mere little boy will be leader over them."—Isaiah 11:6–9; Hosea 2:18.

Just imagine, in the Paradise earth all sicknesses and physical infirmities will also be healed! God's Word assures us: "No resident will say: 'I am sick.'" (Isaiah 33:24) "[God] will wipe out every tear from their eyes, and death will be no more, neither will mourning nor outcry nor pain be anymore. The former things have passed away."—Revelation 21:4.

How It Is Possible for You

Surely your heart must be moved by the promises of God regarding life in his new world of righteousness. And while some may consider the realizing of such blessings too good to be true, they are not too good to come from the hand of our loving Creator.—Psalm 145:16; Micah 4:4.

Of course, there are requirements to be met if we are to live forever in the coming Paradise on earth. Jesus showed a principal one, saying in prayer to God: "This means everlasting life, their taking in knowledge of you, the only true God, and of the one whom you sent forth, Jesus Christ."—John 17:3.

So if we truly want to live in God's new world, we must first learn God's will and then do it. For it is a fact: This "world is passing away and so is its desire, but he that does the will of God remains forever," to enjoy eternally the blessings to be showered down by our loving Creator.—1 John 2:17.

Eternal Happiness—In Heaven or on Earth?

Does your happiness depend primarily on where you live? Most people would readily acknowledge that happiness depends more on factors like good health, a purpose in life, and fine relationships with others. A Bible proverb puts it this way: "Better is a dish of vegetables where there is love than a manger-fed bull and hatred along with it."—Proverbs 15:17.

Sadly, however, our earthly home has a long history of hatred, violence, and other forms of wickedness. But what about heaven, or the spirit realm, where many people hope to go after they die? Has it always been a place of blissful peace and tranquility, without disturbance of any kind, as is commonly supposed?

The Bible teaches that God resides in heaven along with millions of spirit creatures called angels. (Matthew 18:10; Revelation 5:11) These are described as spirit "sons of God." (Job 38:4, 7) Like humans, the angels also have free moral agency; they are not robots. It follows, therefore, that they too can choose to do right or to do wrong. Would angels choose to do wrong? It may come as a surprise to some to learn that thousands of years ago, a considerable number of angels did, in fact, sin against God—they rebelled against him!—Jude 6.

Rebels in Heaven

Sin appeared in the spirit realm because of the rebellion by an angel, who came to be called Satan (Resister) and Devil (Slanderer). This once-obedient angel chose to do wrong of his own free will. Thereafter he became a corrupting influence on other spirit creatures, so that by the time of Noah, prior to the Flood, a large number of them joined Satan in rebellion against God.—Genesis 6:2, footnote; 2 Peter 2:4.

These fallen angels were not evicted from heaven immediately. Rather, their access was tolerated—apparently with certain restrictions—for thousands of years.[4] However, when God's toleration of these evildoers ended, they were "hurled" out of heaven, ultimately to be destroyed. A voice in heaven then said: "On this account be glad, you heavens and you who reside in them!" (Revelation 12:7–12) Evidently, the faithful angels rejoiced greatly that, at last, the heavens were rid of those vile troublemakers!

Considering these generally unknown details, it is apparent that there can be no true peace whenever intelligent creatures disregard God's laws and principles. (Isaiah 57:20, 21; Jeremiah 14:19, 20) On the other hand, when all obey God's law, peace and tranquility prevail. (Psalm 119:165; Isaiah 48:17, 18) So if all humans loved and obeyed God and loved one another, would not the earth be a truly delightful, happy abode? The Bible answers yes!

But what about those who selfishly refuse to change their wicked ways? Will they forever disturb the peace of those who truly want to do God's will? No, God dealt with the wicked angels in heaven, and he will also deal with the wicked people here on earth.

An Earth Swept Clean

"The heavens are my throne, and the earth is my footstool," God said. (Isaiah 66:1) Being the very acme of holiness, God will not allow his "footstool" to be soiled by evil indefinitely. (Isaiah 6:1–3; Revelation 4:8) Just as he purged the heavens of wicked spirits, so he will rid the earth of all wicked people, as the following Bible passages show:

"Evildoers themselves will be cut off, but those hoping in Jehovah are the ones that will possess the earth."—Psalm 37:9.

"The upright are the ones that will reside in the earth, and the blameless are the ones that will be left over in it. As regards the wicked, they will be cut off from the very earth; and as for the treacherous, they will be torn away from it."—Proverbs 2:21, 22.

"It is righteous on God's part to repay tribulation to those who make tribulation for you, but, to you who suffer tribulation, relief along with us at the revelation of the Lord Jesus from heaven with his powerful angels in a flaming fire, as he brings vengeance upon those who do not know God and those who do not obey the good news about our Lord Jesus. These very ones will undergo the judicial punishment of everlasting destruction from be-fore the Lord and from the glory of his strength."—2 Thessalonians 1:6–9.

"The world [of wicked mankind] is passing away and so is its desire, but he that does the will of God remains forever."—1 John 2:17.

Will the Earth Remain Peaceful?

Although the Scriptures clearly show that God's toleration of the wicked has its limits, how can we be sure that evil, once eliminated, will not recur? After all, following the Flood of Noah's day, it soon surfaced again to such an extent that God had to thwart mankind's wicked schemes by confusing their language.—Genesis 11:1–8.

Our main reason for confidence that evil will not arise again is that the earth will no longer be ruled by humans as it was soon after the Flood. Rather, it will be ruled by the Kingdom of God. Ruling from heaven, this Kingdom will be earth's sole government. (Daniel 2:44; 7:13, 14) It will act quickly against anyone who attempts to reintroduce evil. (Isaiah 65:20) In fact, it will eventually destroy the very originator of wickedness—Satan the Devil—along with the demons, the wicked angels that followed him. —Romans 16:20.

Additionally, mankind will have no causes for anxiety about food, clothing, shelter, and employment—the lack of which today drives some into a life of crime. Yes, the entire earth will be transformed into a productive paradise with an abundance for all.—Isaiah 65:21–23; Luke 23:43.

More important, the Kingdom will educate its subjects in a peaceful way of life while at the same time raising them to the very pinnacle of human perfection. (John 17:3; Romans 8:21) Thereafter, humankind will no longer have to struggle with weaknesses and sinful tendencies, making perfect obedience to God both possible and delightful, as it was in the case of the perfect man Jesus. (Isaiah 11:3) In fact, Jesus remained loyal to God even in the face of great temptation and torture—things that will be utterly foreign to life in Paradise.—Hebrews 7:26.

Why Some Do Go to Heaven

Many readers of the Bible, however, are aware of Jesus' words: "In the house of my Father there are many abodes. . . . I am going my way to prepare a place for you." (John 14:2, 3) Does this not contradict the idea of life everlasting on a paradise earth?

These teachings are not contradictory. In fact, one supports the other. To begin with, the Bible states that only a limited number of faithful Christians—namely, 144,000 of them—are raised as spirit creatures to live in heaven. Why are they given this wonderful reward? Because they make up the group that John saw in a vision who "came to life and ruled as kings with the Christ for a thousand years." (Revelation 14:1, 3; 20:4–6) Compared with the billions on earth, the 144,000 truly are a "little flock." (Luke 12:32) Moreover, having experienced the problems common to human-kind, like Jesus they will be able to "sympathize with our weaknesses" as they supervise the rehabilitation of mankind and of the earth. —Hebrews 4:15.

Earth — Mankind's Eternal Home

By providing the ransom sacrifice of Jesus Christ, God began gathering the 144,000 almost 2,000 years ago, and indications are that this group is now complete. (Acts 2:1–4; Galatians 4:4–7) However, Jesus' sacrifice was not for the sins of the 144,000 only, "but also for the whole world's." (1 John 2:2) Hence, all who exercise faith in Jesus have the prospect of eternal life. (John 3:16) Those asleep in the grave but who are in God's memory will be resurrected, not to heaven, but to life on a cleansed earth. (Ecclesiastes 9:5; John 11:11–13, 25; Acts 24:15) What will await them there?

Revelation 21:1–4 answers, saying: "Look! The tent of God is with mankind . . . And he will wipe out every tear from their eyes, and death will be no more, neither will mourning nor outcry nor pain be anymore. The former things have passed away." Imagine—humans being released from death, and the pain and outcry it causes gone forever! At last, Jehovah's original purpose for the earth and humankind will reach its glorious fulfillment.—Genesis 1:27, 28.

Our Choice — Life or Death

Adam and Eve were never given the option of going to heaven. Their choice was either to obey God and live eternally on a paradise earth or to disobey him and die. Sadly, they chose disobedience and therefore returned to the "dust" of the ground. (Genesis 2:16, 17; 3:2–5, 19) It was never God's purpose for the human family in general to die and to populate heaven via the grave.[5] God created myriads of angels to live in heaven; these spirit creatures are not humans who are deceased and who have been resurrected to life in heaven.—Psalm 104:1, 4; Daniel 7:10.

What must we do to receive the blessing of living forever in Paradise on earth? A first step is to study God's Word, the Holy Bible. "This means everlasting life," Jesus said in prayer, "their taking in knowledge of you, the only true God, and of the one whom you sent forth, Jesus Christ."—John 17:3.

Putting that knowledge into practice is another step to everlasting happiness in Paradise. (James 1:22–24) Those who live by God's Word have the prospect of seeing with their own eyes the fulfillment of such thrilling prophecies as the one recorded at Isaiah 11:9, which says: "They [humankind] will not do any harm or cause any ruin in all my holy mountain; because the earth will certainly be filled with the knowledge of Jehovah as the waters are covering the very sea."

From *Knowledge That Leads to Everlasting Life*

"No Part of the World"

Those desiring to please Jehovah and enjoy Kingdom blessings avoid idolatry in any form. The Bible shows that it is wrong to make and worship images, including those of Christ, or of Jesus' mother, Mary. (Exodus 20:4, 5; 1 John 5:21) So, true Christians do not venerate icons, crosses, and images. They also avoid more subtle forms of idolatry, such as acts of devotion to flags and the singing of songs that glorify nations. When pressured to perform such acts, they recall Jesus' words to Satan: "It is Jehovah your God you must worship, and it is to him alone you must render sacred service." (Matthew 4:8–10) Jesus said that his followers are "no part of the world." (John 17:14) This means being neutral in political affairs and living peacefully in harmony with Isaiah 2:4, which says: "He [Jehovah God] will certainly render judgment among the nations and set matters straight respecting many peoples. And they will have to beat their swords into plowshares and their spears into pruning shears. Nation will not lift up sword against nation, neither will they learn war any more."

Being "no part of the world" also means breaking off all association with "Babylon the Great," the world empire of false religion. Unclean worship spread from ancient Babylon until it held harmful spiritual dominion over people earth wide. "Babylon the Great" embraces all religions whose doctrines and practices are out of harmony with the knowledge of God. (Revelation 17:1, 5, 15) No faithful worshipper of Jehovah will engage in interfaith activities by sharing in worship with different religions or by having spiritual fellowship with any part of Babylon the Great. (Numbers 25:1–9; 2 Corinthians 6:14) Consequently, many new Bible students send a letter of resignation to the religious organization to which they belong. This has brought them closer to the true God, as promised: "'Get out from among them, and separate yourselves,' says Jehovah, 'and quit touching the un-clean thing'; 'and I will take you in.'" (2 Corinthians 6:17; Revelation 18:4, 5) Is not such acceptance by our heavenly Father what you keenly desire?

Weighing Annual Observances

A godly life frees us from the often burdensome celebrating of worldly holidays. For instance, the Bible does not reveal the exact day of Jesus' birth. "I thought Jesus was born on December 25!" some may exclaim. This is not possible because he died in the spring of 33 C.E. at 33 1/2 years of age. Moreover, at the time of his birth, shepherds were "living out of doors and keeping watches in the night over their flocks." (Luke 2:8) In the land of Israel, late December is a cold, rainy season during which sheep would be kept in shelters overnight to protect them from the winter weather. Actually, December 25 was set aside by the Romans as the birthday of their sun god. Centuries after Jesus was on earth, apostate Christians adopted this date for the celebration of Christ's birth. Consequently, true Christians do not celebrate Christmas or any other holiday based on false religious beliefs. Because they give Jehovah exclusive devotion, they also do not observe holidays that idolize sinful humans or nations.

The Bible specifically mentions only two birthday observances, both involving men who did not serve God. (Genesis 40:20–22; Matthew 14:6–11) Since the Scriptures do not reveal the birth date of the perfect man Jesus Christ, why should we give special attention to the birthdays of imperfect humans? (Ecclesiastes 7:1) Of course, godly parents do not await a special day to show their children love. A 13-year-old Christian [i.e., Jehovah's Witness] girl remarked: "My family and I have lots of fun. . . . I'm very close to my parents, and when other kids ask why I don't celebrate holidays, I tell them that I celebrate every day." Said a Christian youth aged 17: "In our house, gift-giving is all year long." Greater happiness results when gifts are given spontaneously.

For those pursuing a godly life, there is one day each year to be specially observed. It is the Lord's Evening Meal, often called the Memorial of Christ's death. Concerning it, Jesus commanded his followers: "Keep doing this in remembrance of me." (Luke 22:19, 20; 1 Corinthians 11:23–25) When Jesus instituted this meal on the night of Nisan[6] 14, 33 C.E., he used unleavened bread and red wine, representing his sinless human body and his perfect blood. (Matthew 26:26–29) These emblems are partaken of by Christians anointed with God's holy spirit. They have been taken into the new covenant and the covenant for the Kingdom, and they have a heavenly hope. (Luke 12:32; 22:20, 28–30; Romans 8:16, 17; Revelation 14:1–5) Nevertheless, benefits are experienced by all those present on the evening that corresponds with Nisan 14 on the ancient Jewish calendar. They are reminded of the love shown by Jehovah God and Jesus Christ in the sin-atoning ransom sacrifice that makes eternal life possible for those having divine favor.—Matthew 20:28; John 3:16. . . .

Clearly, living a godly life requires effort. It may result in ridicule from family members or acquaintances. (Matthew 10:32–39; 1 Peter 4:4) But the rewards of living such a life far outweigh any trials. It results in a clean conscience and provides wholesome companionship with fellow wor-shipers of Jehovah. (Matthew 19:27, 29) Then, too, imagine living forever in God's righteous new world (Isaiah 65:17, 18) And what joy there is in complying with Bible counsel and thus making Jehovah's heart rejoice! (Proverbs 27:11) No wonder that living a godly life brings happiness!— Psalm 128:1, 2.

NOTES

Excerpts from *Millennial Dawn,* vol. 1: *The Plan of the Ages* (*Studies in the Scriptures,* vol. 1) by Charles Taze Russell (Allegheny, Pa.: Watch Tower Bible and Tract Society, 1886), 90–92, 93–95.

Excerpts from Jehovah's Witness tract literature, "Life in a Peaceful New World" and "Eternal Happiness—In Heaven or on Earth?" (Copyright © 2001 Watch Tower Bible and Tract Society of Pennsylvania. Used with permission.) All Bible quotations are from the *New World Translation of the Holy Scriptures* (Brooklyn, N.Y.: Watchtower Bible and Tract Society of Pennsylvania, 1984, 1961).

Excerpts from *Knowledge That Leads to Everlasting Life* (Brooklyn, N.Y.: The Watchtower and Tract Society of Pennsylvania, 1995. Used with permission.) All Bible quotations are from the *New World Translation of the Holy Scriptures* (Brooklyn, N.Y.: Watchtower Bible and Tract Society of Pennsylvania, 1984, 1961).

1. The date 1914 derives from multiplying the seven "Gentile times" of Daniel 4 by 360 days, or "one time" as determined by the "time, times, and half a time" of Revelation 12:6, 12:4, rendering 2,520 "days" or prophetic years. The year 606 B.C.E. is taken to be the beginning of Gentile times, when the Israelite kingdom of Judah fell to the Babylonians, and thus 2,520 years from 606 B.C.E. is 1914 C.E. Unfortu-nately, this date for the fall of Judah is at least nine years too early. The complex roots of, justifications for, and revisions of Russell's Endtimes dating are docu-mented by M. James Penton, *Apocalypse Delayed* (Toronto: University of Toronto Press, 1985), 15–23. Penton also provides succinct versions of the Witnesses' origi-nal, revised, and recent eschatological timelines on pp. 197–99. An explication of this prophetic system as it is currently preached by Jehovah's Witnesses can be

found in *You Can Live Forever in Paradise on Earth* (Brooklyn, N.Y.: Watchtower Bible and Tract Society of Pennsylvania, 1989), 138–41.

2. After 1914, the Endtimes anticipation continued, with that date coming to mark the beginning of "this generation" (Matthew 24:34) that would not pass away before the End, a position officially abandoned in 1995. The last date advocated by the Watchtower Society was 1975, which corresponded to the ostensible end of the 6,000-year allotment for human existence. The general state of the world in terms of war, disease, immorality, and race relations has served most recently as evidence confirming the signs of the End.

3. "Jehovah" is a traditional English rendering of the Hebrew YHWH, or "Yahweh," most likely with the vowels of the euphemism *Adonai* ("Lord") substituted, due to a misunderstanding of the medieval Masoretic text of the Hebrew Bible. Jehovah's Witnesses are compelled to vindicate the divine name by spreading specific knowledge of it, rather than generic titles such as "God" or "Lord."

4. For a discussion of why God has tolerated evil in heaven and on earth, see the book *Knowledge That Leads to Everlasting Life*, published by the Watchtower Bible and Tract Society of New York, Inc. [1995] pages 70–9. [Note in original text.]

5. Reflecting the Jehovah's Witnesses' rejection of the immortality of the soul on scriptural terms.

6. A month of the Jewish calendar, corresponding to March–April.

FOR FURTHER READING

Harrison, Barbara Grizzuti, *Visions of Glory: A History and a Memory of Jehovah's Witnesses* (New York: Simon and Schuster, 1978). A former Jehovah's Witness provides a compassionate but candid memoir of her years in the movement.

Holden, Andrew, *Jehovah's Witnesses: Portrait of a Contemporary Religious Movement* (London: Routledge, 2002). A balanced ethnographic study.

Jehovah's Witnesses: The Organization Behind the Name. VHS. (Brooklyn, N.Y.: Watch Tower Bible and Tract Society of Pennsylvania, 1990). An upbeat survey of the inner workings of the Jehovah's Witnesses' activities, especially the production of their publications.

Penton, M. James, *Apocalypse Delayed: The Story of Jehovah's Witnesses* 2nd ed. (Toronto: University of Toronto Press, 1997). A thorough scholarly study of Jehovah's Witness history, belief, and organization.

Watchtower, http://www.watchtower.org. The official Website of the Watch Tower Bible and Tract Society of Pennsylvania, or Jehovah's Witnesses.

Chapter 14

The New Millennium
NRMs and the Year 2000

As the previous two chapters have demonstrated, the concept of a new millennium—a literal or symbolic thousand-year reign of peace that follows a catastrophic, global tribulation—proffered by the Book of Revelation can be attached to any date, or no date. And yet, at the end of the twentieth century, it became inextricably associated with what should have been a prophetically innocuous year in the Gregorian calendar: the year 2000.[1] Such is the power of the phrase "a new millennium" that apocalyptic interest and expectation increased palpably in the latter half of the 1990s, a "millennial stew" fueled by, and probably itself fueling, an explosion of dark predictions from pulpits, a rash of apocalyptically themed movies, television shows, and pop songs, and an apparent rise in "doomsday cults."

While the aftermath of the 1993 Branch Davidian inferno lingered, another shocking event occurred on March 20, 1995. A Japanese apocalyptic group, Aum Shinrikyo, released deadly sarin gas into Tokyo's subway system, killing twelve people and injuring thousands. The next month, on the anniversary of the destruction of the Branch Davidian community in Waco, Timothy McVeigh killed 168 people when he blew up the federal building in Oklahoma City. While it was clearly an earlier date that motivated McVeigh, the leader of Aum Shinrikyo, Shoko Asahara, apparently expected Armageddon in 2000—the sarin attack was to serve both as a preemptive strike against an irredeemably evil and corrupt world (even as it was meant to be a merciful release from it for its victims) and as a distraction for police, who planned to raid Aum's headquarters.[2]

Baseless or not, it was difficult for many to disassociate this increase in religious violence from the advent of a "new millennium" and all of the imagery wedded to that phrase. Moreover, with the end of the Cold War and the dismantling of the Soviet Union, what had once been a clear moral and political order in the world was gone, and some of the stances that had defined America for decades became moot. Although the memory of nuclear threat was still fresh, it was no longer many people's worst fear, especially when so many other crises—AIDS, global warming, urban decay—loomed. What should have been a period of relative security and peace for most Americans was often fraught with a sense of anxiety and purposelessness. Events such as those in Oklahoma City and Tokyo seemed only to confirm their worst suspicions—that the world itself was coming unmoored. On the other hand, to countless Christians, these conditions offered a strange hope: they could be read as signs that the events depicted in the Book of Revelation had commenced. Here we examine two NRMs that had a very different take on the eschatological significance of the state of the world in general and of the year 2000 in particular.

Heaven's Gate was a San Diego group with a keen interest in the coming millennial change and other aspects of the Endtimes. Like Aum Shinrikyo, they saw human existence itself as evil and intolerable and, as discussed in Chapter 3, sought to escape to "The Evolutionary Level Above Human" (referred to as "T.E.L.A.H."). However, their beliefs did not prompt the group to inflict death on others, but rather on themselves: on March 26, 1997, thirty-nine members of Heaven's Gate were found to have killed themselves in a ritualistic fashion; it was the largest mass suicide in American history. "The Class," as they called themselves, wore black pajamas, Nike running shoes, and plastic bags over their heads—presumably to help accelerate the effect of the sleeping pills and alcohol on which they had overdosed. To the Class, this was not suicide, but liberation—it was the rest of humanity who had chosen death by staying in this world.

According to Marshal Herff Applewhite (1931–1997), who had formed the group (then called "Human Individual Metamorphosis" or HIM) in the early 1970s with Bonnie Lu Nettles (1927–1985),[3] the universe as we know it was created as an experimental testing ground for souls to prepare for the next stage of cosmic evolution, T.E.L.A.H. But the experiment had failed, and the earth had long since been controlled by wicked aliens they called the Luciferians. Heaven's Gate members saw themselves as the current incarnations of the souls of Jesus and the early Christian church and thus were the few souls advanced enough to transcend to T.E.L.A.H. with the assistance of the good aliens and their spacecraft. When a photo of the Hale-Bopp comet appeared on the Internet in November 1996 with what was purported to be a Saturn-shaped flying saucer following close behind, this seemed to Applewhite and the Class to be their chance to escape. That the photo was shown to be a hoax could not dissuade them, as they defiantly stated on their Website (excerpted below) just prior to their deaths. The specter of mass suicide also haunted another apocalyptic group awaiting planetary escape by way of UFO, if only in the media's portrayal of it, but on this point it could not have been more different from Heaven's Gate. Chen Tao ("True Way") of Taiwan expected 1999 to be the beginning of a forty-four-year Great Tribulation. This year would be marked by "Noah's Flood" in Eastern Asia, the massacre of "a thousand million" Taiwanese by "devil spirits" who possess people and feed off their "spiritual light energy," and, ultimately, a Chinese nuclear attack on Taiwan. They were led by Master Hon-ming Chen (b. 1956), a former professor of social science who had a lifelong history of religious revelation, first by communicating with God through visions of golden balls of light, later by gazing into a ring worn backwards on his hand.[4] In 1995 it was revealed to him that North America was the "Pure Land of God"[5] and that he and his followers must move there to prepare for the end of the current world cycle. According to Chen's writings, *The Practical Evidence and Study of the World of God and Buddha* (1996) and *God's Descending in Clouds (Flying Saucers) on Earth to Save People* (1997, excerpted below), the earth had been destroyed before in five previous Great Tribulations, the karmic effects of the actions of "Heavenly Devil Kings." In each case, God had saved only the inhabitants of North America, rescuing them in flying saucers.

In 1997, Chen Tao (also known as the God Saves the Earth Flying Saucer Foundation) established God's Salvation Church in San Dimas, California, then scouted locations for the other churches necessary to carry out its work of alerting North Americans to the coming Tribulation. They also sought the reincarnations of Jesus and the Buddha, finding them in the course of their travels in the form of two young boys who were brought into the group.[6] One hundred and fifty members settled in Garland, Texas, which Chen said was an auspicious place, as the name sounded like "God's Land," and which he declared to be the location where God would appear in person to prepare North Americans for their imminent salvation. According to Chen, as the Tribulation approached, the life forces of all material things, animate and inanimate, would become alive and potentially agitated and vengeful. If one did not wish to experience the wrath of these "spirits" in the coming year, it would be best to be compassionate toward everything in one's life, especially by becoming vegan or vegetarian.[7]

Chen Tao members not only opposed suicide as karmically detrimental, but they also opposed harming any living creature, a stance the worldwide media—whom Chen invited to witness his frequent revelatory pronouncements—found difficult to reconcile with the "UFO / suicide cult" identification with which the group had been saddled, due to apparent parallels with Heaven's Gate. Leading up to and including March 31, 1998, when Chen Tao members expected God's physical appearance in Garland, reporters hounded Chen about plans for a mass suicide if God failed to appear. Chen routinely deflected this line of questioning, but on this last date, he attempted to demonstrate that he was, at that time, in fact God in a physical body by staring into the sun. Reporters and many members were unconvinced, and when Chen moved the group again to Lockport, New York, to await divine rescue, only about thirty of the roughly one-hundred and fifty Garland members came with him. After 1999 passed without incident, Chen de-termined that God, in his mercy, had spared the world temporarily, and Chen continued his wait with a handful of devoted followers for God's flying saucers to take the North Americans from their doomed planet and place them on Mars, in the fourth dimension.

Ironically, arguably the most legitimate threat of destruction of the world as we know it due to the calendrical change of the new millennium came from a thoroughly secular and modern source: the computer. Due to memory constraints on the first computers, recording years was restricted to two digits (65 for 1965, for example); this shortcut remained standard practice even as vastly improved storage capacity made the personal computing revolution of the 1980s possible. As the millennial change-over loomed, however, many in the programming industry feared that the temporally illogical backward step from "99" to "00" would cause many systems to crash, including those in some of the world's most vital sectors: banking, transportation, energy delivery, military defense—just about every system of any importance contained an outdated microchip somewhere.

In the 1990s, a massive global effort was launched to head off this "Y2K" ("Year 2000") crisis, but many believed it was too little, too late. Several influential religious observers saw something else in the potential collapse of modern society at the hands of its own vaunted technology: the fulfillment of biblical prophecy and the opportunity for Christ to return triumphantly to a humanity humbled by the devastation of its "perfectible," scientifically based society. As the excerpt from Brenda E. Brasher's *Give Me That Online Religion* illustrates, the glee with which some of these prophets of doom predicted the destruction of society in the course of a global computer malfunction did not prevent many of them from posting their warnings on the Internet. Because the World Wide Web played such a central role in the spread of religious and secular anxiety over Y2K, and also because few if any of these sites remain, Brasher's compendium of Christian attitudes promulgated on the Internet regarding the aftermath of a possible computer-related social collapse serves as a valuable record of actual stances taken in the shadow of the year 2000.

To a great extent, an expansive, fantastic—even magical—vision of science and technology is the uniting aspect of these three movements. In the cases of Heaven's Gate and Chen Tao, besides borrowing the UFO concept from popular culture and science fiction, members of both groups saw a certain kind of "scientism" as capable of expressing spiritual truths. Applewhite described many of his cosmological concepts in terms of the television series *Star Trek*.[8] In its first incarnation as the Soul Light Resurgence Association in Taiwan, Chen Tao members measured spiritual light energy with electronic equipment, not unlike the E-meters of Scientology. These forms of "scientific" knowledge dovetail with both groups' adoption of flying saucer ideologies. As described in Chapter 3, such beliefs seem to expand one's vision and breadth of knowledge of the universe, making it impossible to see it as others do.

The science and technology at the root of the Y2K scare ironically come across to many Americans as just as alien as UFOs. Yet for the prophetically minded, the warnings about the possible collapse of the computerized information network were signs to the righteous concerning the secrets of the Endtimes, offering comfort that the Reign of Christ was at hand and warning them to prepare for the coming upheaval. Yet the Y2K movement differs from the two UFO groups discussed here in that, whereas the latter expected to leave Earth and literally go to a new world, many in the former thought that a computer glitch would bring about the "end of the world as we know it," which some believed could trigger Armageddon and usher in the Messianic age. Hence much of the fascination with Y2K among conservative Christians stemmed from their long-standing war against modern, secular society, which they expected to be soon hoisted on its own technological petard, ushering in the New Society of God's Kingdom. While not overly emphasized, Chen Tao's interest in "soul light" as well as basic Buddhist conceptualizations of selfhood suggest an aspect of New Self appeal for its members. On the other hand, Heaven's Gate members felt such antagonism toward humanness that they subsumed the self entirely, eradicating their gender through surgical castration and by adopting names such as "Srrody," and ultimately leaving behind their human "vessels" as they sought the next evolutionary level. As communal groups, however, both Heaven's Gate and Chen Tao created alternative New Societies as they awaited the great transformation that would leave the current ones, and the world that produced them, behind.

From the Heaven's Gate Website

RED ALERT—HALE-BOPP BRINGS CLOSURE TO HEAVEN'S GATE

As was promised—the keys to Heaven's Gate are here again in Ti and Do (The UFO Two) as they were in Jesus and His Father 2000 yrs. ago

Whether Hale-Bopp has a "companion" or not is irrelevant from our perspective. However, its arrival is joyously very significant to us at "Heaven's Gate." The *joy* is that our Older Member in the Evolutionary Level Above Human (the "Kingdom of Heaven") has made it clear to us that Hale-Bopp's approach is the "marker" we've been waiting for—the time for the arrival of the spacecraft from the Level Above Human to take us home to "Their World"—in the literal Heavens. Our 22 years of classroom here on planet Earth is finally coming to conclusion—"graduation" from the Human Evolutionary Level. We are happily prepared to leave "this world" and go with Ti's crew.

If you study the material on this website you will hopefully understand our joy and what our purpose here on Earth has been. You may even find your "boarding pass" to leave with us during this brief "window."

We are so very thankful that we have been recipients of this opportunity to prepare for membership in Their Kingdom, and to experience Their boundless Caring and Nurturing.

Do's Intro: Purpose–Belief

What Our Purpose Is — The Simple "Bottom Line"

Two thousand years ago, a crew of members of the Kingdom of Heaven who are responsible for nurturing "gardens," determined that a percentage of the human "plants" of the present civilization of this Garden (Earth) had developed enough that some of those bodies might be ready to be used as "containers" for soul deposits. Upon instruction, a member of the Kingdom of Heaven then left behind His body in that Next Level (similar to putting it in a closet, like a suit of clothes that doesn't need to be worn for awhile), came to Earth, and moved into (or incarnated into), an adult human body (or "vehicle") that had been "prepped" for this particular task. The body that was chosen was called Jesus. The member of the Kingdom of Heaven who was instructed to incarnate into that body did so at His "Father's" (or Older Member's) instruction. He "moved into" (or took over) that body when it was 29 or 30 years old, at the time referred to as its baptism by John the Baptist (the incarnating event was depicted as ". . . the Holy Spirit descended upon Him in bodily form like a dove"—Luke 3:22). [That body (named Jesus) was tagged in its formative period to be the receptacle of a Next Level Representative, and even just that "tagging" gave that "vehicle" some unique awareness of its coming purpose.]

The sole task that was given to this member from the Kingdom of Heaven was *to offer the way leading to membership into the Kingdom of Heaven* to those who recognized Him for who He was and chose to follow Him. "The Kingdom of Heaven is at hand" meant—"since I am here, and I am from that Kingdom, if you leave everything of this world and follow me, I can take you into my Father's Kingdom." Only those individuals who had received a "deposit" containing a soul's beginning had the capacity to believe or recognize the Kingdom of Heaven's Representative. They could get to His Father only through total reliance upon Him. He later sent His students out with the "Good news of the Kingdom of Heaven is at hand," and His followers could then help gather the "flock" so that the "Shepherd" might teach others what was required of them to enter His Father's House—His Father's Kingdom—the Kingdom of Heaven—in the literal and physical Heavens—certainly not among humans on Earth. Leaving behind this world included: family, sensuality, selfish desires, your human mind, and even your human body if it be required of you—all mammalian ways, thinking, and behavior. Since He had been through this metamorphic transition Himself from human to Level Above Human —under the guidance of His Father—He was qualified to take others through that same discipline and transition. Remember, the One who incarnated in Jesus was sent for one purpose only, to say, "If you want to go to Heaven, I can take you through that gate—it requires everything of you."

Our mission is exactly the same. I am in the same position to today's society as was the One that was in Jesus then. My being here now is actually a continuation of that last task as was promised, to those who were students 2000 years ago. They are here again, continuing in their own overcoming, while offering the same transition to others. Our only purpose is to offer the discipline and "grafting" required of this transition into membership in My Father's House. My Father, my Older Member, came with me this time for the first half of this task to assist in the task because of its present difficulty.

Looking to us, and desiring to be a part of my Father's Kingdom, can offer to those with deposits that chance to connect with the Level Above Human, and begin that transition. Your separation from the world and reliance upon the Kingdom of Heaven through its Representatives can open to you the opportunity to become a new creature, one of the Next Evolutionary Level, rightfully belonging to the Kingdom of Heaven.

Why It Is Difficult to Believe or Accept Us

We don't know if you believe in the real existence of negative or "lower" forces. If you do, then you may be able to understand or relate to some of what we are about to say. It seems that how your "programming" permits you to see or identify those forces, determines the limit of your acceptance or understanding. Many believe that there are "evil" acts or even "evil" individuals, but would draw the line before they would believe in evil spirits, evil discarnates, negative influences, malevolent space aliens, "Luciferians," or Satan and his fallen angels.

The generally accepted "*norms*" of today's societies—world over— are designed, established, and maintained by the individuals who were at one time "students" of the Kingdom of Heaven—"angels" in the making —who "flunked out" of the classroom. Legends and scriptures refer to them as fallen angels. The current civilization's records use the name Satan or Lucifer to describe a single fallen angel and also to "nickname" any "evil presence." If you have experienced some of what our "classroom" requires of us, you would know that these "presences" are real and that the Kingdom of God even permits them to "attack" us in order for us to learn their tricks and how to stay above them or conquer them. The space aliens, or Luciferians, use the discarnate spirits (the minds that are disembodied at the death of a body) as their primary servants—against potential members of the Kingdom of God. These "influences," or discarnates, are constantly "programming" every human "plant" (vehicle or body), to accept a set of beliefs and norms for behavior during a lifetime. From our point of view, this "programming" finds that body, and the vast majority of all human bodies, barely usable by students of the Kingdom of Heaven.

As the above example can serve to testify, the "lower forces" would—through their "norm" concept—what is "socially acceptable," what is politically correct—have you *not* believe in spirits, spirit possession, negative space aliens, Satan, etc. They would have you believe that to even dabble in these ideas is of the "occult," satanic, or at the least, giving credence to "fringe" topics. That's where they would also categorize any mental search of Eastern religions, astrology, metaphysics, paranormal, UFOs, etc., etc. In other words, they (these space aliens) don't want themselves "found out," so they condemn any exploration. They want you to be a perfect servant to society (THEIR society—of THEIR world)—to the "acceptable establishment," to humanity, and to false religious concepts. Part of that "stay blinded" formula goes like this: "Above all, be married, a good parent, a reasonable church goer, buy a house, pay your mortgage, pay your insurance, have a good line of credit, be socially committed, and graciously accept death with the hope that 'through His shed blood,' or some other equally worthless religious precept, you will go to Heaven after your death."

Many segments of society, especially segments of the religious, think that they are *not* "of the world," but rather that their "conversion" experience finds them "*outside of* worldliness." The next statement that we will make will be the "Big Tester," the one that the "lower forces" would use to clearly have you discredit or disregard us. That statement is: Unless you are currently an active student or are attempting to become a student of the present Representative from the Kingdom of Heaven—you ARE STILL "of the world," having done *no significant* separation from worldliness, and you are still serving the *opposition* to the Kingdom of Heaven. This statement sounds—to humans who have been so carefully programmed by the "lower forces"—arrogant, pompous, or egotistical at the least—as if by taking this stand we had something to gain—as if we were seeking recognition as "Deity" or as self-appointed prophets.

That Luciferian programming *has truly been effective,* for we don't even want to voice to you the statement in question. However, believe it or not, it is only for your sake—the sake of prospective recipients of the Kingdom of Heaven—that we *must* "tell the truth," openly identify to you as Representatives of the Kingdom of Heaven, well aware of the "fallout" of that position.

The hard facts or bold statements in a nutshell, that are so difficult to accept or "digest"—come down to: If you want or ever expect to go to Heaven—here is your window. That window opportunity requires: 1) an incarnate (as human) Representative of the Kingdom of Heaven; 2) that all who hope to enter Heaven become active students of that Representative while the Representative is present; 3) those who endure the "transition classroom" until it ends (adequately bonding or "grafting" to that Representative) will go with that Representative—literally LEAVE the human kingdom and Earth as He is about to do. Staying behind, for any significant period, could jeopardize that "graft." That window to Heaven will not open again until another civilization is planted and has reached sufficient maturity (according to the judgment of the Next Level).

We can't blame you for "buying into" the "Luciferian" program. What else has been available during those periods when no Representative was present? Almost nothing—save some warnings in the Scriptures, i.e., Luke 20:34–36, Luke 21:23, Mark 12:25, and Mark 13:17–19. Check these out.

Another fact is that what someone is into during the time a Representative is *not* present really doesn't matter that much, except that they are found unprepared when One comes—the only time when the Kingdom of Heaven can be offered to you.

The dilemma is *we are here* and most humans are thoroughly "hooked" to humanity. However, the same "grace" that was available at the end of the Representative's mission 2000 years ago is available now with our presence. If you quickly choose to take these steps toward separating from the world, and look to us for help, you *will see* our Father's Kingdom.

It is clear to all of us, that to the Anti-Christ—those propagators of sustained faithfulness to mammalian humanism—we are, and will be seen as, their Anti-Christ. This is certainly to be expected, and it will not delay our return to our Father's Kingdom. It might even accelerate that return.

We will, between now and our departure, do everything we can for those who want to go with us. But we cannot allow them to interfere with or delay our return to Him.

The Present Representative
Do

From "Disappearance of the Spiritual Life of Earth and the Madness of the Human-Devil Realm"

Hon-ming Chen

Man has limited span of life, and so does the planet. It is an unavoidable fact. When aged, people will have their spiritual vitality and physical strength on the wane gradually. Once faced with the line of death, they will have to suffer great pains both mentally and physically. So does the life of the earth: entering into the ending period, it begins to decline, and when annihilation period comes, natural disasters and man-made calamities become more and more. They are all related with the disturbance from the realm of the devils. The more and greater is the power from the realm of devils, the clearer it is how great the karmic impediment is that living beings have built up. In the same way, the decline of the life of the earth can also be detected in the deterioration of every magnetic field of energy on the land.

How long the life of a planet can last is related with the causality of its own. We have previously mentioned that the material universe that we live in has exploded for [*sic*] fifteen times. As a matter of fact, how long a planet can sustain its life for human evolution on it has to do with God's omnipotence and control of all beings. Of course, God would like to prolong the life of planets, but the result of self-destruction of human evolution also comes from the great natural law of causal retribution. After all, the end is made by human beings collectively. There is no one to blame for that. People should reflect on themselves and ask themselves why they have failed to escape such a drastic destiny of ending in the great tribulation of nuclear war since far back in time and space. Why haven't they made any progress?

The kingdom of God has moved from the East to America in the West. It has been a year since the three-and-a-half years of salvation before the great tribulation began.[9] The kingdom of God operated in Taiwan, East Asia, for only a whole year. Why did God operated [*sic*] the salvation for only a year in the East? As a matter of fact, it was related to the collective Karma of human sins. The one who blamed the heaven and other people instead of reflecting on and repenting of her own depraved nature from the time with no beginning, who grudged that the heaven didn't give her more fame and fortune, and who forced God, the Heavenly Father, away, is also one who betrayed Jesus Christ two thousand years ago—Judas. For two thousand years, his depraved character hasn't changed. God has given her many chances to evolve and to repent, but the root of her original depraved nature was still re-activated at the ending period of the world. God is pure and holy. He takes any human beings as His own children. If any of His children force him away, he would just leave with tears, because their evil nature cannot accommodate God's most positive and most up-right spiritual light. The other sons and daughters of God should be brave in holding on to justice and follow God and leave. At the ending period of the world, God saves all the brothers and sisters in His own church (preaching place, *tao-tsan*) first, lest they might have been betrayed and murdered by devils. It is for sure that those who have deep-rooted sins and karma but refuse to repent shall lose their life in the East. They shall find no way to come to the place of God's Kingdom in America.

Why will the disappearance of the spiritual life of earth bring about the madness of the human-devil realm? First, we should know that human spiritual light energy is three million degrees. In the normal situation, human beings' main spiritual light can respond to the heavenly magnetic field and absorb the energy above three million degrees in order to maintain the basic nature of human beings. What is the basic nature of man? For example, in the chaotic times of wars and confusion without food, a human being of three million degrees of spiritual light energy would rather starve to death than eat human meat. The spiritual light energy less than three million degrees belongs to the animal realms. When a man's spiritual light energy drops below three million degrees, his evil root of depravity, such as greed, anger, and stupidity, becomes re-activated. The lower the spiritual light energy drops, the stronger the bestial nature grows, and the higher the evilness grows. Then, any brutal things might happen.

Except in America, where the magnetic field of God's kingdom operates, in such areas as Asia, Africa, Europe, Oceania, Australia, and New Zealand, the spiritual light energy drops by 100 thousand degrees in average every month. By May of 1997, it shall drop to 2,700 thousand degrees. As the year of 1999 comes near, the energy decrease is very formidable. The maintenance of more than three million degrees in the magnetic field of America is to provide a place of evolution in physical body for those whose accumulated karma is less heavy as well as those who are willing to repent. It is a decided fact that four-fifths of the world population shall die in the great tribulation. Whether it is more than four-fifths to survive or less depends on the degrees of people's repentance. Those who repent shall be saved. As the gospel of the coming of God's kingdom on earth shall be preached to all over the world in the next two years, any souls, any one who wants to evolve, will try to come to America. Those with heavy karmic obstacles—that is, those combined with [i.e., possessed by] devils —will find any excuse to make themselves die in the great tribulation of 1999 or earlier. Why? Because they have been possessed and totally controlled by their previous souls which had become heavenly devil kings. The tragedy is ready to happen.

In May of 1999, the earth will have no spiritual light energy left. People's previous souls of heavenly devil kings will come to capture and suck their main spiritual light because there'll be no higher energy to suck. When the people's main spiritual light energy lowers to 1,800 thousand degrees and cannot be sucked any longer, these heavenly devil kings will become mad and try all means to depart form the physical body they have occupied. In order to get rid of it, they will try to destroy it. At this time, anyone combined with the devil will respond to heavenly devil kings and ask them to destroy their physical body; otherwise, the karma of the three souls in the physical body[10] will make use of those heavenly devils, which have returned, to do the job for them. In a word, the devil can depart from the human body only by killing the body they have taken up. As the year of 1999 comes nearer, the social disorder and confusion will become more serious, and people's desire for fame, fortune, food, and lust will grow stronger. We will see many people who have become unhuman. For example, crimes of incest, drug-addiction, murders, and kidnapping are becoming more brutal. It is at this moment that we can imagine how it looks like when tigers, lions, leopards, or wolves are tearing apart their preys and devouring them in the animal world. We cannot deny that in some places, prosperity seems like the last glow of health before passing away. Under scrutiny, is it still so? Will this kind of situation last till the second half of 1998? Why don't you keep alert and wait to see the outcome!

The madness of the devil realm also means madness of people too, since man has no longer been man. Now, people still have food to eat, and self-destruction is not yet to come. But once the natural disaster brings out famines, it might happens [sic] that people begin to eat people, parents eat children, and siblings kill each other. A normal man (about three million degrees of energy) would rather kill himself than eat another human being, let alone eating his own kinsmen. It is the madness and tragedy of the human-devil realm.

Here I want to remind you that: with the great tribulation in 1999 coming nearer, if you are still sober and want to leave Asia, Europe, or Africa for America, you may confront various reasons from your relatives to stop you. These reasons seem to make sense, but once you refuse them, they might force you to stay. After 1999, it will become impossible for anyone to leave even if you desire to leave, because at that time your spiritual energy will have been consumed up by the previous souls of devil or debt-claimants.

You should be alert to the paradoxical saying that "Here I was born as a so-and-so, and I shall die as a so-and-so." People should acknowledge the truth that "Born as offsprings [*sic*] of God and Buddha, we should return to their side even after we die." However, to keep your physical body alive makes it certain for you to evolve and witness the history of God's great power of descending on earth to save all living beings.

From *Give Me That Online Religion*

Brenda E. Brasher

"Y2K: The Technological Tribulation"

Across the World Wide Web, a trend to interpret Y2K through the lens of divine judgment ran rampant, with Protestant Christians leading the way. Some equated cyberspace with the Tower of Babel. In a Web post by the Rev. Jerry Falwell, cyberspace was referred to as a "tower unto heaven." Falwell claimed that just as in the biblical story of Babel, the goal toward which humankind directed its technical prowess had gotten it into trouble:

> As the world prepares to crash into the 21st Century, with all the predicted crises and catastrophes which may begin happening at 12:01 am on January 1, 2000, we must remember that a similar international event occurred long ago. It occurred when the masses decided to circumvent God's plan of salvation and build a tower into Heaven.
>
> http://www.trbc.org/media/sermontexts/980830.html

The fact that this text was posted on the Web (attached to the walls of Babel?) introduces an ironic humor to his protest, which Falwell evidently misses.

A second biblical parallel that cyber-prophets employed to describe Y2K was to depict it as an element of the Tribulation, the period of strife, civil war, and global chaos that Christian premillennialists associate with the end of history. Fundamentalist pastors such as Jack Van Impe preached that Y2K fulfilled biblical prophecy and was a "sign of the times." Van Impe was so convinced this was the case that he and his wife, Rexella, made a video titled *2000 Time Bomb* that they marketed on the Web. The ad copy on the Web describing the eighty-minute video used stark, premillennialist language and images to describe Y2K:

> The so-called "millenium [*sic*] bug" could scramble the electronic mind of computers worldwide in the year 2000 . . . and the universal panic inspired could be the catalyst for the rise of the antichrist, the mark of the beast "666" system[11] for buying and selling, and the advent of the great tribulation! See how the effects of this predicted computer catastrophe coincide with the Bible prophecy regarding the Lord and the latter days of time on this earth! Will you be ready to protect your home, family, career, savings for the future? This powerful video prepares you for the coming of chaos and offers hope for the future.
>
> http://www.jvim.com/catalog/i2000tbv.html

Though he refrained from mentioning Y2K by name, Falwell was a leader among those who interpreted Y2K as an end-times phenomenon:

> In fulfillment of Bible prophecy, the world today is beginning to speak the same language. We have become an urban society with nearly six billion persons mostly living in large cities. We are satellite and internet connected. We are fast moving toward a cashless economy . . . a one world government . . . court . . . and one world church. We are building a universal city with a one world church whose tower reaches into heaven. But, the Trinity has come down and looked us over. And it seems that God doesn't like what He sees. He may be preparing to confound our language, to jam our communications, scatter our efforts and judge us for our sin and rebellion against His lordship. We are hearing from many sources that January 1, 2000 will be a fateful day in the history of the world. And, as brilliant and scientifically

advanced as we are, it all slipped up on us without fanfare and in the most simplistic manner.

http://www.trbc.org/media/sermontexts/980830.html

Not all online Christian evangelical voices were quite so pessimistic. Some evangelical Christians considered the potential catastrophe of Y2K an excellent opportunity to demonstrate the communal value of their beliefs. These technological Noahs built cyber-arks of information and resources they hope would carry society through any technology deluge. Many moderate online evangelicals used the Web to publish information about potential Y2K problems and encourage people to do what they could to minimize Y2K risks to themselves and others. A parachurch evangelical Christian media enterprise, the Christian Broadcasting Network (CBN), used television, books, and videos along with cyberspace to disseminate Y2K warnings, each carefully anchored in a biblical passage. Their main recommendation was that people stay calm but be prepared. They recommended that among other preparations, obtaining copies of important financial records; stockpiling goods and supplies; and preparing to do without heat, water, or electricity for an extended period.[12]

The Joseph Project was another such effort. According to its Website, the sole intent of the project was to minimize the impact of Y2K on global populations, as a testament to their faith.

> The Joseph Project 2000, a Christian-led nonprofit, seeks to prevent and respond to the potential impacts of the Year 2000 computer problem in a biblically balanced and professional manner, honoring and glorifying God in all we do.
>
> http://www.josephproject2000.org

Though Joseph 2000 was clearly on the bandwagon of the Web as cyberark, its founder, evangelical Christian Bill Bright, also believed that Y2K was an excellent opportunity for evangelism.

> We realize there are many other issues to consider, such as how to prepare and serve our staff members (especially those ministering overseas) where Y2K problems may be much worse. Therefore, we are supplying information and web links through which they can obtain information to evaluate the problem where they minister and make their own decisions. We are also taking steps to ensure that electronic fund transfers proceed with minimal

problems. Having said that, we realize that the psychological issues may outweigh the technical. Americans used to living fifty years in a society with few potential nationwide disasters may feel a great deal of anxiety leading up to January 1, 2000. Therefore, we seek secondly to bolster faith of believers and thirdly to compassionately witness to nonbelievers.

http://www.josephproject2000.org/billbright.html

A Website titled "God's Wilderness" was representative of the extreme pessimism at the other end of the spectrum of religious responses to Y2K. Presuming that Y2K would be a catalyst for world disaster, the beginning of a technological tribulation that would make urban life unlivable, these Y2K pessimists fled the cities and established technology-proof living compounds in the American backcountry. But how could a small, obscure, poorly funded group of individuals inform others of their decision to forsake contemporary technology—much less urge interested parties to join them—except by extending an invitation via cyberspace? Even the most extreme Y2K technophobes came up with no satisfactory alternative to the Web, so they published the news of their intention to break with technosociety by way of the global bulletin board.

After many years of living in the northwoods, and after most of our children were "up and out" we felt led of the LORD to sell some of the God's Wilderness land. We just wanted to sell bare land. Because there were already other Christian families in the area we simply placed a small add in World Magazine asking for "Christian Home-schooling families to purchase Northern Wilderness land." When interested people began to look at the land they informed us about Y2K. . . . We have no desire to commercialize on Y2K. It takes more than just a desire to relocate, more than even the money to do it. We believe the most important factor is that families KNOW that the LORD is leading them to make the move.

http://www.lakenet.com/~dwhnjh/helpag-9.html

The film *Titanic* became a mega-hit as the Y2K crisis gathered steam. But instead of being a straightforward reprise of the disastrous sinking of the technologically dazzling ocean liner, the Y2K saga was an inversion of it. In the film, after the ship rammed an iceberg, news that the unsinkable *Titanic* was going down was restricted to a few, while everyone on board could see that the ship was sinking. In the case of Y2K, warnings reverberated throughout cyberspace and the nonvirtual world that the computer environment was about to crash, while everyone saw that things contin-ued to work. On December 31, 1999, and January 1, 2000, there was scarcely a com-puter gurgle. Faster than the hula hoop, Y2K was declared passé, and the year 2000 was labeled a nonevent. Perhaps that is why, post-*Titanic*, ship travel never regained its cultural prominence, while post-Y2K the world silently reembraced cyber-eternity. As for the prophets who had barked out warnings that cyber-eternity was over, with nary an apology they be-gan to bray about other signs of the end times.

NOTES

Excerpt from the Heaven's Gate Website (1997; currently mirrored at www.psy-www.com/psyrelig/hg/index.html)

Excerpt from "Disappearance of the Spiritual Life of Earth and the Madness of the Human-Devil Realm," in *God's Descending In Clouds (Flying Saucers) on Earth to Save People*, by "God—The Supreme Being" (self-published by Hon-ming Chen, 1997), 73–77.

Excerpt from *Give Me That Online Religion* by Brenda E. Brasher (San Francisco: Jossey-Bass, 2001), 56–61. Reprinted by permission of Rutgers University Press.

1. There are various reasons why the year 2000 ought not to have had true millenarian significance: because our calendar begins with the year 1 and not 0, the third millennium of the Christian era technically began in 2001; because the birth of Jesus was miscalculated by Bishop James Ussher, the timeline should more appropriately begin somewhere between 6 and 4 B.C.E.; the end of the *second* mil-lennium holds little particular significance in biblical prophecy (some claim that of the 6,000 years prophesied for the earth's existence, 4,000 were for the Jews, while the last 2,000 would be for the Christians); and so on. One prophetic calcu-lation, however, added one biblical generation, forty years (citing Matthew 24:34), to Israel's capturing of the Old City of Jerusalem in the Six Day War of 1967 to get 2007 as the date of Christ's Second Coming, meaning that the seven-year Tribu-lation would have begun in 2000. See M. J. Agee, *Exit 2007: The Secrets Revealed* (Yorba Linda, Calif.: Archer, 1992).

2. Charles S. Strozier, introduction to *The Year 2000: Essays on the End*, ed. Charles S. Strozier and Michael Flynn (New York: New York University Press, 1997), p. 5. For a fuller examination of Aum Shinrikyo, see Robert Jay Lifton, *De-stroying the World to Save It: Aum Shinrikyo, Apocalyptic Violence, and the New Global Terrorism* (New York: Henry Holt, 1999).

3. Nettles's role in Heaven's Gate and Applewhite's relationship with her is too

complex to treat comprehensively here. They met in a hospital, though there are at least three different accounts of why they were each there. In 1973, they came to the realization that they were the two witnesses of Revelation 11 who would be killed and resurrected. Despite the obvious gender relationship, Applewhite regarded Nettles as the "Older Member" and his "Father," as an acknowledgment of Nettles's evolutionary advancement and "true divinity"; they called themselves, variously, Do and Ti and Bo and Peep. Nettles died in 1985.

4. Chen had immersed himself at various points in his life in Buddhist, Taoist, and Christian literature, and had also followed the teachings of an emergent UFO NRM in Taiwan. In 1993 he and other defectors broke with that group to form the Soul Light Resurgence Association to explore techniques that would improve the power and purity of one's "spiritual light energy," a reflection of one's karmic status and determinant of one's position in life following rebirth.

5. Pure Land is a Chinese form of Buddhism focused on Amida, a Buddha of Infinite Light.

6. Chen himself claimed to be the reincarnation of Jesus' father, Joseph.

7. Two Buddhist concepts are intertwined here. One of the precepts of the Buddha's Noble Eightfold Path is "Right Action," which proscribes harm to any living being, including animals that could be used for food. At the same time, folk Buddhism, as well as popular Taoist practice, maintains a belief that much misfortune is caused by "angry ghosts" or spirits disgruntled by some injustice done to them, who must be appeased before the ghosts' targets can find peace.

8. Bizarrely, the brother of Nichelle Nichols, who played Lieutenant Uhura on the show, was among the Heaven's Gate dead.

9. The time referred to at Revelation 13:15 as half of the seven-year period of Tribulation, when the Antichrist unites the world under a false peace.

10. The three souls are the main soul light, the conscious soul, and the physical soul. As Chen notes in his text, this tripartite division of the soul derives from Chinese antiquity. *God's Descending in Clouds (Flying Saucers) on Earth to Save People*, by "God—The Supreme Being" (Hon-ming Chen, 1997), 17.

11. "Mark of the beast 666" is a reference to a belief popular among Christian fundamentalists that an evil entity marked with the number 666 would appear at the end of time. [Note in original text; see Revelation 13:18.]

12. The 700 Club, http://www.cbn.org/the700club/. Accessed May 3, 1999. [Note in original text.]

FOR FURTHER READING

Boyer, Paul, *When Time Shall Be No More: Prophecy Belief in Modern American Culture* (Cambridge, Mass.: Belknap Press of Harvard University Press, 1992.) The classic overview of the roots and forms of American millennialism.

Center for Millennial Studies at Boston University, http://www.mille.org. The Center's official Website.

Daniels, Ted, ed., *A Doomsday Reader: Prophets, Predictors, and Hucksters of Salvation* (New York: New York University Press, 1999). An anthology of primary materials from a variety of apocalyptic movements.

Robbins, Tom, and Susan Palmer, eds., *Millennium, Messiahs, and Mayhem: Contemporary Apocalyptic Movements* (New York: Routledge, 1997). A collection of scholarly essays examining aspects of apocalypticism at the end of the twentieth century.

Strozier, Charles, and Michael Flynn, eds., *The Year 2000: Essays on the End* (New York: New York University Press, 1997). A collection of scholarly and philosophical essays on the significance of the approaching year 2000.

Thompson, Damian, *The End of Time: Faith and Fear in the Shadow of the Millennium* (Hanover, N.H.: University Press of New England, 1996). A rich presentation of the global historical roots of millennial expectation and some of its cultural manifestations in the build-up to the third millennium of the Common Era.

Constructing the New Religious Threat
Anticult and Countercult Movements

Douglas E. Cowan

From the Christian perspective, the so-called new age
cults represent the most recent manifestation of an age-
old struggle—the battle between good and evil, between
God and God's adversary, Satan. The phenomena described in this book are neither random nor accidental:
they are profoundly patterned. As simplistic as it may
sound to some, they indicate a demonic conspiracy to
subvert the true gospel of Jesus Christ through human
agents whose eyes have been blinded by the evil one.
      —Ronald Enroth, *Youth, Brainwashing and the
                                          Extremist Cults*

Even though the term "cult" has limited utility, it is so
embedded in popular culture that those of us concerned
about helping people harmed by group involvements or
preventing people from being so harmed cannot avoid
using it. Whatever the term's limitations, it points us in a
meaningful direction.
      —Michael Langone, The American Family Foundation

Constructing and Deconstructing the New Religious Threat

In the cultural chorus that seeks to warn late modern society of the puta-
tive threat represented by NRMs, a number of different voices have come
together over the past several decades. Former members occasionally offer

harrowing tales of their time in this or that "cult." In the wake of parents' concern over the unpopular and often misunderstood religious choices made by their children, an organized, secular anticult movement has arisen, dedicated to "rescuing" those who have been "deceived" by a wide variety of religious leaders, groups, and movements. Religiously orientated countermovements, on the other hand, have responded to the appearance of spiritual competitors in time-honored fashion—with accusations of heresy, blasphemy, idolatry, and sundry spiritual deception. Although there are occasional Roman Catholic contributions to this particular field, by far the majority of religious countermovement literature has been produced by a Christian "countercult" made up of evangelical Protestants who regard the appearance of NRMs as a "clear and present danger."[1] Finally, in a variety of incarnations, there is the mass media, a powerful social institution that has clearly demonstrated itself no ally of NRMs.

For a generation now, scholars of religion have added their voices as well, addressing the issue of NRMs from a wide variety of academic perspectives: anthropology, history, philosophy, psychology, and sociology. In some cases, the questions they sought to answer were reasonably straightforward. What empirical evidence is there, for example, that a mysterious process called "brainwashing" was responsible for the dramatic rise of so-called religious cults? Although fewer social scientists now accept the brainwashing hypothesis than did, perhaps, a few decades ago, the debate continues over issues of influence, thought control, and milieu management. Other research questions, however, are more broadly construed. What social and cultural factors contribute to the appearance of NRMs? How do these movements evolve, mature, and, in many cases, disappear? If they are not "brainwashed," then why *do* adherents choose to join new, often controversial religious movements? What accounts for often very high attrition rates in these movements? How do NRMs adapt in order to maintain a level of cultural appeal? And, since this is the point at which many media reports take initial notice of them, what is there to say about NRMs and violence?

Distinguishing Late Modern Anticult and Countercult Movements

Often, when the secular anticult and the evangelical countercult are considered together, the latter is subsumed as a subset of the former. As I have argued elsewhere,[2] however, though both share concerns about the presence of NRMs in society, the differences between them are important enough to warrant more careful distinction. In this section, I would like to discuss these differences in terms of three interrelated areas: (1) the social origins of countercult and anticult movements; (2) the key conceptualizations that underpin their work; and (3) the objectives each pursues.

Origins: Noticing New Religious Movements

Only four years after the initial appearance of the *Book of Mormon* in 1830, Eber D. Howe self-published the first polemic exposé of the nascent Church of Jesus Christ of Latter-day Saints (LDS), entitled *Mormonism Unvailed* [*sic*].[3] "For climacteric comicality," wrote George Hamilton Combs (1864–1951), more than a generation later, "Mormonism should be awarded the palm."[4] Combs, a Disciples of Christ minister from Kansas City, Missouri, also dismissed Mary Baker Eddy's *Science and Health with Key to the Scriptures* as "such a hodge-podge of crudities [as] was never found between the covers of one book,"[5] concluding, "pass can this delusion none too swiftly to that oblivion which is its doom."[6] In his contribution to the well-known series of booklets called *The Fundamentals,* William Moorehead, a professor at the United Presbyterian Theological Seminary in Xenia, Ohio, characterized the teachings of Charles Taze Russell's *Millennial Dawn,* foundational for the group that would become the Jehovah's Witnesses (see Chapter 13), as "the climax in audacity and falsehood" and opined that they were "calculated to subvert the faith of Christians by substituting for the truth of Jesus Christ the calamitous doctrines of Mr. Russell."[7] A century after Eber Howe challenged the legitimacy of the LDS Church, Jan Karen van Baalen, in *The Chaos of Cults,* the first encyclopedic categorization of new religious "threats" to the dominance of Protestant Christianity, lamented that "Mormonism, Christian Science, Unity, and similar non-Christian cults are allowed to list their services and hours of worship on the same bulletin boards at the entrance of cities and towns, and in hotel lobbies, with evangelical churches whose every tenet these cults not merely deny but combat." He warned "that it would be well to stop this practice."[8]

In the domain of religious interaction, countermovement polemic such as this is hardly new. Indeed, as I have noted elsewhere, "one of the perspectives from which the social history of religious development can be written is that of the clash between movements and countermovements."[9]

In the late nineteenth and early twentieth centuries, what became the evangelical countercult movement emerged out of a long tradition of defending the truth of Christian faith from what were regarded as sundry spiritual imposters. Indeed, in the late twentieth century, while the secular anticult movement may have been able to generate more media coverage through its often lurid tales of "brainwashing" and "deprogramming," evangelical Protestants alarmed by the presence of new players on the spiritual block were the first to attempt organized countermovement categorization of new or alternative religious movements in North America. Indeed, when NRMs did anything but "pass into oblivion," as Combs had hoped, professional countercult organizations emerged, including the Christian Research Institute (founded by Walter R. Martin), the Spiritual Counterfeits Project (which began as an outreach of the Berkeley Christian Coalition), Personal Freedom Outreach, and Evangelical Ministries to New Religions. With the advent of the Internet, evangelical countercult apologetics has now grown into something of a cottage industry, with participants ranging from those who have academic training in theology and religious studies, to those whose only claim to expertise is former membership in a suspect group, to those who have neither training nor experience but participate simply by replicating online the work of others.

While the secular anticult movement emerged under similar circumstances of expanding religious pluralism, it did so for very different reasons. In the late 1960s and early 1970s, parents and friends alarmed by the often baffling religious choices made by their loved ones sought ways to make sense of these choices and to combat them. As sons and daughters left the pews of their youth and joined such NRMs as the Children of God (now The Family International; see Chapter 7), the Hare Krishnas, the Unification Church (see Chapter 6), or the Divine Light Mission, as they began to practice meditation with Transcendental Meditation groups or auditing with the Church of Scientology, questions arose not only about why these choices were being made, but how to "rescue" young men and women from what came increasingly to be regarded as "destructive cults."

However, despite the impression that the "cultic" threat was somehow both omnipresent and omnipotent, as Anson D. Shupe, Jr., and David G. Bromley point out, "most of the new religions had a maximum of only a few thousand members each; thus, no one of them provided a sufficiently large or visible presence to create the amount of alarm which the [anticult movement] needed to coalesce and survive on a national level."[10] That is, before the secular anticult could institutionalize and professionalize, a controlling metaphor was required, a floating cultural signifier that could be readily attached to any and all suspect groups regardless of their parent tradition, religious beliefs and practices, or social behavior. As I discuss more fully in the next section, the secular anticult found this signifier in the well-known "brainwashing hypothesis."

The larger secular anticult movement grew out of an array of loosely connected (if at all) and essentially grassroots groups, many of which focused on a particular religious movement as opposed to the growing number of alternative religious choices. One such group was Free the Children of God (FREECOG), founded in 1972 with the help of Ted Patrick, "who later initiated the practice of deprogramming."[11] According to Shupe and Bromley, the formation of FREECOG served a number of important social functions: creating solidarity among those affected by their children's membership in NRMs; disseminating information about suspect groups and emerging countermeasures; and acting as a referral agency for bewildered friends and parents who suddenly found themselves faced with this situation, and as a reflexive forum for sharing successes and failures in what many saw as a desperate fight to rescue their loved ones.[12] All of these roles have been institutionalized in the secular anticult as it exists today. Two years after its formation, FREECOG expanded its mandate beyond the Children of God and became the Citizens Freedom Foundation (CFF), at the time the largest anticult organization in the country. Throughout the 1970s a number of such groups emerged, many of which, as Shupe and Bromley note, shared by their very names in the floating signifier of brainwashing: "Free Minds, Return to Personal Choice, Citizens Engaged in Reuniting Families, Citizens Organized for the Public Awareness of Cults, and the National Ad Hoc Committee Engaged in Freeing Minds."[13] It was not until the 1980s, however, with the formation of the American Family Foundation (AFF) and the Cult Awareness Network (CAN), that the secular anticult movement gained a national presence. Today, CAN has ceased to operate as a secular anticult institution, but the AFF remains the most prominent organization in the movement.

Epistemology: Understanding New Religious Movements

In order to understand both the secular anticult and the evangelical countercult movements, we must first examine how each movement defines a "cult." How these two movements conceive of NRMs grounds all other aspects of their existence, their motivation, their methodology, and their desired outcomes. As noted above, in broad terms the secular anti-cult movement proceeds according to various versions of the "brainwash-ing," "thought reform," or "mind control" hypothesis—that is, the belief that members of suspect groups ("cults") somehow have had their cog-nitive capacities impaired through "unethically manipulative methods" of persuasion.[14] The Christian countercult, on the other hand, many of whose members explicitly reject the "brainwashing" hypothesis, constructs its understanding of "cults" theologically, and evaluates suspect groups in terms of a normative framework of evangelical Protestantism. While there are minor variations in terms of which groups ought to be considered "dangerous cults" and why, these general distinctions serve as an analytic point of departure.

Regarded as one of the leading intellectuals of the secular anticult movement,[15] Margaret Thaler Singer chose to define the problem of sus-pect groups in terms of a "cultic relationship" or "cultic milieu" rather than "cult" per se. In Cults in Our Midst, Singer offered a definition based on three interrelated sets of criteria: "1. The origin of the group and the role of the leader. 2. The power structure, or relationship between the leader (or leaders) and the followers. 3. The use of a coordinated program of persuasion (which is called thought reform or, more commonly, brain-washing)."[16] Expanding on her first criterion, Singer declared that "cult leaders typically . . . are self-appointed, persuasive persons who claim to have a special mission in life or to have special knowledge . . . Cult leaders tend to be determined and domineering and are often described as char-ismatic. . . . Cult leaders center veneration on themselves."[17] Explaining the relationship between leaders and followers, Singer wrote, "Cults are authoritarian in structure. . . . [They] appear to be innovative and exclu-sive . . . [and they] tend to have a double set of ethics."[18] Finally, she main-tained that "Cults tend to be totalistic, or all-encompassing, in controlling their members' behavior and also ideologically totalistic, exhibiting zealotry and extremism in their worldview. . . . Cults tend to require mem-bers to undergo a major disruption or change in life-style."[19] Interviewed in 1998 for an article on "cults" in a homemakers' weekly magazine, Singer warned that "anyone could be in a cult without knowing it. 'They're not all religious,' she says. 'People forget that we have psychology cults, flying saucer cults, martial arts cults and political cults.'"[20] Not insignificantly, in terms of the cultural construction of a new religious threat, the article was titled: "Cults, The Next Wave: Almost Everyone Is Vulnerable."

In "Cults 101," Michael D. Langone, the executive director of the American Family Foundation and editor of many of its publications, deploys a similarly broad definition, listing twelve "statements" that he contends "often characterize manipulative groups." Visitors to the AFF Website (www.csj.org) are encouraged to "place a checkmark beside all items that characterize the group in question. If you check many of these items, and particularly if you check most of them, you might consider examining the group more closely."[21] Suspect groups, Langone suggests, are "focused on a living leader to whom members seem to display excessively zealous, unquestioning commitment," and are "preoccupied" both "with bringing in new members" and "with making money." They are "elitist, claiming a special, exalted status for [themselves], [their] leader(s), and members"; they have "a polarized us-versus-them mentality, which causes conflict with the wider society"; and their leaders are "not accountable to any authorities."

Following the argument of sociologists Rodney Stark and William Sims Bainbridge that useful definitions are derived from empirically measurable *attributes* (characteristics or phenomena that are *always* present in a particular group) rather than subjectively determined *correlates* (aspects of a thing which *may or may not* be present),[22] observers might reasonably wonder just when the criteria suggested by Singer and Langone indicate a problematic organization and when they do not. First, obviously, many religious movements no longer have a "living leader" on whom devotion may be lavished. Further, when does devotion to an organization or to the religious, philosophical, or transformative principles it represents cross the line between "appropriate" and "excessive" zeal? A number of Eastern religious traditions have a long and time-honored history of devotion to a personal guru as an essential part of one's spiritual development and enlightenment process. Because "what may appear inappropriate or even manipulative to one person hardly registers on another's perceptual radar,"[23] the notion of "zeal" is a notoriously slippery concept often used to bootleg the notion of "fanaticism" into a discussion.

For example, for parents who have raised their children in nonreligious households, even a mild interest on the part of those children in things religious—the content of sacred scriptures, the teachings of different religious teachers, the rituals and practices of different faith traditions—can trigger fears of zealotry and fanaticism. Conversely, if a young man brought up in a staunchly Christian home decides at some point that his spiritual path is Hinduism—especially when it takes the form of a controversial group such as the International Society for Krishna Consciousness (the Hare Krishnas)—the dramatic shift in religious sensibilities can easily trigger similar fears. In addition, a number of social groups —both religious and non-religious—are "preoccupied with bringing in new members." When does this indicate a "cult" and when not?

Finally, as I have noted elsewhere, many "well-established religious traditions employ what Langone calls 'mind-numbing techniques,' in which he includes 'meditation, chanting, [and] speaking in tongues.'"[24] When do these criteria characterize "cults" and when not? How many of Langone's "characteristics" must be present and to what degree? How do observers determine when these same criteria are not meant to indicate dangerous, manipulative groups? In fact, because the secular anticult movement confuses correlates with attributes, "there is no stability of definition; they present instead what Stark and Bainbridge have called the 'un-ideal type,' a labeling process more suited to the political evaluation of unpopular groups than a dispassionate analysis of their social and cultural location."[25]

Langone at least implicitly recognizes the problems inherent in the secular anticult's conceptualization. "I have had to point out why the United States Marine Corps is not a cult so many times," he writes in "How the United States Marine Corps Differs from Cults," "that I carry a list to lectures and court appearances."[26] As I have noted elsewhere, "the fact that he has had to point out the differences that many times indicates the fundamentally ambiguous nature—and corresponding futility—of the American Family Foundation definition."[27]

No such ambiguity exists among the evangelical Christian countercult. Rather than depend on the kind of subjective correlates that inform the secular anticult definition—though, when useful, these are occasionally deployed to reinforce their case[28]—countercult apologists predicate their definition of "cult" on normative claims to the uniqueness and insuperability of evangelical Christianity. That is, what they often characterize as "orthodox Christianity" is the rod and rule by which all other religious phenomena are to be measured. In 1955, for example, Walter Ralston Martin, founder of the Christian Research Institute (CRI), one of the most prominent countercult think tanks, and regarded by many as the most influential countercult apologist of the post–World War II period, defined "cultism, in short," as "any major deviation from orthodox Christianity, relative to cardinal doctrines of the Christian faith." More than four decades later, Gretchen Passantino, co-founder with Martin of CRI, wrote in the fourth edition of Martin's magnum opus, *The Kingdom of the Cults*, that "*doctrinal* aberration should distinguish cults from Christianity, not social aberration."[29] In *The Lure of the Cults*, Ronald Enroth, an evangelical sociologist and co-founder of the countercult umbrella organization Evangelical Ministries to New Religions, declares that "any group, movement, or teaching may be considered cultic to the degree it deviates from biblical, orthodox Christianity."[30] Similarly, for Jay Howard, a "cult expert" and founder of the Association for Theological Studies (the Website for which is called "Focus on the Faulty"), states bluntly that a "cult" is "any group promoting a person or set of teachings that rejects the historic, central teachings of the Christian church"[31]—a definition which, presumably, would render two-thirds of the world's population "cultic."

By consistently treating statements of faith as statements of fact, these particular definitions beg the question: How do they know? How is the definition of "cult" deployed by the evangelical countercult any less subjective than that provided by the secular anticult? In point of fact, it isn't. Although the constituents of its construction are manifestly different, the countercult definition is as socially and subjectively constructed as that of the anticult—though few countercult apologists would consider it so.

As I have noted elsewhere, according to the "brainwashing" or "thought control" model of "cultic" involvement deployed by the secular anticult movement, "since no one in their right mind, operating with full cognitive information and consent, would make the kind of life choices made by those who join new and controversial religious movements, those who do join must, therefore, have had their ability to make such choices inhibited."[32] Inadequate diet, endless rounds of chanting, long hours of witnessing or tract-passing in the face of too few hours of restful sleep, and the inevitable, interminable, and, in many ex-member accounts, inescapable indoctrination sessions—all combine to impair an individual's ability to make rational, self-guided choices.

The evangelical Christian countercult, on the other hand, places its opposition to NRMs squarely in the domain of cosmological conflict, "one more skirmish line in ongoing battle between God and Satan."[33] Douglas Groothuis, an associate professor at the theologically conservative Denver Seminary, writes of the New Age Movement that "despite whatever good intentions New Agers may have, it is Satan, the spiritual counterfeiter himself, who ultimately inspires all false religion," continuing that real Christians "are in combat conditions, with no demilitarized zones available this side of heaven."[34] In response to the perceived "*culting* of America," Ron

Rhodes, a former colleague of Walter Martin at the Christian Research Institute, declares that "if Christians do not act, *the cults will.* The war is on—and you as a Christian will either be a soldier in the midst of the conflict or a casualty on the sidelines. Which will it be?"[35]

Objective: Countering New Religious Movements

The objectives of both the secular anticult and the evangelical counter-cult are grounded firmly in their respective conceptualizations of the "cult problem." Both groups attempt to maintain a countervailing pressure to what they regard as a significant social problem, but each characterizes differently the dangers represented by "cults," as well as the responsible social action to be taken in the face of those dangers. While both groups believe that their task is to "rescue" those who have been ensnared by unscrupulous religious groups, each understands the particulars of that process in terms of its own conceptualization. Because those in the secular anticult movement predicate their understanding of "cultic involvement" on the notion of "brainwashing" or "thought control," their task is to "free" the adherent, to effect his or her successful *exit* from the group in question. In the 1970s, 1980s, and even into the 1990s, this often meant "coercive deprogramming," a term coined by Ted Patrick in 1971. Paid sometimes thousands of dollars by anxious parents and family members, coercive deprogrammers violently kidnapped members of NRMs, held them against their will in remote locations, and subjected them to lengthy personal degradation, disparagement of their beliefs, and accusations that they had been brainwashed. As Anson Shupe and Susan E. Darnell note, in the terms of the CAN bankruptcy, "the precipitating, but not lone, event that hastened its demise was a civil suit brought against both CAN and a trio of coercive deprogrammers who unsuccessfully tried to remove a legal adult, Mr. Jason Scott, from a United Pentecostal congregation."[36]

Fortunately, coercive deprogramming has been recognized in the United States for the felony and denial of constitutionally guaranteed religious freedom that it is. This does not mean, however, that countermovement efforts have ceased. Rather, they have attempted to make a transition from violent, coercive deprogramming to allegedly more benign forms of intervention such as "exit counseling" and "thought reform consultation."[37] Indeed, some members of the secular anticult movement, such as "thought reform consultant" Carol Giambalvo, now claim that their intention is "*not* to get someone out of a cult," but merely to "give the group member the information that enables them to make a fully informed choice."[38] However, Giambalvo, a former deprogrammer, maintains that the "desired outcome" of the intervention may still be the adherent's exit from the suspect group. Also, since the concept of "unethically manipulative" persuasion as a basic characteristic of the "cultic relationship" has not changed, and since the terms "mind control," "brainwashing," "coercive persuasion," and "thought reform" are all used as functional equivalents, any claim by the secular anticult movement that it has abandoned its primary agenda to facilitate exit from suspect groups seems disingenuous at best. Although, in the wake of several high-profile legal actions such as the one that bankrupted the old CAN, the secular anticult process of facilitating exit from NRMs has been reconceptualized as "exit counseling," it is still popularly remembered for its more ignominious history of "deprogramming"—the forcible removal, detention, and coercion of adult converts at the request of friends and family members.

Because the evangelical countercult is based on an alternative religious vision, exit is seen as only part of the process; success in countercult terms is understood as *migration from* the suspect group *to* evangelical Christianity. This migration is informed by two principle objectives, what I have termed elsewhere "apologetic-evangelistic" and "apologetic-reinforcement."[39] In apologetic evangelism adherents of suspect groups are confronted with information intended to convince them to leave the group they are in and convert to evangelical Protestantism. In *The Culting of America*, for example, Rhodes writes that "through the use of apologetics we can provide well-reasoned evidences to the non-believer [that is, the non-believer in Rhodes' type of evangelical Christianity] as to why he ought to choose Christianity rather than any other religion. Apologetics can be used to show the unbeliever that all other options in the smorgasbord of world religions *are not really options at all*, since they are false."[40] Groothuis concurs; indeed, he believes that unless one's worldview conforms to the tenets of evangelical Christianity, it is false.

Negative apologetics presents *reasons against* non-Christian perspectives. It assumes that . . . if non-Christian world views are largely based on false ideas, the weakness of those world views can be highlighted through argumentation. . . . Any world view not based on the truth of God's revelation in the Bible will prove itself faulty at key points. . . . Negative apologetics says, "Your perspective doesn't make sense; and it doesn't fit the facts. Therefore, you shouldn't believe it."[41]

Obviously, for the evangelical Christian, the concomitant effect of demonstrating the alleged superiority of one's own religious worldview over another is the reinforcement of personal belief in evangelical Christianity. Indeed, as I have argued elsewhere, boundary-maintenance of this kind is one of the two main functions of evangelical countercult apologetics.[42]

In *Strange Gods*, Bromley and Shupe concluded that, despite both anticult and countercult alarmism, which was often supported by sensationalist media, there really was "no avalanche of rapidly growing cults," "no mysterious brainwashing process," and "no compelling reason to believe that all modern gurus and spiritual leaders are complete charlatans."[43] Their conclusions, however, have done little to mitigate the concerns of the secular anticult and the evangelical countercult, both of which continue to respond to what they regard as imminent religious threats in late modern society.

NOTES

1. Ron Rhodes, *The Culting of America* (Eugene, Ore.: Harvest House, 1994), 26.

2. Much of this section has been revised and adapted from Douglas E. Cowan, "Exits and Migrations: Foregrounding the Christian Counter-cult," *Journal of Contemporary Religion* 17 (3): 339–54; and idem., *Bearing False Witness? An Introduction to the Christian Countercult* (Westport, Conn.: Praeger, 2003): esp. 15–28.

3. Eber D. Howe, *Mormonism Unvailed* (Painesville, Ohio: Author, 1834).

4. George Hamilton Combs, *Some Latter-day Religions* (Chicago: Fleming H. Revell, 1899), 205.

5. Ibid., 235

6. Ibid., 243.

7. William G. Moorehead, "Millennial Dawn: A Counterfeit of Christianity," in *The Fundamentals: A Testimony to the Truth*, ed. R. A. Torrey et al. (1917; reprint, Grand Rapids, Mich.: Baker, 1996), 110, 117.

8. Jan Karel van Baalen, *The Chaos of Cults: A Study in Present-Day Isms*, 3d ed. (Grand Rapids, Mich.: Wm. B. Eerdmans, 1960), 6.

9. Douglas E. Cowan, "Contested Spaces: Movement, Countermovement, and E-Space Propaganda," in *Religion Online: Finding Faith on the Internet*, ed. Lorne L. Dawson and Douglas E. Cowan (New York: Routledge, 2004), 255.

10. Anson D. Shupe, Jr., and David G. Bromley, *The New Vigilantes: Deprogrammers, Anti-Cultists, and the New Religions* (Beverly Hills, Calif.: Sage, 1980), 28–29. This section on the social history of the secular anticult movement relies heavily on the seminal work of a generation of scholars. Interested readers are encouraged to consult James A. Beckford, *Cult Controversies* (New York: Tavistock,

1985); idem., "Politics and the Anti-Cult Movement," *Annual Review of the Social Sciences of Religion* 3 (1979): 169–90; David G. Bromley, ed., *Falling from the Faith: Causes and Consequences of Religious Apostasy* (Newbury Park, Calif.: Sage, 1988); David G. Bromley and Phillip E. Hammond, eds., *The Future of New Religious Movements* (Macon, Ga: Mercer University Press, 1987); David G. Bromley and Anson D. Shupe, Jr., *Strange Gods: The Great American Cult Scare* (Boston: Beacon Press, 1981); Anson Shupe and David G. Bromley, eds., *Anti-Cult Movements in Cross-Cultural Perspective* (New York: Garland, 1994); Anson D. Shupe, Jr., David G. Bromley, and Donna L. Oliver, *The Anti-Cult Movement in America: A Bibliography and Historical Survey* (New York: Garland, 1984); and Anson D. Shupe, Jr., Bert L. Hardin, and David G. Bromley, "A Comparison of Anti-Cult Movements in the United States and West Germany," in *Of Gods and Men: New Religious Movements in the West,* ed. Eileen Barker (Macon, Ga.: Mercer University Press, 1983), 177–93.

11. Shupe and Bromley, *The New Vigilantes,* 90. See also Ted Patrick, with Tom Dulack, *Let Our Children Go!* (New York: Dutton, 1976).

12. Shupe and Bromley, *The New Vigilantes,* 90–91.

13. Anson Shupe and David G. Bromley, "The Modern American Anti-Cult Movement 1971–91: A Twenty-Year Retrospective," in *Anti-Cult Movements in Cross-Cultural Perspective,* 6.

14. Michael D. Langone, "Cults and Mind Control" (1988), archived at www.csj.org/infoserv_ articles/langone_ michael_cultmindctr.htm.

15. See Charlotte Allen, "Brainwashed! Scholars of Cults Accuse Each Other of Bad Faith," *Lingua Franca* 8/9 (December 1998/January 1999): 26–36.

16. Margaret Singer, with Janja Lalich, *Cults in Our Midst* (San Francisco: Jossey-Bass, 1995), 7.

17. Ibid., 8 (emphasis in original).

18. Ibid., 9 (emphasis in original).

19. Ibid., 10 (emphasis in original).

20. Margaret Singer, quoted in Robert Hoshowsky, "Cults, The Next Wave: Almost Everyone Is Vulnerable," *Homemaker's Magazine,* March 1998, 55.

21. Michael D. Langone, "Cults 101: Checklist of Cult Characteristics" (1999); archived at www.csj.org/infoserv_ cult101/checklis.htm.

22. For example, consider the definition of a "chair": a piece of furniture that includes a seating surface, some kind of supporting structure, and a backrest— *attributes* that are always present in chairs. *Correlates,* on the other hand, may or may not be present. Some chairs are padded, some aren't; some chairs are blue, others red; some chairs have three legs, others four. None of these, however, could be used definitively to identify a "chair." See Rodney Stark and William Sims Bainbridge, *The Future of Religion: Secularization, Revival, and Cult Formation* (Berkeley: University of California Press, 1985), 19–20.

23. Cowan, "Exits and Migrations," 342.

24. Ibid. See also Langone, "Cults 101."

25. Cowan, "Exits and Migrations," 342; see Stark and Bainbridge, *The Future of Religion*, 19–20.

26. Michael D. Langone, " How the United States Marine Corps Differs from Cults" (1999); archived at www.csj.org/infoserv_cult101/marine.htm.

27. Cowan, *Bearing False Witness?*, 19.

28. See, for example, Norman L. Geisler and Ron Rhodes, *When Cultists Ask: A Popular Handbook on Cultic Misinterpretations* (Grand Rapids, Mich.: Baker Books, 1997), 9–18.

29. The CRI definition is in Walter R. Martin, *The Rise of the Cults* (Grand Rapids, Mich: Zondervan, 1955), 12. Passantino's definition is in Bob Passantino and Gretchen Passantino, "Critiquing Cult Mind-Control Model," in Martin, *The Kingdom of the Cults*, 4th ed., ed. Hank Hanegraaff (Minneapolis: Bethany House, 1997), 55 (emphasis in original).

30. Ronald Enroth, *The Lure of the Cults* (Chappaqua, N.Y.: Christian Herald, 1979), 20.

31. Jay Howard, with Timothy Fink and Nathan Unseth, *Confronting the Cultist in the New Age* (Old Tappan, N.J.: Power Books, 1990), 23.

32. Cowan, "Exits and Migrations," 344.

33. Ibid., 344.

34. Douglas R. Groothuis, *Confronting the New Age: How to Resist a Growing Religious Movement* (Downers Grove, Ill.: InterVarsity, 1988), 38, 39.

35. Rhodes, *The Culting of America*, 219 (emphasis in original).

36. See Shupe and Darnell, "CAN, We Hardly Knew Ye: Sex, Drugs, Deprogrammers' Kickbacks, and Corporate Crime in the (old) Cult Awareness Network," in *The Cult Awareness Network: Anatomy of a Hate Group*, ed. Thomas C. Whittle (N.p.: Freedom Magazine, n.d.).

37. See Anson Shupe and Susan E. Darnell, "The Attempted Transformation of a Deviant Occupation into a Therapy: Deprogramming Seeks a New Identity," paper presented at the 2003 annual meeting of the Society for the Scientific Study of Religion / Religious Research Association; archived at www.cesnur.org/2003/shupe_darnell.htm.

38. Carol Giambalvo, "From Deprogramming to Thought Reform Consultation," paper presented at the 1998 American Family Foundation Conference; archived at www.csj.org/studyindex/studyintervention/study_deprog_threfrmconsult.htm.

39. Cowan, "Exits and Migrations," 349; idem., *Bearing False Witness?*, 26.

40. Rhodes, *The Culting of America*, 230.

41. Groothuis, *Confronting the New Age*, 67 (emphasis in original).

42. Cowan, *Bearing False Witness?*, 45–46, 160–64.

43. Bromley and Shupe, *Strange Gods*, 2, 3.

Index

Abductees. *See* Aliens; UFOs (unidentified flying objects)

Abduction Study Conference, 77–82

Adamski, George, 66, 95

Adolescents and young adults, NRMs and, 2, 4, 164, 166, 317, 320

Adventism: vs. Catholic Church/Pope, 259, 260, 261–262, 265; Health ministry, 261, 278; history of, 260–262; Sabbath and, 260, 261; separation of church and state, 261, 262; Seventh-day Adventists (SDA), 3, 260–262, 275, 279. *See also* Failed prophecy, reinterpretation of; Jesus Christ, Second Coming; Miller, William; Millerites; White, Ellen G.

African diaspora religions, 21, 202; Candomblé, 183; Vodou, 3, 183, 110. *See also* Afrocentrism; Black nationalism; Rastafarianism; Santería

African Initiated/Independent Churches (AICs), 6

Afro–Caribbean religions. *See* African diaspora religions

Afrocentrism, 3, 13, 207, 209. *See also* Black nationalism; Rastafarianism

AIDS, 169, 298

Akasa, 55–56

Alchemy, 46

Alfred Hitchcock Presents (series), 74

Ali, Noble Drew, 225

Aliens, 13; Heaven's Gate and, 298, 304–306; UFO experiencers/religious groups and, 64–65, 66, 67, 68, 69, 70, 71–94

Alternative religions. *See* New Religious Movements (NRMs)

America in Prophecy (book), 262, 266–270. *See also* Adventism; White, Ellen G.

American Family Foundation (AFF), 5, 317, 321, 323, 324. *See also* Anticult/countercult movement

American Muslim Mission, 228

Amsterdam, Peter, 166. *See also* Family, The

Anti-Christ, 306, 315n. 9

Anticult/countercult movement, 1, 4, 7, 8, 15, 317–330; and the Association for Theological Studies, 325; and deprogramming, 5, 320, 321, 326, 327; and Evangelical Ministries to New Religions, 320, 325; and Personal Freedom Outreach, 320; and Spiritual Counterfeits Project, 320; distinction between, 4, 318, 320, 322, 324–326, 327; definitions of "cults" in, 321–326; objectives, 319, 326–328; origins, 319–321; United States Marine Corps, as distinguished from "cults," 324. *See also* American Family Foundation (AFF); Brainwashing; Christian Research Institute (CRI); Citizens Freedom Foundation (CFF); Concerned Relatives; Cult Awareness Network (CAN); Deprogramming; Free Our Children from the Children of God (FREECOG); Howard, Jay; Langone, Michael D.; Martin, Walter R.; Patrick, Ted; Rhodes, Ron; Singer, Margaret Thaler

Apocalypticism, 13, 164, 165, 166, 206, 210, 242, 244, 316; Adventists and, 259–260, 261–262, 263, 274, 279; Chen Tao and, 299–300, 307, 310; Jehovah's Witnesses and, 279, 280, 281, 282, 283–285, 296n. 2; The Family and, 164, 165, 166; the Tribulation, 299, 307, 311, 314n. 1, 315n. 9; year 2000 and, 297–298, 301, 311–313. *See also* Anti–Christ; Armageddon; Babylon; Branch Davidians; Koresh, David; New World type; Millennialism/millenarianism; Nuclear war; Revelation, Book of (Bible)

Applewhite, Marshal Herff, 67, 298, 301, 314n. 3; as "Do," 302, 306, 314n. 3; as Jesus, 298, 304. *See also* Heaven's Gate

Nation of Islam (NOI), 3, 240; blacks as Original Man/People, 226, 228, 229, 231, 233, 239; black separatism, 227, 230; Fruit of Islam, 227, 238; God as black man, 226; history of, 224–227, 240; Jews and, 226, 228; and Mecca, 227, 234, 236; men and women in, 236–237; mythology ("Yacub's History"), 226, 229–230, 233–236; and Negroes, 231–232, 236, 237, 239; theology, 226, 240; whites as devils/evil, 226, 228, 231, 234–235, 239. *See also* Fard, Wallace D.; Islam; Muhammad, Elijah; Science, NRMs' use of; X, Malcolm

Native American religions, 21

Needleman, Jacob, 1

Neo-pagan traditions, 99, 100, 101, 105, 107, 117n. 1, 117n. 4, 118. *See also* Wicca

Nettles, Bonnie Lu Truesdale, 67, 298, 314n. 3; as Heavenly Father, 302, 304, 314n. 3; as "Ti," 302, 314n. 3. *See also* Heaven's Gate

New Age movement, 4, 20, 21, 66, 69, 82, 83, 100, 317, 325; Theosophy and, 49; Wicca and, 100

New Family type, 10, 12, 13; Anticult/countercult movement and, 15; Branch Davidians as, 264; The Family, as, 17, 167; Jehovah's Witnesses as, 283; Peoples Temple as, 244; Rastafarianism as, 210; Santería as, 186; sociology and, 16; Unification Church as, 139, 143; Wicca as, 101. *See also* Nexuses of novelty

New New Religions (Japan), 6, 134

New Religious Movements (NRMs): in Africa, 6; as alternative religions, 1, 2, 3; as churches, 2, 8, 9; as cults, 1, 2, 8, 9, 140, 278, 297, 300, 317–330; as emergent religions, 1, 3; in Europe, 6, 99; in the former Soviet Union, 6; in Japan, 6, 119, 120, 297; leaders as charismatic, 2, 165, 263, 271, 322; in the 1960s, 1, 2, 3, 4, 7, 18n. 4, 140, 320; in the 1970s, 2, 4, 6, 7, 140, 164–165, 167, 320; from the nineteenth century, 3, 6, 25; as sects, 1, 2, 6, 8, 9; typologies, 8–14; use of term, 1, 2, 3–4. *See also* Adolescents and young adults, NRMs and; Anticult/countercult movement; Conversion, NRMs and; Gender, NRMs and; Marriage, NRMs and; Scholars of NRMs; Sex, NRMs and; Sociology of NRMs; Violence, NRMs and; Women, NRMs and

New Self type, 10, 11–12, 13, 15; Chen Tao as, 301; Christian Science as, 29, 37–39; Falun Gong as, 20n. 23; The Family as, 167; Heaven's Gate as counter to, 301–302; Jehovah's Witnesses as counter to, 283; Nation of Islam as, 228; psychology and, 15, 16; Rastafarianism as, 210; Soka Gakkai as, 121; Transcendental Meditation as, 20n. 23; Wicca as, 17, 101. *See also* Nexuses of novelty

New Society type, 10, 12, 13, 15; Branch Davidians as, 264; Chen Tao as, 302; Christians awaiting Y2K crisis as, 301; Heaven's Gate as, 302; Jehovah's Witnesses as, 282–283; Nation of Islam as, 229; Peoples Temple as, 17, 243; Rastafarianism as, 209; Soka Gakkai as, 121; Theosophy as, 49; Wicca as, 101; Y2K crisis as ushering in, 301. *See also* Nexuses of novelty; Racism; Zion

Newton, Huey, 254n. 1

New Understanding type, 10, 11, 12, 13; Adventism as, 263–264; apocalypticism and, 263–264; Christian Science as, 17, 29; countercult theology and, 15; The Family as, 167; Soka Gakkai as, 120–121; Theosophy as, 17, 49; UFO religious groups as, 17, 68, 69, 70, 301; Wicca as, 101. *See also* Nexuses of novelty

New World Order, 274

New World type, 10, 13; Adventism as, 263; Branch Davidians as, 17, 263; Chen Tao as, 301; The Family as, 167; Heaven's Gate as, 17, 301; Jehovah's Witnesses as, 17, 282–283, 286–288; Peoples Temple as, 244; Rastafarianism as, 210; Soka Gakkai as, 121; Theosophy as, 49; Unification Church as, 143; Wicca as, 102; Y2K crisis as ushering in, 301. *See also* Apocalypticism; Nexuses of novelty

Nexuses of novelty, 11, 13, 14, 15, 16

1960s. *See* New Religious Movements

1970s. *See* New Religious Movements

Nixon, Richard, 141

Nuclear war, 119, 166, 210, 242, 298, 299, 307

Occultism, 2, 46, 66, 106, 183, 305

Ocean of Theosophy, The (book), 49–50, 52–62. *See also* Judge, William Q.; Theosophy

About the Editors

Dereck Daschke is Assistant Professor of Philosophy and Religion at Truman State University, specializing in the areas of religion and culture and the psychology of religion. His publications on the psychology of apocalypticism, biblical prophecy, and mysticism have appeared in the *Journal of Psychology and Christianity, American Imago,* and the four-volume *Psychology and The Bible.*

W. Michael Ashcraft is Associate Professor of Religion at Truman State University. He is the author of *The Dawn of the New Cycle: Point Loma Theosophists and American Culture* and former chairman of the New Religious Movements Group of the American Academy of Religion.